# America's Top Military Careers,
## Third Edition

### The Official Guide to Occupations in the Armed Forces

This book is a complete reprint of *Military Careers: A Guide to Military Occupations and Selected Military Career Paths* as produced by the U.S. Department of Defense. It includes all the content of the original book and is published by JIST Works, Inc., Indianapolis, Indiana 46216.

**America's Top Military Careers, Third Edition**
The Official Guide to Occupations in the Armed Forces

---

## Other Books in the *America's Top Jobs®* Series:

- *America's Top Jobs® for College Graduates*, by J. Michael Farr
- *America's Top Jobs® for People Without College Degrees*, by J. Michael Farr
- *America's Fastest Growing Jobs*, by J. Michael Farr
- *America's Top White-Collar Jobs®*, by J. Michael Farr
- *America's Top Medical, Education, & Human Services Jobs®*, by J. Michael Farr
- *America's Top 300 Jobs*
- *America's Top Federal Jobs*
- *Career Guide to America's Top Industries*

Please see the back of this book for ordering information and details on other JIST titles.

---

Published by JIST Works, Inc.
8902 Otis Avenue
Indianapolis, IN 46216-1033
Phone: 1-800-648-JIST   Fax: 1-800-JIST-FAX   E-mail: editorial@jist.com
Visit our World Wide Web site for catalog and free information: www.jist.com/jist

Cover design by Aleata Howard

Printed in the United States of America

03 02 01 00        9 8 7 6 5 4 3 2 1

Library of Congress Cataloging-in-Publication Data

This edition, distributed by JIST Works, Inc., is an unabridged reprint of *Military Careers* compiled by the United States Department of Defense, Washington, D.C. We have been careful to provide accurate information throughout this book, but it is possible that errors and omissions have been introduced. Please consider this in making any career plans or other important decisions. Trust your own judgment above all else and in all things.

ISBN 1-56370-706-3

# Foreword

The Department of Defense recruits and trains approximately 365,000 enlisted members and officers each year, making it one of the largest employers in the U.S. *Military Careers has* been developed to help educators and youth learn about the many career opportunities the military has to offer. The book is a compendium of military occupational, training, and career information and is designed for use by students desiring to explore the military world of work. The document is an important career information resource that is part of the Armed Services Vocational Aptitude Battery (ASVAB) Career Exploration Program. This program assists individuals in understanding their aptitudes, interests, and personal preferences and matching these characteristics to civilian and military occupations.

This second edition of *Military Careers* is organized into two major sections: Military Occupations and Military Career Paths. The result is a single reference source for educators and students to use for learning about the diverse opportunities available to young people in the military. Military Occupations contains descriptions of 152 enlisted and officer occupations. Students who have taken the ASVAB can use their scores to estimate their chances of qualifying for enlisted occupations based on their aptitudes. Military Career Paths describes the typical duties and assignments a person might expect when advancing along the path of a 20-year military career. While the Military Occupations section presents an overview of the typical job duties in a military occupation, the Military Career Paths section presents a more comprehensive description of work performed at various stages of a military career.

Many individuals contributed to the development and production of *Military Careers*. Specifically, we wish to thank Dr. Jeff rey Worst, Ms. Dana Pao, Ms. Signe George, Mr. Jehu Barnes, and Ms. Denise Lawson of Booz-Allen and Hamilton Inc. Their contributions are most appreciated.

Various members of the Department of Defense have contributed to this publication. Mrs. Elaine Seliman and Ms. Mary Quenette of the Defense Manpower Data Center (DMDC) in Rosslyn, VA conducted analyses for producing the graphs associated with the enlisted occupational titles. In addition, members of DMDC in Seaside, CA contributed to the production of the document. Mr. Reynold Wong designed the cover, Mrs. Gretchen Glick assisted with the editing and proofing, Mr. Randy Marks assisted in designing the document, and Mr. Les Willis provided current military opportunities information. Members of the ManpowerAccession PolicyWorking Group helped to gatherservice-specific information and reviewed the contents for accuracy and currency. The Directorate for Accession Policy, Office of the Assistant Secretary of Defense (Force Management Policy), headed by Dr. W. S. Sellman, provided policy oversight for the program.

Finally, the project was directed by Dr. Janet Wall, DMDC, Testing Division, Seaside, CA. Herguidance and leadership were instrumental in the quality, accuracy, and utility of this book.

Frederick Pang
Assistant Secretary of Defense
(Force Management Policy)

# Contents

# Military Officer Occupations

# Job Opportunities in the Armed Forces

*Editors' Note: The following information is reprinted from the Department of Labor's* Occupational Outlook Handbook *and includes the most current information available about job outlook statistics for the military from the Bureau of Labor Statistics.*

## Significant Points

- *Opportunities should be good in all branches of the Armed Forces through the year 2006 for applicants meeting the desired standards.*
- *The needs of the military always come first, so hours and working conditions can vary substantially.*
- *Some training or duty assignments may be hazardous, even in peacetime.*

## Nature of the Work

Maintaining a strong National defense encompasses such diverse activities as running a hospital, commanding a tank crew, programming computers, operating a nuclear reactor, and repairing and maintaining a helicopter. The military's occupational diversity provides educational opportunities and work experience in literally hundreds of occupations. Military personnel hold managerial and administrative jobs; professional, technical, and clerical jobs; construction jobs; electrical and electronics jobs; mechanical and repair jobs; and many others. The military provides training and work experience for people who serve a single enlistment of 3 to 6 years of active duty, those who embark on a career that lasts 20 years or more, and those who serve in the Army, Navy, Marine, Air Force, and Coast Guard Reserves and Army and Air National Guard.

There are more than 360 basic and advanced military occupational specialties for enlisted personnel and almost as many for officers. Over 75 percent of these occupational specialties have civilian counterparts. A brief discussion of the major military occupational groups follows.

*Infantry, gun crews, and seamanship specialists* are the front line of the Armed Forces. Officers plan and direct military operations, oversee security activities, and serve as combat leaders and pilots. Enlisted personnel serve as infantry or weapons specialists, aircraft crew members, armored and amphibious vehicle crew, artillery, gunnery, or rocket specialists, and combat engineers. Some of these specialties involve skills that can be applied to a number of civilian occupations such as police officers, commercial pilots, and heavy equipment operators. In addition, people in this category learn how to work as team members and develop leadership, managerial, and supervisory skills.

Military personnel assigned to *electronic equipment repair occupations* are responsible for maintaining and repairing many different types of equipment. Officers oversee the regular maintenance and repair of avionics, communications, radar, and air traffic control equipment. Enlisted personnel repair radio, navigation, missile guidance, and flight control equipment as well as telephone and data processing equipment. Many of these skills are directly transferable to jobs in the civilian sector.

*Communications and intelligence specialists* in the military have civilian scientific, engineering, and investigative counterparts. Officers serve as intelligence gatherers and interpreters, cryptologists, information analysts, translators, and in related intelligence occupations. Enlisted personnel work as computer programmers, air traffic controllers, interpreters and translators, radio, radar, and sonar operators, and interrogation and investigative specialists.

Military *medical and dental occupations* all have civilian counterparts. Holding the rank of health care officer are physicians, dentists, optometrists, nurses, therapists, veterinarians, pharmacists, and others in health diagnosing and treating occupations. Enlisted personnel are trained to work as medical laboratory technologists and technicians, radiological technologists, emergency medical technicians, dental assistants, optical assistants, pharmaceutical assistants, sanitation specialists, and veterinary assistants. Health professions training obtained in the military is usually recognized in the civilian sector and service-trained health professionals are eligible to apply for certification or registration in the civilian sector, which is often a hiring prerequisite.

Military experience in *other technical and allied specialty occupations* is often directly transferable to civilian life. Officers in this field work as meteorologists, mapping directors, television and motion picture directors, and band directors. Enlisted personnel are trained to work as photographers, motion picture camera operators, mapping and surveying specialists, illustrators, weather data collectors, explosives disposal specialists, divers, and musicians.

*Functional support and administrative occupations* in military service require the same skills as similar jobs in private businesses and government agencies. Officers in this category work as directors, executives, adjutants, administrative officers, personnel managers, training administrators, budget officers, finance officers, public affairs officers, accountants, hospital administrators, inspectors, computer systems managers, and lawyers. Enlisted personnel in this category work as accounting, payroll, personnel, and postal clerks; computer programmers and operators; chaplain assistants; counseling aides; typists; and storekeepers.

Those in *electrical and mechanical equipment repair occupations* maintain aircraft, motor vehicles, and ships. Officers oversee the maintenance of aircraft, missiles, conventional and nuclear-powered ships, trucks, earth-moving equipment, and other vehicles. Enlisted personnel serve as mechanics, engine specialists, and boiler technicians. They also install and maintain wire communications systems such as telephones. Skills obtained in these jobs are readily transferable to those in the civilian sector.

Military personnel assigned to *craft occupations* are skilled craft workers. Officers serve as civil engineers and architects and manage the work of enlisted personnel who work as carpenters, construction equipment operators, metalworkers, machinists, plumbers, welders, electricians, and heating and air-conditioning specialists.

Military personnel in *service and supply occupations* handle food service, security, and personal services and supply. Officers work as logistics officers, supply managers, transportation and traffic managers, and procurement officers. Enlisted personnel include military police, correctional specialists, criminal investigators, firefighters, and food preparation and other service workers. They operate or service transportation equipment such as trucks, ships, boats, airplanes, and helicopters, and act as quartermasters, supply specialists, and cargo specialists. Many of these skills can be transferred to civilian occupations.

## Working Conditions

Military life is much more regimented than civilian life, and one must be willing to accept the discipline. It is important to remember that signing an enlistment contract obligates you to serve for a specified period of time.

Dress and grooming requirements are stringent, and rigid formalities govern many aspects of everyday life. For instance, officers and enlisted personnel do not socialize together, and commissioned officers are saluted and addressed as "sir" or "ma'am." These and other rules encourage respect for superiors whose commands must be obeyed immediately and without question.

The needs of the military always come first. As a result, hours and working conditions can vary substantially. However, most military personnel not deployed on a mission usually work 8 hours a day, 5 days a week. While off duty, military personnel usually do not wear their uniforms and are free to participate in family and recreational activities like most civilians. Some assignments, however, require night and weekend work, or require people to be on call at all hours. All may require substantial travel. Depending on the service, assignments may require long periods at sea, sometimes in cramped quarters or lengthy overseas assignments in countries offering few amenities. Some serve tours in isolated parts of the world, where they are subject to extreme cold or heat and the possibility of hostilities breaking out at any time. Others, such as sailors on carrier flight deck duty, have jobs that are hazardous even in noncombat situations.

During wartime, many military personnel engage in combat, and find themselves in life or death situations. They rely on countless hours of training to produce teamwork that is critical to the success or failure of an operation, and to protecting the lives of the individuals in their unit. Rapidly advancing military technology has made warfare more precise and lethal, further increasing the need for teamwork. Noncombatants may also face danger if their duties bring them close to a combat zone. Even in peacetime, most members of the combat arms branches of the military participate in hazardous training activities.

Ship and air crews travel extensively, while others in the military are stationed at bases throughout the country or overseas. Military personnel are usually transferred to a new duty station every few years.

Military personnel enjoy more job security than their civilian counterparts. Satisfactory job performance generally assures one of steady employment and earnings, and many of their requirements such as meals, clothing, and living quarters are provided for them.

## Employment

In 1997, about 1.48 million individuals were on active duty in the Armed Forces—about 483,000 in the Army; 405,000 in the Navy; 383,000 in the Air Force; 172,000 in the Marine Corps, and 35,000 in the Coast Guard.

Military personnel are stationed throughout the United States and in many countries around the world. California, Texas, North Carolina, and Virginia accounted for more than 1 in 3 military jobs. About 249,000 were stationed outside the United States in 1997. Over 100,000 of these were stationed in Europe (mainly in Germany) and in the Western Pacific area.

Table 1 shows the occupational composition of enlisted personnel in 1997. Nearly 4 out of 10 held jobs that involved communications, electronic, mechanical, or related equipment, a reflection of the highly technical nature of the fighting forces today. Table 2 shows the occupational composition of officer personnel in 1997. Officers—who accounted for about 20 percent of all military personnel—are concentrated in activities in which they serve as ships' officers, aircraft pilots and crew members, and infantry or artillery officers. Officers also serve in administrative, support, engineering and maintenance, and medical and dental positions.

## Qualifications, Training, and Advancement

*General enlistment qualifications.* As it has since 1973, the military expects to meet its personnel requirements through volunteers. Enlisted members must enter a legal agreement called an enlistment contract, which usually involves a commitment to 8 years of service. Depending on the terms of the contract, 2 to 6 years are spent on active duty, the balance in the reserves. The enlistment contract obligates the service to provide the agreed-upon options—job, rating, pay, cash bonuses for enlistment in certain occupations, medical and other benefits, occupational training, and continuing education. In return, enlisted personnel must serve satisfactorily for the specified period of time.

Requirements for each service vary, but certain qualifications for enlistment are common to all branches. Enlistees must be between the ages of 17 and 35, must be a U.S. citizen or immigrant alien holding permanent resident status, must not have a felony record, and must possess a birth certificate. Applicants who are 17 must have the consent of a parent or legal guardian before entering the service. Air Force enlisted personnel must enter active duty before their 28th birthday. Applicants must pass both a written examination—the Armed Services Vocational Aptitude Battery—and meet certain minimum physical standards such as height, weight, vision, and overall health. All branches prefer high school graduation or its equivalent and require it for certain enlistment options. In 1997, over 9 out of 10 enlistees were high school graduates. Single parents are generally not eligible to enlist.

Table 1.  Military enlisted personnel by broad occupational category and branch of military service, 1997

| Occupational Group | Total | Army | Navy | Marine Corps | Air Force |
|---|---|---|---|---|---|
| Total | 1,195,745 | 397,583 | 340,537 | 153,943 | 303,682 |
| Infantry, gun crews, and seamanship specialists | 211,312 | 115,287 | 40,273 | 36,318 | 19,436 |
| Electronic equipment repairers | 108,963 | 25,949 | 42,098 | 8,829 | 32,087 |
| Communications and intelligence specialists | 104,627 | 38,312 | 33,961 | 11,074 | 21,280 |
| Health care specialists | 83,089 | 30,893 | 27,199 | (¹) | 24,870 |
| Other technical and allied specialists | 33,712 | 11,464 | 6,820 | 3,670 | 11,538 |
| Functional support and administration | 195,114 | 65,888 | 37,456 | 25,152 | 66,614 |
| Electrical/mechanical equipment repairers | 236,245 | 53,519 | 87,847 | 23,943 | 70,936 |
| Craftworkers | 47,566 | 7,621 | 19,838 | 4,075 | 14,038 |
| Service and supply handlers | 108,346 | 46,759 | 17,608 | 21,144 | 22,837 |
| Non-occupational | 68,991 | 1,893 | 27,314 | 19,738 | 20,046 |

[1] The Marine Corps employs no medical personnel.  Their medical services are provided by the Navy.

SOURCE:  U.S. Department of Defense

**Table 2. Military officer personnel by broad occupational category and branch of service, 1997**

| Occupational Group | Total | Army | Navy | Marine Corps | Air Force |
|---|---|---|---|---|---|
| Total | 226,398 | 77,810 | 56,069 | 17,968 | 74,551 |
| General officers and executives | 2,072 | 310 | 220 | 698[1] | 844[3] |
| Tactical operations officers | 86,653 | 31,611 | 21,548 | 8,434 | 25,060 |
| Intelligence officers | 11,774 | 5,351 | 2,271 | 720 | 3,434 |
| Engineering and maintenance officers | 29,313 | 9,269 | 6,277 | 1,744 | 12,023 |
| Scientists and professionals | 10,595 | 2,834 | 2,214 | 457 | 5,090 |
| Medical officers | 39,754 | 15,049 | 11,070 | (²) | 13,635 |
| Administrators | 14,185 | 4,603 | 2,949 | 1,665 | 4,968 |
| Supply, procurement, and allied officers | 19,651 | 7,844 | 3,157 | 2,171 | 6,479 |
| Non-occupational | 9,866 | 180 | 5,555 | 2,020 | 2,111 |

[1]The Marine Corps includes colonels as general officers. There were 79 generals in the Marine Corps in 1997.

[2]The Marine Corps employs no medical personnel. Their medical services are provided by the Navy.

[3]There were 274 general officers and 570 executives, not elsewhere classified, in the Air Force in 1997.

SOURCE: U.S. Department of Defense

People thinking about enlisting in the military should learn as much as they can about military life before making a decision. This is especially important if you are thinking about making the military a career. Speaking to friends and relatives with military experience is a good idea. Determine what the military can offer you and what it will expect in return. Then talk to a recruiter, who can determine if you qualify for enlistment; explain the various enlistment options; and tell you which military occupational specialties currently have openings for trainees. Bear in mind that the recruiter's job is to recruit promising applicants into the military, so the information he or she gives you is likely to stress the positive aspects of military life.

Ask the recruiter to assess your chances of being accepted for training in the occupation or occupations of your choice, or, better still, take the aptitude exam to see how well you score. The military uses the aptitude exam as a placement exam, and test scores largely determine an individual's chances of being accepted into a particular training program. Selection for a particular type of training depends on the needs of the service, general and technical aptitudes, and personal preference. Because all prospective recruits are required to take the exam, those who do so before committing themselves to enlist have the advantage of knowing in advance whether they stand a good chance of being accepted for training in a particular specialty. The recruiter can schedule you for the Armed Services Vocational Aptitude Battery without any obligation. Many high schools offer the exam as an easy way for students to explore the possibility of a military career, and the test also provides insight into career areas where the student has demonstrated aptitudes and interests.

*Enlistment contract.* If you decide to join the military, the next step is to pass the physical examination and then enter into the enlistment contract. This involves choosing, qualifying, and agreeing on a number of enlistment options such as length of active duty time, which may vary according to the enlistment option. (Most active duty programs have enlistment options ranging from 3 to 6 years, although there are some 2-year programs.) The contract will also state the date of enlistment and other options such as bonuses and types of training to be received. If the service is unable to fulfill its part of the contract (such as providing a certain kind of training) the contract may become null and void.

All services offer a "delayed entry program" by which an enlistee can delay entry into active duty for up to 1 year. High school students can enlist during their senior year and enter a service after graduation. Others choose this program because the job training they desire is not currently available but will be within the coming year, or because they need time to arrange personal affairs.

Women are eligible to enter almost all military specialties. Although many women serve in medical and administrative support positions, women also work as mechanics, missile maintenance technicians, heavy equipment operators, fighter pilots, and intelligence officers. Only occupations involving a high probability of direct exposure to combat are excluded—for example, the artillery and infantry branches of the Army.

People planning to apply the skills gained through military training to a civilian career should look into several things before selecting their military occupation. First, they should determine how good the prospects are for civilian employment in jobs related to the military specialty that interests them. Second, they should know the prerequisites for the related civilian job. Many occupations require a license, certification, or a minimum level of education. In such cases, it is important to determine whether military training is sufficient to enter the civilian equivalent or, if not, what additional training will be required.

Other *Handbook* statements discuss the job outlook for civilian occupations for which military training is helpful. Additional information often can be obtained from school counselors.

*Training programs for enlisted personnel.* Following enlistment, new members of the Armed Forces undergo recruit training. Better known as "basic" training, recruit training provides a 6- to 11-week introduction to military life with courses in health, first aid, and military skills and protocol. Days and nights are carefully structured and include rigorous physical exercises designed to improve strength and endurance.

Following basic training, most recruits take additional training at technical schools that prepare them for a particular military occupational specialty. The formal training period generally lasts from 10 to 20 weeks, although training for certain occupations—nuclear power plant operator for example—may take as much as 1 year. Recruits not assigned to classroom instruction receive on-the-job training at their first duty assignment.

Many service people get college credit for the technical training they receive on duty, which, combined with off-duty courses, can lead to an Associates degree through community college programs such as the Community College of the Air Force.

In addition to on-duty training, military personnel may choose from a variety of educational programs. Most military installations have tuition assistance programs for people wishing to take courses during off-duty hours. These may be correspondence courses or degree programs offered by local colleges or universities. Tuition assistance pays up to 75 percent of college costs. Also available are courses designed to help service personnel earn high school equivalency diplomas. Each service branch provides opportunities for full-time study to a limited number of exceptional applicants. Military personnel accepted into these highly competitive programs receive full pay, allowances, tuition, and related fees. In return, they must agree to serve an additional amount of time in the service. Other very selective programs enable enlisted personnel to qualify as commissioned officers through additional military training.

*Officer training.* Officer training in the Armed Forces is provided through the Federal service academies (Military, Naval, Air Force, and Coast Guard); the Reserve Officers Training Corps (ROTC); Officer Candidate School (OCS) or Officer Training School (OTS); the National Guard (State Officer Candidate School programs); the Uniformed Services University of Health Sciences; and other programs. All are very selective and are good options for those wishing to make the military a career.

Federal service academies provide a 4-year college program leading to a bachelor of science degree. The midshipman or cadet is provided free room and board, tuition, medical care, and a monthly allowance. Graduates receive regular or reserve commissions and have a 5-year active duty obligation, or longer if entering flight training.

To become a candidate for appointment as a cadet or midshipman in one of the service academies, most applicants obtain a nomination from an authorized source (usually a Member of Congress). Candidates do not need to know a Member of Congress personally to request a nomination. Nominees must have an academic record of the requisite quality, college aptitude test scores above an established minimum, and recommendations from teachers or school officials; they must also pass a medical examination. Appointments are made from the list of eligible nominees.

Appointments to the Coast Guard Academy are made strictly on a competitive basis. A nomination is not required.

ROTC programs train students in about 950 Army, 60 Navy and Marine Corps, and 550 Air Force units at participating colleges and universities. Trainees take 2 to 5 hours of military instruction a week in addition to regular college courses. After graduation, they may serve as officers on active duty for a stipulated period of time, at the convenience of the service. Some may serve their obligation in the Reserves or Guard. In the last 2 years of an ROTC program, students receive a monthly allowance while attending school and additional pay for summer training. ROTC scholarships for 2, 3, and 4 years are available on a competitive basis. All scholarships pay for tuition and have allowances for subsistence, textbooks, supplies, and other fees.

College graduates can earn a commission in the Armed Forces through OCS or OTS programs in the Army, Navy, Air Force, Marine Corps, Coast Guard, and National Guard. These officers must serve their obligation on active duty.

Persons with training in certain health professions may qualify for direct appointment as officers. In the case of health professions students, financial assistance and internship opportunities are available from the military in return for specified periods of military service. Prospective medical students can apply to the Uniformed Services University of Health Sciences, which offers free tuition in a program leading to an M. D. degree. In return, graduates must serve for 7 years in either the military or the Public Health Service.

Direct appointments also are available for those qualified to serve in other special duties, such as the judge advocate general (legal) or chaplain corps.

Flight training is available to commissioned officers in each branch of the Armed Forces. In addition, the Army has a direct enlistment option to become a warrant officer aviator.

*Advancement opportunities.* Each service has different criteria for promoting personnel. Generally, the first few promotions for both enlisted and officer personnel come easily; subsequent promotions are much more competitive. Criteria for promotion may include time in service and grade, job performance, a fitness report (supervisor's recommendation), and written examinations. People who are passed over for promotion several times generally must leave the military.

## Job Outlook

Opportunities should be good in all branches of the Armed Forces through the year 2006 because many qualified youth prefer civilian employment. About 190,000 enlisted personnel and 15,000 officers must be recruited each year to replace those who complete their commitment or retire. Educational requirements will continue to rise as military jobs become more technical and complex; high school graduates and applicants with a college background will be sought to fill the ranks of enlisted personnel.

America's strategic position is stronger than it has been in decades. Although there have been reductions in personnel due to the reduction in the threat from Eastern Europe and Russia, the number of active duty personnel is now expected to remain about constant through 2006. The Armed Forces' goal is to maintain a sufficient force to fight and win two major regional conflicts occurring at the same time. However, political events could cause these plans to change.

## Earnings, Allowances, and Benefits

*Starting salaries.* Annual salaries by rank and years of service of military personnel are shown in table 3. Most enlisted personnel started as recruits at Grade E-1 in 1997; however, those with special skills or above-average education started as high as Grade E-4. Most warrant officers started at Grade W-1 or W-2, depending upon their occupational and academic qualifications and the branch of service. Most commissioned officers started at Grade O-1; highly trained officers—for example, physicians, engineers, and scientists—started as high as Grade O-3 or 0-4.

*Allowances.* In addition to basic pay, military personnel receive free room and board (or a tax-free housing and subsistence allowance), medical and dental care, a military clothing allowance, military supermarket and department store shopping privileges, 30 days of paid vacation a year (referred to as leave), and travel opportunities. Other allowances are paid for foreign duty, hazardous duty, submarine and flight duty, and employment as a medical officer.

Athletic and other recreational facilities—such as libraries, gymnasiums, tennis courts, golf courses, bowling centers, and movies—are available on many military installations.

Military personnel are eligible for retirement benefits after 20 years of service.

*Veterans' benefits.* The Veterans Administration (VA) provides numerous benefits to those who have served at least 2 years in the Armed Forces. Veterans are eligible for free care in VA hospitals for all service-connected disabilities regardless of time served; those with other medical problems are eligible for free VA care if they are unable to pay the cost of hospitalization elsewhere. Admission to a VA medical center depends on the availability of beds, however. Veterans are also eligible for certain loans, including home loans.

**Table 3.  Military basic pay by grade for active duty personnel with fewer than 2 years service at grade, 1997**

| Rank and title | | | | *Basic monthly pay* |
|---|---|---|---|---|
| **Army** | **Navy and Coast Guard** | **Air Force** | **Marine Corps** | |
| Commissioned officers: | | | | |
| O-6 Colonel | Captain | Colonel | Colonel | $3,638.40 |
| O-5 Lieutenant Colonel | Commander | Lieutenant Colonel | Lieutenant Colonel | 2,910.30 |
| O-4 Major | Lieutenant Commander | Major | Major | 2,452.80 |
| O-3 Captain | Lieutenant | Captain | Captain | 2,279.40 |
| O-2 1st Lieutenant | Lieutenant (JG) | 1st Lieutenant | 1st Lieutenant | 1,987.80 |
| O-1 2nd Lieutenant | Ensign | 2nd Lieutenant | 2nd Lieutenant | 1,725.90 |
| | | | | |
| Warrant officers: | | | | |
| W-2 Chief Warrant Officer | Chief Warrant Officer | | Chief Warrant Officer | 1,848.60 |
| W-1 Warrant Officer | Warrant Officer | NONE | Warrant Officer | 1,540.20 |
| | | | | |
| Enlisted personnel: | | | | |
| E-6 Staff Sergeant | Petty Officer 1st Class | Technical Sergeant | Staff Sergeant | 1,360.80 |
| E-5 Sergeant | Petty Officer 2nd Class | Staff Sergeant | Sergeant | 1,194.30 |
| E-4 Corporal / Specialist | Petty Officer 3rd Class | Senior Airman | Corporal | 1,113.60 |
| E-3 Private First Class | Seaman | Airman 1st Class | Lance Corporal | 1049.70 |
| E-2 Private | Seaman Apprentice | Airman | Private 1st Class | 1010.10 |
| E-1 Private | Seaman Recruit | Airman Basic | Private | 900.90 |
| E-1[1] | | | | 833.40 |

[1]Fewer than 4 months active duty.

SOURCE: U.S. Department of Defense

Veterans, regardless of health, can convert a military life insurance policy to an individual policy with any participating company in the veteran's State of residence. In addition, job counseling, testing, and placement services are available.

Veterans who participate in the New Montgomery GI Bill Program receive educational benefits. Under this program, Armed Forces personnel may elect to deduct from their pay up to $100 a month to put toward their future education for the first 12 months of active duty. Veterans who serve on active duty for three years or more, or two years active duty plus four years in the Selected Reserve or National Guard, will receive $427.87 a month in basic benefits for 36 months. Those who enlist and serve for less than 3 years will receive $347.65 a month. In addition, each service provides its own additional contributions to put toward future education. This sum becomes the service member's educational fund.

Upon separation from active duty, the fund can be used to finance an education at any VA-approved institution. VA-approved schools include many vocational, correspondence, business, technical, and flight training schools; community and junior colleges; and colleges and universities.

Information on educational and other veterans' benefits is available from VA offices located throughout the country.

## Sources of Additional Information

Each of the military services publishes handbooks, fact sheets, and pamphlets describing entrance requirements, training and advancement opportunities, and other aspects of military careers. These publications are widely available at all recruiting stations, most State employment service offices, and in high schools, colleges, and public libraries.

# After the Service: Veterans in the Workforce

The following information is reprinted from the U.S. Office of Personnel Management. For more detailed information about Federal hiring preferences for veterans, visit their web site at http://www.opm.gov/employ/vetguide.pdf.

## Veterans' Employment Opportunities Act of 1998

The Veterans' Employment Opportunities Act of 1998 allows preference eligibles or veterans who have been separated under honorable conditions from the armed forces with 3 or more years of continuous active service to compete for vacancies under merit promotion procedures when an agency accepts applications from outside its own workforce.

What the new law does:
- Requires all merit promotion announcements open to applicants outside the hiring agencies' workforce to indicate that veterans eligible under this new law can apply. However, the new law does not require the application of veterans' preference to selections made under merit promotion;
- Permits these eligible veterans to be hired under an excepted service appointing authority. Eligible veterans are able to compete for competitive service jobs open to all sources;
- Permits a preference eligible to file a formal complaint with the U.S. Department of Labor if he or she believes that an agency has violated his or her veterans' preference entitlements;
- Makes violation of veterans' preference entitlements a prohibited personnel practice;
- Extends veterans' preference requirements to certain activities in the Government Accounting Office, Executive Office of the President, Judicial and Legislative branches of Government;
- Requires the Federal Aviation Administration to apply veterans' preference during RIF procedures.

Benefits of the hiring authority:
- Allows qualified veterans no longer eligible under the VRA authority to be appointed to Federal jobs;
- Provides benefits similar to other excepted authorities (incl. permanent employment, career ladder promotions, health and life insurance benefits, and the ability to compete for Federal jobs when an agency is seeking candidates outside its own workforce);
- Protections in RIF and adverse actions
- No time-in-grade requirements for promotions
- No grade limits on the appointment

Note: "active service" under this law means active duty in a uniformed service and includes full-time training duty, annual training duty, full-time national Guard, and attendance, while in the active service, at a school designated as a service school by law or by the Secretary concerned.

---

### Veterans Lead the Way

Every year, almost 200,000 service members leave the military and join over 15 million other veterans in the civilian labor force—all with a host of skills. These veterans stand ready and willing to meet the challenges and demands of working in the twenty-first century's rapidly changing, global economy.

With the help of the Veterans' Employment and Training Service, veterans have formed innovative labor-management partnerships to place qualified veterans in high-tech apprenticeship programs or directly into jobs. Combining classroom and on-the-job training, these apprenticeship programs help veterans qualify in many high-tech jobs, including computer programming and systems analysis, computer and telecommunications network installation, and high- and low-voltage utility system repair. These programs can be used as models for other training programs targeting older workers, youths, workers who have lost their jobs because of technological change, and others.

Excerpted from futurework: Trends and Challenges for Work in the 21st Century, U.S. Department of Labor, 1999.

# Introduction to Military Careers

Your future. It's coming just ahead. One of the important decisions you will need to make concerning your future is what type of career you might want to enter. In today's world, where there are hundreds of occupations to choose from, it is important to spend some time investigating different occupations that you might be interested in pursuing. Career information resources are a good place to start because they contain detailed descriptions of occupations, including the type of duties performed, amount of education/training required, career advancement opportunities, and working conditions.

*Military Careers* is the leading career information resource for the military world-of-work. This book describes 152 enlisted and officer occupations. It contains information about the type of work performed, as well as employment, training, and career advancement opportunities for Army, Navy, Air Force, Marine Corps, and Coast Guard occupations. Because many military occupations are comparable to one or more civilian occupations, civilian counterparts are listed for all applicable military occupations.

*Military Careers* is organized into two sections:

• Military Occupations
• Military Career Paths

Military Occupations provides descriptions of 91 enlisted and 61 officer occupations. The section provides valuable information for each occupation, such as primary work activities, training provided, and work environment.

The Military Career Paths section describes the typical duties and assignments a person could expect when advancing along the path of a 20-year military career. In total, this section describes the career paths of 23 enlisted and 13 officer occupations from Military Occupations.

While the Military Occupations section presents an overview of the typical job duties for a military occupation, Military Career Paths presents a more comprehensive description of work performed at various stages of a military career.

## EXPLORING CAREERS

"What will I do when I finish high school?" is a question all young people must answer sooner or later. For some, the answer is, "Get a job." For others, the answer is, "Go to college or seek further training." Although making this first decision is a major step in the lifelong process of developing a career, it will not be the last.

Some people believe that once they have decided which occupation to enter, they will follow it for the rest of their lives. That is not necessarily true. The decision on which occupation to enter does not have to be permanent. People and jobs change over time. For example, people reevaluate their careers because their interests and values change, because new technology alters the skills necessary for a certain career, or because of changing economic factors.

You may now be asking yourself, "But how do I go about exploring what careers might be best for me?" There are two basic steps to career exploration:

* Learning about yourself
* Learning about careers

The following paragraphs explain how to go about career exploration using this two-step process.

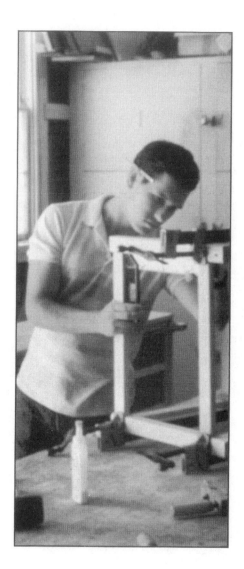

## LEARNING ABOUT YOURSELF

The first step is to spend some time finding out about yourself. Your interests, values, and abilities are important in making career plans. They help you think about what you might want in a career and what you are likely to enjoy. Your counselor can help you begin to clarify your interests, values, and abilities and may also be able to give you tests that measure interests and abilities.

An important resource for learning more about yourself is *Exploring Careers: The ASVAB Workbook.* Copies of this book are available to all students who have taken the Armed Services Vocational Aptitude Battery (ASVAB). Ask your counselor for details on the ASVAB and on obtaining a copy of the Workbook. Below are some things for you to consider when learning about yourself.

### Interests

What do you enjoy doing or would you like to do? Do you like to work on car engines? Perhaps you enjoy writing stories or drawing pictures. Do you prefer to work by yourself or as part of a group? Exploring your interests is helpful at the beginning of the career planning process; knowing your interests will help you to identify careers to investigate.

Your interests are also important to your career development and enjoyment of life. Working in an occupation that interests you makes it easier to work harder and advance in a career. One way to learn more about your interests is to take an "interest inventory." *Exploring Careers: The ASVAB Workbook* contains such an inventory, the *Interest-Finder™.*

### Values

What do you consider most important or desirable in life? We all place a high value on having food to eat and a place to sleep. We also have values that affect what we want from our careers. Some people want careers that pay high salaries almost immediately, even if the work is not very interesting. Others are willing to accept careers with lower wages if the work is challenging and exciting. Many consider having flexible hours or opportunities to travel very important. Some people value having time to pursue nonwork-related interests such as being with their families. Understanding your values is important in planning your future. The ASVAB Workbook contains several exercises that can help you clarify your values.

### Abilities

What do you do well? Are there school subjects in which you get particularly good grades? Are you physically strong and well-coordinated? Can you communicate well with others? Have you worked to develop a skill such as playing a musical instrument? Your abilities can help you find occupations in which you may have a successful career. But just because you do not have the abilities for a certain occupation now does not mean that you cannot acquire them. Additional courses and training may help you to develop your abilities.

Also, it is possible that your interests and abilities may not always match. People are usually interested in things they do well, but this is not always the case. For example, you may be interested in becoming an electronics technician but may not have the manual dexterity to make the precise adjustments needed to keep electronic equipment functioning. However, with additional training, you may acquire the skills needed to become an electrical engineer or a computer programmer who helps to design electronic equipment.

Each year, many high school students take the ASVAB. The ASVAB is a test that measures a person's academic and occupational abilities. ASVAB scores, combined with information about your interests, achievements, values, and other test results, may help you select appropriate areas for career exploration.

*Exploring Careers: The ASVAB Workbook* will help you develop the necessary skills for learning more about yourself. It can help you identify your interests, clarify your work values, and better understand your abilities. You can use these skills again and again as you explore different career opportunities.

## LEARNING ABOUT OCCUPATIONS

Next, you will need to take the information you have learned about yourself and compare it to information about different occupations. This process will allow you to identify occupations that match your interests, values, and abilities.

There are many ways to learn about the broad variety of careers open to you for exploration. To explore the military world-of-work, use the Military Occupations section of this book. It describes 152 different occupations offered by the Army, Navy, Air Force, Marine Corps, and Coast Guard.

The Military Career Paths section of this book can help you learn about career progression. Military Career Paths explains the typical duties and assignments a person could expect when advancing along the path of a 20-year military career.

The *Occupational Outlook Handbook* (OOH) provides occupational descriptions for about 250 civilian occupations. In addition, many schools have a computerized system that provides local, state, and national occupational information for individuals exploring the world-of-work. Your counselor, teachers, or librarians can direct you to these and other resources.

One of these resources is the ASVAB Career Exploration System (ACES). This new computer software is designed to supplement *Exploring Careers: The ASVAB Workbook* by giving the user the capability to generate a list of occupations that best match his or her interests, values, and abilities on-line. This system currently automates Chapter 2: What are your Interests? and Chapter 5: The OCCU-FIND, of the ASVAB Workbook.

While exploring various careers, you need to be constantly asking yourself, "How well does this career match my current interests, values, and abilities?" and "Will this career lead to a lifestyle I desire?" Other questions you might want to ask yourself are:

- What do people do in this career?

- In what type of environment do people in this career work?

- What kind and how much training is needed to enter this career?

- What are the opportunities for obtaining work in this career?

Chances for a rewarding career are improved if personal and career characteristics are similar.

## HOW TO USE MILITARY CAREERS

After learning something about yourself, explore the various career opportunities described in the Military Occupations section. Begin by reading the introduction on page 3 for information on how to use this section.

If one of the careers in the Military Occupations section is of particular interest to you, go to the Military Career Paths section to see if there is a description of its career path. Read the introduction on page 307 for information on how to use this section of the book. Even if there are no careers described of interest to you, you may want to browse through this section to learn about the various occupations and added responsibilities people encounter as they progress through a career.

# Military
# Occupations

# Introduction to Military Occupations

Military Occupations provides an overview of the military world-of-work and was developed specifically to help students explore different military occupations. This section is divided into two parts—military enlisted occupations and military officer occupations.

Enlisted personnel carry out the fundamental operations of the military. They are people like the infantrymen, dental specialists, mechanics, graphic designers and illustrators, computer systems specialists, and air traffic controllers in the military work force. Enlisted personnel are usually high school graduates and are required to meet minimum physical and aptitude standards before enlisting. Enlistment qualifications are described on page 14.

The enlisted occupations section provides general information and descriptions of 91 enlisted occupations. Each enlisted occupational description contains valuable information such as the primary work activities, training provided, employment opportunities, and civilian counterparts. Descriptions of the enlisted occupations can be found on pages 55 to 170. A graph is included for each occupation so you can estimate your chance of qualifying for the occupation. To use these graphs, you must have ASVAB test results. See your counselor or local recruiter for information on how to take the ASVAB.

Officers are the leaders of the military and usually are college graduates. Their roles are like those of corporate managers or executives. Officers develop plans, set objectives, and lead other officers and enlisted personnel in attaining their goals. Young men and women hoping to become officers must meet the minimum entrance requirements set by each military service. The qualifications required for being commissioned as an officer are described on page 181.

The officer occupations section provides general information on being an officer and descriptions of 61 officer occupations. Each officer occupation contains important information similar to that provided for enlisted occupations. For a description of how to read the officer occupations, read pages 174 and 175. Descriptions of the officer occupations can be found on pages 219 to 302.

You may also find the indexes on pages 401 through 427 helpful. If there is a civilian occupation of interest to you, the indexes will help you learn if the military has a similar occupation.

# Military Enlisted Occupations

# How to Read the Enlisted Occupational Descriptions

The purpose of *Military Careers* is to introduce students, parents, and counselors to the military world-of-work. *Military Careers* can be used to explore the many employment and training opportunities available in the enlisted and officer forces of the Army, Navy, Air Force, Marine Corps, and Coast Guard.

*Military Careers* contains descriptions of 152 military occupations. The enlisted occupational section of *Military Careers* contains descriptions of 91 enlisted military occupations. Each enlisted description has standard sections as shown in the example on the opposite page. An explanation for each section of the description is also provided.

When reading any of the 91 enlisted descriptions, remember that it is a summary of similar job specialties across two or more of the military services. For example, the Divers description in the sample represents 18 distinct diving specialties across four services. Therefore, individual job specialties may differ somewhat from the general occupations described in this book. If you are interested in learning more about a particular service or occupation, you should contact a recruiter for details.

**1 Occupational Title**
The occupational title names the military occupation. An alphabetical listing of titles is in the index beginning on page 420.

**2 Military Service Representation**
The military services listed next to the title offer employment and training opportunities in the occupation. Not all services offer every occupation described in *Military Careers*.

**3 Summary**
The summary contains background information about the military occupation.

**4 What They Do**
"What They Do" describes the main work activities performed by workers in the occupation. Because job specialties vary from one service to another, some of the activities listed may not apply to all services.

**5 Physical Demands**
Some military occupations place physical demands on workers. For example, strength for moderate or heavy lifting is a common physical demand noted in *Military Careers*. Other physical demands include running, climbing, swimming, clear speech, and special vision or hearing requirements.

**6 Special Requirements**
Special requirements must be met to enter certain occupations. Typing ability, fluency in a foreign language, and successful completion of certain high school courses are examples of special qualifications. This section also identifies combat occupations from which women are excluded by law at the time of this publication.

**7 Helpful Attributes**
"Helpful Attributes" include interests, school subjects taken, experience, and other personal characteristics that may be helpful for training and working in the military occupation. These attributes are not requirements.

**8 Work Environment**
"Work Environment" describes the typical work settings and conditions for the occupation. Work settings may be indoors or outdoors, on land, aboard ships, or in aircraft.

**9 Training Provided**
The military provides job training to all new workers. Most job training is provided in a classroom setting. For some occupations, training is provided on the job. In "Training Provided," the length of classroom training and course content are summarized. Course content and length of training may vary for each service. When applicable, this section also names the services that offer apprenticeship programs certified by the Department of Labor.

**10 Civilian Counterparts**
Most military occupations are comparable to one or more civilian occupations because they require similar duties and training. "Civilian Counterparts" identifies these civilian occupations and the kinds of companies or organizations in which they are located. The *Dictionary of Occupational Titles* (DOT) Code Index, beginning on page 408, provides a complete listing of counterpart civilian occupations for each military occupation.

**11 Opportunities**
"Opportunities" contains information on the total number of enlisted personnel working in the occupation and the average annual need for new personnel. Military career advancement in the occupation is also summarized in this section.

**12 ASVAB Qualification Graph**
The ASVAB is a test offered in most high schools and postsecondary schools. If you have taken the ASVAB, you can use your Military Careers Score with these graphs.

For each of the 91 enlisted occupations described in *Military Careers*, a graph is included that relates your Military Careers Score to military occupations. See page 8 for instructions on using these graphs.

**① DIVERS**

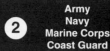

**②** Army
Navy
Marine Corps
Coast Guard

**③** Sometimes, military tasks such as ship repair, construction, and patrolling must be done under water. Divers in the military perform this work. They usually specialize either as scuba divers, who work just below the surface, or as deep sea divers, who may work for long periods of time in depths up to 300 feet.

**④ What They Do**

Divers in the military perform some or all of the following duties:

- Inspect and clean ship propellers and hulls
- Patch damaged ship hulls using underwater welding equipment
- Patrol the waters below ships at anchor
- Salvage (recover) sunken equipment
- Assist with underwater construction of piers and harbor facilities
- Survey rivers, beaches, and harbors for underwater obstacles
- Use explosives to clear underwater obstacles

**⑤ Physical Demands**

Divers must be good swimmers and physically strong.

**⑥ Special Requirements**

Although there are women divers, some specialties in this occupation are open only to men.

**⑦ Helpful Attributes**

Helpful school subjects include shop mechanics and building trades. Helpful attributes include:

- Interest in underwater diving
- Ability to stay calm under stress
- A high degree of self-reliance

**⑧ Work Environment**

Divers work under water. However, they plan and prepare for work on land or aboard ships. Because diving is not usually a full-time job, divers often have another job specialty in which they work.

**⑨ Training Provided**

Job training consists of 5 to 13 weeks of classroom instruction, including practice in diving and repair work. Training length varies depending on specialty. Course content typically includes:

- Principles of scuba diving
- Underwater welding and cutting
- Use and care of hand and power tools
- Maintenance of diving equipment

Further training occurs on the job and through advanced courses.

**⑩ Civilian Counterparts**

Civilian divers work for oil companies, salvage companies, underwater construction firms, and police or fire rescue units. They perform duties similar to divers in the military.

**⑪ Opportunities**

The services have about 350 divers. On average, they need about 10 new divers each year. After job training, divers work in teams headed by experienced divers. Eventually, they may become master divers and supervise diving operations.

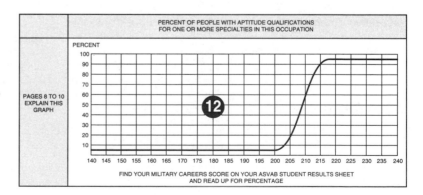

PAGES 8 TO 10 EXPLAIN THIS GRAPH

PERCENT OF PEOPLE WITH APTITUDE QUALIFICATIONS FOR ONE OR MORE SPECIALTIES IN THIS OCCUPATION

PERCENT

⑫

FIND YOUR MILITARY CAREERS SCORE ON YOUR ASVAB STUDENT RESULTS SHEET AND READ UP FOR PERCENTAGE

# How to Use the ASVAB Graph

## What is the ASVAB?

The ASVAB is a test that can help you with educational and career planning. ASVAB scores can be used to explore occupations that interest you. For each of the 91 enlisted occupations described in the occupations section of *Military Careers*, a graph is included that relates ASVAB scores to enlisted military occupations. The officer occupational descriptions do not include an ASVAB graph because the ASVAB is not used in the selection process for officers. Using the graphs in this book and your ASVAB results, you can estimate your chances of qualifying for entry into enlisted military occupations. If you have not taken the ASVAB and would like to, ask your school counselor for information on how to do so.

## Which ASVAB Score Should I Use?

On your Student Results Sheet, you will find a section marked ASVAB Scores (see sample on opposite page). At the bottom of this section is your Military Careers Score. You can use this score to estimate your chances of qualifying for any of the enlisted occupations in this book.

## What is my Military Careers Score?

Each of the enlisted military occupations described in this book requires a minimum aptitude score. The minimum score required may vary from occupation to occupation. The Military Careers Score is based on your math, verbal, mechanical, and electronic abilities, as indicated by your ASVAB Scores. By using your Military Careers Score with the graphs found in the enlisted occupational descriptions, you can estimate your chances of qualifying for any of the enlisted occupations described.

For those students in the 10th or 11th grade, it is important to remember that your Military Careers Score may improve as you get older and receive more schooling. If you took the ASVAB when you were in the 10th grade, and then again in the 12th grade, your later Military Careers Score would probably be higher. An improved Military Careers Score would allow you to qualify for a greater number of enlisted occupations. Therefore, in order to have the best possible chance of qualifying for an occupation, you should stay in school, get your high school diploma, and then take the ASVAB again.

## How Do I Use My Military Careers Score?

Using your Military Careers Score to estimate your chances of qualifying for military occupations described in this book involves four steps. To help you learn these steps, a sample ASVAB graph is provided on the opposite page. Pretend the graph is from an occupational description that interests you.

### STEP 1

On your Student Results Sheet, in the section marked ASVAB Scores, find your Military Careers Score. For example, the sample Student Results Sheet on the opposite page shows you have obtained a Military Careers Score of "200."

### STEP 2

Find your score on the bottom line of the ASVAB graph. In this example, the arrow points to your score of "200" on the sample graph. (You will need to estimate the location of your score if it falls between the numbers shown on the bottom line of the graph.)

## Sample *Military Careers* ASVAB Graph

PAGES 8 TO 10 EXPLAIN THIS GRAPH

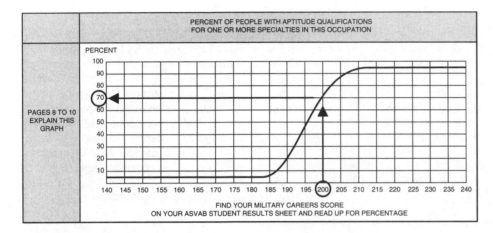

PERCENT OF PEOPLE WITH APTITUDE QUALIFICATIONS FOR ONE OR MORE SPECIALTIES IN THIS OCCUPATION

PERCENT

FIND YOUR MILITARY CAREERS SCORE
ON YOUR ASVAB STUDENT RESULTS SHEET AND READ UP FOR PERCENTAGE

### STEP 3

Read up in a straight line from your score until you come to the curve drawn on the graph.

### STEP 4

Now, follow straight across to the left from the curve to the number on the side of the graph. The number indicates the percentage of people with a particular Military Careers Score who qualify for this military occupation. In the example, 70 percent of the people who obtained a Military Careers Score of "200" qualified for this occupation. This means your score of "200" gives you an estimated 70 percent chance of qualifying for one or more job specialties in the occupation. Turn to the next page for further explanation of what the percentage means.

## Sample ASVAB Results Sheet

PUBLIC JANE Q
GRADE 11                    SEX F
SSN 987-65-4321
TEST DATE 9/10/95
BETA HIGH SCHOOL
ANYTOWN                     IL

# ASVAB STUDENT RESULTS SHEET
ARMED SERVICES VOCATIONAL APTITUDE BATTERY

**Percentile Scores**

| ASVAB Scores | Same Grade/ Same Sex | Same Grade/Same Sex Percentile Score Bands | Same Grade/ Opposite Sex |
|---|---|---|---|
| | | 1   5   10   20   30   40   50   60   70   80   90   95   99 | |
| **Academic Ability** (AA = VA + MA) | 50 | [ - ] | 53 |
| **Verbal Ability** (VA = WK + PC) | 51 | [----] | 51 |
| **Math Ability** (MA = AR + MK) | 54 | [-- | 56 |
| Word Knowledge (WK) | 47 | [---- -] | 44 |
| Paragraph Comprehension (PC) | 67 | [------------] | 74 |
| Arithmetic Reasoning (AR) | 55 | [----] | 52 |
| Mathematics Knowledge (MK) | 52 | [--- | 59 |
| General Science (GS) | 56 | [------] | 43 |
| Auto & Shop Information (AS) | 81 | [-------] | 43 |
| Mechanical Comprehension (MC) | 65 | [ ] | 37 |
| Electronics Information (EI) | 60 | [----- ] | 38 |
| Numerical Operations (NO) | 78 | [----] | 89 |
| Coding Speed (CS) | 62 | [----------] | 82 |
| **ASVAB Codes** 3,4 | | | |
| **Military Careers Score** 200 | | | |

(SEE BACK OF SHEET FOR EXPLANATION)

### Explanation of Your ASVAB Scores

**ASVAB SCORES**

When you took the Armed Services Vocational Aptitude Battery (ASVAB), there were 10 tests. These tests are listed under the column "ASVAB Scores." Two examples are Word Knowledge and Coding Speed. Also, three additional scores are provided: Academic Ability (AA), Verbal Ability (VA) and Math Ability (MA). All of these ASVAB scores are described on the back of this sheet.

**PERCENTILE SCORES**

Your ASVAB scores are reported as percentiles. Percentile scores show how well you did in relation to others. ASVAB scores compare you to a national sample of students. Two types of percentile scores are reported: same grade/same sex and same grade/opposite sex scores. If you are in grades 10, 11 or 12, your same grade/same sex score compares you with students of your own grade and sex. In contrast, your same grade/opposite sex score compares you with students of your own grade and the opposite sex. Postsecondary students are compared with two-year college students. Suppose an 11th grade female obtained a same grade/same sex score of 60 on Verbal Ability. This means she scored the same or better than 60 out of every 100 females at her grade level in the national sample.

As mentioned above, scores are provided that compare you with students of your own and opposite sex. Because life experiences of girls and boys can vary, they can score somewhat differently on tests. Being male or female, however, does not limit your career or educational choices. Using gender-based scores may broaden the range of career and educational areas you are considering. For help in exploring careers, ask your counselor for *Exploring Careers: The ASVAB Workbook*. Also, if you need help understanding your scores, see your counselor.

SEE YOUR COUNSELOR FOR FURTHER HELP IN INTERPRETING YOUR ASVAB SCORES

TURN THIS SHEET OVER TO LEARN MORE ABOUT YOUR ASVAB SCORES

| ASVAB Codes | 3,4 |
|---|---|
| Military Careers Score | 200 |

(See Back of Sheet for Explanation)

## What Does the ASVAB Percent Mean?

In the example below, your Military Careers Score of "200" gave you an estimated 70 percent chance of qualifying for one or more job specialties in the occupation. A 70 percent chance of qualifying is similar to a weather forecaster's prediction of a 70 percent chance of rain. This prediction means that, under certain weather conditions, it rains 70 times out of 100. The ASVAB percentage means that 70 out of every 100 people who obtain a Military Careers Score of "200" have the aptitude to qualify for one or more of the occupations in the example.

When using the ASVAB graphs, remember that ASVAB estimates are not precise measures. No test can provide a completely accurate measure of aptitudes. Your scores may change somewhat if you take the ASVAB again. For example, students who take the ASVAB during their sophomore or junior year usually find that their scores improve somewhat if they retake the ASVAB during their senior year.

Also, keep in mind that aptitude is only one of several qualifications needed to enter occupations in the military. For example, specific physical requirements must be met to qualify for some occupations. The next section of this book describes some of the other requirements.

The ASVAB information in *Military Careers* is provided so that you may explore your chances of qualifying for military occupations. Specific information about whether you qualify for a particular service job specialty is available through a local service recruiter.

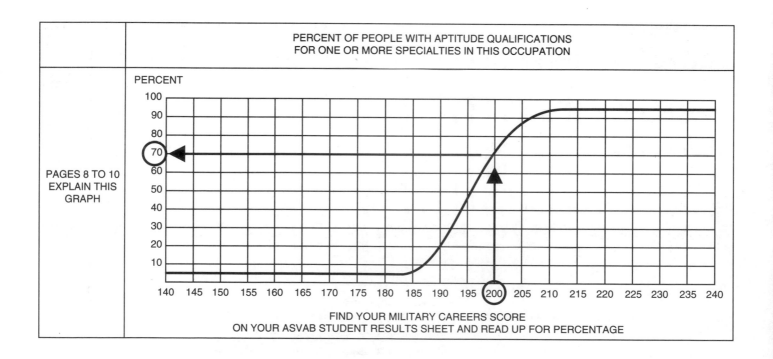

# General Information on Enlisted Occupations

# General Information on Enlisted Occupations

For almost 45 years, the military's personnel requirements and overall strategies had been shaped by the need to be prepared to deal with a short-notice, global war with the former Soviet Union. Given the dramatic developments in Eastern Europe, the former Soviet Union, and Africa, the military services are refocusing their strategy on a peacetime mission and on readiness for regional conflicts and contingencies. As the military plans for the next century, it will reduce the number of enlisted military personnel on active duty.

Although the active-duty military services have declined in size, they still need substantial numbers of new recruits to fill the many entry-level jobs that are available.

Enlisted members are the supervisors and workers who carry out and maintain the basic operations of the military. Their roles are like those of company employees and supervisors. Enlisted members serve in occupations as diverse as computer programmers, automotive and heavy equipment mechanics, medical care technicians, and personnel specialists. As supervisors, enlisted members are responsible for the well-being of other enlisted members and for the care of equipment and property under their control. Overall, the services have available a broad range of enlisted occupations that require personnel with various types of knowledge, skills, and abilities.

## MILITARY ENLISTED OCCUPATIONS

Besides being the single largest employer in the nation, the military offers the widest choice of career opportunities. Together, the five services offer training and employment in over 2,000 enlisted job specialties. To help you explore the enlisted world-of-work, these specialties are grouped into 91 enlisted occupations in this book. These 91 occupations are organized into 12 broad groups:

- Human Services
- Media and Public Affairs
- Health Care
- Engineering, Science, and Technical
- Administrative
- Service
- Vehicle and Machinery Mechanic
- Electronic and Electrical Equipment Repair
- Construction
- Machine Operator and Precision Work
- Transportation and Material Handling
- Combat Specialty

Figure 1 shows the distribution of enlisted members across the 12 occupational groups.

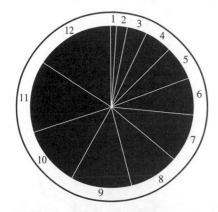

**Figure 1**
**Distribution of Enlisted Personnel by Occupational Group**

1. Human Services
2. Media and Public Affairs
3. Health Care
4. Engineering, Science, and Technical
5. Administrative
6. Service
7. Vehicle and Machinery Mechanic
8. Electronic and Electrical Equipment Repair
9. Construction
10. Machine Operator and Precision Work
11. Transportation and Material Handling
12. Combat Specialty

---

| Table 1 – General Enlistment Qualifications* |
|---|

**Age:** Must be between 17 and 35 years. Consent of parent or legal guardian required if 17.

**Citizenship Status:** Must be either (1) U.S. citizen, or (2) an immigrant alien legally admitted to the U.S. for permanent residence and possessing immigration and naturalization documents.

**Physical Condition:** Must meet minimum physical standards listed below to enlist. Some military occupations have additional physical standards.

| Height – | | Maximum | Minimum |
|---|---|---|---|
| | For males: | 6'8"/203.2 cm | 5'0"/152.4 cm |
| | For females: | 6'8"/203.2 cm | 4'10"/147.3 cm |

Weight – There are minimum and maximum weights for the various services according to height, wrist size, and/or percentage of body fat.

| | | Maximum | Minimum |
|---|---|---|---|
| | For males: | 255 lb/115.66 kg | 100 lb/45.35 kg |
| | For females: | 227 lb/102.96 kg | 90 lb/40.82 kg |

Vision – The requirements are specific for each service and are determined by job specialty. In general, service members must have at least 20/400 or 20/200 vision if it can be corrected to 20/20 with eyeglasses or contacts lenses. The vision requirements are also based on depth perception as well as color blindness.

Overall Health – Must be in good health and pass a medical exam. Certain diseases or conditions may exclude persons from enlistment; for example, diabetes, severe allergies, epilepsy, alcoholism, and drug addiction.

**Education:** High school graduation is desired by all services and is a requirement under most enlisted options.

**Aptitude:** Must make the minimum entry score on the Armed Services Vocational Aptitude Battery (ASVAB). Minimum entry scores vary by service and occupation.

**Moral Character:** Must meet standards designed to screen out persons likely to become disciplinary problems. Standards cover court convictions, juvenile delinquency, arrests, and drug use.

**Marital Status and Dependents:** May be either single or married; however, single persons with one or more minor dependents are not eligible for enlistment into military service.

**Waivers:** On a case-by-case basis, exceptions (waivers) are granted by individual services for some of the above qualification requirements.

---

\* Each service sets its own enlistment qualification requirements. If you are interested in a specific service's enlistment requirements, see the "Service Information on Enlisted Occupations" section beginning on page 31, or contact a military recruiter.

In order to function as a self-sufficient community, the military must employ individuals with many different skills and abilities. The services need auto, ship, and aircraft mechanics to keep their many forms of transportation moving; food service specialists to provide meals for thousands of soldiers; and computer programmers to maintain information and communication systems. Therefore, the military has a wide spectrum of occupations.

Over 75 percent of all military occupations have counterparts in the civilian world-of-work. For example, dental hygienist, air traffic controller, computer programmer, aircraft mechanic, and technician occupations exist in both the military and civilian work forces.

The services offer training and an opportunity to progress in each occupation. No matter which occupation newly enlisted personnel enter, they will find a well-defined career path leading to higher pay and increased responsibility.

## ENLISTMENT

Enlisted personnel are usually high school graduates and must meet minimum standards such as physical and aptitude requirements before enlisting. The general qualifications required for enlistment are shown in Table 1. If you are interested in a specific service's enlistment requirements or programs, see the "Service Information on Enlisted Occupations" section beginning on page 31.

### Service Obligation

Joining the military involves entering into a legal contract called an enlistment agreement. The service agrees to provide a job, pay, benefits, and occupational training. In return, the enlisted member agrees to serve for a certain period of time, which is called the service obligation. The standard service obligation is eight years, which is divided between active military duty and reserve duty. Depending on the enlistment program selected, enlisted members spend two to six years on active duty with the balance of the eight-year obligation period spent in reserve status.

### Enlistment Programs

Enlistment programs vary by service. The services adjust the programs they offer to meet changing recruiting needs. Major enlistment options include cash bonuses for enlisting in certain occupations and guaranteed choice of job training and assignments. Currently, all services also offer a Delayed Entry Program (DEP), an option that is used by many high school students who wish to enlist now but wait a short while before entering into active duty. By enlisting under the DEP option, an applicant delays entry into active duty for up to one year. High school students often enlist under the DEP during their senior year and enter a service after graduation. Other qualified applicants choose the DEP because the job training they desire is not currently available but will be within the next year.

### Enlistment Contracts

The enlistment contract specifies the enlistment program selected by the applicant. It contains the enlistment date, term of enlistment, and other options, such as a training program guarantee or a cash bonus. If, for any reason, the service cannot meet its part of the agreement (for example, to provide a specific type of job training), then the applicant is no longer bound by the contract. If the applicant accepts another enlistment program, a new contract is written.

### High School Graduates

The military encourages young people to stay in high school and graduate. Research has shown that high school graduates are more likely to adjust to military life and complete an initial tour of duty. Therefore, the services accept very few non-high school graduates.

## ENLISTING IN THE MILITARY

Enlisting in the military involves a four-step process.

### Step 1: Talking with a Recruiter

If you are interested in applying for one of the military services, you must talk with a recruiter from that service. Recruiters can provide detailed information about the employment and training opportunities in their service, as well as answer specific questions about service life, enlistment options, and other topics. They can also provide details about their service's enlistment qualification requirements.

If you decide to apply for entry into the service, and the recruiter identifies no problems (such as a severe health problem), the recruiter will examine your educational credentials. The recruiter will then schedule you for enlistment processing.

### Step 2: Qualifying for Enlistment

Full enlistment processing occurs at one of the more than 60 Military Entrance Processing Stations (MEPS) located around the country. At the MEPS, applicants take the ASVAB, if they have not already done so, and receive medical examinations to determine if they are qualified to enter the service. The ASVAB may also be administered at Mobile Examining Team (MET) sites.

ASVAB results are used to determine if an applicant qualifies for entry into a service, and if the applicant has the specific aptitude level required to enter job specialty training programs. If you have taken the ASVAB at your school, you can use your scores to determine if you qualify for entry into the military services, provided the scores are not more than two years old. Applicants with current ASVAB scores are not required to take the ASVAB a second time.

### Step 3: Meeting with a Service Classifier

A service classifier is a military career information specialist who helps applicants select military occupations. For example, if you are applying for entry, the classifier would inform you of service job training openings that match your aptitudes and interests. Specifically, the classifier would enter your ASVAB scores into a computerized reservation system. Based on your scores, the system would show the career fields and training programs for which you qualify and when job training would be available.

After discussing job training options with the classifier, you would select an occupation and schedule an enlistment date. Enlistment dates may be scheduled up to one year in the future to coincide with job training openings. This option is called the Delayed Entry Program (DEP) as described on the previous page.

Following selection of a military training program, you would sign an enlistment contract and take the oath of enlistment. If you chose the DEP option, you would return home until your enlistment date.

### Step 4: Enlisting in the Service

After completing enlistment processing, applicants who select the immediate enlistment option receive their travel papers and proceed to a military base for basic training. Applicants who select the DEP option return to the MEPS on their scheduled enlistment date. At that time, applicants officially become "enlistees" (also known as "recruits") and proceed to a military base.

In the uncommon event that your guaranteed training program, through no fault of your own, is not available on the reserved date, you have three options:

- Make another reservation for the same training and return at a later date to enter the service

- Select another occupation and job training option

- Decide not to join the service and be free from any obligation.

## MILITARY TRAINING

The military operates one of the largest training systems in the world. The five services sponsor nearly 300 technical training schools offering more than 10,000 separate courses of instruction.

Education and training provided by the services offer service members valuable opportunities for career development. The services spend billions of dollars each year training service members for jobs ranging from air traffic controller to medical service technician. The main purpose of training is to prepare individuals to perform jobs in the service. Training also helps individuals meet personal goals and prepares them to assume greater responsibility in the service work force.

The military generally provides four kinds of training for its personnel:

- Recruit training

- Job training

- Advanced training

- Leadership training.

### Recruit Training

Recruit training, popularly called basic training, is a rigorous orientation to the military. Depending on the service, recruit training lasts from six to ten weeks and provides a transition from civilian to military life. The services train recruits at selected military bases across the country. Where an enlistee trains depends on the service and the job training to be received. Through basic training, recruits gain the pride, knowledge, discipline, and physical conditioning necessary to serve as members of the Army, Navy, Air Force, Marine Corps, and Coast Guard.

Upon reporting for basic training, recruits are divided into training groups of 40 to 80 people. They then meet their drill instructor, receive uniforms and equipment, and move into assigned quarters.

During basic training, recruits receive instruction in health, first aid, and military skills. They also improve their fitness and stamina by participating in rigorous daily exercises and conditioning. To measure their conditioning progress, recruits are tested on sit-ups, push-ups, running, and body weight.

Recruits follow a demanding schedule throughout basic training; every day is carefully structured with time for classes, meals, physical conditioning, and field instruction. Some free time (including time to attend religious services) is available to recruits during basic training. After completing basic training, recruits normally proceed to job training.

### Job Training

Through job training, also called technical or skill training, recruits learn the skills they will need to perform their job specialties. The military provides its personnel with high-quality training because lives and mission success depend on how well people perform their duties. Military training produces highly qualified workers, and for this reason many civilian employers consider military training excellent preparation for civilian occupations.

The type of job specialty determines the length of training. Most training lasts from 10 to 20 weeks, although some specialties require over one year of training.

Military training occurs both in the classroom and on the job. Classroom training emphasizes hands-on activities and practical experience, as well as textbook learning. For example, recruits who will be working with electronic equipment practice operating and repairing the equipment, in addition to studying the principles of electronics.

At their first assignments, enlisted members continue to learn on the job. Experienced enlisted members and supervisors help service men and women further develop their skills. In addition, the military offers refresher courses and advanced training to help military personnel maintain and increase their skills. As personnel advance in rank, they continue their training with leadership and management courses.

Three services, the Army, Navy, and Marine Corps, offer apprenticeship programs for some job specialties. These programs consist of classroom and on-the-job training that meet U.S. Department of Labor apprenticeship standards. After completing an apprenticeship program, personnel receive a Department of Labor apprenticeship certificate. To military commanders and civilian employers, these certificates demonstrate that the worker has acquired specific skills and qualifications.

For each of the 91 enlisted occupations described in the Military Occupations section of this book, a summary of the typical training content and length is provided.

### Advanced Training

Hundreds of advanced training courses have been developed by the services to improve the technical skills of the enlisted work force. These courses offer instruction in skills not covered in initial training. An automobile mechanic, for example, may take advanced instruction in troubleshooting (identifying engine problems) or preventive maintenance techniques. Advanced training also includes courses covering new or additional job-related equipment. An auto mechanic may go to school to learn how to repair a new type of vehicle, or a radiological technician may take instruction in the use of ultrasound equipment. Advanced training is especially important in high technology areas where military technicians are constantly being exposed to newer and more sophisticated equipment. Other advanced courses provide instruction in supervising and managing the daily operations of military units, such as repair shops or medical facilities.

Some advanced training involves classroom training, but the services also provide enlisted members with a wide choice of self-study correspondence courses. Some of these are general courses and address most duties of a job. Other courses are designed to cover highly complex tasks or job-related skills. Self-study courses are particularly important to individual career advancement. Completing a self-study course can provide a service member with the job skills and knowledge to perform more advanced job duties. Self-study courses also include material that prepares enlisted personnel to take the competitive examinations required to advance through the noncommissioned officer (NCO) ranks.

### Leadership Training

Each service has schools and courses to help supervisors be more effective in managing the day-to-day operations of their units. These classes are designed primarily for noncommissioned officers. Courses include instruction in leadership skills, service regulations, and management techniques needed to train and lead other service members.

## CAREER DEVELOPMENT, GUIDANCE AND COUNSELING

Almost every military base has an education center. At these centers, counselors are available with information about education and training (military and civilian) and requirements for career advancement. They can also provide information about retraining for other military occupations.

Counselors coordinate the services' education programs and help service men and women set educational goals. They can explain the many opportunities available and help service members enroll in programs or courses. The counselors help enlisted personnel tailor their educational programs to meet their career goals.

### Continuing Education

The services recognize the value of education, both military and civilian. Military training helps enlisted personnel perform their job duties and develop leadership and supervisory skills. Continuing civilian education, regardless of the subject, also helps an enlisted person to become a more well-rounded individual, better prepared to deal with the challenges of service life. The services offer many programs to help and encourage enlisted men and women to continue their civilian educations. Enlisted personnel may enroll in courses to earn college degrees,

improve work skills, or simply for personal enjoyment. Each service's training department offers self-study courses on many different topics in which any enlisted person can enroll. If you are interested in a specific service's continuing education program, see the "Service Information on Enlisted Occupations" section beginning on page 31.

### Defense Activity for Nontraditional Education Support (DANTES)

DANTES is an organization within the Department of Defense designed to support education in all of the services. It helps develop and administer education programs. In addition to supporting individual service programs, DANTES also offers many different programs for active-duty service members. The College Level Examination Program (CLEP) allows service members to obtain college credits through examination without attending courses. The Independent Study Program allows enlisted personnel to take high school through graduate-level self-study courses offered by accredited colleges and universities.

### Service Members Opportunity Colleges (SOCs)

The Service Members Opportunity Colleges are a consortium of colleges and universities that help enlisted personnel satisfy the requirements for college

degrees. SOCs began in the early 1970s to help expand and improve postsecondary educational opportunities for military personnel and veterans. This civilian/military partnership consists of more than 1,000 colleges and universities, the Department of Defense, the military services, and is supported by 12 national higher education associations. Because enlisted personnel are frequently reassigned, they can find it difficult to complete their coursework for a degree at one college or university. In this program, participating colleges and universities accept credits earned at other schools and award credit for some military training courses. Through SOCs, enlisted personnel can more easily complete the requirements for a college degree. For additional information on SOCs, call 800-368-5622 or 202-667-0079.

### Other College Programs

The services offer tuition assistance programs that pay from 75 to 100 percent of the fees for off-duty study in most courses at accredited schools, depending upon the availability of funds. Enlisted personnel can use these courses to pursue bachelor's or advanced degrees. The services also have agreements with many colleges and universities that allow the schools to hold classes on the base. Similar programs also offer courses at overseas locations and aboard ships.

**Figure 2**
**Enlisted Insignia of the United States Armed Forces**

## ENLISTED CAREER ADVANCEMENT

A military career is more than just a job. The military offers the opportunity to advance in exciting careers. Motivated men and women advance by improving their job skills and taking on greater responsibility. Advancement means recognition for a job well done, a promotion to more responsible duties, and increased military rank and pay grade. Pay grade and length of service determine a service member's pay. Figure 2 shows the insignias for the ranks of each service. It also depicts the relationship between rank and pay grade.

### Enlisted Promotion

Men and women in the lower pay grades (E-1 to E-3) usually advance to the next grade based on their length of service and time in their present pay grade. They must also receive their commanding officer's approval and be satisfactorily progressing in their training and job performance. Only individuals who show superior performance may be promoted to E-4.

All enlisted personnel are led, supervised, and evaluated by senior enlisted personnel and officers. Factors that qualify an enlisted person for promotion include:

- Length of service
- Time in present pay grade
- Job performance
- Leadership ability
- Awards or commendations
- Job specialty
- Educational achievement through technical, on-the-job, or civilian instruction.

Each service sets minimum standards for the length of service and time in current pay grade that must be met before a person can compete for promotion to the next higher pay grade.

| SERVICE / PAY GRADE | ARMY | NAVY | AIR FORCE | MARINE CORPS | COAST GUARD |
|---|---|---|---|---|---|
| E-9 | COMMAND SERGEANT MAJOR / SERGEANT MAJOR | MASTER CHIEF PETTY OFFICER | CHIEF MASTER SERGEANT | SERGEANT MAJOR / MASTER GUNNERY SERGEANT | MASTER CHIEF PETTY OFFICER |
| E-8 | FIRST SERGEANT / MASTER SERGEANT | SENIOR CHIEF PETTY OFFICER | SENIOR MASTER SERGEANT | FIRST SERGEANT / MASTER SERGEANT | SENIOR CHIEF PETTY OFFICER |
| E-7 | SERGEANT FIRST CLASS | CHIEF PETTY OFFICER | MASTER SERGEANT | GUNNERY SERGEANT | CHIEF PETTY OFFICER |
| E-6 | STAFF SERGEANT | PETTY OFFICER FIRST CLASS | TECHNICAL SERGEANT | STAFF SERGEANT | PETTY OFFICER FIRST CLASS |
| E-5 | SERGEANT | PETTY OFFICER SECOND CLASS | STAFF SERGEANT | SERGEANT | PETTY OFFICER SECOND CLASS |
| E-4 | CORPORAL / SPECIALIST | PETTY OFFICER THIRD CLASS | SENIOR AIRMAN | CORPORAL | PETTY OFFICER THIRD CLASS |
| E-3 | PRIVATE FIRST CLASS | SEAMAN | AIRMAN FIRST CLASS | LANCE CORPORAL | FIREMAN / SEAMAN |
| E-2 | PRIVATE | SEAMAN APPRENTICE | AIRMAN | PRIVATE FIRST CLASS | FIREMAN APPRENTICE / SEAMAN APPRENTICE |
| E-1 | No Insignia / PRIVATE | SEAMAN RECRUIT | No Insignia / AIRMAN BASIC | No Insignia / PRIVATE | No Insignia / SEAMAN RECRUIT |

Figure 3 shows the average time an enlisted member has been in the military (time-in-service) when he or she is promoted to each pay grade. For example, it takes an average of one year to reach pay grade E-3 and nine years to reach E-6. The time-in-service and advancement information shown is developed from data provided by each of the services.

Good performance reports are essential to continue along a career path. Although a good performance report does not automatically qualify an individual for promotion, a less than satisfactory rating severely limits chances for promotion. By selecting from among qualified individuals for promotion to each rank, the services try to ensure that the best qualified personnel are promoted. Because the number of enlisted positions is limited by Congress, the competition for promotion at the senior levels is intense. Changes in the number of personnel in a particular specialty, or in the armed services as a whole, can also affect promotion.

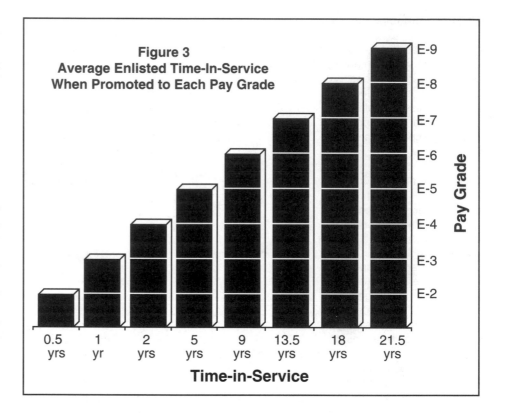

**Figure 3**
**Average Enlisted Time-In-Service**
**When Promoted to Each Pay Grade**

### Enlisted Commissioning Programs

Officers and enlisted personnel advance along separate career paths. However, each service has programs that enable selected enlisted personnel to become commissioned officers. The entrance standards for these programs are high, and the competition is strong.

Typically, there are two ways for enlisted personnel to earn commissions: through direct appointment and acceptance to officer training and through service programs that send enlisted personnel to college full-time to obtain a degree. Direct appointment programs usually require an outstanding performance record and a college degree. Individuals selected for these programs go to officer training schools operated by their service. Enlisted personnel selected to complete their college degree attend college through an ROTC program or one of the service academies. After completing officer training, these individuals are awarded commissions as officers in their respective services.

## DUTY ASSIGNMENT

The five services have similar systems for assigning personnel to jobs. Each system is designed to satisfy the staffing needs of the particular service. For example, if the service needs a machinist at a remote location, a service member trained as a machinist is assigned there. However, at the same time, the services also attempt to meet the desires of the individual service member and provide opportunities for career development. The duty assignment process determines where enlisted personnel work, how often they move, and the opportunities open to them.

### Assignment Decisions

The services use noncommissioned officers who are familiar with a particular occupation to manage assignments for people in that job. Although they cannot always meet each person's needs or desires, these noncommissioned officers try to make duty assignments that will enhance each service member's career.

Each service tries to give enlisted members job assignments in different types of organizations. Gaining a range of experience is more important to people at supervisory levels, because with each assignment, service members learn more about their jobs and gain confidence in their abilities to react effectively to unexpected events or to assume greater responsibility.

### Possible Location

All services require their members to travel. Enlisted personnel are stationed in each of the 50 states and in countries all over the world. They are routinely reassigned after two-, three-, or four-year tours of duty. To many people, this is one of the attractive parts of service life and, in fact, many men and women join for the opportunity to travel, live in foreign countries, and see different parts of the United States.

Nearly three-quarters of all service personnel are assigned to duty in the United States. Each service also has personnel stationed overseas; many personnel are located in Europe, in countries such as Great Britain, Italy, and Germany. Enlisted personnel are also assigned to the Pacific and Far East, in countries such as Japan, South Korea, and Australia. During their careers, many service members will serve at least one overseas assignment. Several of the services have programs that allow enlisted personnel returning from overseas to select the location in the United States where they will be stationed.

### Length of Tours

The time that an enlisted person spends at a particular duty assignment is called a "tour." The length of a tour varies by service and geographic location. Typically, a tour lasts from three to four years, although there are many exceptions.

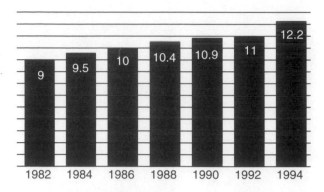

**Figure 4
Percentage of Active
Duty Enlisted Women
1982-1994**

## WOMEN IN THE MILITARY

Military women make important contributions to national defense. As shown in Figure 4, military women have increased in numbers to 12.2 percent of active duty personnel.

Not only has the percentage of women risen, but also women's opportunities in the military have expanded. Women are currently eligible to enter almost 90 percent of all military job specialties. Examples of the many occupations women occupy include airplane navigator, helicopter pilot, radio intelligence operator, computer programmer, environmental health and safety specialist, and power plant operator.

In 1994, the Department of Defense decided to open more than 80,000 additional positions to women.

Historically, women have not been assigned to duty that involves a high probability of exposure to direct combat. This policy is currently being reviewed.

## RESERVE FORCES

Seven different forces make up the Reserves—the Army, Navy, Air Force, Marine Corps, and Coast Guard Reserves and the Army and Air National Guard. Currently, approximately 900,000 Americans serve as Reservists. Each year, the military needs about 160,000 new Reservists.

The Reserves are important to our overall national defense. In a national emergency, Reservists can be called up immediately to serve on active duty, because they are highly trained by the services and drill regularly.

During peacetime, the Reserves perform many functions to support active-duty forces in our country's defense, such as reconnaissance, rescue missions, air defense for the continental U.S., installation and repair of communications equipment, and transport of troops, material, and medical support.

### Enlistment

To enlist in the Reserves, applicants must meet physical, aptitude, citizenship, educational, and moral requirements similar to those that active-duty applicants must meet. They must also be between 17 and 35 years of age. Parental consent is required for 17-year-olds. Specific age standards vary by service.

Reservists normally enlist for eight years. They serve an initial period on active duty while completing basic training and receiving job training. After the training period, which usually lasts several months, Reservists return to civilian life. For the remainder of their service obligation, they attend training sessions and perform work in their job specialty one or two days per month (usually on weekends or in the evening) with their local unit. Once a year (often during the summer), Reservists participate in an active-duty training session of 10 to 14 days.

### Pay and Promotions

Reservists are paid at the same rate as active-duty members for the time they spend working or training. Pay grade and length of service determine their rate of pay.

The Reserves have promotion systems similar to, but separate from, the regular services. Reservists compete only with other Reservists for promotion; advancement is based on performance and length of service.

### Training

The military generally offers the same basic and initial job training to Reservists as it does to active-duty members. Reservists may attend the same schools and complete similar training programs. Besides basic training and initial job training, Reservists may enroll in advanced training courses by correspondence or may attend regular service training classes.

## PAY AND BENEFITS

Military personnel in all five services are paid according to the same pay scale and receive the same basic benefits. Military pay and benefits are set by Congress, which normally grants a cost-of-living pay increase once each year. In addition to pay, the military provides many of life's necessities, such as food, clothing, and housing, or pays monthly allowances for them. The following sections describe military pay, allowances, and benefits in more detail.

### Enlisted Pay Grades

Enlisted members can progress through nine enlisted pay grades during their career. Pay grade and length of service determine a service member's pay. Figure 2, on page 23, shows the relationship between pay grade and rank in each service and also illustrates the insignia for the ranks.

### GI Bill Benefits

Individuals who have entered active duty since June 30, 1985, have been automatically enrolled in the Montgomery GI Bill Program unless they have chosen not to participate. Those enrolled in the program have their basic pay reduced by $100 per month for their first 12 months of service. Upon completion of three years of continuous active duty, individuals are eligible for $433 per month for 36 months, for a maximum of $14,400 in basic benefits for full-time schooling (individuals who complete a two-year obligation will receive $325 per month for 36 months).

### Basic Pay

The major part of an enlisted member's paycheck is basic pay. Pay grade and total years of service determine an enlisted member's basic pay. Table 2 contains information on annual basic pay as of 1995. Cost-of-living increases generally occur once a year.

### Incentives and Special Pay

The military offers incentives and special pay (in addition to basic pay) for certain types of duty. For example, incentives are paid for submarine and flight duty. Other types of hazardous duty with monthly incentives include parachute jumping, flight deck duty, and explosives demolition. In addition, the military gives special pay for sea duty, diving duty, special assignments, duty in certain foreign places, and duty in areas subject to hostile fire. Depending on the service, bonuses are also paid for entering certain occupations.

## Table 2 – 1995 Basic Pay for Enlisted Members (Annual Figures)

| Pay Grade | Years of Services | | | | | | | | |
|---|---|---|---|---|---|---|---|---|---|
| | Under 2 yrs. | 2 | 3 | 4 | 6 | 8 | 10 | ... | 26 |
| E-9 | * | * | * | * | * | * | $30,740 | ... | $39,575 |
| E-8 | * | * | * | * | * | $25,776 | 26,518 | ... | 35,341 |
| E-7 | $17,996 | $19,429 | $20,146 | $20,855 | $21,564 | 22,252 | 22,964 | ... | 31,799 |
| E-6 | 15,484 | 16,877 | 17,579 | 18,328 | 19,015 | 19,699 | 20,423 | ... | 23,209 |
| E-5 | 13,586 | 14,789 | 15,509 | 16,182 | 17,248 | 17,950 | 18,659 | ... | 19,699 |
| E-4 | 12,672 | 13,385 | 14,173 | 15,264 | 15,869 | 15,869 | * | ... | * |
| E-3 | 11,941 | 12,596 | 13,097 | 13,615 | * | * | * | ... | * |
| E-2 | 11,491 | * | * | * | * | * | * | ... | * |
| E-1 | 10,253 | * | * | * | * | * | * | ... | * |
| Less than 4 months | 9,482 [1] | * | * | * | * | * | * | ... | * |

[1] E-1 Basic Pay for the first four months is about $790 per month ($9,482 on an annual basis).

*Military Personnel with this many years of service will probably not be in this pay grade. (Pay scale between 10 and 26 years not shown.)

## Allowances

Most enlisted members, especially in the first year of service, live in military housing and eat in military dining facilities free of charge. Those living off base receive quarters (housing) and subsistence (food) allowances in addition to their basic pay. As of 1995, the monthly housing allowance ranges from $184 to $600, depending on pay grade and number of dependents. The food allowance ranges from $193 to $313 per month, depending on living circumstances. Because allowances are not taxed as income, they provide a significant tax savings in addition to their cash value.

When added up, housing and food allowances, together with their tax savings, are substantial additions to basic pay. Table 3 contains information on the total value of basic pay, allowances, and tax savings, called Regular Military Compensation. The table represents the amount of pay a civilian worker would need to earn to realize the same "take home" pay as a service member. These figures provide a more realistic basis of comparison between military and civilian wages than do the figures in Table 2.

### Table 3 – 1995 Regular Military Compensation (Annual Figures)

| Pay Grade | Under 2 yrs | 2 | 3 | 4 | 6 | 8 | 10 | ... | 26 |
|---|---|---|---|---|---|---|---|---|---|
| E-9 | * | * | * | * | * | * | $43,869 | ... | $52,565 |
| E-8 | * | * | * | * | * | $38,145 | 38,865 | ... | 47,433 |
| E-7 | * | * | * | * | $33,115 | 33,793 | 34,498 | ... | 43,204 |
| E-6 | $26,186 | $27,639 | $28,345 | $29,069 | 297645 | 30,439 | 31,153 | ... | * |
| E-5 | 23,270 | 24,491 | 25,197 | 25,848 | 26,894 | 27,591 | 28,295 | ... | * |
| E-4 | 20,935 | 21,668 | 22,470 | 23,530 | 24,111 | * | * | ... | * |
| E-3 | 19,622 | 20,275 | 20,776 | 21,292 | * | * | * | ... | * |
| E-2 | 18,242 | * | * | * | * | * | * | ... | * |
| E-1 | 16,565 | * | * | * | * | * | * | ... | * |
| Less than 4 months | 15,564 | * | * | * | * | * | * | ... | * |

E-1 Regular Military Compensation reflects basic pay, allowances, and the value of the tax advantage for allowances.

*Military Personnel with this many years of service will probably not be in this pay grade. (Pay scale between 10 and 26 years not shown.)

## Employment Benefits

Military personnel receive substantial benefits in addition to their pay and allowances. While they are in the service, enlisted members' benefits include health care, vacation, legal assistance, recreational programs, educational assistance, and commissary/exchange (military store) privileges. Families of service members also receive some of these benefits. Table 4 contains a summary of these employment benefits.

## Retirement Benefits

The military offers one of the best retirement programs in the country. After 20 years of active duty, personnel may retire and receive a monthly payment equal to 40 percent of their average basic pay for their last five years of active duty. Persons who retire with more than 20 years of service receive higher pay. Other retirement benefits include medical care and commissary/exchange privileges.

## Veterans' Benefits

Veterans of military service are entitled to certain veterans' benefits set by Congress and provided by the Veterans Administration. In most cases, these include guarantees for home loans, hospitalization, survivor benefits, educational benefits, disability benefits, and assistance in finding civilian employment.

### Table 4 – Summary of Enlisted Employment Benefits

| | |
|---|---|
| **Vacation** | Leave time of 30 days per year. |
| **Medical, Dental, and Eye Care** | Full medical, hospitalization, dental, and eye care services for enlistees and most health care costs for family members. |
| **Continuing Education** | Voluntary educational programs for undergraduate and graduate degrees or for single courses, including tuition assistance for programs at colleges and universities. |
| **Recreational Programs** | Programs include athletics, entertainment, and hobbies:<br><br>Softball, basketball, football, swimming, tennis, golf, weight training, and other sports<br><br>Parties, dances, and entertainment<br><br>Club facilities, snack bars, game rooms, movie theaters, and lounges<br><br>Active hobby and craft clubs, book and music libraries. |
| **Exchange and Commissary Privileges** | Food, goods, and services are available at military stores, generally at lower costs than regular retail stores. |
| **Legal Assistance** | Many free legal services are available to assist with personal matters. |

# Service Information on Enlisted Occupations

# Army

## OVERVIEW

Today's "Army of Excellence" is a modern and powerful military force redesigning to a goal of 69,000 officers, 11,500 warrant officers, and 450,000 enlisted soldiers. Army men and women work in many types of jobs, ranging from general administration to the operation and maintenance of the Army's many thousands of weapons, vehicles, aircraft, and highly technical electronic systems.

Soldiers, working as a team, perform the Army's mission of protecting the security of the United States and its vital resources. The Army stands constantly ready to defend American interests and the interests of our allies through land-based operations anywhere in the world.

The Army needs approximately 80,000 to 90,000 new enlistees each year. Those who enlist into the Army will find hundreds of challenging career opportunities that can offer a lifetime of security and excitement to them and their families.

## ENLISTMENT

Enlistment in the Army may be for two, three, four, five, or six years. Applicants must be from 17 to 35 years old, American citizens or registered aliens, and in good health and physical condition. To determine what careers they are best suited for, all applicants must take the Armed Services Vocational Aptitude Battery (ASVAB). The ASVAB is offered at most high schools and at military enlistment processing sites.

In most cases, qualified applicants can be guaranteed their choice of training or duty assignment. There are often combinations of guarantees that are particularly attractive to those who are qualified. For those who wish to be guaranteed a specific school, a particular area of assignment, or both, the Army offers the Delayed Entry Program (DEP). An applicant for the DEP can reserve a school or an assignment choice as much as one year in advance of entry into active duty. Other enlistment programs include the Army Civilian Acquired Skills Program, which gives recognition to those skills acquired through civilian training or experience. This program allows enlisted members with previously acquired training to be promoted more quickly than they ordinarily would be. In some cases, the Army also offers enlistment bonuses.

Enlistment programs and options vary from time to time. Local Army recruiters always have the latest information and are ready to answer inquiries without obligation.

## TRAINING

Initial Army training is provided in two phases: basic training and Advanced Individual Training (job training).

### Basic Training

Basic training is a rigorous eight-week orientation for men and women entering the Army. Basic training transforms new enlistees from civilians into soldiers. During basic training, new soldiers gain the discipline, spirit, pride, knowledge, and physical conditioning necessary to perform Army duties.

Army basic training is given in several locations throughout the country, including training centers in South Carolina, Georgia, Kentucky, Alabama, Oklahoma, and Missouri.

Upon reporting for basic training, new soldiers are assigned to a training company and are issued uniforms and equipment. They are introduced to their training leaders, otherwise known as drill sergeants. Drill sergeants are experienced noncommissioned officers who direct soldiers' training to ensure that they are successful.

Army basic training stresses teamwork. Soldiers are trained in groups known as squads or platoons. These groups range from nine to approximately 80 soldiers; they are small enough that each soldier can be recognized for his or her special abilities. Such groups tend to become closely knit teams and develop group pride and camaraderie during the eight weeks of rigorous training they experience together.

Basic training is conducted on a demanding schedule, but each soldier progresses at the rate he or she can handle best. Soldiers attend a variety of classes and field instruction that include military training, weapons familiarization, physical conditioning, and military drills. All training emphasizes team work and therefore includes classes in human relations. These classes help trainees from different backgrounds learn to work closely together. Only limited personal time is available during basic training, but there is plenty of time for receiving and answering mail, for personal care, and for attending religious services.

### Job Training (Advanced Individual Training)

After basic training, Army soldiers go directly to Advanced Individual Training in the occupational field that they have chosen and qualified for, where they learn a specific Army job. Advanced Individual Training schools are located at many Army bases throughout the country.

The Army offers skills training in a wide range of career fields that include programs maintenance, administration, electronics, health care, construction, and combat specialty occupations, to name a few.

Advanced Individual Training students generally attend traditional classes very similar to those in a high school or college. These classes are supplemented with demonstrations by highly qualified instructors and by practical exercises that use "hands-on" training, Army equipment, or Army procedures in a way that prepares students for their jobs. Many soldiers also receive on-the-job training, learning job skills by working at a job with other soldiers under the guidance of qualified instructors.

Some Advanced Individual Training courses are registered with the U.S. Department of Labor as certified apprenticeship training programs. Generally, this training qualifies participants for both federal and state apprenticeship programs and helps secure future civilian employment in their chosen trade.

## ADVANCEMENT

Every job in the Army has a career path leading to increased pay and responsibility with well-defined promotion criteria. After six months of service, new soldiers advance to Private (E-2). The next step in the promotion ladder is Private First Class (E-3), which occurs after the 12th month. Promotion to Corporal or Specialist (E-4) occurs after established time-in-grade and time-in-service requirements are met. These times vary, but every soldier can ordinarily expect to become a corporal within his or her first three years of service. Starting with grade E-5, promotions to Sergeant through Sergeant Major are accomplished on a competitive basis. At each grade, there are minimum periods of time in service and time in grade that must be met before a soldier can be considered for promotion. In some cases, there also are educational requirements that must be met for promotion.

The Army offers a number of ways to advance beyond enlisted status as either a warrant officer or commissioned officer. These programs usually are reserved for only the best qualified soldiers. Warrant officers perform duties similar to commissioned Army officers. Many warrant officers are directly appointed from the enlisted grades as vacancies occur. These opportunities usually exist in the technical fields, especially those involving maintenance of equipment. Other opportunities are available in Army administration, intelligence, and law enforcement. Unique among the Armed Forces is the Army's Warrant Officer Aviator Program. Qualified personnel may enlist for Warrant Officer Candidate School and, upon completion, receive flight training and appointment as Army warrant officer aviators.

Enlisted soldiers may also compete for a limited number of selections to attend Officer Candidate School (OCS) or the United States Military Academy. Upon graduating from OCS or the academy, soldiers receive officer commissions. For soldiers with college degrees, there are opportunities for direct commissioning.

## EDUCATION PROGRAMS

For enlisted personnel, the Army has a well-defined system for progressive service school training. Soldiers are often able to volunteer for this schooling or, in some cases, they are selected on a competitive basis.

As a soldier progresses in his or her career, advanced technical training opportunities are offered. These courses include, but are not limited to, advanced noncommissioned officer courses at the staff sergeant grade level and the Sergeants Major Academy at the E-8 and E-9 levels.

Civilian education is stressed as a means to improve both the soldier's work performance and preparedness for life in a technical and competitive society. The Army Continuing Education System provides counseling, academic services, and vocational-technical services at little or no cost. In a few cases, the Army sends its soldiers to college, but generally they are encouraged to pursue college training during off-duty time.

Army personnel are also eligible to participate in educational assistance programs with the government, such as the Montgomery GI Bill, which can provide up to $14,400 for future educational needs. Additionally, the Army College Fund may add additional monetary incentives to qualified soldiers' accounts to total $30,000 for education.

## FOR FURTHER INFORMATION

Students who wish to learn more about specific military jobs and careers are encouraged to use this manual to its fullest. In addition, many career information systems found in high schools and libraries have information about Army careers. The most up-to-date information about Army programs or careers is always available from an Army recruiter. For the Army recruiter nearest you, check the Yellow Pages or call 1-800-USA-ARMY for details. There is no obligation.

# Navy

## OVERVIEW

The Navy plays an important role in helping to maintain the freedom of the seas. It defends the right of our country and its allies to travel and trade freely on the world's oceans and helps protect our country during times of international conflict. Navy sea and air power make it possible for our country to use the oceans when and where our national interests require it.

The Navy is a large and diverse organization. It is made up of about 400,000 officers and enlisted people. Navy personnel operate and repair more than 340 ships and over 6,000 aircraft; they serve in such diverse fields as radio operators, dental specialists, seamen, computer programmers, photographers, ship electricians, and boiler technicians and work in many other exciting careers. Navy people serve on ships at sea, on submarines under the sea, in aviation positions on land and sea, and at shore bases around the world.

The Navy recruits about 60,000 officers and enlisted people each year to fill openings in Navy career fields.

## ENLISTMENT

To qualify for enlistment in Navy programs, men and women must be between the ages of 17 and 34. Parental consent is required for all 17-year-olds. In the nuclear field, the maximum enlistment age is 23, due to extensive training requirements. Since most Navy programs require enlistees to be high school graduates, the Navy prefers young people to graduate first before entering the Navy.

Enlistees must be citizens of the United States or immigrant aliens with immigration and naturalization papers. A physical examination and the Armed Services Vocational Aptitude Battery (ASVAB) test must be completed.

Initial enlistment in the Navy usually is for four years. However, two-, three-, five-, or six-year enlistments are also available for men and women, depending on the programs they select.

After going through the enlistment process at a Military Entrance Processing Station, Navy people usually are placed in the Delayed Enlistment Program (DEP). Recruits in the DEP are guaranteed training assignments. The DEP allows enlistees to finish high school, take care of personal business, or just relax before reporting for duty.

There is extra pay in the Navy for sea duty, submarine duty, demolition duty, diving duty, work as a crew member of an aviation team, or jobs that require special training. Because the nuclear field is such a critical and unique area of the Navy, quicker promotions are earned and bonuses are available when the training in this field is completed and also when sailors with nuclear training reenlist.

## TRAINING

The Navy is known for the excellent training it provides. The Navy provides both recruit training and job training.

### Recruit Training

The first assignment for every Navy enlistee is recruit training. It is a tough eight-week period of transition from civilian to Navy life. It provides the discipline, knowledge, and physical conditioning necessary to continue serving in the Navy.

Navy recruit training centers are located in Orlando, Florida; Great Lakes, Illinois; and San Diego, California. Women recruits train only at Orlando. After reporting, recruits are placed into training companies, issued uniforms and equipment, and assigned living quarters.

The recruit's day starts at 0530 (5:30 a.m.). Taps (lights out) is at 2130 (9:30 p.m.). During weekdays, the daily schedule is based on 11 periods of physical fitness and classroom instruction, each lasting 40 minutes.

Physical fitness training includes push-ups, sit-ups, sit-reach, distance running, water survival, and swimming instruction. Recruits are tested for physical fitness at the beginning and end of recruit training. The test requirements differ slightly for men and women.

Recruits are given classroom and field instruction covering more than 30 subjects, including aircraft and ship familiarization, basic deck seamanship, career incentives, decision-making, time management, military drill, Navy mission and organization, military customs and courtesies, and the chain of command.

### Job Training

After recruit training, most Navy people go directly to the technical school (called class A school) they signed up for at the Military Entrance Processing Station.

The Navy has more than 60 job fields from which enlistees may choose. They are grouped in occupational categories similar to the 127 occupations described in *Military Careers*.

Navy class A schools are located on military bases throughout the United States, including Great Lakes, Illinois; San Diego, California; Newport, Rhode Island; Millington, Tennessee; and Pensacola, Florida. They range in length from a few weeks to many months, depending on the complexity of the subject.

Those who complete recruit training and are still undecided about what career path they want to take in the Navy can begin an on-the-job apprenticeship training program. One such program for men is the Subfarer Program, which trains men to serve aboard submarines. The Divefarer Program trains personnel in diving specialties, and the Aircrew Program trains enlistees in inflight maintenance and tactical crew duties in naval aircraft.

When apprentices finish on-the-job training, they should have an idea of what type of job (rating) they want to pursue during the rest of their Navy service. They may then apply to class A school for training in that rating. Advanced training in most job fields is available later in a Navy person's career.

The Office of Education Credit of the American Council on Education regularly reviews and evaluates Navy training and experience. It has recommended that colleges and universities award credits for nearly all Navy courses.

## ADVANCEMENT

Like other branches of the service, the Navy has nine enlisted pay grades, from E-1 to E-9. A new enlistee entering the Navy is an E-1 (Seaman Recruit). After about six months in the Navy, the E-1 normally is eligible for advancement to E-2 (Seaman Apprentice).

Navy promotions are based on: 1) job performance, 2) competitive examination grades, 3) recommendations of supervisors, 4) length of service, and 5) time in present level of work. It is impossible to predict exactly when promotions will occur; however, every job in the Navy has a defined career path leading to supervisory positions.

People with highly developed skills in certain critical occupations may enter the Navy at advanced pay grades. Some people qualify for one of the specialized technical training programs in the electronics or nuclear fields, where advancement is often rapid.

Enlisted petty officer ratings (E-4 through E-9) are not to be confused with Navy commissioned officer rankings. Most Navy enlisted personnel are not college graduates, while most Navy commissioned officers have college degrees. However, the Navy does offer several programs that allow enlisted personnel to advance to officer status.

Two Navy programs, Limited Duty Officer (LDO) and Warrant Officer (WO), permit career enlisted Navy people to advance to commissioned officer status without a college education. Enlisted Navy people interested in officer commissions through these two programs should start planning for them early in their careers. These commissions are limited to successful career petty officers; the competition is keen and the standards are high.

The Enlisted Commissioning Program enables an eligible enlisted man or woman with previous college credits and between 4 and 11 years of active service to earn a bachelor's degree in 24 months or less while assigned to Naval Reserve Officers' Training Corps (NROTC) college. Because these students may not actually have to participate in the NROTC program at college, they earn their commissions as Navy officers after graduating from Officer Candidate School (OCS).

## EDUCATION PROGRAMS

The Navy believes that the more education people receive, the better equipped they are to perform their jobs and fulfill personal goals. A program called Navy Campus provides opportunities for enlisted members to take continuing education classes throughout their Navy careers. Through Navy Campus, enlisted members can pursue all levels of education and training, from high school equivalency to vocational certificate to college degree, wherever they are stationed. Navy Campus offers on-duty and off-duty study to provide a complete package of educational benefits to Navy people. They can enroll in any combination of Navy Campus programs and keep adding credits toward a civilian college degree or vocational certificate of their choice.

The Navy offers enlisted members two officer preparatory programs to improve their academic status so they may compete for a commissioning program such as the NROTC or the United States Naval Academy in Annapolis, Maryland. These preparatory programs are the Broadened Opportunity for Officer Selection and Training (BOOST) and the Naval Academy Preparatory School (NAPS).

The United States Naval Academy offers a fully subsidized four-year college education—plus a monthly salary. About 1,300 people are selected for the Naval Academy each year from nominations by Senators, Representatives, the President and Vice President of the United States, and the Secretary of the Navy.

Candidates must be U.S. citizens, aged 17 to 22, and single with no children. Enlisted Navy men and women applying to the academy must have served at least one year of active duty by the date of entrance. Graduates receive a bachelor of science degree and a commission.

## FOR FURTHER INFORMATION

The occupational information provided in *Military Careers* can be useful in exploring career opportunities in the Navy. Many career information systems found in high schools and libraries have similar information about military careers. However, to learn more detailed information about the latest training and enlistment programs, contact your local Navy recruiter. There is no obligation. The Navy toll free number for recruiting information is 1-800-327-NAVY.

# Air Force

## OVERVIEW

The mission of the Air Force is to defend the United States through control and exploitation of air and space. The Air Force flies and maintains aircraft, such as long-range bombers, supersonic fighters, Airborne Warning and Control System (AWACS) aircraft, and many others, whenever and wherever necessary, to protect the interests of America and American allies. Almost 400,000 highly trained officers and airmen make up today's Air Force. Some pilot aircraft—everything from helicopters to the Space Shuttle. Many others do the jobs that support the Air Force's flying mission; they may work as firefighters, aircraft mechanics, security police, or air traffic controllers, or in many other Air Force career fields. The Air Force currently recruits about 30,000 to 40,000 men and women each year to fill openings in hundreds of challenging Air Force careers.

## ENLISTMENT

Applicants for enlistment in the Air Force must be in good health, possess good moral character, and make the minimum scores on the Armed Services Vocational Aptitude Battery (ASVAB) required for Air Force enlistment. They must also be at least 18 years of age. (Individuals who are 17 years of age may enlist if they are married, have parental consent to enlist, or have been emancipated by the courts.)

Prior to taking the oath of enlistment, qualified applicants may be guaranteed either to receive training in a specific skill or to be assigned within a selected aptitude area. The Guaranteed Training Enlistment Program guarantees training and initial assignment in a specific job skill. The Aptitude Area Program guarantees classification into one of four aptitude areas (mechanical, administrative, general, or electronic); specific skills within these aptitude areas are selected during basic training.

After choosing one of these programs, applicants will enter the Delayed Entry Program (DEP). DEP enlistees become members of the Air Force Inactive Reserve with a delayed date for active-duty enlistment. They do not participate in any military activities or earn pay or benefits while in the DEP. The individual agrees to enter active duty on a certain date, and the Air Force agrees to accept him or her (if still qualified) and provide training and initial assignment in the aptitude area or job specified.

## TRAINING

The Air Force provides two kinds of training to all enlistees: basic training and job training.

### Basic Training

All Air Force Basic Military Training (BMT) is conducted at Lackland Air Force Base (AFB) in San Antonio, Texas. BMT teaches enlistees how to adjust to military life, both physically and mentally, and promotes pride in being a member of the Air Force. It lasts six weeks and consists of academic instruction, confidence courses, physical conditioning, and marksmanship training. Trainees who enlist with an aptitude-area guarantee receive orientation and individual counseling to help choose a job specialty compatible with Air Force needs and with their aptitudes, education, civilian experience, and desires. After graduation from BMT, recruits receive job training in their chosen specialty.

### Job Training

All BMT graduates go directly to one of the Air Education and Training Command's Technical Training Centers for formal, in-residence training. In-residence job training is conducted at Keesler AFB, Biloxi, Mississippi; Lackland AFB, San Antonio, Texas; Sheppard AFB, Wichita Falls, Texas; Goodfellow AFB, San Angelo, Texas; and several other locations nationwide. In formal classes and practice sessions, airmen learn the basic skills needed for the first assignment in their specialty.

Air Force training does not end with graduation from basic training and technical training school. After three months at their first permanent duty station, airmen begin on-the-job training (OJT). OJT is a two-part program consisting of self-study and supervised job performance. Airmen enroll in skill-related correspondence courses to gain broad knowledge of their Air Force job, and they study technical orders and directives to learn specific tasks they must perform. They also work daily with their trainers and supervisors who coach them during hands-on task performance. Through OJT, they develop the job skills needed to progress from apprentice airmen to skilled noncommissioned officers (NCOs). Airmen also complete advanced training and supplemental formal courses throughout their careers to increase their skills in using specific equipment or techniques.

## MANAGEMENT TRAINING

In addition to becoming skilled in their specialties, Air Force airmen and NCOs are also leaders and supervisors. Schools in the professional military education (PME) system teach airmen and NCOs to be more effective in the operation of the Air Force. PME is a progressive system consisting of leadership schools for airmen, NCO academies for intermediate NCOs, and the Senior NCO Academy for selected Master Sergeants and Senior Master Sergeants. Through PME, airmen and NCOs develop management abilities that are valuable in any chosen career, military or civilian.

## ADVANCEMENT

Typically, Airman Basic (pay grade E-1) is the initial enlisted grade. However, there are several programs available that may qualify individuals for enlistment at a higher initial grade. These programs include: successful completion of a Civil Air Patrol program and receipt of the Billy Mitchell, Amelia Earhart, or Carl Spaatz Award; successful completion of at least three years of a Junior Reserve Officer Training Corps (JROTC) program (any service); receipt of a Boy Scout Eagle Scout or Girl Scout Gold Award; or completion of certain levels of course work at accredited colleges or universities.

Every job in the Air Force has a defined career path leading to supervisory positions. Airman Basic enlistees are normally promoted to Airman (E-2) upon completion of six months of service and to Airman First Class (E-3) after 16 months of service. Promotion to Senior Airman (E-4) usually occurs at the three-year point of service. However, some airmen qualify for accelerated promotion. Local Air Force recruiters have all the details on qualifications for accelerated promotions and advanced enlistment grades.

Promotions to the higher enlisted grades of Staff Sergeant (E-5), Technical Sergeant (E-6), Master Sergeant (E-7), and Senior and Chief Master Sergeant (E-8 and E-9) are competitive. Eligible airmen compete with others worldwide in the same grade and skill, based on test scores, performance ratings, decorations, and time in service and grade. All airmen receive a promotion score that shows how they stand in relation to others in their specialty and where improvement may be needed. Additionally, E-8 and E-9 candidates are reviewed by an evaluation board.

Chief Master Sergeants occupy the top enlisted grade, and they have great responsibility and prestige in the Air Force. They have the management ability to head several enlisted specialties related to their own skill, or they may be the top enlisted expert in a highly technical field.

Normally, enlisted airmen and commissioned officers advance along separate career fields. However, the Air Force offers three programs through which airmen can receive commissions: the Air Force ROTC Scholarship Commissioning Program, the Airman Education and Commissioning Program, and the Air Force Academy. The Air Force ROTC Scholarship Commissioning Program allows airmen to complete their college degrees and earn officer commissions through Air Force ROTC scholarships. If selected for the program, the individual is transferred from active duty into the Air Force Reserve, then attends college (at the same time enrolling in the college's Air Force ROTC program) for completion of degree requirements. This highly competitive program pays tuition, fees, and a monthly allowance.

Airmen can also apply for a commission as an Air Force officer under the Airman Education and Commissioning Program (AECP) or by acceptance to the United States Air Force Academy. Enlisted personnel who possess bachelor's degrees or who can complete degree requirements under AECP in areas of critical need may be accepted into the Officer Training School. They are commissioned upon graduation.

Each year Regular airmen on active duty and airmen serving in the Air Force Reserve and Air National Guard receive appointments to the Air Force Academy. There are 85 appointments available for Regular airmen and another 85 for those in the Air Force Reserve or Air National Guard. All candidates are considered for admission on a competitive basis. Examination results and previous performance determine selection. Graduates from the Air Force Academy receive bachelor of science degrees and are commissioned as Second Lieutenants in the active duty Air Force.

## EDUCATION PROGRAMS

The Air Force has many education programs to help men and women pursue their educational goals while serving in the Air Force. These programs are in addition to veterans' educational benefits set up by the federal government for members of all services. All Air Force bases have education service centers, where trained counselors help airmen decide on a program or combination of programs and help them enroll. Some of these programs are:

### Community College of the Air Force

The Community College of the Air Force (CCAF) offers education programs directly related to Air Force specialties; graduates are awarded an associate degree. The college works with Air Force training schools, regional accrediting agencies, and hundreds of cooperating civilian colleges and universities. Since the technical nature of most Air Force courses places them on a level with college study, airmen earn fully recognized college credits for most of what they learn in job training and on-the-job training. They can combine those credits with attendance at off-duty courses from civilian colleges to earn a two-year accredited associate degree in applied sciences from CCAF. The college offers more than 80 fields of study, ranging from police science to environmental services technology. Registration is free, and CCAF establishes a special study program for each student. Professional, industrial, and governmental organizations that issue licenses and certifications and set standards for civilian work recognize Air Force training and education through CCAF.

### The College Level Examination Program

This program allows airmen to receive credit for selected college courses by examination. The program is free, and education services centers maintain a current list of college tests available.

### The Extension Course Institute

The Extension Course Institute (ECI) is the Air Force's correspondence school. It offers, free of charge, nearly 400 courses to some 250,000 students who register for ECI each year. These courses include everything from fundamentals of solid state devices to apprentice carpentry. Air Force personnel may voluntarily enroll in courses such as auto mechanics, plumbing, carpentry, or electrical wiring simply for background knowledge.

### Tuition Assistance

The Air Force will pay up to 75 percent of the tuition costs of most college courses. College programs are offered on all Air Force bases, with local college professors coming to the base at most installations.

## FOR FURTHER INFORMATION

Local Air Force recruiters have the latest information on enlistment programs and career opportunities; contact them if you have any questions. High school guidance counselors can also give you advice on Air Force ROTC programs and the USAF Academy.

# Marine Corps

## OVERVIEW

The Marine Corps has become one of the most elite fighting forces in the world. Since its creation on November 10, 1775, the U.S. Marine Corps has allowed America to project power far from its shores. Against the Barbary pirates off the coast of Tripoli, Libya, the Marines, from 1801 through 1805, launched a series of punitive raids in retaliation for attacks on U.S. ships. The attacks ceased. Almost 200 years later, when Saddam Hussein sent his forces into Kuwait in August 1990, the Marines rushed to the region, arriving just seven days after President Bush ordered U.S. forces to respond. The Marines brought the first heavy tanks and artillery to prevent Hussein's advance into Saudi Arabia.

The Marines are a part of the Department of the Navy and operate in close cooperation with U.S. naval forces at sea. The Marine Corps' mission is unique among the services. Marines serve on U.S. Navy ships, protect naval bases, guard U.S. embassies, and provide a quick, ever-ready strike force to protect U.S. interest anywhere in the world. All Marines can move on short notice to match up with equipment stored on floating bases on the world's oceans. In the post-Cold War world, this remains an essential capability for the U.S. With their inherent flexibility and global reach, the Marines serve as America's force of choice to met the main threats of the 1990s.

To perform the many duties of the Marine Corps, approximately 174,000 officers and enlisted Marines fly planes and helicopters; operate radar equipment; drive armored vehicles; gather intelligence; survey and map territory; maintain and repair radios, computers, jeeps, trucks, tanks, and aircraft; and perform hundreds of other challenging jobs. Each year, the Marine Corps recruits approximately 41,000 enlisted men and women to fill openings in its numerous career fields. The Marine Corps training programs offer practical, challenging, and progressive skill development. The Marine Corps stresses professional education for all ranks and emphasizes the development of mental strength as well as traditional physical prowess. In this way, the Marine Corps provides the Nation with a modern well-armed force that is both "tough" and "smart."

## ENLISTMENT

Marine Corps enlistment terms are for three, four, five, or six years, depending on the type of enlistment program. Young men and women enlisting in the Marine Corps must meet exacting physical, mental, and moral standards. Applicants must be between the ages of 17 and 29, American citizens or registered aliens, and in good health to ensure that they can meet the rigorous physical training demands. The Armed Services Vocational Aptitude Battery (ASVAB), described in this guide, is used by the Marine Corps to assess each person's vocational aptitudes and academic abilities. Some applicants for enlistment may have taken the ASVAB while still in high school. For those applicants who have not previously taken the ASVAB, a Marine recruiter can arrange for them to do so.

Applicants for enlistment can be guaranteed training and duty assignment with a wide variety of options, depending upon the degree of education and the qualifications they possess. Women are eligible to enlist in all occupational fields, with the exception of combat arms—infantry, artillery, and tank and amphibian tractor crew members.

In addition to regular enlistment, the Marine Corps offers special enlistment programs.

### Delayed Entry Program

Students who wish to complete the Marine Corps enlistment process before graduating from high school or a community college may enlist in the Marine Corps Delayed Entry Program (DEP). Enlistment in the DEP allows applicants to postpone their initial active-duty training for up to a full year. Enlisting in the DEP has two principal benefits: the student can finish high school or community college, and the highly desirable enlistment programs that are available in limited numbers, such as all computer specialties and many aviation specialties, can be reserved early.

### Musician Enlistment Option Program

The Musician Enlistment Option Program gives graduates with musical talent an opportunity to serve in Marine Corps bands or the Marine Corps Drum and Bugle Corps. The program's incentives include formal school training, accelerated promotions, and duty station choices.

### Enlistment Options Program

The Enlistment Options Program guarantees well-qualified applicants, before they enlist, assignment to one of 25 occupational fields. The occupational fields contain every job available in the Marine Corps, ranging from combat arms to motor transport to high technology avionics, electronics, and computer science. Some enlistment options feature cash bonuses as well as formal training programs.

### Quality Enlistment Program

The Quality Enlistment Program is for highly qualified young men and women for enlistment and assignment primarily to technical occupational fields. The program provides incentives, including choice of geographic assignment, to all qualified high school graduates or seniors who enlist for six years.

## TRAINING

Marine Corps training occurs in two sections: recruit training and job training.

### Recruit Training

Upon completing the enlistment process, all applicants enter Marine Corps recruit training. Young men undergo recruit training either at Parris Island, South Carolina, or in San Diego, California. All young women attend recruit training at Parris Island. Recruit training is rigorous, demanding, and challenging. The overall goal of recruit training is to instill in the recruits the military skills, knowledge, discipline, pride, and self-confidence necessary to perform as United States Marines.

In the first several days at the recruit depot, a recruit is assigned to a platoon, receives a basic issue of uniforms and equipment, is given an additional physical, and takes further assignment classification tests. Each platoon is led by a team of three Marine drill instructors. A typical training day for recruits begins with reveille at 0500 (5:00 a.m.), continues with drill, physical training, and several classes in weapons and conduct, and ends with taps at 2100 (9:00 p.m.).

### Job Training

Upon graduation from recruit training, each Marine takes a short vacation, then reports to the School of Infantry for combat skills training. Upon graduation from the School of Infantry, Marines then report either to a new command for formal school training or to the on-the-job training to which he or she has been assigned. The Marine Corps sends students to over 200 basic formal schools and to over 300 advanced formal schools. The length of formal school varies from four weeks to over a year, depending on the level of technical expertise and knowledge required to become proficient in certain job skills. For example, different military occupational specialties (MOSs) within the electrical and electronic repair occupational field require from 10 to 50 weeks to complete; different MOSs in the vehicle and machinery mechanic occupational field require from six to 18 weeks to complete.

Marines assigned to an MOS within the combat specialty occupational field conduct most of their training outdoors. Marines receiving training in highly technical MOSs receive most of their training in a classroom. The main thrust of Marine Corps training is toward "hands-on" training and practical application of newly acquired skills. As soon as possible after classroom instruction is completed, students are placed in an actual work environment to obtain practical experience and to develop confidence. After completing entry-level MOS training, most Marines are assigned to operational units of the Fleet Marine Forces to apply their skills. Marines assigned to the more technical MOSs may require more advanced training prior to their first operational duty assignment.

Job performance requirements in a number of MOSs are comparable to requirements needed for journeyman certification in civilian occupations. A Marine assigned to these MOSs may apply for status as a registered apprentice.

## ADVANCEMENT

Advancement is directly linked to an individual's performance in an MOS and development as a Marine. Each Marine is evaluated based on job performance, experience, and ability to apply newly learned skills. While promotion criteria rely heavily upon individual job performance, Marines are also in competition with others of the same rank in the same MOS. Promotion becomes increasingly competitive as Marines advance in rank. The normal time-in-grade requirements for promotion are as follows: Private to Private First Class, six months; Private First Class to Lance Corporal, eight months; Lance Corporal to Corporal, eight months; and Corporal to Sergeant, 24 months. Promotions above Sergeant to the staff noncommissioned officer (SNCO) ranks are determined by promotion boards.

The Meritorious Promotion System is used to recognize Marines who demonstrate outstanding job performance and professional competence. Marines recommended for meritorious promotion are carefully screened for accelerated advancement. Qualified enlisted Marines can compete for and be accepted into the officer corps through several different programs. Competition is keen, and only the best qualified Marines are accepted.

### The Enlisted Commissioning Program

This program provides the opportunity for enlisted Marines with two years of college to apply for assignment to the Officer Candidates School and subsequent appointment as unrestricted commissioned officers.

### Enlisted Commissioning Education Program

The Marine Corps Enlisted Commissioning Education Program provides to selected enlisted Marines (who have had no college experience) the opportunity to earn baccalaureate degrees by attending a college or university as full-time students. Marines in this program who obtain their baccalaureate degrees and subsequently complete officer candidate training are commissioned as Second Lieutenants.

### The Warrant Officer Program

Warrant officers are technical specialists who are assigned to duties only in their area of expertise. All other officers are said to be "unrestricted" and are assigned to a wide variety of assignments during their career. The Warrant Officer Program provides for the selection and appointment to permanent warrant officer those qualified applicants who are in the grade of Sergeant or above at the time of application.

## EDUCATION PROGRAMS

All Marines on active duty are encouraged to continue their education by taking advantage of service schools and Marine Corps funded off-duty courses at local civilian colleges. Three educational assistance programs are available to enlisted Marines.

The Marine Corps has developed an extensive professional military education program to provide Marine leaders with the skill, knowledge, understanding, and confidence that will better enable Marines to make sound military decisions.

### Tuition Assistance Program

The Marine Corps Tuition Assistance Program provides Marines with financial assistance to pursue educational programs at civilian secondary and postsecondary institutions during off-duty time. Tuition assistance may only be used to fund courses at a higher academic level than the degree or diploma currently held by the Marine.

### Servicemembers' Opportunity Colleges

The Servicemembers' Opportunity Colleges (SOC) is a consortium of colleges and universities that have agreed to help military personnel gain access to higher education by minimizing residency requirements, recognizing nontraditional education attainment, such as the College Level Examination Program (CLEP) tests, easing the transfer of college credit of similarly accredited institutions, and granting credit for formal military training.

### College After the Corps

Marines are also eligible to participate in educational assistance programs with the Government, such as the Montgomery G.I. Bill, which can provide up to $14,400 for future educational needs. The Marine Corps College Fund may add monetary incentives to qualified Marines' accounts to total no more than $30,000 for education.

## FOR FURTHER INFORMATION

The above information provides the general scope of enlistment policies, recruit training, follow-on training, and educational opportunities found in the Marine Corps today. Young men and women who are interested in joining the Marine Corps can contact a Marine recruiter by calling 1-800-MARINES.

# Coast Guard

## OVERVIEW

The Coast Guard constantly performs its mission of protecting America's coastlines and inland waterways by enforcing customs and fishing laws, combating drug smuggling, conducting search and rescue missions, maintaining lighthouses, and promoting boating safety. The Coast Guard is part of the Department of Transportation; in time of war it may be placed in the Department of Defense under the command of the Navy. A vital part of the Armed Services, the Coast Guard has participated in every major American military campaign. With a work force of 7,000 commissioned or warrant officers, and 28,000 enlisted members, Coast Guard personnel perform in many different occupations to support the missions of the Coast Guard. Each year, the Coast Guard has openings for about 4,000 new enlistees in a wide range of challenging careers,

## ENLISTMENT

Applicants for enlistment in the Coast Guard must be physically qualified, possess high moral character, and make at least the minimum required scores on the Armed Services Vocational Aptitude Battery (ASVAB). Coast Guard regular enlistments are for four or six years of active duty. Provided openings are available, qualified enlistees may be guaranteed an assignment to a geographical region (not an individual unit). Guaranteed geographic assignments cannot be used in conjunction with a guaranteed school. Qualified applicants may also enlist up to 12 months prior to beginning active duty. Coast Guard recruits must be at least 17 years old and must not have reached their 28th birthday on the day of enlistment.

## COAST GUARD RESERVE

There are approximately 8,000 Coast Guard Reservists. For those without prior service, enlistment into the Coast Guard Reserve is for a period of eight years. The Coast Guard has four programs for individuals with no prior service experience. Three of the programs are for individuals who are at least 17 and who have not reached their 28th birthday. The other program is for individuals who are at least 26 but have not reached their 36th birthday. The programs all include a period of basic training and class A school or on-the-job training and then release from initial active duty for training. Upon completion, these reservists return to their home and drill with their Reserve units monthly. One of the four programs is a direct petty officer program for persons who possess specialized civilian skills and can convert these skills to the various ratings in the Coast Guard Reserve. Reservists augment the regular Coast Guard component on a regular basis, keeping the spirit of the "One Coast Guard Family."

## TRAINING

Two types of training are provided to Coast Guard recruits: recruit training and job training.

### Recruit Training

After completing the enlistment process, all Coast Guard recruits attend recruit training, or "boot camp," at Cape May, New Jersey. Boot camp lasts approximately eight weeks; it is designed to provide a transition from civilian life to that of service with the Coast Guard. The course is demanding, both physically and mentally. Coast Guard recruit training instills in each trainee a sense of teamwork and discipline. Coast Guard history, missions, customs, and basic discipline are all part of the training course. Boot camp includes physical training, classroom work, and practical application of the subjects studied.

### Job Training

The Coast Guard maintains basic petty officer (class A) schools for formal training in specific occupational specialties. Courses of study in these class A schools vary from 8 to 42 weeks, depending on the rating or specialty area taught. Each school provides a course of study that leads to advancement to the Petty Officer Third Class level. Specialty schools in the other services can be used by Coast Guard personnel in addition to, or in place of, Coast Guard schools for training in certain ratings. Upon successful completion of class A school, the graduate becomes a qualified specialist and can expect assignment to a field unit for duty and further on-the-job training in his or her specialty.

Opportunities for additional professional training are available to qualified, career-oriented personnel in the form of advanced petty officer (class B) and special (class C) schools. These advanced schools range in length from a few weeks to several months, depending on the skills taught. Senior enlisted personnel in certain ratings are also eligible to compete for assignment to special degree programs within their occupational specialty areas.

## ADVANCEMENT

The Coast Guard enlisted rating structure consists of paths of advancement from pay grade E-1 through E-9. Two general apprenticeships are available within pay grades E-1 through E-3: Fireman (FN) and Seaman (SN). Approximately 25 occupational fields, called ratings, exist in pay grades E-4 through E-9.

Every job in the Coast Guard has a career path leading to increased pay and responsibility—with well-defined promotion criteria. A Coast Guard Seaman Recruit (E-1) is promoted to Seaman Apprentice (E-2) upon completion of basic training. Eligibility for promotion to Seaman or Fireman (E-3) is based on four requirements: adequate time-in-grade, successful demonstration of military and professional qualifications, recommendation of the commanding officer, and completion of correspondence courses.

To earn petty officer ratings (E-4 through E-9), an individual must, in addition to the requirements above, pass the Coast Guard-wide competitive examination for the rating.

A Coast Guard enlisted member can expect to spend the majority of his or her career within the 48 contiguous states, primarily on the East, West, or Gulf Coast. The Coast Guard also has a number of units on the Great Lakes and along the Midwest's river system. At some point in his or her career, a Coast Guard member should expect to serve one or more tours of duty in an overseas assignment. Tour lengths vary from one to four years, depending upon the location of the assignment, the nature of the duty, and the preferences of the individual. The amount of sea duty varies according to the individual's rating and might range from a slight majority to a small fraction of the career. The Coast Guard, the smallest of the military forces, prides itself on its ability to give personal consideration to the needs of its members in the personnel assignment process.

## EDUCATION PROGRAMS

The Coast Guard believes strongly in the continued education of its members. The Coast Guard offers several education assistance programs, including:

### Tuition Assistance Program

The Coast Guard sponsors a tuition assistance program for off-duty education within the limits of available funds. This program allows Coast Guard personnel, both officer and enlisted, to enroll in off-duty courses at accredited colleges, universities, junior colleges, high schools, and commercial schools. Seventy-five percent of the tuition is paid by the Coast Guard for all courses not in excess of six credits per semester (or quarter) or for any course not extending beyond one semester or a maximum of 17 weeks, whichever is longer.

### Physician's Assistant Program

The physician's assistant program is a two-year, full-time course of study at Sheppard AFB, Wichita Falls, Texas. The program includes 12 months of study and 12 months of clinical rotation at an Air Force hospital. Upon successful completion, Coast Guard graduates receive their certificates as physician's assistants and a direct commission as Ensigns. Completion of the program results in a bachelor's degree in Health Science.

### Electronics Technology Course

The advanced electronics training program for enlisted personnel is conducted at several locations throughout the country. While the specific courses of study utilized by the Coast Guard vary somewhat from school to school, they all provide a practical and theoretical mix of current state-of-the-art electronics. Electronics technology institutions prepare a Coast Guard member for duty as an engineer's assistant. During their careers, engineer's assistants participate in the design and specification of equipment and equipment modification at headquarters, headquarters' units, district offices, larger shore units, and aboard major vessels. The programs at these institutions are all full-time resident courses and, in most cases, result in the awarding of an associate degree.

### Pre-commissioning Program for Enlisted Personnel (PPEP)

The Pre-commissioning Program for Enlisted Personnel enables selected enlisted personnel to attend college on a full-time basis for up to two years, receive a bachelor's degree, attend Officer Candidate School (OCS), and upon graduation from OCS, receive a commission. The program provides an upward mobility mechanism for qualified enlisted personnel to become commissioned officers. The number of PPEP selections made annually will be determined at the time of selection.

## FOR FURTHER INFORMATION

Although the preceding section gives a general overview of the Coast Guard and its programs, it by no means covers the wide range of opportunities available in the Coast Guard. Use *Military Careers* to begin exploring career possibilities in the Coast Guard. Your local Coast Guard recruiter would be pleased to supply you with current, more detailed career information. There is no obligation. The Coast Guard toll-free information number is 1-800-424-8883.

# Enlisted Occupational Descriptions

# Human Services Occupations

- Caseworkers and Counselors
- Religious Program Specialists

# CASEWORKERS AND COUNSELORS

Army
Navy
Air Force
Marine Corps
Coast Guard

Just like some civilians, some military personnel can develop problems with drug or alcohol abuse. Others may develop depression or other emotional problems. Caseworkers and counselors help military personnel and their families to overcome social problems. They work as part of a team that may include social workers, psychologists, medical officers, chaplains, personnel specialists, and commanders.

## What They Do

Caseworkers and counselors in the military perform some or all of the following duties:

- Interview personnel who request help or are referred by their commanders
- Identify personal problems and determine the need for professional help
- Counsel personnel and their families
- Administer and score psychological tests
- Teach classes on human relations
- Keep records of counseling sessions and give reports to supervisors

## Helpful Attributes

Helpful school subjects include health, biology, psychology, sociology, social science, and speech. Helpful attributes include:

- Interest in working with people
- Patience in dealing with problems that take time and effort to overcome
- Sensitivity to the needs of others

## Training Provided

Job training consists of 8 to 10 weeks of classroom instruction, including practice in counseling. Course content typically includes:

- Orientation to counseling and social service programs
- Interviewing and counseling methods
- Treatments for drug and alcohol abuse
- Psychological testing techniques

Further training occurs on the job and through advanced courses.

## Work Environment

Caseworkers and counselors usually work in offices or clinics.

## Civilian Counterparts

Civilian caseworkers and counselors work in rehabilitation centers, hospitals, schools, and public agencies. Their duties are similar to duties in the military. Civilian caseworkers and counselors, however, are usually required to have a college degree in social work, psychology, or counseling. They may be called group workers, human relations counselors, or drug and alcohol counselors.

## Physical Demands

Caseworkers and counselors need to speak clearly and distinctly in order to teach classes and work with personnel who have problems.

## Opportunities

The services have about 800 caseworkers and counselors. On average, they need about 100 new caseworkers and counselors each year. After job training, caseworkers and counselors work under close supervision. With experience, they work more independently and may supervise other caseworkers.

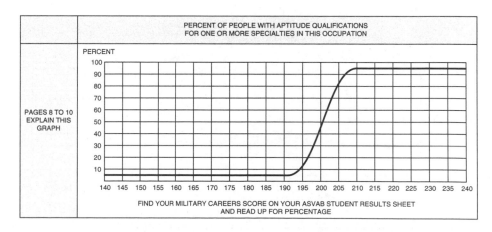

PERCENT OF PEOPLE WITH APTITUDE QUALIFICATIONS
FOR ONE OR MORE SPECIALTIES IN THIS OCCUPATION

PAGES 8 TO 10 EXPLAIN THIS GRAPH

PERCENT

FIND YOUR MILITARY CAREERS SCORE ON YOUR ASVAB STUDENT RESULTS SHEET AND READ UP FOR PERCENTAGE

# RELIGIOUS PROGRAM SPECIALISTS

The military has personnel from many religions and faiths. The military provides chaplains and religious program specialists to help meet the spiritual needs of its personnel. Religious program specialists assist chaplains with religious services, religious education programs, and related administrative duties. Turn to page 356 for more information about religious program specialists.

## What They Do

Religious program specialists in the military perform some or all of the following duties:

- Assist chaplains in planning and preparing religious programs and activities
- Assist chaplains in conducting religious services
- Prepare religious, educational, and devotional materials
- Organize charitable and public service volunteer programs
- Maintain relations with religious communities and public service organizations
- Perform administrative duties for chaplains, such as scheduling appointments, handling correspondence, maintaining files, and handling finances

## Physical Demands

The ability to speak clearly and distinctly is required to enter this occupation.

## Helpful Attributes

Helpful school subjects include English, public speaking, accounting, and typing. Helpful attributes include:

- Interest in religious guidance
- Sensitivity to the needs of others
- Knowledge of various religious customs and beliefs
- Ability to express ideas clearly and concisely
- Interest in administrative work

## Work Environment

Religious program specialists in the military usually work indoors. They also serve aboard ships or with land and air units in the field.

## Training Provided

Job training consists of 7 to 8 weeks of classroom instruction. Course content typically includes:

- Principles of religious support programs
- Guidance and counseling techniques
- Leadership skills
- Office procedures

## Civilian Counterparts

Civilian religious program specialists help manage churches and religious schools. Their duties are similar to those performed by military religious program specialists, including planning religious programs and preparing religious educational materials. They are also called directors of religious activities.

## Opportunities

The services have about 1,300 religious program specialists. On average, they need about 80 new specialists each year. After job training, religious program specialists help chaplains and supervisors with administrative matters. With experience, they gain more responsibility for organizing activities and working in the local community. In time, they may supervise other specialists.

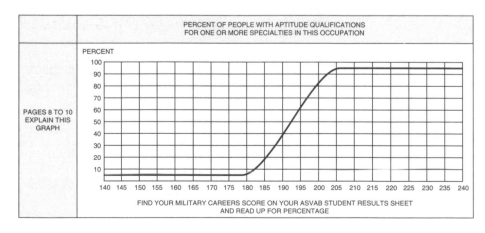

PERCENT OF PEOPLE WITH APTITUDE QUALIFICATIONS FOR ONE OR MORE SPECIALTIES IN THIS OCCUPATION

PAGES 8 TO 10 EXPLAIN THIS GRAPH

PERCENT

FIND YOUR MILITARY CAREERS SCORE ON YOUR ASVAB STUDENT RESULTS SHEET AND READ UP FOR PERCENTAGE

# Media and Public Affairs Occupations

- **Audiovisual and Broadcast Directors**
- **Music Directors**
- **Public Information Officers**

# AUDIOVISUAL AND BROADCAST TECHNICIANS

Television and film productions are an important part of military communications. Films are used for training in many military occupations. They are also used to record military operations, ceremonies, and news events. These productions require the teamwork of many technicians. Audiovisual and broadcast technicians perform many specialized tasks, ranging from filming to script editing to operating audio recording devises.

## What They Do

Audiovisual and broadcast technicians in the military perform some or all of the following duties:

- Work with writers, producers, and directors in preparing and interpreting scripts
- Plan and design production scenery, graphics, and special effects
- Operate media equipment and special effect devises including cameras, sound recorders, and lighting
- Follow script and instructions of film or TV directors to move cameras, zoom, pan, or adjust focus

## Training Provided

Job training consists of 7 to 52 weeks of instruction. Training length varies depending on specialty. Course content typically includes:

- Motion picture equipment operation
- Audio recording
- Scripting and special effects techniques
- Maintenance of public address sound equipment

Further training occurs on the job and through advanced courses.

## Helpful Attributes

Helpful school subjects include photography, graphics, art, speech and drama. Helpful attributes include:

- Interest in creative and artistic work
- Preference for working as part of a team
- Experience in school plays or making home movies

## Physical Demands

Normal color vision and the ability to speak clearly are required for some specialties in this area.

## Civilian Counterparts

Civilian audiovisual and broadcast technicians work for film production companies, government audiovisual studios, radio and television stations, and advertising agencies. Their duties are similar to those performed by military journalists and newswriters. They may be called motion picture camera operators, audiovisual production specialists, sound mixers, recording engineers, and broadcasting and recording technicians.

## Work Environment

Audiovisual and broadcast technicians work in studios or outdoors on location. They sometimes work from aircraft or ships. They travel and work in all climates.

## Opportunities

The services have about 1,300 audiovisual and broadcast technicians. On average, they need about 160 new audiovisual and broadcast technicians each year. After job training, new technicians assist with various production processes. With experience, they work more independently and, in time, may direct audiovisual productions.

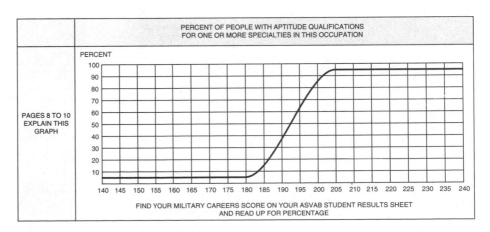

PERCENT OF PEOPLE WITH APTITUDE QUALIFICATIONS FOR ONE OR MORE SPECIALTIES IN THIS OCCUPATION

PAGES 8 TO 10 EXPLAIN THIS GRAPH

PERCENT

FIND YOUR MILITARY CAREERS SCORE ON YOUR ASVAB STUDENT RESULTS SHEET AND READ UP FOR PERCENTAGE

# BROADCAST JOURNALISTS AND NEWSWRITERS

Army
Navy
Air Force
Marine Corps
Coast Guard

The military publishes newspapers and broadcasts television and radio programs for its personnel and the public. These services are an important source of general information about people and events in the military. Broadcast journalists and newswriters write and present news programs, music programs, and radio talk shows. Turn to page 328 for more information about broadcast journalists and newswriters.

## What They Do

Broadcast journalists and newswriters in the military perform some or all of the following duties:

- Gather information for military news programs and publications

- Write radio and TV scripts

- Develop ideas for news articles

- Arrange and conduct interviews

- Collect information for commercial media use

- Select photographs and write captions for news articles

- Write news releases, feature articles, and editorials

## Work Environment

Broadcast journalists and newswriters work in broadcasting studios on land or aboard ships, or sometimes outdoors, depending upon the research needed for their articles.

## Training Provided

Job training consists of 9 to 12 weeks of classroom instruction. Course content typically includes:

- Newswriting and research

- Newspaper format and layout

- Photojournalism (writing news stories featuring pictures)

- Radio and television programming and production

## Physical Demands

Normal color vision and the passing of a voice audition are required for some specialties in this area.

## Helpful Attributes

Helpful school subjects include English, journalism, speech, typing, and media communications. Helpful attributes include:

- Ability to keep detailed and accurate records

- Interest in researching facts and issues for news stories

- Ability to write clearly and concisely

- Strong, clear speaking voice

## Civilian Counterparts

Broadcast journalists and newswriters work for newspapers, magazines, wire services, and radio and television stations. Their duties are similar to those performed by military journalists and newswriters. They may be employed as newscasters, disc jockeys, writers, directors, producers, editors, or correspondents.

## Opportunities

The military has about 1,800 broadcast journalists and newswriters. On average, the services need about 130 new broadcast journalists and newswriters each year. After job training, they research and announce news stories and music programs. Eventually, they may become editors or editorial assistants or managers of broadcasting stations.

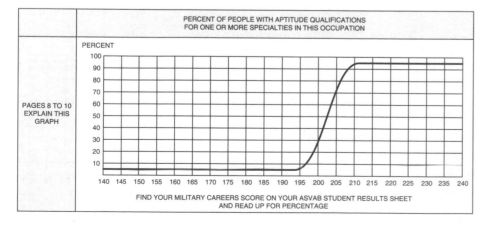

PAGES 8 TO 10 EXPLAIN THIS GRAPH

PERCENT OF PEOPLE WITH APTITUDE QUALIFICATIONS FOR ONE OR MORE SPECIALTIES IN THIS OCCUPATION

PERCENT

100
90
80
70
60
50
40
30
20
10

140  145  150  155  160  165  170  175  180  185  190  195  200  205  210  215  220  225  230  235  240

FIND YOUR MILITARY CAREERS SCORE ON YOUR ASVAB STUDENT RESULTS SHEET AND READ UP FOR PERCENTAGE

# GRAPHIC DESIGNERS AND ILLUSTRATORS

Army
Navy
Air Force
Marine Corps

The military produces many publications, such as training manuals, newspapers, reports, and promotional materials. Graphic artwork is used in these publications and for signs, charts, posters, and TV and motion picture productions. Graphic designers and illustrators produce graphic artwork, drawings, and other visual displays.

## What They Do

Graphic designers and illustrators in the military perform some or all of the following duties:

- Produce computer-generated graphics
- Draw graphs and charts to represent budgets, numbers of troops, supply levels, and office organization
- Develop ideas and design posters and signs
- Help instructors design artwork for training courses
- Draw illustrations of parts of the human body for medical training
- Draw cartoons for filmstrips and animation for films
- Make silkscreen prints
- Work with TV and film producers to design backdrops and props for film sets

## Physical Demands

Coordination of eyes, hands, and fingers are needed to draw sketches.

Normal color vision is required to work with paints, watercolors, and other art materials.

## Helpful Attributes

Helpful school subjects include art, drafting, and geometry. Helpful attributes include:

- Interest in artwork or lettering
- Ability to convert ideas into visual presentations
- Neatness and an eye for detail

## Work Environment

Graphic designers and illustrators usually work in offices on land or aboard ships.

## Training Provided

Job training consists of about 12 weeks of classroom instruction including practice in preparing graphic designs and illustrations. Course content typically includes:

- Introduction to graphics, lettering, drawing, and layout techniques
- Illustration and television graphic techniques
- Theory and use of color

The Army, Navy, and Marine Corps offer certified apprenticeship programs for some specialties in this occupation.

## Civilian Counterparts

Civilian graphic designers and illustrators work for government agencies, advertising agencies, print shops, and engineering firms. They also work for many large organizations that have their own graphics departments. Their duties are similar to military graphic designers and illustrators. They may be known as commercial artists or graphic arts technicians.

## Opportunities

The services have about 800 graphic designers and illustrators. On average, they need about 90 new designers and illustrators each year. After job training, graphic designers prepare tables, signs, and graphics under close supervision. With experience, they help formulate and produce more complex designs. In time, they may supervise others and lead large projects. Eventually, they may manage graphics departments.

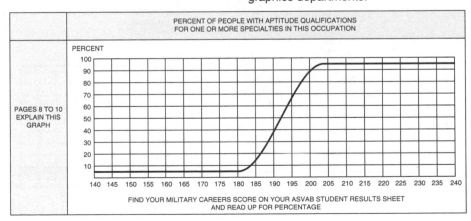

PAGES 8 TO 10 EXPLAIN THIS GRAPH

PERCENT OF PEOPLE WITH APTITUDE QUALIFICATIONS FOR ONE OR MORE SPECIALTIES IN THIS OCCUPATION

PERCENT

FIND YOUR MILITARY CAREERS SCORE ON YOUR ASVAB STUDENT RESULTS SHEET AND READ UP FOR PERCENTAGE

# INTERPRETERS AND TRANSLATORS

Some members of te military must be able to read and understand the many languages of the world. Information from foreign language newspapers, magazines, and radio broadcasts is important to the nation's defense. Interpreters and translators convert written or spoken foreign languages into English or other languages. They usually specialize in a particular foreign language.

## What They Do

Interpreters and translators in the military perform some or all of the following duties:

- Translate written and spoken foreign language material to and from English, making sure to preserve the original meaning

- Interrogate (question) prisoners of war, enemy deserters, and civilian informers in their native languages

- Record foreign radio transmissions using sensitive communications equipment

- Prepare written reports about the information obtained

- Translate foreign documents, such as battle plans and personnel records

- Translate foreign books and articles describing foreign equipment and construction techniques

## Physical Demands

Normal hearing and the ability to speak clearly and distinctly are usually required to enter this occupation.

## Special Requirements

Fluency in a foreign language is required to enter most specialties within this occupation. Although there are women interpreters and translators, some specialties in this occupation are open only to men.

## Helpful Attributes

Helpful school subjects include speech, communications, and foreign languages. Helpful attributes include:

- Talent for foreign languages
- Interest in working with people
- Interest in reading and writing

## Work Environment

Interpreters and translators normally work on military bases, aboard ships, or in airplanes.

## Training Provided

Job training consists of 7 to 20 weeks of classroom instruction including practice in interpretation. Training length varies depending on specialty. Longer training is necessary for specialties that do not require foreign language fluency prior to entry. For these specialties, foreign language training for 6 to 12 months is provided. Course content typically includes:

- Interrogation (questioning) methods
- Use and care of communications equipment
- Procedures for preparing reports

Further training occurs on the job and through advanced courses.

## Civilian Counterparts

Civilian interpreters and translators work for government agencies, embassies, universities, and companies that conduct business overseas. Their work is similar to the work of military interpreters and translators.

## Opportunities

The military has about 6,700 interpreters and translators. On average, the services need about 600 new interpreters and translators each year. After job training, interpreters and translators work under the direction of more experienced workers and supervisors. With experience, they work more independently. In time, interpreters and translators may become directors of translation for large bases.

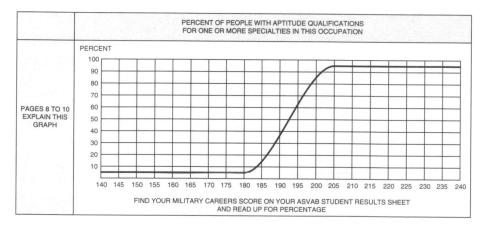

PAGES 8 TO 10 EXPLAIN THIS GRAPH

PERCENT OF PEOPLE WITH APTITUDE QUALIFICATIONS FOR ONE OR MORE SPECIALTIES IN THIS OCCUPATION

PERCENT

100 90 80 70 60 50 40 30 20 10

140 145 150 155 160 165 170 175 180 185 190 195 200 205 210 215 220 225 230 235 240

FIND YOUR MILITARY CAREERS SCORE ON YOUR ASVAB STUDENT RESULTS SHEET AND READ UP FOR PERCENTAGE

# MUSICIANS

Music is an important part of military life. Service bands and vocal groups have a strong tradition of performing at ceremonies, parades, concerts, festivals, and dances. Musicians and singers perform in service bands, orchestras, and small groups. They perform many types of music, including marches, classics, jazz, and popular music.

## What They Do

Musicians in the military perform some or all of the following duties:

- Play in or lead bands, orchestras, combos, and jazz groups

- Sing in choral groups or as soloists

- Perform for ceremonies, parades, concerts, festivals, and dances

- Rehearse and learn new music when not performing

- Play brass, percussion, woodwind, or string instruments

## Special Requirements

To qualify for a service band, applicants must pass one or more auditions. They must be fairly accomplished musicians and have good music sight-reading ability.

## Helpful Attributes

Helpful school subjects include band, music theory, harmony, and other music courses. Helpful attributes include:

- Poise when performing in public

- Ability to play more than one instrument

- Ability to sing

## Work Environment

Musicians play indoors in theaters, concert halls, and at dances; outdoors at parades and open-air concerts. They also travel regularly.

## Training Provided

Although musicians must be musically proficient to enter the service, music training is given to new band members. Job training consists of 11 to 24 weeks of classroom instruction, including practice playing instruments. Training length varies depending on musical specialty. Course content typically includes:

- Music theory

- Group instrumental techniques

- Sight-reading musical scores

- Dance band techniques

Further training occurs on the job through regular rehearsals and individual practice.

## Civilian Counterparts

Civilian musicians work for many types of employers, including professional orchestras, bands, and choral groups. They work in nightclubs, concert halls, theaters, and recording studios.

## Opportunities

The services have about 3,600 musicians. On average, they need about 200 new musicians each year. After job training, musicians are assigned to band units located with U.S. forces around the world. They perform as members of bands and vocal groups. In time, they may become heads of their instrument sections and, possibly, bandleaders or orchestra conductors. The most outstanding performers are selected for the official service bands or orchestras of their service.

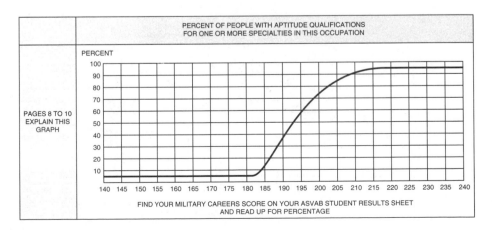

PERCENT OF PEOPLE WITH APTITUDE QUALIFICATIONS FOR ONE OR MORE SPECIALTIES IN THIS OCCUPATION

PAGES 8 TO 10 EXPLAIN THIS GRAPH

PERCENT

FIND YOUR MILITARY CAREERS SCORE ON YOUR ASVAB STUDENT RESULTS SHEET AND READ UP FOR PERCENTAGE

# PHOTOGRAPHIC SPECIALISTS

The military uses photographs for many purposes, such as intelligence gathering and news reporting. The services operate photographic laboratories to develop the numerous photos taken by the military. Photographic specialists take and develop still color or black and white photographs.

## What They Do

Photographic specialists in the military perform some or all of the following duties:

- Select camera, film, and other equipment needed for photo assignments

- Determine camera angles, lighting, and any special effects needed

- Take still photos of people, events, military equipment, land areas, and other subjects

- Develop, duplicate, or retouch film negatives, photos, or slides

- Maintain photographic equipment

## Physical Demands

Normal color vision is required to produce accurate color prints.

## Work Environment

Photographic specialists work both indoors and outdoors while photographing their subjects. They may take photos from aircraft or ships. They process photographs in photographic laboratories on bases or aboard ships.

## Training Provided

Job training consists of 7 to 24 weeks of classroom instruction, including practice in taking and developing photographs. Length of training varies depending on the specialty. Course content typically includes:

- Photographic processing and reproduction

- Principles of photojournalism

- Operation and maintenance of photographic equipment

Further training occurs on the job and through advanced courses.

## Helpful Attributes

Helpful school subjects include photography, chemistry, art, and mathematics. Helpful attributes include:

- Ability to recognize and arrange interesting photo subjects

- Accuracy and attention to detail

## Civilian Counterparts

Civilian photographic specialists work for photography studios, newspapers, magazines, advertising agencies, commercial photograph developers, and large businesses. They perform duties similar to military specialists. Depending on the specialty, they may be known as photojournalists, aerial or still photographers, film developers, automatic print developers, or print controllers.

## Opportunities

The services have about 2,000 photographic specialists. On average, the services need about 120 new specialists each year. After job training, specialists work under supervision. With experience, they are given more responsibility and, eventually, may supervise other photographic specialists.

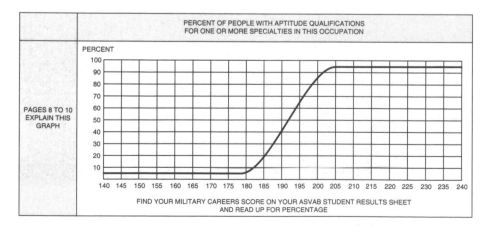

PAGES 8 TO 10 EXPLAIN THIS GRAPH

PERCENT OF PEOPLE WITH APTITUDE QUALIFICATIONS FOR ONE OR MORE SPECIALTIES IN THIS OCCUPATION

PERCENT

FIND YOUR MILITARY CAREERS SCORE ON YOUR ASVAB STUDENT RESULTS SHEET AND READ UP FOR PERCENTAGE

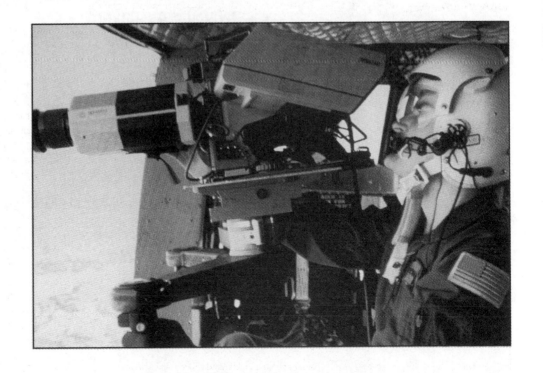

# Health Care Occupations

- **Dietitians**
- **Pharmacists**
- **Physical and Occupational Therapists**
- **Physician Assistants**
- **Registered Nurses**
- **Speech Therapists**

# CARDIOPULMONARY AND EEG TECHNICIANS

Military health care includes medical treatment for heart, lung, and brain disorders. Physicians need sophisticated tests to help diagnose and treat these problems. Cardiopulmonary and EEG (electroencephalograph) technicians administer a variety of diagnostic tests of the heart, lungs, blood, and brain. They operate complex electronic testing equipment.

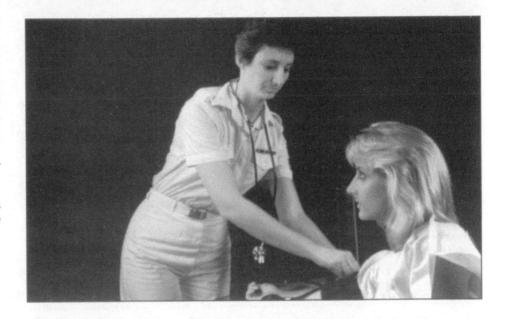

## What They Do

Cardiopulmonary and EEG technicians in the military perform some or all of the following duties:

- Take patients' blood pressure readings
- Attach electrodes or microphones to patients' bodies
- Help physicians revive heart attack victims
- Adjust settings and operate test equipment
- Watch dials, graphs, and screens during tests
- Talk to physicians to learn what tests or treatments are needed
- Keep records of test results and discuss them with medical staff
- Operate electrocardiographs, electroencephalographs, and other test equipment

## Helpful Attributes

Helpful school subjects include algebra, chemistry, biology, or related courses. Helpful attributes include:

- Interest in electronic equipment
- Ability to follow strict standards and procedures
- Interest in learning how the heart, lungs, and blood work together
- Ability to keep accurate records

## Work Environment

Cardiopulmonary and EEG technicians usually work in hospitals and clinics. In combat situations, they may work in mobile field hospitals.

## Physical Demands

Normal color vision is required for some specialties in order to set up and monitor equipment.

## Training Provided

Job training consists of 26 to 30 weeks of classroom instruction. Course content typically includes:

- Diagnostic procedures
- Operation and maintenance of diagnostic equipment
- Preparation of patients for testing
- Methods of resuscitation

Further training occurs on the job and through advanced courses.

## Civilian Counterparts

Civilian cardiopulmonary and EEG technicians work in hospitals, clinics, and physicians' offices. Their duties are similar to those performed in the military. They may specialize in either cardiovascular (heart), pulmonary (lungs), or electroencephalographic (brain) testing.

## Opportunities

The services have about 1,700 cardiopulmonary and EEG technicians. On average, they need 60 new technicians each year. After job training, new technicians are assigned to hospitals and clinics, where they work under the supervision of physicians and senior technicians. With experience, they may supervise others and assist in managing clinics.

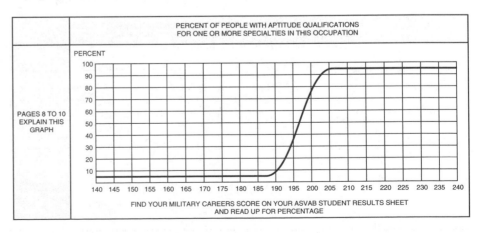

PERCENT OF PEOPLE WITH APTITUDE QUALIFICATIONS FOR ONE OR MORE SPECIALTIES IN THIS OCCUPATION

PAGES 8 TO 10 EXPLAIN THIS GRAPH

PERCENT

FIND YOUR MILITARY CAREERS SCORE ON YOUR ASVAB STUDENT RESULTS SHEET AND READ UP FOR PERCENTAGE

Dental care is one of the health services provided to all military personnel. It is available in military dental clinics all over the world. Dental specialists assist military dentists in examining and treating patients. They also help manage dental offices.

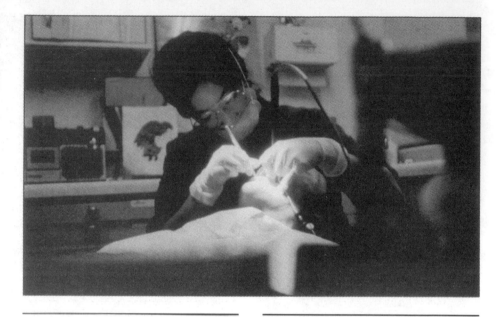

## What They Do

Dental specialists in the military perform some or all of the following duties:

- Help dentists perform oral surgery
- Prepare for patient examinations by selecting and arranging instruments and medications
- Help dentists during examinations by preparing dental compounds and operating dental equipment
- Clean patients' teeth using scaling and polishing instruments and equipment
- Operate dental X-ray equipment and process X-rays of patients' teeth, gums, and jaws
- Provide guidance to patients on daily care of their teeth
- Perform administrative duties, such as scheduling office visits, keeping patient records, and ordering dental supplies

## Civilian Counterparts

Civilian dental specialists work in dental offices or clinics. Their work is similar to work in the military. They typically specialize in assisting dentists to treat patients, provide clerical support (dental assistants), or clean teeth (dental hygienists).

## Physical Demands

Dental specialists must sometimes stand for long periods.

## Special Requirements

A minimum age of 18 is required for this occupation.

## Helpful Attributes

Helpful school subjects include biology and chemistry. Helpful attributes include:

- Good eye-hand coordination
- Ability to follow spoken instructions and detailed procedures
- Interest in working with people

## Training Provided

Job training consists of 9 to 14 weeks of classroom instruction, including practice in dental care tasks. Course content typically includes:

- Preventive dentistry
- Radiology (X-ray) techniques
- Dental office procedures
- Dental hygiene procedures

Further training occurs on the job and through advanced courses. The Navy offers a certified apprenticeship program for one specialty in this occupation.

## Work Environment

Dental specialists in the military usually work indoors in dental offices or clinics. Some specialists may be assigned to duty aboard ships.

## Opportunities

The military has about 3,200 dental specialists. On average, the services need about 350 new specialists each year. After job training, new specialists are assigned to dental offices or clinics, where they work under the supervision of dentists. With experience, dental specialists perform more difficult tasks involving patient care. In time, they may become responsible for assisting dental officers in the management of dental programs.

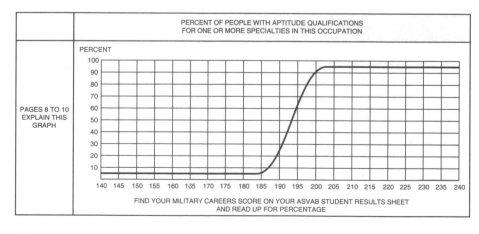

PERCENT OF PEOPLE WITH APTITUDE QUALIFICATIONS FOR ONE OR MORE SPECIALTIES IN THIS OCCUPATION

PAGES 8 TO 10 EXPLAIN THIS GRAPH

PERCENT

FIND YOUR MILITARY CAREERS SCORE ON YOUR ASVAB STUDENT RESULTS SHEET AND READ UP FOR PERCENTAGE

# MEDICAL CARE TECHNICIANS

Army
Navy
Air Force
Coast Guard

The military provides medical care to all men and women in the services. Medical care technicians work with teams of physicians, nurses, and other health care professionals to provide treatment to patients. They help give patients the care and treatment required to help them recover from illness or injury. They also prepare rooms, equipment, and supplies in hospitals and medical clinics.

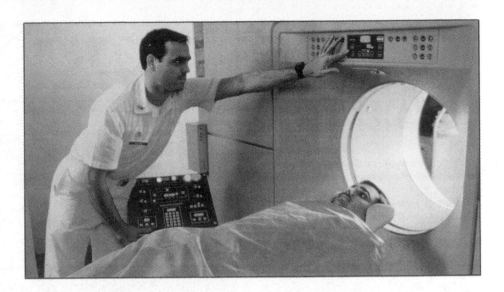

## What They Do

Medical care technicians in the military perform some or all of the following duties:

- Provide bedside care in hospitals, including taking the body temperature, pulse, and respiration rate of patients

- Feed, bathe, and dress patients

- Prepare patients, operating rooms, equipment, and supplies for surgery

- Make casts, traction devices, and splints according to physicians' instructions

- Give medication to patients under the direction of physicians and nurses

## Physical Demands

Some specialties in this area require sufficient strength to lift and move patients, and some require a normal skin condition to guard against infection.

## Helpful Attributes

Helpful school subjects include general science, biology, and psychology. Helpful attributes include:

- Interest in helping others

- Ability to work under stressful or emergency conditions

- Ability to follow directions precisely

## Work Environment

Medical care technicians work in hospitals and clinics on land or aboard ships. In combat situations, they may work in mobile field hospitals.

## Training Provided

Job training consists of 7 to 52 weeks of classroom instruction, including practice in patient care. Training length varies depending on specialty. Course content may include:

- Patient care techniques

- Emergency medical techniques

- Methods of sterilizing surgical equipment

- Plaster casting techniques

Further training occurs on the job and through advanced courses.

## Civilian Counterparts

Civilian medical care technicians work in hospitals, nursing homes, rehabilitation centers, psychiatric hospitals, or physicians' offices. They perform similar duties to those performed in the military. They may be called nurses aides, orderlies, operating room technicians, orthopedic assistants, or practical nurses.

## Opportunities

The services have about 8,950 medical care technicians. On average, they need about 480 new medical care technicians each year. After job training, new technicians are assigned to hospitals or medical units where they work under close supervision. In time, they may advance to supervisory positions and help train others.

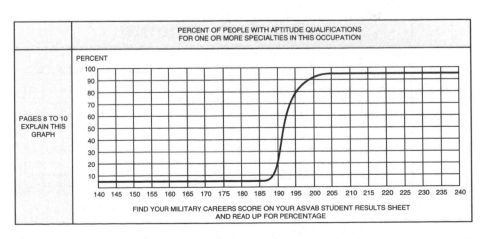

PERCENT OF PEOPLE WITH APTITUDE QUALIFICATIONS FOR ONE OR MORE SPECIALTIES IN THIS OCCUPATION

PAGES 8 TO 10 EXPLAIN THIS GRAPH

PERCENT

FIND YOUR MILITARY CAREERS SCORE ON YOUR ASVAB STUDENT RESULTS SHEET AND READ UP FOR PERCENTAGE

# MEDICAL LABORATORY TECHNICIANS

**Army**
**Navy**
**Air Force**
**Coast Guard**

Medical laboratories are an important part of the military health care system. The staffs of medical laboratories perform clinical tests required to detect and identify diseases in patients. Medical laboratory technicians conduct tests on the tissue, blood, and body fluids of medical patients.

## What They Do

Medical laboratory technicians in the military perform some or all of the following duties:

- Use lab equipment to analyze specimens (samples) of tissue, blood, and body fluids
- Examine blood and bone marrow under microscopes
- Test specimens for bacteria or viruses
- Draw blood from patients
- Assist in collecting specimens at autopsies (medical examinations of the dead)
- Record and file results of laboratory tests

## Training Provided

Job training consists of 12 to 36 weeks of classroom and on-the-job instruction, including practice in testing specimens. Training length varies depending on specialty. Course content typically includes:

- Medical laboratory procedures
- Study of human parasites and diseases
- Laboratory administration and record keeping

## Helpful Attributes

Helpful school subjects include biology, chemistry, and algebra. Helpful attributes include:

- Interest in scientific and technical work
- Ability to follow detailed procedures precisely

## Physical Demands

Normal color vision is required to work with colored chemicals and dyes.

## Work Environment

Medical laboratory technicians work in medical centers, clinics, and hospitals on land or aboard ships.

## Civilian Counterparts

Civilian medical laboratory technicians usually work for privately owned laboratories, hospitals, clinics, or research institutions. They perform duties similar to military medical laboratory technicians.

## Opportunities

The military has about 4,500 medical laboratory technicians. On average, the services need about 400 new technicians each year. After job training, technicians perform routine laboratory tests under close supervision. With experience, they do more complex testing and analysis and work more independently. After demonstrating job proficiency, medical laboratory technicians help train new technicians and supervise laboratory personnel. In time, they may advance to laboratory management positions.

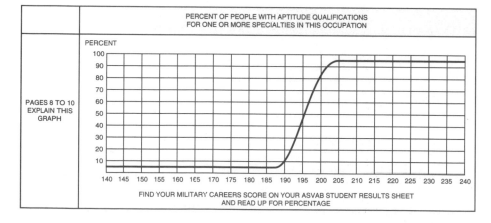

PERCENT OF PEOPLE WITH APTITUDE QUALIFICATIONS FOR ONE OR MORE SPECIALTIES IN THIS OCCUPATION

PAGES 8 TO 10 EXPLAIN THIS GRAPH

PERCENT

FIND YOUR MILITARY CAREERS SCORE ON YOUR ASVAB STUDENT RESULTS SHEET AND READ UP FOR PERCENTAGE

# MEDICAL RECORD TECHNICIANS

Medical records are important for health care delivery. To provide proper treatment, physicians need complete and accurate information about patient symptoms, test results, illnesses, and prior treatments. Medical record technicians prepare and maintain patient records, reports, and correspondence.

## What They Do

Medical record technicians in the military perform some or all of the following duties:

- Fill out admission and discharge records for patients entering and leaving military hospitals

- Assign patients to hospital rooms

- Prepare daily reports about patients admitted and discharged

- Organize, file, and maintain medical records

- Type reports about physical examinations, illnesses, and treatments

- Prepare tables of medical statistics

- Maintain libraries of medical publications

## Work Environment

Medical record technicians work in admissions or medical records sections of hospitals and clinics. They work in land-based facilities and aboard ships.

## Helpful Attributes

Helpful school subjects include general science and business administration. Helpful attributes include:

- Interest in work requiring accuracy and attention to detail

- Ability to communicate well

- Interest in using computers and other office machines

## Training Provided

Job training consists of 6 to 18 weeks of classroom instruction. Training length varies depending on specialty. Course content typically includes:

- Medical terminology

- Medical records preparation and maintenance

- Maintenance of medical libraries

- Basic typing skills

## Civilian Counterparts

Civilian medical record technicians usually work for hospitals, clinics, and government health agencies. They perform duties similar to military medical record technicians. However, civilian medical record technicians tend to specialize in areas such as admissions, ward, or outpatient records. Those working in admission or discharge units are called admitting or discharge clerks.

## Opportunities

The services have about 4,000 medical record technicians. On average, they need about 200 new technicians each year. After training, new technicians are assigned to hospitals or clinics, where they work under close supervision. With experience, they may assume supervisory positions and may manage medical record units or admission or discharge units.

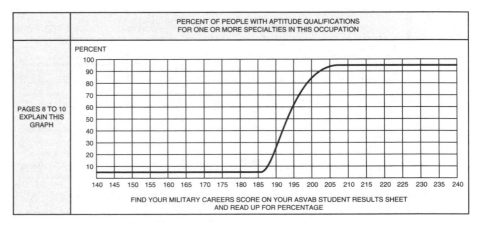

PAGES 8 TO 10 EXPLAIN THIS GRAPH

PERCENT OF PEOPLE WITH APTITUDE QUALIFICATIONS
FOR ONE OR MORE SPECIALTIES IN THIS OCCUPATION

PERCENT

FIND YOUR MILITARY CAREERS SCORE ON YOUR ASVAB STUDENT RESULTS SHEET
AND READ UP FOR PERCENTAGE

# MEDICAL SERVICE TECHNICIANS

In emergencies or in combat, physicians are not always immediately available to treat the injured or wounded. When a physician is not available, medical service technicians provide basic and emergency medical treatment. They also assist medical officers in caring for sick and injured patients. Turn to page 344 for more information about medical service technicians.

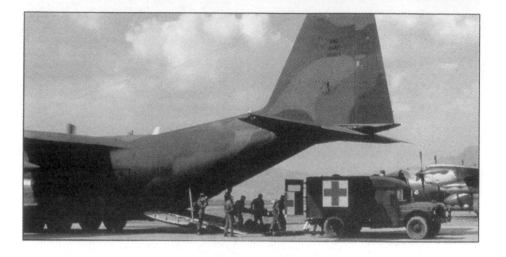

## What They Do

Medical service technicians in the military perform some or all of the following duties:

- Examine and treat emergency or battlefield patients
- Interview patients and record their medical histories
- Take patients' temperature, pulse, and blood pressure
- Prepare blood samples for laboratory analysis
- Keep health records and clinical files up to date
- Give shots and medicines to patients

## Helpful Attributes

Helpful school subjects include chemistry, biology, psychology, general science, and algebra. Helpful attributes include:

- Interest in helping and caring for others
- Ability to communicate effectively
- Ability to work under stressful conditions

## Work Environment

Medical service technicians usually work in hospitals and clinics on land or aboard ships. Medical service technicians may give emergency medical treatment in the field.

## Training Provided

Job training consists of 16 to 54 weeks of classroom instruction, depending on specialty. Course content typically includes:

- Emergency medical treatment
- Basic nursing care
- Study of the human body
- Minor surgical procedures
- Clinical laboratory procedures
- Methods for diagnosing diseases

Further training occurs on the job and through advanced courses.

## Physical Demands

Medical service technicians may have to lift and carry wounded or injured personnel during emergency situations. Air medical evacuation specialists must pass a flight physical exam.

## Civilian Counterparts

Civilian medical service technicians work in hospitals, clinics, nursing homes, and rehabilitation centers. They perform duties similar to those performed by medical service technicians in the military. Civilian medical service technicians are known for the type of work they do: emergency medical technicians treat victims of accidents, fire, or heart attacks; medical assistants work for physicians and perform routine medical and clerical tasks; medication aides give shots and medicine under the close supervision of physicians; and physician assistants perform routine examinations and treatment for physicians.

## Opportunities

The services have about 26,000 medical service technicians. On average, they need about 3,500 new technicians each year. After job training, technicians are assigned to serve in their medical specialty. They work under the direction and supervision of medical officers and experienced medical service technicians. Eventually, they may advance to supervisory positions and help manage a medical facility.

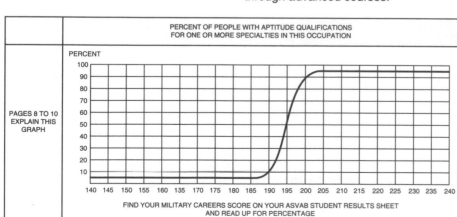

PAGES 8 TO 10 EXPLAIN THIS GRAPH

PERCENT OF PEOPLE WITH APTITUDE QUALIFICATIONS FOR ONE OR MORE SPECIALTIES IN THIS OCCUPATION

PERCENT

100 90 80 70 60 50 40 30 20 10

140 145 150 155 160 135 170 175 180 185 190 195 200 205 210 215 220 225 230 235 240

FIND YOUR MILITARY CAREERS SCORE ON YOUR ASVAB STUDENT RESULTS SHEET AND READ UP FOR PERCENTAGE

# OPTOMETRIC TECHNICIANS

Optometry, or vision care, is one of the many health benefits available to military personnel. The military operates its own clinics to examine eyes and fit glasses or contact lenses. Optometric technicians assist optometrists in providing vision care. They work with patients and manage clinic offices.

## What They Do

Optometric technicians in the military perform some or all of the following duties:

- Perform screening tests of patients' vision and record results
- Order eyeglasses and contact lenses from prescriptions
- Measure patients for eyeglass frames
- Fit eyeglasses to patients
- Make minor repairs to glasses
- Place eyedrops and ointment into patients' eyes
- Keep records in optometry offices

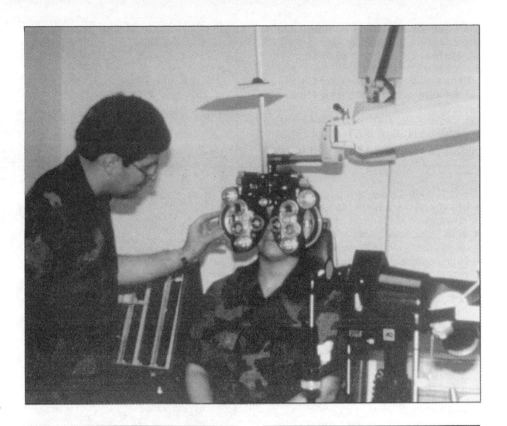

## Helpful Attributes

Helpful school subjects include algebra, geometry, biology, and related courses. Helpful attributes include:

- Interest in helping people
- Interest in work requiring accuracy and attention to detail
- Ability to communicate effectively

## Training Provided

Job training consists of 9 to 13 weeks of classroom instruction, including practice in optometric procedures. Course content typically includes:

- Preparing and fitting glasses and contact lenses
- Vision testing
- Maintenance of optometric instruments

Further training occurs on the job.

## Physical Demands

Normal color vision is required for some specialties to use optometric instruments.

## Work Environment

Optometric technicians normally work in optometric clinics.

## Civilian Counterparts

Civilian optometric technicians work in private optometry offices, clinics, and government health agencies. They perform duties similar to those performed by military optometric technicians. Optometric technicians are also called optometric assistants.

## Opportunities

The services have about 500 optometric technicians. On average, they need 60 new technicians each year. After training, new technicians give simple vision tests under close supervision and perform office duties. As they gain experience, they work with less supervision and perform more difficult tasks. In time, they may help to manage optometric clinics.

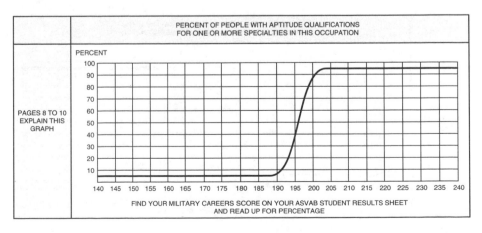

PERCENT OF PEOPLE WITH APTITUDE QUALIFICATIONS FOR ONE OR MORE SPECIALTIES IN THIS OCCUPATION

PAGES 8 TO 10 EXPLAIN THIS GRAPH

FIND YOUR MILITARY CAREERS SCORE ON YOUR ASVAB STUDENT RESULTS SHEET AND READ UP FOR PERCENTAGE

Prescription drugs and medicines are important to medical treatment. Patients and physicians depend on military pharmacies to fill their prescriptions accurately. Pharmacy technicians prepare and dispense prescribed drugs and medicines under the supervision of pharmacists or physicians. They also maintain pharmacy supplies and records.

## What They Do

Pharmacy technicians in the military perform some or all of the following duties:

- Read physicians' prescriptions to determine the types and amount of drugs to prepare
- Weigh and measure drugs and chemicals
- Mix ingredients in order to produce prescription medications
- Prepare labels for prescriptions
- Dispense medications to patients
- Keep records of drugs prescribed
- Store shipments of drugs and medications

## Helpful Attributes

Helpful school subjects include algebra, chemistry, biology, physiology, anatomy, and typing. Helpful attributes include:

- Interest in body chemistry
- Ability to work using precise measurements and standards
- Ability to follow strict procedures and directions

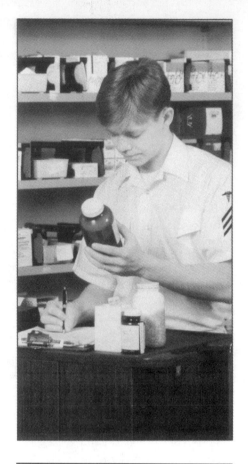

## Training Provided

Job training consists of 12 to 17 weeks of classroom instruction. Course content typically includes:

- Pharmacy laws and regulations
- Drug types and uses
- Mixing and dispensing drugs

## Physical Demands

Normal color vision is required as is the ability to speak clearly. Some specialties may involve heavy lifting.

## Work Environment

Pharmacy technicians usually work in hospitals and clinics on land or aboard ships. They may also work in field hospitals.

## Civilian Counterparts

Civilian pharmacy technicians work in pharmacies, drug stores, hospitals, and clinics under the direction of pharmacists. They are usually known as pharmacy helpers and generally do not have responsibility for the compounding and dispensing of drugs. They perform simple tasks, such as storing supplies, cleaning equipment, and delivering prescriptions. While military pharmacy technicians generally have more job responsibilities than civilian pharmacy helpers, they do not have the qualifications needed to become civilian pharmacists. Pharmacists must complete a college pharmacy degree program, pass a state board exam, and serve in a pharmacy internship.

## Opportunities

The services have about 2,300 pharmacy technicians. On average, they need about 200 new technicians each year. After job training, new technicians work under the supervision of experienced pharmacy technicians and pharmacists. With experience, they work more independently. Eventually, they may supervise other technicians and may manage military pharmacies.

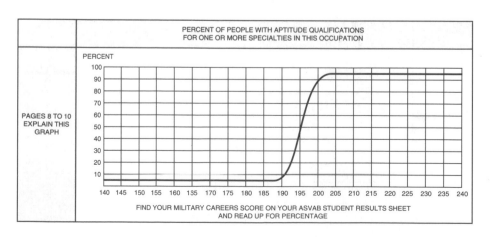

PAGES 8 TO 10 EXPLAIN THIS GRAPH

PERCENT OF PEOPLE WITH APTITUDE QUALIFICATIONS FOR ONE OR MORE SPECIALTIES IN THIS OCCUPATION

PERCENT

100 90 80 70 60 50 40 30 20 10

140 145 150 155 160 135 170 175 180 185 190 195 200 205 210 215 220 225 230 235 240

FIND YOUR MILITARY CAREERS SCORE ON YOUR ASVAB STUDENT RESULTS SHEET AND READ UP FOR PERCENTAGE

# PHYSICAL AND OCCUPATIONAL THERAPY SPECIALISTS

**Army**
**Navy**
**Air Force**
**Coast Guard**

Physical and occupational therapy consists of treatment and exercise for patients disabled by illness or injury. Physical and occupational therapy specialists assist in administering treatment aimed at helping disabled patients regain strength and mobility and preparing them to return to work.

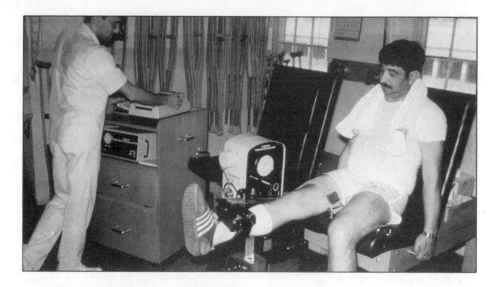

## What They Do

Physical and occupational therapy specialists in the military perform some or all of the following duties:

- Test and interview patients to determine their physical and mental abilities
- Assist physical and occupational therapists in planning therapy programs and exercise schedules
- Fit artificial limbs (prostheses) and train patients in their use
- Provide massages and heat treatments to patients
- Teach patients new mobility skills
- Set up and maintain therapeutic equipment such as exercise machines and whirlpools

## Physical Demands

Therapy specialists may have to lift and support patients during exercises and treatments.

## Helpful Attributes

Helpful school subjects include general science, biology, physiology, and psychology. Helpful attributes include:

- Interest in working with and helping people
- Patience to work with people whose injuries heal slowly
- Ability to communicate effectively

## Work Environment

Therapy specialists work in hospitals, clinics, and rehabilitation centers.

## Training Provided

Job training consists of 11 to 31 weeks of classroom instruction, including practice in applying therapy techniques. Course content typically includes:

- Anatomy, physiology, and psychology (the study of the body, body functions, and the mind)
- Methods of therapy, including massage, electric therapy, and radiation therapy
- Handling and positioning of patients
- Principles of rehabilitation

Further training occurs on the job and through advanced courses.

## Civilian Counterparts

Civilian therapy specialists work in hospitals, rehabilitation centers, nursing homes, schools, and community health centers. They perform duties similar to military therapy specialists. Civilian therapy specialists often specialize in treating a particular type of patient, such as children, the severely disabled, the elderly, or those who have lost arms or legs (amputees).

## Opportunities

The services have about 700 physical and occupational therapy specialists. On average, they need about 70 new specialists each year. After job training, therapy specialists provide routine therapy care under the direction of supervisors. With experience, they work with patients with more serious problems. Eventually they may advance to supervisory positions.

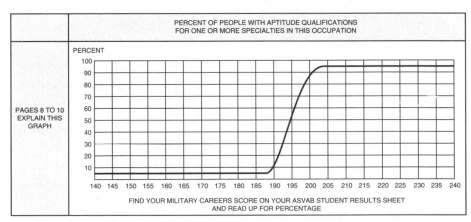

PERCENT OF PEOPLE WITH APTITUDE QUALIFICATIONS FOR ONE OR MORE SPECIALTIES IN THIS OCCUPATION

PAGES 8 TO 10 EXPLAIN THIS GRAPH

PERCENT

FIND YOUR MILITARY CAREERS SCORE ON YOUR ASVAB STUDENT RESULTS SHEET AND READ UP FOR PERCENTAGE

# RADIOLOGIC (X-RAY) TECHNICIANS

Radiology (the use of X-rays) is a health care service provided to men and women in the military. X-ray photographs help physicians detect injuries and illnesses. Radiology is also used to treat some diseases, such as cancer. Radiologic technicians operate X-ray and related equipment used in diagnosing and treating injuries and diseases. They work as part of a medical team of physicians and specialists to provide health care to patients. Turn to page 354 for more information about radiologic technicians.

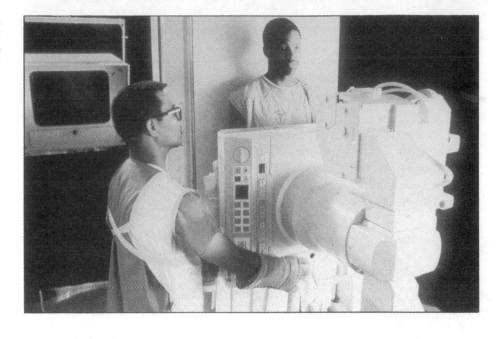

## What They Do

Radiologic technicians in the military perform some or all of the following duties:

- Read requests or instructions from physicians to determine each patient's X-ray needs
- Position patients under radiologic equipment
- Operate X-ray equipment
- Adjust X-ray equipment to the correct time and power of exposure
- Process X-ray pictures
- Prepare and administer radioactive solutions to patients
- Keep records of patient treatment

## Work Environment

Radiologic technicians work in hospitals and clinics. In combat situations, they may work in mobile field hospitals. They follow strict safety procedures to minimize exposure to radiation.

## Training Provided

Job training consists of 12 to 19 weeks of classroom instruction, including practice with radiologic equipment. Extensive on-the-job training is also provided. Training length varies depending on specialty. Course content typically includes:

- Operation of X-ray equipment
- Radioactive isotope therapy
- X-ray film processing
- Anatomy and physiology

Additional training occurs through advanced courses.

## Helpful Attributes

Helpful school subjects include algebra, biology, and other science courses. Helpful attributes include:

- Interest in activities requiring accuracy and attention to detail
- Ability to follow strict standards and procedures
- Interest in helping others

## Civilian Counterparts

Civilian radiologic technicians work in hospitals, diagnostic clinics, and medical laboratories. They perform duties similar to military radiologic technicians. They may specialize in various areas of radiology and may be called X-ray technologists or nuclear medical technologists.

## Opportunities

The military has about 2,500 radiologic technicians. On average, the services need about 200 new technicians each year. After job training, technicians start taking routine X-rays. With experience, they may specialize in nuclear medicine and administer radiation and radioisotopic treatment and therapy. In time, they may advance to become supervisors of radiologic units.

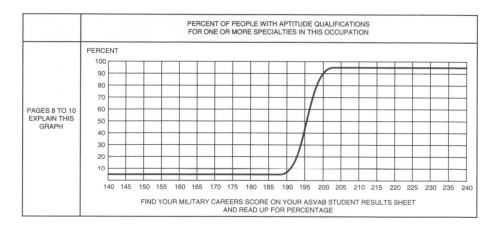

PERCENT OF PEOPLE WITH APTITUDE QUALIFICATIONS
FOR ONE OR MORE SPECIALTIES IN THIS OCCUPATION

PAGES 8 TO 10 EXPLAIN THIS GRAPH

PERCENT

FIND YOUR MILITARY CAREERS SCORE ON YOUR ASVAB STUDENT RESULTS SHEET
AND READ UP FOR PERCENTAGE

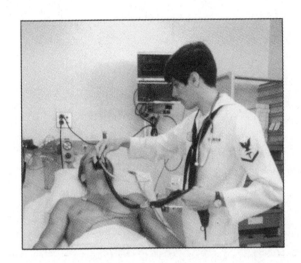

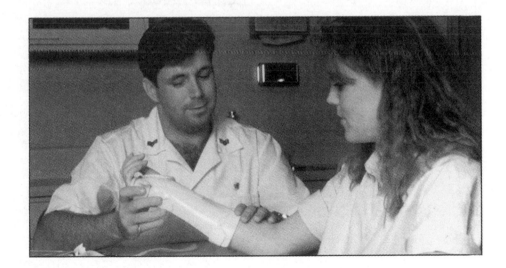

# Engineering, Science, and Technical Occupations

- **Air Traffic Controllers**
- **Chemical Laboratory Technicians**
- **Communications Equipment Operators**
- **Computer Programmers**
- **Emergency Management Specialists**
- **Environmental Health and Safety Specialists**
- **Intelligence Specialists**
- **Meteorological Specialists**
- **Non-Destructive Testers**
- **Ordnance Specialists**
- **Radar and Sonar Operators**
- **Radio Intelligence Operators**
- **Space Operations Specialists**
- **Surveying, Mapping, and Drafting Technicians**

# AIR TRAFFIC CONTROLLERS

Every day, hundreds of military airplanes and helicopters take off and land all over the world. Their movements are closely controlled in order to prevent accidents. Air traffic controllers direct the movement of aircraft into and out of military airfields. They track aircraft by radar and give voice instructions by radio. Turn to page 320 for more information about air traffic controllers.

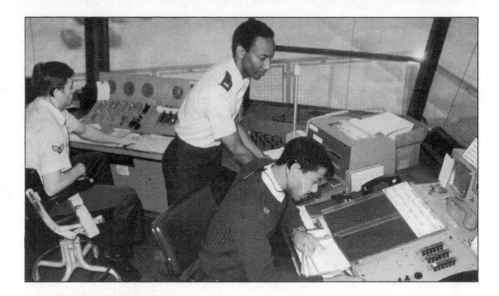

## What They Do

Air traffic controllers in the military perform some or all of the following duties:

- Operate radio equipment to issue takeoff, flight, and landing instructions to pilots

- Relay weather reports, airfield conditions, and safety information to pilots

- Use radar equipment to track aircraft in flight

- Plot airplane locations on charts and maps

- Compute speed, direction, and altitude of aircraft

- Maintain air traffic control records and communication logs

## Physical Demands

Normal color vision, normal hearing and a clear speaking voice are required to enter this occupation. Controllers must pass a special physical exam.

## Helpful Attributes

Helpful school subjects include English, general mathematics, and typing. Helpful attributes include:

- Ability to work under stress

- Skill in math computation

- Ability to make quick, decisive judgments

- Ability to remain alert while performing repetitive tasks

## Special Requirements

Certification by the Federal Aviation Administration (FAA) normally must be obtained during training.

## Work Environment

Air traffic controllers work in land-based and shipboard control centers.

## Training Provided

Job training consists of 7 to 13 weeks of classroom instruction. Training length varies depending on specialty. Course content typically includes:

- Air traffic control fundamentals

- Visual and instrument flight procedures

- Radar and other landing approach procedures

- Communication procedures

Additional training occurs on the job. Aircraft carrier air traffic controllers receive specialized training.

## Civilian Counterparts

Civilian air traffic controllers work for the FAA in airports and control centers around the country. They perform duties similar to military air traffic controllers. They may specialize in specific areas, such as aircraft arrivals, departures, ground control, or en route flights.

## Opportunities

The services have about 3,800 air traffic controllers. On average, they need 800 new controllers each year. After job training, new controllers normally perform duties such as ground control or work in airfields with light air traffic. With experience, they perform more difficult controller duties. In time, they may become supervisors of other controllers.

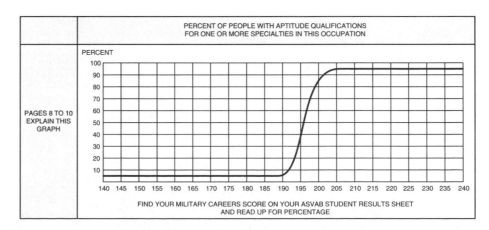

PERCENT OF PEOPLE WITH APTITUDE QUALIFICATIONS FOR ONE OR MORE SPECIALTIES IN THIS OCCUPATION

PAGES 8 TO 10 EXPLAIN THIS GRAPH

PERCENT

FIND YOUR MILITARY CAREERS SCORE ON YOUR ASVAB STUDENT RESULTS SHEET AND READ UP FOR PERCENTAGE

# CHEMICAL LABORATORY TECHNICIANS

Army
Navy
Coast Guard

Fuels and oils must be free of water and other contaminants to be safely used in aircraft or vehicles. The same is true for chemicals and other materials used by the military. Chemical laboratory technicians test fuels, oils, chemicals, and other materials for quality, purity, and durability.

## What They Do

Laboratory technicians in the military perform some or all of the following duties:

- Obtain petroleum test samples from storage tanks, barges, and tankers
- Test fuels and oils for water, sediment, and other contaminants using laboratory equipment
- Analyze chemicals for strength, purity, and toxic qualities
- Perform chemical and physical tests on clothing, food, paints, and plastics
- Keep detailed laboratory records and files

## Physical Demands

Normal color vision is required to perform chemical tests.

Some specialties may require moderate to heavy lifting.

## Work Environment

Chemical laboratory technicians work in laboratories on military bases and aboard ships.

## Training Provided

Job training consists of 2 to 13 weeks of instruction, including practice in testing different products. Training length varies depending on specialty. Course content typically includes:

- Testing methods
- Use of lab equipment, such as centrifuges and spectrometers
- Physical and chemical properties of fuel, oils, and other products

Further training occurs on the job and through advanced courses. The Army and the Navy offer certified apprenticeship programs for one specialty in this occupation.

## Helpful Attributes

Helpful school subjects include chemistry and mathematics. Helpful attributes include:

- Interest in performing technical work
- Interest in working with chemicals and lab equipment
- Ability to follow detailed procedures

## Civilian Counterparts

Civilian chemical laboratory technicians work for petroleum refineries, chemical companies, manufacturing firms, and government agencies. They perform duties similar to military laboratory technicians. Civilian chemical laboratory technicians specialize in particular industries, such as petroleum, food processing, or medical drugs. They also may be called fuel and chemical laboratory technicians or laboratory testers.

## Opportunities

The services have about 1,000 chemical laboratory technicians. On average, they need about 100 new laboratory technicians each year. After job training, laboratory technicians work in testing laboratories under close supervision. With experience, they work more independently and perform more complex analyses. In time, laboratory technicians may supervise or manage test laboratories.

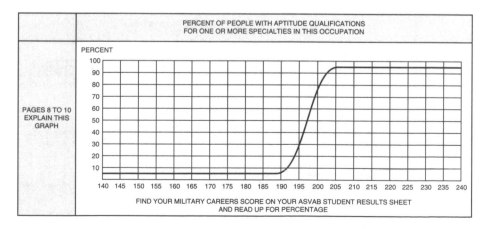

PAGES 8 TO 10 EXPLAIN THIS GRAPH

PERCENT OF PEOPLE WITH APTITUDE QUALIFICATIONS FOR ONE OR MORE SPECIALTIES IN THIS OCCUPATION

PERCENT

FIND YOUR MILITARY CAREERS SCORE ON YOUR ASVAB STUDENT RESULTS SHEET AND READ UP FOR PERCENTAGE

# COMMUNICATIONS EQUIPMENT OPERATORS

Army
Navy
Air Force
Marine Corps
Coast Guard

The ability to link air, sea, and ground forces through communication systems is critical in the military. Communications equipment operators enable these messages to be transmitted and received.

## What They Do

Communications equipment operators in the military perform some or all of the following duties:

- Transmit, receive, and log messages according to military procedures
- Encode and decode classified messages
- Operate different types of telephone switchboards
- Install, maintain, and operate communications equipment
- Monitor and respond to emergency calls

## Physical Demands

Normal color vision, normal hearing, and the ability to speak clearly and distinctly are required to enter some specialties in this occupation. Operators must often sit for long periods.

## Training Provided

Job training consists of 9 to 22 weeks of instruction, including practice with equipment. Course content typically includes:

- Use of various types of communications equipment
- Procedures for setting up communications equipment
- Maintenance and care of communications equipment

Further training occurs on the job and through advanced courses. The Army, Navy, and Marine Corps offer certified apprenticeship programs for some specialties in this occupation.

## Work Environment

Communications equipment operators may work either indoors or outdoors, depending on the specialty. They may be assigned to ships, aircraft, land bases, or mobile field units.

## Helpful Attributes

Helpful school subjects include typing, English, and speech. Helpful attributes include:

- Interest in working with communications equipment
- Interest in working with codes
- Ability to remain calm in an emergency

## Civilian Counterparts

Civilian communications equipment operators work in airports, harbors, police stations, fire stations, telephone companies, telegraph companies, and many businesses. They may also work aboard ships. Their duties are similar to duties assigned to military communications equipment operators, although civilian communications equipment operators do not usually work in field units. They may be called radio operators, telephone operators, radiotelephone operators, switchboard operators or teletype operators, depending on their specialty.

## Opportunities

The military has about 43,900 communications equipment operators. On average, the services need about 4,650 new operators each year. After job training, communications equipment operators prepare and send messages, work at switchboards, and type and file messages under supervision. With experience, they work more independently. In time, they may become supervisors of communications centers.

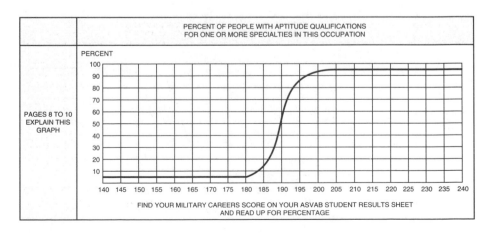

PAGES 8 TO 10 EXPLAIN THIS GRAPH

PERCENT OF PEOPLE WITH APTITUDE QUALIFICATIONS FOR ONE OR MORE SPECIALTIES IN THIS OCCUPATION

PERCENT

FIND YOUR MILITARY CAREERS SCORE ON YOUR ASVAB STUDENT RESULTS SHEET AND READ UP FOR PERCENTAGE

# COMPUTER PROGRAMMERS

The military is one of the largest users of data processing equipment in the world. Information about communications, personnel, finance, and supply is kept in its many high-speed computers. This information is important for planning and management. Computer programmers plan and prepare instructions, called programs, that command computers to solve problems and organize data. Turn to page 330 for more information about computer programmers.

## What They Do

Computer programmers in the military perform some or all of the following duties:

- Organize and arrange computer programs into logical steps which direct computers to solve problems

- Determine and analyze computer systems requirements

- Code programs into languages that computers can read, such as COBOL and FORTRAN

- Design, test, and debug computer programs

- Review and update old programs as new information is received or changes are needed

## Work Environment

Computer programmers normally work in office settings. Some work aboard ships, in missile facilities, or in space command centers.

## Training Provided

Job training consists of 10 to 13 weeks of classroom instruction, including practice in program coding. Course content typically includes:

- Program structuring, coding, and debugging

- Analysis and design of computer systems

- Preparation of block diagrams, flow charts, and program codes

- FORTRAN, COBOL, and other computer programming languages

Further training occurs on the job and through advanced courses in specific computer systems and languages.

## Helpful Attributes

Helpful school subjects include math, business administration, and computer science. Helpful attributes include:

- Ability to understand math concepts

- Interest in solving problems using rules of logic

- Interest in computers

## Civilian Counterparts

Civilian computer programmers work for such organizations as manufacturing firms, banks, data processing organizations, government agencies, and private corporations. These employers handle large amounts of information that programmers help organize for convenient use. Civilian computer programmers perform duties similar to those in the military. They may also be called computer systems analysts.

## Opportunities

The military has about 2,800 computer programmers. On average, the services need about 200 new programmers each year. After job training, programmers are assigned to data processing units. Programmers may work alone or with systems specialists. With experience, programmers may advance to supervisory positions, such as programming chiefs.

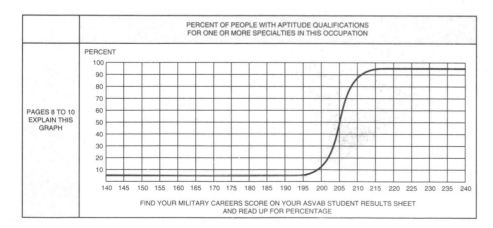

PERCENT OF PEOPLE WITH APTITUDE QUALIFICATIONS
FOR ONE OR MORE SPECIALTIES IN THIS OCCUPATION

PAGES 8 TO 10 EXPLAIN THIS GRAPH

PERCENT

FIND YOUR MILITARY CAREERS SCORE ON YOUR ASVAB STUDENT RESULTS SHEET
AND READ UP FOR PERCENTAGE

# EMERGENCY MANAGEMENT SPECIALISTS

The military prepares for emergencies or natural disasters by developing detailed warning, control, and evacuation plans. Emergency management specialists prepare emergency plans and procedures for all types of disasters, such as floods, earthquakes, hurricanes, or enemy attack.

## What They Do

Emergency management specialists in the military perform some or all of the following duties:

- Assist in preparing and maintaining disaster operations plans
- Train military and civilian personnel on what to do in an emergency
- Operate and maintain nuclear, biological, and chemical detection and decontamination equipment
- Conduct surveys to determine needs in the event of an emergency
- Monitor disaster preparedness activities and training operations

## Helpful Attributes

Helpful school subjects include algebra, chemistry, physics, geometry, and trigonometry. Helpful attributes include:

- Ability to communicate effectively
- Ability to plan and organize
- Ability to work calmly under stress

## Work Environment

Emergency management specialists work indoors when conducting training sessions and preparing disaster plans. Sometimes they work outdoors while operating decontamination equipment and monitoring disaster training.

## Training Provided

Job training consists of 8 to 10 weeks of classroom instruction, including practice in the use of nuclear, biological, and chemical detection and decontamination equipment. Course content typically includes:

- Defensive procedures for nuclear, biological, and chemical warfare
- Preparation of emergency plans

Further training occurs on the job and through advanced courses.

## Physical Demands

Normal color vision is needed to identify chemical agents.

## Civilian Counterparts

Civilian emergency management specialists work for federal, state, and local governments, including law enforcement and civil defense agencies. They perform duties similar to military emergency management specialists.

## Opportunities

The services have about 8,000 emergency management specialists. On average, they need 700 new specialists each year. After job training, some prepare emergency plans under close supervision. With experience, they work more independently and assist in surveys and inspections. Other specialists conduct inspections and operate decontamination equipment. Eventually, they may become supervisors of emergency management programs.

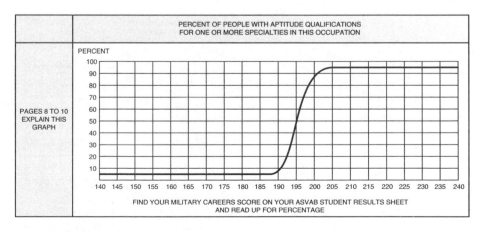

PAGES 8 TO 10 EXPLAIN THIS GRAPH

PERCENT OF PEOPLE WITH APTITUDE QUALIFICATIONS FOR ONE OR MORE SPECIALTIES IN THIS OCCUPATION

PERCENT

FIND YOUR MILITARY CAREERS SCORE ON YOUR ASVAB STUDENT RESULTS SHEET AND READ UP FOR PERCENTAGE

# ENVIRONMENTAL HEALTH AND SAFETY SPECIALISTS

Each military base is a small community. The health and well-being of the residents and surrounding land is a major concern of the services. Keeping military work places and living areas sanitary helps to prevent illness. Environmental health and safety specialists inspect military facilities and food supplies for the presence of disease, germs, or other conditions hazardous to health and the environment.

## What They Do

Environmental health and safety specialists in the military perform some or all of the following duties:

- Monitor storage, transportation, and disposal of hazardous waste
- Analyze food and water samples to ensure quality
- Conduct health and safety investigations of living quarters and base facilities
- Provide training on industrial hygiene, environmental health, and occupational health issues
- Monitor noise and radiation levels at job sites

## Helpful Attributes

Helpful school subjects include algebra, biology, chemistry, and general science. Helpful attributes include:

- Interest in gathering information
- Preference for work requiring attention to detail
- Interest in protecting the environment

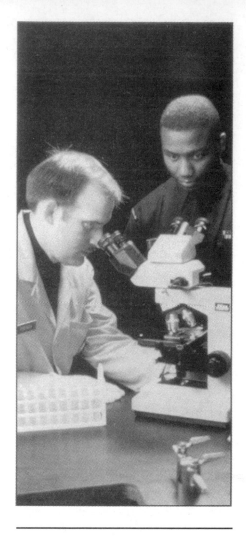

## Work Environment

Environmental health specialists work indoors while inspecting food facilities and buildings. They work outdoors while inspecting waste disposal facilities and field camps.

## Physical Demands

Normal color vision is required to inspect foods for quality and freshness.

## Training Provided

Job training consists of 11 to 19 weeks of classroom instruction, including practice in making health and sanitation inspections. Training length varies depending on specialty. Course content typically includes:

- Identification of health hazards
- Inspection of food products and food service operations
- Inspection of wastewater and waste disposal facilities

Further training occurs on the job and through advanced courses.

## Special Requirements

Some specialties require a minimum age of 18 to enter this occupation.

## Civilian Counterparts

Most civilian environmental health and safety specialists work for local, state, and federal government agencies. Their duties are similar to the duties of military environmental health specialists. They may be called food and drug inspectors, public health inspectors, health and safety inspectors, or industrial hygienists.

## Opportunities

The services have about 2,700 environmental health and safety specialists. On average, they need about 250 new specialists each year. After job training, environmental health and safety specialists help to make inspections. With experience, they work more independently and may supervise other environmental health and safety specialists. Eventually, they may become superintendents of environmental health programs at large military bases.

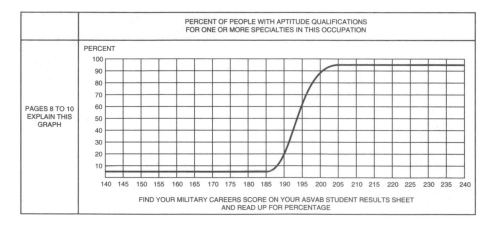

PAGES 8 TO 10 EXPLAIN THIS GRAPH

PERCENT OF PEOPLE WITH APTITUDE QUALIFICATIONS FOR ONE OR MORE SPECIALTIES IN THIS OCCUPATION

PERCENT

FIND YOUR MILITARY CAREERS SCORE ON YOUR ASVAB STUDENT RESULTS SHEET AND READ UP FOR PERCENTAGE

# INTELLIGENCE SPECIALISTS

Military intelligence is information needed to plan for our national defense. Knowledge of the number, location, and tactics of enemy forces and potential battle areas is needed to develop military plans. To gather information, the services rely on aerial photographs, electronic monitoring using radar and sensitive radios, and human observation. Intelligence specialists gather and study the information required to design defense plans and tactics.

## What They Do

Intelligence specialists in the military perform some or all of the following duties:

- Study aerial photographs of foreign ships, bases, and missile sites
- Study foreign troop movements
- Operate sensitive radios to intercept foreign military communications
- Study land and sea areas that could become battlegrounds in time of war
- Store and retrieve intelligence data using computers
- Study foreign military codes
- Prepare intelligence reports, maps, and charts

## Training Provided

Job training consists of 9 to 24 weeks of classroom instruction, including practice in intelligence gathering. Training length varies depending on specialty. Course content typically includes:

- Planning aerial and satellite observations
- Preparing maps and charts
- Analyzing aerial photographs
- Preparing intelligence reports
- Using computer systems

Further training occurs on the job and through advanced courses.

## Helpful Attributes

Helpful school subjects include typing, algebra, geometry, trigonometry, and geography. Helpful attributes include:

- Interest in reading maps and charts
- Interest in gathering information and studying its meaning
- Ability to organize information
- Ability to think and write clearly

## Physical Demands

Normal color vision is required for some specialties in order to work with color-coded maps.

## Work Environment

Intelligence specialists work in offices on land and aboard ships, and in tents when in the field.

## Civilian Counterparts

Civilian intelligence specialists generally work for federal government agencies such as the Central Intelligence Agency or the National Security Agency. Their duties are similar to those performed by military intelligence specialists. The analytical skills of intelligence specialists are also useful in other fields, such as research or business planning.

## Opportunities

The services have about 16,250 intelligence specialists. On average, they need about 1,250 new specialists each year. After job training, intelligence specialists collect information and prepare maps and charts under close supervision. With experience, they are given more responsibility for organizing and studying intelligence data. Eventually, they may become chiefs of intelligence units.

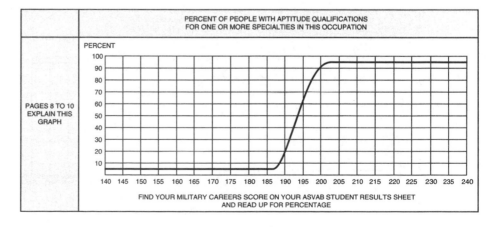

PERCENT OF PEOPLE WITH APTITUDE QUALIFICATIONS FOR ONE OR MORE SPECIALTIES IN THIS OCCUPATION

PAGES 8 TO 10 EXPLAIN THIS GRAPH

PERCENT

FIND YOUR MILITARY CAREERS SCORE ON YOUR ASVAB STUDENT RESULTS SHEET AND READ UP FOR PERCENTAGE

# METEOROLOGICAL SPECIALISTS

Army
Navy
Air Force
Marine Corps
Coast Guard

Weather information is important for planning military operations. Accurate weather forecasts are needed to plan troop movements, airplane flights, and ship traffic. Meteorological specialists collect information about weather and sea conditions for use by meteorologists. They make visual observations and take readings from weather equipment, radar scans, and satellite photographs.

## What They Do

Meteorological specialists in the military perform some or all of the following duties:

- Launch weather balloons to record wind speed and direction
- Identify the types of clouds present and estimate cloud height and amount of cloud cover
- Take readings of barometric pressure, temperature, humidity, and sea conditions
- Operate radio equipment to receive information from satellites
- Plot weather information on maps and charts
- Forecast weather based on readings and observations

## Work Environment

Meteorological specialists usually work in offices either on land or aboard ships. They work outdoors when making visual weather observations and launching weather balloons.

## Helpful Attributes

Helpful school subjects include geography, mathematics, and physical science. Helpful attributes include:

- Interest in working with formulas, tables, and graphs
- Ability to communicate effectively
- Interest in learning how weather changes
- Interest in gathering and organizing information

## Physical Demands

Normal color vision is required to use color-coded maps and weather charts.

Some specialties may involve heavy lifting.

## Training Provided

Job training consists of 7 to 18 weeks of classroom instruction. Training length varies depending on specialty. Course content typically includes:

- Basic meteorology (study of weather) and oceanography (study of the ocean)
- Methods for plotting weather data
- Analyzing radar and satellite weather information
- Preparation of weather reports

Advanced training in weather forecasting is available for some specialties. The Marine Corps offers a certified apprenticeship program for one specialty in this occupation.

## Civilian Counterparts

Civilian meteorological specialists work for government agencies (such as the U.S. Weather Service), commercial airlines, radio and television stations, and private weather forecasting firms. They perform duties similar to military meteorological specialists. Civilian meteorological specialists may also be called oceanographer assistants and weather clerks.

## Opportunities

The services have about 1,500 meteorological specialists. On average, they need about 200 new specialists each year. After job training, new specialists collect weather information under the supervision of experienced workers. With experience, they perform more complex collection and analysis tasks and may become weather forecasters. Eventually, they may become managers of weather observation units.

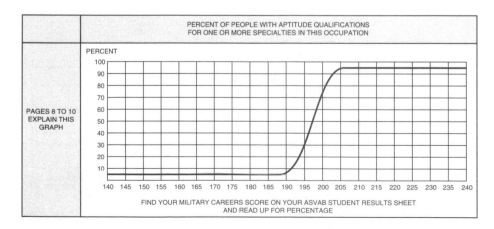

PERCENT OF PEOPLE WITH APTITUDE QUALIFICATIONS
FOR ONE OR MORE SPECIALTIES IN THIS OCCUPATION

PAGES 8 TO 10 EXPLAIN THIS GRAPH

PERCENT

100
90
80
70
60
50
40
30
20
10

140 145 150 155 160 165 170 175 180 185 190 195 200 205 210 215 220 225 230 235 240

FIND YOUR MILITARY CAREERS SCORE ON YOUR ASVAB STUDENT RESULTS SHEET
AND READ UP FOR PERCENTAGE

# NON-DESTRUCTIVE TESTERS

Navy
Air Force
Marine Corps
Coast Guard

Military equipment is often placed under heavy stress. An airplane's landing gear absorbs heavy runway impact. Submarine hulls withstand tremendous pressure in the ocean depths. In time, stress may cause structural weakening or damage. Non-destructive testers examine metal parts for stress damage. They use X-rays, ultrasonics, and other testing methods that do not damage (are non-destructive to) the parts tested.

## What They Do

Non-destructive testers in the military perform some or all of the following duties:

- Inspect metal parts and joints for wear and damage
- Take X-rays of aircraft and ship parts
- Examine X-ray film to detect cracks and flaws in metal parts and welds
- Operate ultrasonic, atomic absorption, and other kinds of test equipment
- Conduct oil analysis and heat damage tests to detect engine wear
- Prepare inspection reports

## Training Provided

Job training consists of 9 to 13 weeks of classroom instruction, including practice in testing metal parts. Course content typically includes:

- Methods for inspecting parts and welds
- Operation of X-ray and film processing equipment
- Operation of ultrasonic test equipment
- Preparation of test reports

## Helpful Attributes

Helpful school subjects include math and metal shop. Helpful attributes include:

- Thoroughness and dependability
- Interest in operating test equipment
- Interest in machines and how they work

## Special Requirements

Applicants must be 18 or older.

## Work Environment

Non-destructive testers work indoors in laboratories and aircraft hangars. They also work outdoors in shipyards and in the field.

## Civilian Counterparts

Civilian non-destructive testers work for commercial testing laboratories, airlines, aircraft maintenance companies, and industrial plants. They perform duties similar to military non-destructive testers and may be called radiographers.

## Physical Demands

Normal color vision is required to read color-coded diagrams.

## Opportunities

The military has about 900 non-destructive testers. On average, the services need about 50 new testers each year. After job training, testers are assigned to testing units, where they perform tests under supervision. With experience, they work more independently. In time, non-destructive testers may become supervisors of testing laboratories or maintenance units.

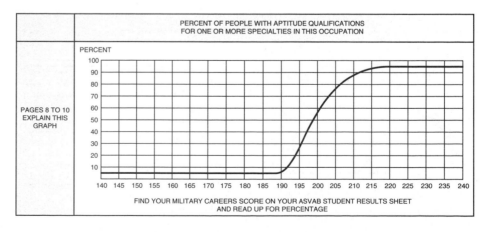

PERCENT OF PEOPLE WITH APTITUDE QUALIFICATIONS FOR ONE OR MORE SPECIALTIES IN THIS OCCUPATION

PAGES 8 TO 10 EXPLAIN THIS GRAPH

PERCENT

FIND YOUR MILITARY CAREERS SCORE ON YOUR ASVAB STUDENT RESULTS SHEET AND READ UP FOR PERCENTAGE

# ORDNANCE SPECIALISTS

Ordnance is a military term for ammunition and weapons. Ordnance includes all types of ammunition, missiles, toxic chemicals, and nuclear weapons. Ammunition and weapons are hazardous materials which must be handled carefully and stored properly. Ordnance specialists transport, store, inspect, prepare, and dispose of weapons and ammunition.

## What They Do

Ordnance specialists in the military perform some or all of the following duties:

- Load nuclear and conventional explosives and ammunition on aircraft, ships, and submarines

- Inspect mounted guns, bomb release systems, and missile launchers to determine need for repair or destruction

- Assemble and load explosives such as torpedoes

- Defuse unexploded bombs

- Locate, identify, and dispose of chemical munitions

## Physical Demands

Ordnance specialists may have to lift and carry artillery shells and other heavy ordnance.

## Special Requirements

Although there are women ordnance specialists, some specialties in this occupation are open only to men.

## Helpful Attributes

Helpful school subjects include general science and shop mechanics. Helpful attributes include:

- Interest in working with guns and explosives

- Ability to remain calm under stress

- Ability to maintain concentration

## Training Provided

Job training consists of 15 to 25 weeks of classroom instruction, including practice in ordnance maintenance. Training length varies depending on specialty. Course content typically includes:

- Maintenance of nuclear weapons

- Handling, testing, and maintenance of missiles and rockets

Further training occurs on the job and through advanced courses. The Army, Navy, and Marine Corps offer certified apprenticeship programs for some specialties in this occupation.

## Work Environment

Ordnance specialists work both indoors and outdoors. They work in repair shops while assembling explosives and repairing weapons. They work outdoors while repairing equipment in the field and loading weapons on tanks, ships, or aircraft.

## Civilian Counterparts

There are no direct civilian counterparts for many of the military ordnance specialties. However, there are many occupations that are related. For example, civilians work for government agencies and private industry doing ordnance research and development. Others work for police or fire departments as bomb-disposal experts. Some also work as gunsmiths or work for munitions manufacturers and firearms makers. Ordnance specialists may also be called bomb disposal experts.

## Opportunities

The services have about 9,000 ordnance specialists. On average, they need about 450 new ordnance specialists each year. After job training, ordnance specialists work under close supervision. With experience, they work more independently and perform more complex duties. In time, they may become trainers or supervisors. Eventually, they may become managers of weapons maintenance units.

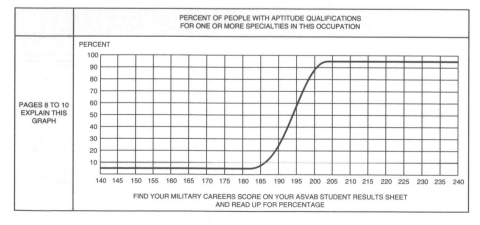

PERCENT OF PEOPLE WITH APTITUDE QUALIFICATIONS
FOR ONE OR MORE SPECIALTIES IN THIS OCCUPATION

PERCENT

PAGES 8 TO 10 EXPLAIN THIS GRAPH

FIND YOUR MILITARY CAREERS SCORE ON YOUR ASVAB STUDENT RESULTS SHEET
AND READ UP FOR PERCENTAGE

# RADAR AND SONAR OPERATORS

Radar and sonar devices work by bouncing radio or sound waves off objects to determine their location and measure distance. They have many uses, such as tracking aircraft and missiles, determining positions of ships and submarines, directing artillery fire, forecasting weather, and aiding navigation. Radar and sonar operators monitor sophisticated radar and sonar equipment. They normally specialize in either radar or sonar. Turn to page 352 for more information about radar and sonar operators.

## What They Do

Radar and sonar operators in the military perform some or all of the following duties:

- Detect and track position, direction, and speed of aircraft, ships, submarines, and missiles

- Plot and record data on status charts and plotting boards

- Set up and operate radar equipment to direct artillery fire

- Monitor early warning air defense systems

- Send and receive messages using radios and electronic communication systems

## Special Requirements

Although there are women radar and sonar operators, some specialties in this occupation are open only to men.

## Helpful Attributes

Helpful school subjects include geometry, algebra, and science. Helpful attributes include:

- Ability to concentrate for long periods

- Interest in working with electronic equipment

## Work Environment

Radar and sonar operators in the military primarily work indoors in security-controlled areas. They work in operations centers and command posts either on land or aboard aircraft, ships, or submarines. Some may work in a mobile field radar unit.

## Physical Demands

Normal color vision is required to enter this occupation.

Specialties involving flying require passing a special physical exam.

## Training Provided

Job training consists of 7 to 12 weeks of classroom instruction and practice operating radar or sonar equipment. Training length varies by specialty. Course content typically includes:

- Operation and maintenance of various types of radar and sonar equipment

- Identification of ships, submarines, aircraft, and missiles

- Computation and recording of aircraft or missile speed, direction, and altitude

Further training occurs on the job and through advanced courses.

## Civilian Counterparts

There are no direct civilian counterparts to military radar and sonar operators. However, workers in civilian occupations that use radar and sonar equipment in their jobs include weather service technicians, air traffic controllers, ship navigators, and ocean salvage specialists.

## Opportunities

The services have about 12,000 radar and sonar operators. On average, they need about 500 new operators each year. After job training, new operators use radar or sonar equipment under close supervision. With experience, they work more independently and may eventually become supervisors of ground, airborne, or shipboard radar or sonar units.

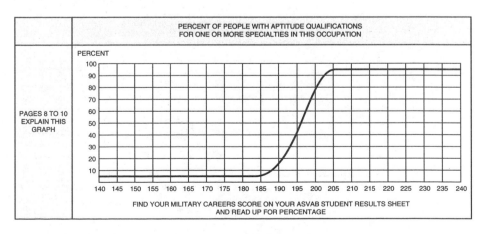

PERCENT OF PEOPLE WITH APTITUDE QUALIFICATIONS FOR ONE OR MORE SPECIALTIES IN THIS OCCUPATION

PAGES 8 TO 10 EXPLAIN THIS GRAPH

PERCENT

FIND YOUR MILITARY CAREERS SCORE ON YOUR ASVAB STUDENT RESULTS SHEET AND READ UP FOR PERCENTAGE

# RADIO INTELLIGENCE OPERATORS

Army
Navy
Air Force
Marine Corps
Coast Guard

Knowing about the military forces of foreign governments helps our military experts plan the nation's defense. One way of learning about foreign military forces is to listen to their radio transmissions. Troop locations, battle tactics, and other secrets can be learned from listening to foreign military units sending messages to one another. Radio intelligence operators intercept, identify, and record foreign radio transmissions.

## What They Do

Radio intelligence operators in the military perform some or all of the following duties:

- Record radio signals coming from foreign ships, planes, and land forces
- Study radio signals to understand the tactics used by foreign military forces
- Tune radios to certain frequencies and adjust for clear reception
- Locate the source of foreign radio signals using electronic direction-finding equipment
- Translate Morse code signals into words and type them for review by superiors
- Keep logs of signal interceptions

## Work Environment

Radio intelligence operators may work indoors or outdoors, depending on assignment. They may also work in airplanes, ships, and land vehicles.

## Physical Demands

Radio intelligence operators may have to sit for long periods and listen to radio transmissions.

## Special Requirements

Although there are women radio intelligence operators, some specialties in this occupation are open only to men.

## Helpful Attributes

Helpful school subjects include math, speech, typing, and foreign languages. Helpful attributes include:

- Interest in working with radio equipment
- Interest in finding clues that help answer questions
- Ability to remain alert while doing repetitive tasks
- A long attention span

## Training Provided

Job training consists of 17 to 24 weeks of classroom instruction, including practice in operating radio equipment. Course content typically includes:

- Use of specialized radio receivers
- Security operations
- Morse code

Further training occurs on the job and through advanced courses.

## Civilian Counterparts

Civilian radio intelligence operators work for government agencies like the National Security Agency, the Central Intelligence Agency, and the Federal Bureau of Investigation. They also work in related jobs for private electronics and communications companies. They perform duties similar to military radio intelligence operators and may also be called electronic intelligence operations specialists.

## Opportunities

The military has about 7,200 radio intelligence operators. On average, the services need about 900 new intelligence operators each year. After job training, radio intelligence operators typically perform routine radio monitoring work under close supervision. With experience, they work more independently analyzing radio signals. In time, they may advance to positions of increased responsibility, such as supervising other radio intelligence operators.

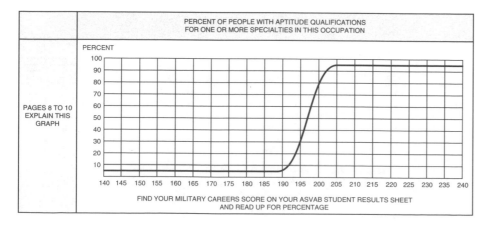

PERCENT OF PEOPLE WITH APTITUDE QUALIFICATIONS FOR ONE OR MORE SPECIALTIES IN THIS OCCUPATION

PAGES 8 TO 10 EXPLAIN THIS GRAPH

PERCENT

FIND YOUR MILITARY CAREERS SCORE ON YOUR ASVAB STUDENT RESULTS SHEET AND READ UP FOR PERCENTAGE

# SPACE OPERATIONS SPECIALISTS

Orbiting satellites and other space vehicles are used for communications, weather forecasting, and collecting intelligence data. In the future, more and more military operations will involve space systems. Space operations specialists use and repair spacecraft ground control command equipment, including electronic systems that track spacecraft location and operation.

## What They Do

Space operations specialists in the military perform some or all of the following duties:

- Transmit and verify spacecraft commands using aerospace ground equipment
- Monitor computers and telemetry display systems
- Analyze data to determine spacecraft operational status
- Repair ground and spacecraft communication equipment
- Assist in preparing spacecraft commands to meet mission objectives
- Operate data-handling equipment to track spacecraft

## Helpful Attributes

Helpful school subjects include physics, geometry, algebra, and trigonometry. Helpful attributes include:

- Interest in operating electronic equipment and systems
- Interest in working as part of a team
- Ability to work with formulas to solve math problems
- Interest in space exploration

## Work Environment

Space operations specialists work in space operations centers.

## Physical Demands

Normal color vision is required to enter this occupation.

## Training Provided

Job training consists of 17 to 30 weeks of classroom instruction, including practice in spacecraft command and control operations. Course content typically includes:

- Operation of electronic transmitting, receiving, and computing equipment
- Analysis of data that indicate spacecraft operational status
- Application of electronic and satellite system principles
- Alignment of ground and spacecraft communication systems
- Space command and control system operational procedures

The Navy offers a certified apprenticeship program for one specialty in this occupation.

## Civilian Counterparts

Civilian space operations specialists work for the National Aeronautics and Space Administration (NASA), the U.S. Weather Service, and private satellite communications firms. They perform duties similar to military space operations specialists.

## Opportunities

The military has about 2,800 space operations specialists. On average, the services need about 300 new specialists each year. After job training, space operations specialists are assigned to space operations centers, where they use and repair space systems equipment under close supervision. After gaining experience, they work more independently and may help train new workers. Eventually, space operations specialists may advance to become supervisors of space operations centers.

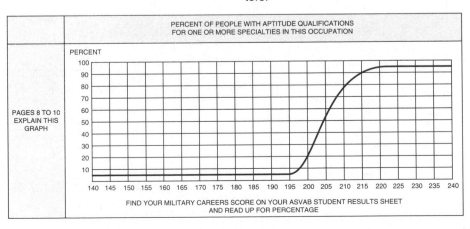

PAGES 8 TO 10 EXPLAIN THIS GRAPH

PERCENT OF PEOPLE WITH APTITUDE QUALIFICATIONS FOR ONE OR MORE SPECIALTIES IN THIS OCCUPATION

PERCENT

FIND YOUR MILITARY CAREERS SCORE ON YOUR ASVAB STUDENT RESULTS SHEET AND READ UP FOR PERCENTAGE

# SURVEYING, MAPPING, AND DRAFTING TECHNICIANS

Army
Navy
Air Force
Marine Corps
Coast Guard

The military builds and repairs many airstrips, docks, barracks, roads, and other projects each year. Surveying, mapping, and drafting technicians conduct land surveys, make maps, and prepare detailed plans and drawings for construction projects. Surveys and maps are also used to locate military targets and plot troop movements.

## What They Do

Surveying, mapping, and drafting technicians in the military perform some or all of the following duties:

- Draw maps and charts using drafting tools such as easels, templates, and compasses

- Make scale drawings of roads, airfields, buildings, and other military projects

- Conduct land surveys and compute survey results

- Draw diagrams for wiring and plumbing of structures

- Build scale models of land areas that show hills, lakes, roads, and buildings

- Piece together aerial photographs to form large photomaps

## Work Environment

Surveying, mapping, and drafting technicians work both indoors and outdoors in all climates and weather conditions. Those assigned to engineering units sometimes work outdoors with survey teams. Those assigned to intelligence units may work on ships as well as on land.

## Physical Demands

Good depth perception is required to study aerial photos through stereoscopes. Normal color vision is required to work with color-coded maps and drawings.

## Helpful Attributes

Helpful school subjects include algebra, geometry, and trigonometry. Helpful attributes include:

- Ability to convert ideas into drawings

- Interest in maps and charts

- Ability to print and draw neatly

- Interest in working with drafting equipment

## Training Provided

Job training consists of 9 to 31 weeks of classroom instruction, depending on specialty. Course content typically includes:

- Surveying and drafting techniques

- Aerial photo interpretation

- Architectural and structural drawing

Further training occurs on the job and through advanced courses. The Army and Marine Corps offer certified apprenticeship programs for some specialties in this occupation.

## Civilian Counterparts

Civilian surveying, mapping, and drafting technicians work for construction, engineering, and architectural firms and government agencies such as the highway department. Their work is used for planning construction projects such as highways, airport runways, dams, and drainage systems. Surveyors and mapmakers are also called cartographers, cartographic technicians, and photogrammetrists.

## Opportunities

The military has about 4,000 surveying, mapping, and drafting technicians. On average, the services need about 450 surveying, mapping, and drafting technicians each year. After job training, technicians make simple drawings, trace photos, perform basic survey duties, or help make maps under close supervision. With experience, they work more independently. Eventually, they may supervise mapmaking laboratories, surveying teams, or construction units.

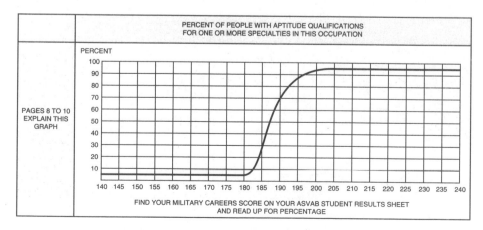

PAGES 8 TO 10 EXPLAIN THIS GRAPH

PERCENT OF PEOPLE WITH APTITUDE QUALIFICATIONS FOR ONE OR MORE SPECIALTIES IN THIS OCCUPATION

PERCENT

FIND YOUR MILITARY CAREERS SCORE ON YOUR ASVAB STUDENT RESULTS SHEET AND READ UP FOR PERCENTAGE

# Administrative Occupations

- **Administrative Support Specialists**
- **Computer Systems Specialists**
- **Finance and Accounting Specialists**
- **Flight Operations Specialists**
- **Legal Specialists and Court Reporters**
- **Personnel Specialists**
- **Postal Specialists**
- **Preventive Maintenance Analysts**
- **Recruiting Specialists**
- **Sales and Stock Specialists**
- **Supply and Warehousing Specialists**
- **Training Specialists and Instructors**
- **Transportation Specialists**

# ADMINISTRATIVE SUPPORT SPECIALISTS

Army
Navy
Air Force
Marine Corps
Coast Guard

The military must keep accurate information for planning and managing its operations. Paper and electronic records are kept on equipment, funds, personnel, supplies, and all other aspects of the military. Administrative support specialists record information, type reports, and maintain files to assist in the operation of military offices. Turn to page 316 for more information about administrative support specialists.

## What They Do

Administrative support specialists in the military perform some or all of the following duties:

- Type letters, reports, requisition (order) forms, and official orders
- Proofread written material for spelling, punctuation, and grammatical errors
- Organize and maintain files and publications
- Order office supplies
- Greet and direct office visitors
- Sort and deliver mail to office workers
- Schedule training and leave for unit personnel
- Answer phones and provide general information
- Take meeting notes

## Work Environment

Administrative support specialists work in office settings, both on land and aboard ships.

## Helpful Attributes

Helpful school subjects include English, math, business administration, and typing. Helpful attributes include:

- Interest in keeping organized and accurate records
- Preference for office work
- Interest in operating typewriters, computers, and other office machines
- Ability to organize and plan

## Training Provided

Job training consists of 6 to 10 weeks of classroom instruction, including practice in various office functions. Course content typically includes:

- English grammar, spelling and punctuation
- Typing and clerical skills
- Setting up and maintaining filing and publication systems
- Preparing forms and correspondence in military style

Further training occurs on the job.

## Civilian Counterparts

Civilian administrative support specialists work in most business, government, and legal offices. They perform duties similar to military administrative support specialists and are called clerk typists, secretaries, general office clerks, administrative assistants, or office managers.

## Opportunities

The military has about 44,930 administrative support specialists. On average, the services need about 3,100 new specialists each year. After job training, specialists develop their skills under close supervision. As they gain experience, specialists are assigned more difficult tasks and work more independently. In time, they may supervise and eventually manage an office. With experience and additional training, they may become secretaries, legal specialists, personnel specialists, or enter related fields.

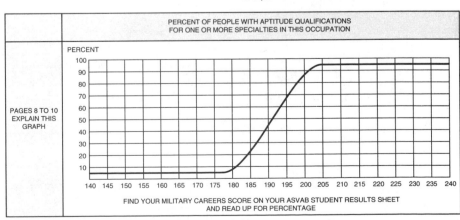

PERCENT OF PEOPLE WITH APTITUDE QUALIFICATIONS FOR ONE OR MORE SPECIALTIES IN THIS OCCUPATION

PAGES 8 TO 10 EXPLAIN THIS GRAPH

PERCENT

FIND YOUR MILITARY CAREERS SCORE ON YOUR ASVAB STUDENT RESULTS SHEET AND READ UP FOR PERCENTAGE

# COMPUTER SYSTEMS SPECIALISTS

Army
Navy
Air Force
Marine Corps
Coast Guard

The military services use computers to store and process data on personnel, weather, finances, and many other operations. Before any information can be processed, computer systems must be set up, data entered, and computers operated. Computer systems specialists ensure information is entered, stored, processed, and retrieved in a way that meets the military services' needs.

## What They Do

Computer systems specialists in the military perform some or all of the following duties:

- Identify computer user problems and coordinate to resolve them

- Install, configure, and monitor local and wide area networks, hardware, and software

- Compile, enter, and process information

- Provide customer and network administration services, such as passwords, electronic mail accounts, security, and troubleshooting

## Helpful Attributes

Helpful school subjects include typing and computer science. Helpful attributes include:

- Interest in work requiring accuracy and attention to detail

- Ability to communicate effectively

- Interest in working with computer equipment

## Training Provided

Job training consists of 7 to 13 weeks of classroom instruction. Training length varies depending on specialty. Course content typically includes:

- Use of computer consoles and peripheral equipment

- Computer systems concepts

- Planning, designing, and testing computer systems

## Work Environment

Computer systems specialists work in offices or at computer sites on military bases or aboard ships.

## Physical Demands

Computer systems specialists may sit and key information for long periods.

## Civilian Counterparts

Civilian computer systems specialists work for a wide variety of employers, such as banks, hospitals, retail firms, manufacturers, government agencies, and firms that design and test computer systems. They perform duties similar to those performed in the military. They may also be called network support technicians, computer operators, or data processing technicians. Most civilian computer systems specialists require a four-year college degree.

## Opportunities

The services have about 14,100 computer systems specialists. On average, they need about 1,300 new computer system specialists each year. After job training, computer systems specialists are assigned to work under the direction of experienced computer systems officers. With experience, they may become managers of computer facilities.

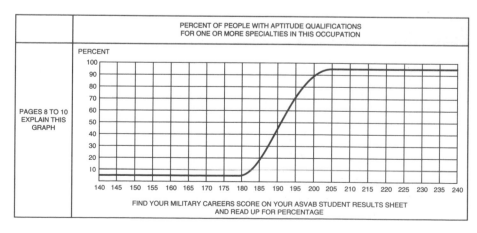

PAGES 8 TO 10 EXPLAIN THIS GRAPH

PERCENT OF PEOPLE WITH APTITUDE QUALIFICATIONS FOR ONE OR MORE SPECIALTIES IN THIS OCCUPATION

PERCENT

FIND YOUR MILITARY CAREERS SCORE ON YOUR ASVAB STUDENT RESULTS SHEET AND READ UP FOR PERCENTAGE

# FINANCE AND ACCOUNTING SPECIALISTS

Millions of paychecks are issued and large amounts of materials are purchased by the services each year. To account for military spending, exact financial records must be kept of these transactions. Finance and accounting specialists organize and keep track of financial records. They also compute payrolls and other allowances, audit accounting records, and prepare payments for military personnel.

## What They Do

Finance and accounting specialists in the military perform some or all of the following duties:

- Record details of financial transactions on accounting forms
- Audit financial records
- Prepare pay and travel vouchers, (checks), earnings and deductions statements, bills, and financial accounts and reports
- Disburse cash, checks, advance pay, and bonds
- Organize information on past expenses to help plan budgets for future expenses

## Special Qualifications

Depending on the specialty, entry into this occupation may require courses in mathematics, bookkeeping, or accounting.

## Training Provided

Job training consists of 6 to 12 weeks of classroom instruction, including practice in accounting techniques. Course content typically includes:

- Accounting principles and procedures
- Preparation and maintenance of financial reports and budgets
- Statistical analyses to interpret financial data
- Computation of pay and deductions

## Work Environment

Finance and accounting specialists work in offices on land or aboard ships.

## Helpful Attributes

Helpful school subjects include mathematics, statistics, bookkeeping, and accounting. Helpful attributes include:

- Ability to work with numbers
- Interest in operating office machines such as computers, calculators, and bookkeeping machines
- Interest in work requiring accuracy and attention to detail

## Civilian Counterparts

Civilian finance and accounting specialists work for all types of businesses and government agencies. They perform duties similar to military finance and accounting specialists. Civilian finance and accounting specialists are also called accounting clerks, audit clerks, bookkeepers, or payroll clerks.

## Opportunities

The services have about 8,000 finance and accounting specialists. On average, they need about 750 new specialists each year. After job training, finance and account specialists perform simple routine accounting and finance activities under the direction of supervisors. With experience, they are given more difficult tasks, such as auditing, and may become responsible for checking the work of others. In time, finance and accounting specialists may become supervisors or managers of accounting units or pay and finance centers.

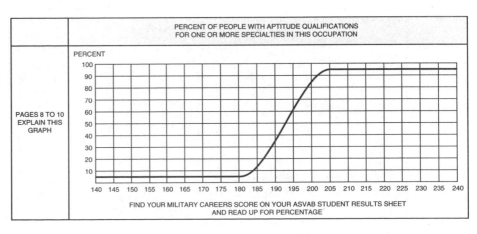

PERCENT OF PEOPLE WITH APTITUDE QUALIFICATIONS FOR ONE OR MORE SPECIALTIES IN THIS OCCUPATION

PAGES 8 TO 10 EXPLAIN THIS GRAPH

PERCENT

FIND YOUR MILITARY CAREERS SCORE ON YOUR ASVAB STUDENT RESULTS SHEET AND READ UP FOR PERCENTAGE

# FLIGHT OPERATIONS SPECIALISTS

Army
Navy
Air Force
Marine Corps
Coast Guard

The services operate one of the largest fleets of aircraft in the world. Hundreds of transport, passenger, and combat airplanes and helicopters fly missions every day. Accurate flight information keeps operations safe and efficient. Flight operations specialists prepare and provide flight information for air and ground crews.

## What They Do

Flight operations specialists in the military perform some or all of the following duties:

- Help plan flight schedules and air crew assignments

- Keep flight logs on incoming and outgoing flights

- Keep air crew flying records and flight operations records

- Receive and post weather information and flight plan data, such as air routes and arrival and departure times

- Coordinate air crew needs, such as ground transportation

- Plan aircraft equipment needs for air evacuation and dangerous cargo flights

- Check military flight plans with civilian agencies

## Work Environment

Flight operations specialists work indoors in flight control centers or air terminals.

## Physical Demands

The ability to speak clearly and distinctly is required.

## Helpful Attributes

Helpful school subjects include general math and typing. Helpful attributes include:

- Interest in work involving computers

- Ability to use typewriters and office machines

- Interest in work that helps others

- Ability to keep accurate records

## Training Provided

Job training consists of 7 to 14 weeks of classroom instruction. Training length varies depending on specialty. Course content typically includes:

- Introduction to aviation operations

- Procedures for scheduling aircraft and assigning air crews

- Flight planning and airfield operations

- Preparing flight operations reports and records

Further training occurs on the job and through advanced courses.

## Civilian Counterparts

Civilian flight operations specialists work for commercial and private airlines and air transport companies. They perform duties similar to military flight operations specialists.

## Opportunities

The services have about 3,200 flight operations specialists. On average, they need about 300 new specialists each year. After training, new specialists keep logs and type schedules. With experience, they schedule air crews. In time, they may plan flight operations and supervise others.

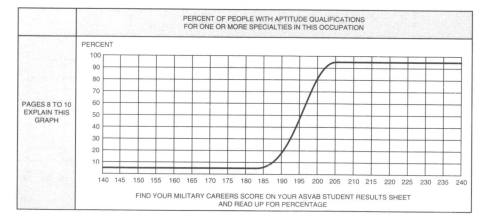

PAGES 8 TO 10 EXPLAIN THIS GRAPH

PERCENT OF PEOPLE WITH APTITUDE QUALIFICATIONS FOR ONE OR MORE SPECIALTIES IN THIS OCCUPATION

PERCENT

FIND YOUR MILITARY CAREERS SCORE ON YOUR ASVAB STUDENT RESULTS SHEET AND READ UP FOR PERCENTAGE

# LEGAL SPECIALISTS AND COURT REPORTERS

The military has its own judicial system for prosecuting lawbreakers and handling disputes. Legal specialists and court reporters assist military lawyers and judges in the performance of legal and judicial work. They perform legal research, prepare legal documents, and record legal proceedings.

## What They Do

Legal specialists and court reporters in the military perform some or all of the following duties:

- Research court decisions and military regulations
- Process legal claims and appeals
- Interview clients and take statements
- Prepare trial requests and make arrangements for courtrooms
- Maintain law libraries and trial case files
- Type text from stenotyped records, shorthand notes, or taped records of court proceedings
- Prepare records of hearings, investigations, court-martials, and courts of inquiry

## Training Provided

Job training consists of 6 to 10 weeks of instruction. Course content typically includes:

- Legal terminology and research techniques
- How to prepare legal documents
- High speed transcription
- Military judicial processes

## Helpful Attributes

Helpful school subjects include business mathematics, typing, speech, and shorthand. Helpful attributes include:

- Interest in the law and legal proceedings
- Ability to keep organized and accurate records
- Ability to listen carefully

## Special Requirements

Some specialties require the ability to type at a rate of 25–50 words per minute.

## Physical Demands

Good hearing and clear speech are needed to record and read aloud court proceedings. A clear speaking ability is necessary to interview clients.

## Civilian Counterparts

Civilian legal specialists and court reporters work for private law firms, banks, insurance companies, government agencies, and local, state, and federal courts. They perform duties similar to military legal specialists and court reporters. Civilian legal specialists and court reporters may also be called legal assistants, clerks, paralegal assistants, and court clerks or recorders.

## Work Environment

Legal specialists and court reporters work in military law offices and courtrooms.

## Opportunities

The services have about 2,500 legal specialists and court reporters. On average, they need about 210 new specialists and court reporters each year. After training, they work under an attorney or legal office. With experience, legal specialists and court reporters perform more demanding activities. In time, they may become supervisors of other legal specialists and court reporters.

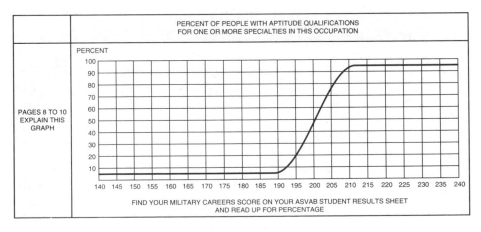

PERCENT OF PEOPLE WITH APTITUDE QUALIFICATIONS FOR ONE OR MORE SPECIALTIES IN THIS OCCUPATION

PAGES 8 TO 10 EXPLAIN THIS GRAPH

FIND YOUR MILITARY CAREERS SCORE ON YOUR ASVAB STUDENT RESULTS SHEET AND READ UP FOR PERCENTAGE

# PERSONNEL SPECIALISTS

Personnel management helps individuals develop their military careers. It also serves the military's need to fill jobs with qualified workers. Personnel specialists collect and store information about the people in the military, such as training, job assignment, promotion, and health information. They work directly with service personnel and their families. Turn to page 348 for more information about personnel specialists.

## What They Do

Personnel specialists in the military perform some or all of the following duties:

- Organize, maintain, and review personnel records

- Enter and retrieve personnel information using computer terminals

- Assign personnel to jobs

- Prepare organizational charts, write official correspondence, and prepare reports

- Provide career guidance

- Assist personnel and their families who have special needs

- Provide information about personnel programs and procedures to service men and women

## Work Environment

Personnel specialists normally work in office settings on land or aboard ships.

## Training Provided

Job training consists of 7 to 9 weeks of classroom instruction. Course content typically includes:

- Basic typing skills

- Preparation of military correspondence and forms

- Personnel records management

- Computer update and retrieval procedures

Further training occurs on the job and through advanced courses.

## Helpful Attributes

Helpful school subjects include English, speech, business administration, and typing. Helpful attributes include:

- Ability to follow detailed procedures and instructions

- Ability to compose clear instructions or correspondence

- Interest in working closely with others

## Civilian Counterparts

Civilian personnel specialists work for all types of organizations, including industrial firms, retail establishments, and government agencies. They perform duties similar to military personnel clerks. However, specific jobs vary from company to company.

## Opportunities

The services have about 15,200 personnel specialists. On average, they need about 1,300 new specialists each year. After job training, specialists process personnel actions and add information to records. In time, they may supervise other personnel specialists and eventually may manage personnel offices.

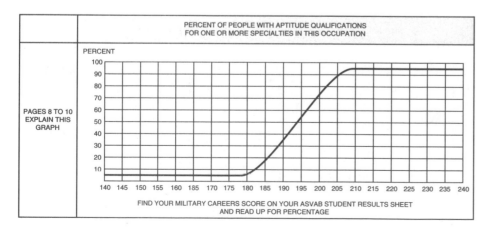

PAGES 8 TO 10 EXPLAIN THIS GRAPH

PERCENT OF PEOPLE WITH APTITUDE QUALIFICATIONS FOR ONE OR MORE SPECIALTIES IN THIS OCCUPATION

PERCENT

FIND YOUR MILITARY CAREERS SCORE ON YOUR ASVAB STUDENT RESULTS SHEET AND READ UP FOR PERCENTAGE

# POSTAL SPECIALISTS

The military operates its own postal service for official military communications and messages. In addition, it delivers mail to thousands of service men and women all over the world. Postal specialists process incoming and outgoing mail between military and civilian postal systems. They also sell stamps and money orders and provide services to postal customers.

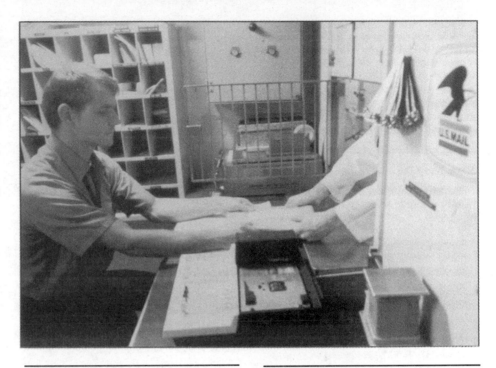

## What They Do

Postal specialists in the military perform some or all of the following duties:

- Process mail using metering and stamp-canceling machines
- Weigh packages, using scales, to determine postage due
- Examine packages to ensure that they meet mailing standards
- Process and sort registered, certified, and insured mail
- Receive payment for and issue money orders and stamps
- Prepare postal reports and claims for lost or damaged mail

## Training Provided

Job training consists of 3 to 4 weeks of classroom instruction. Course content typically includes:

- Post office operations and procedures
- Mail and postal item processing and sorting
- Domestic and international mail delivery procedures
- Use of metering, stamp canceling, and other machines
- Postal reports and the processing of customer claims and complaints

Further training occurs on the job and through advanced courses.

## Helpful Attributes

Helpful school subjects include English and mathematics. Helpful attributes include:

- Courteous manner and patience
- Ability to check names and numbers with speed and accuracy
- Preference for work requiring attention to detail

## Physical Demands

Postal specialists may have to lift and carry heavy sacks of mail or large packages.

## Civilian Counterparts

Civilian postal specialists work for the United States Postal Service and for private courier or express mail firms. They perform many of the same duties as military postal specialists. They are usually called postal clerks.

## Work Environment

Postal specialists work in post offices and mailrooms on land or aboard ships.

## Opportunities

The military has about 7,600 postal specialists. On average, the services need about 700 new specialists each year. After job training, they work alone in small mail rooms or with other postal specialists in larger postal centers. With experience, they may help train new workers and may become supervisors of other postal specialists. Eventually, they may become superintendents of postal centers.

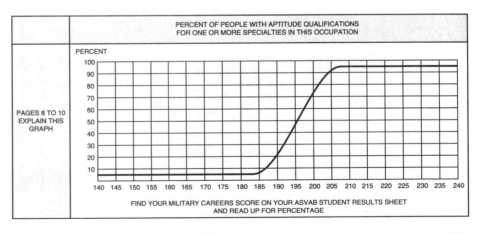

PERCENT OF PEOPLE WITH APTITUDE QUALIFICATIONS FOR ONE OR MORE SPECIALTIES IN THIS OCCUPATION

PAGES 8 TO 10 EXPLAIN THIS GRAPH

FIND YOUR MILITARY CAREERS SCORE ON YOUR ASVAB STUDENT RESULTS SHEET AND READ UP FOR PERCENTAGE

# PREVENTIVE MAINTENANCE ANALYSTS

Regular maintenance extends the time aircraft, vehicles, and machinery can be used. To make sure military equipment is well maintained, the services prepare detailed maintenance schedules. Preventive maintenance analysts promote equipment maintenance. They watch schedules and notify mechanics about upcoming maintenance needs.

## What They Do

Preventive maintenance analysts in the military perform some or all of the following duties:

- Review maintenance schedules and notify mechanics about the types of service needed
- Compare schedules to records of maintenance work actually performed
- Prepare charts and reports on maintenance activities
- Calculate how many mechanics and spare parts are needed to maintain equipment
- Operate computers and calculators to enter or retrieve maintenance data

## Physical Demands

Normal color vision is required to read and interpret maintenance charts and graphs in some specialties.

Some specialties require the ability to speak clearly.

## Helpful Attributes

Helpful school subjects include general mathematics and algebra. Helpful attributes include:

- Interest in working with numbers and statistics
- Preference for work requiring attention to detail
- Ability to use mathematical formulas
- Interest in working with computers

## Work Environment

Preventive maintenance analysts usually work in office settings.

## Training Provided

Job training consists of 4 to 15 weeks of classroom instruction. Training length varies depending on specialty. Course content typically includes:

- Equipment maintenance management concepts
- Accounting procedures
- Statistical reporting methods
- Parts and supply inventory control procedures

## Civilian Counterparts

Civilian preventive maintenance analysts work for government agencies, airlines, and large transportation firms. They also work for firms with large numbers of machines. They perform duties similar to military preventive maintenance analysts.

## Opportunities

The services have about 5,000 preventive maintenance analysts. On average, they need 500 new analysts each year. After job training, new analysts work under close supervision. As they gain experience, they are given more responsibility and more difficult work assignments. Eventually, they may become supervisors of maintenance control units.

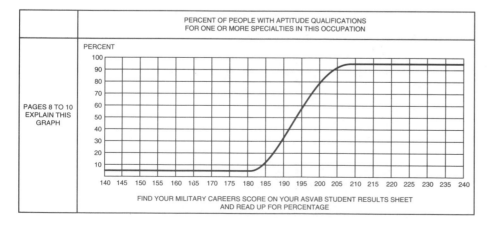

PERCENT OF PEOPLE WITH APTITUDE QUALIFICATIONS FOR ONE OR MORE SPECIALTIES IN THIS OCCUPATION

PAGES 8 TO 10 EXPLAIN THIS GRAPH

PERCENT

FIND YOUR MILITARY CAREERS SCORE ON YOUR ASVAB STUDENT RESULTS SHEET AND READ UP FOR PERCENTAGE

# RECRUITING SPECIALISTS

Army
Navy
Air Force
Marine Corps
Coast Guard

Each year, the military services enlist approximately 200,000 young men and women. Attracting young people with the kinds of talent needed to succeed in today's military is a large task. Recruiting specialists provide information about military careers to young people, parents, schools, and local communities. They explain service employment and training opportunities, pay and benefits, and service life.

## What They Do

Recruiting specialists in the military perform some or all of the following duties:

- Interview civilians interested in military careers
- Describe military careers to groups of high school students
- Explain the purpose of the ASVAB (Armed Services Vocational Aptitude Battery) and test results to students and counselors
- Participate in local job fairs and career day programs
- Talk about the military to community groups
- Counsel military personnel about career opportunities and benefits

## Work Environment

Recruiting specialists work in local recruiting offices, on high school campuses and career centers, and in local communities. They may have to travel often.

## Training Provided

Job training consists of 4 to 6 weeks of classroom instruction. Course content typically includes:

- Recruiting procedures
- Interviewing techniques
- Public speaking techniques
- Community relations practices

Further training occurs on the job and through advanced courses.

## Helpful Attributes

Helpful school subjects include the social sciences, speech, psychology, and English. Helpful attributes include:

- Interest in working with youths
- Ability to speak before groups
- Ability to work independently

## Civilian Counterparts

Civilian recruiting specialists work for businesses of all kinds searching for talented people to hire. Recruiters also work for colleges seeking to attract and enroll talented high school students.

## Opportunities

The services have about 6,000 recruiting specialists. Normally, personnel must be in the service for several years before they are eligible to become recruiters. About 50 military personnel become recruiters each year. Recruiters may choose to make a career of recruiting and, in time, may supervise one or more recruiting offices. Many recruiters, however, spend only a few years in recruiting, and make their careers in other occupations.

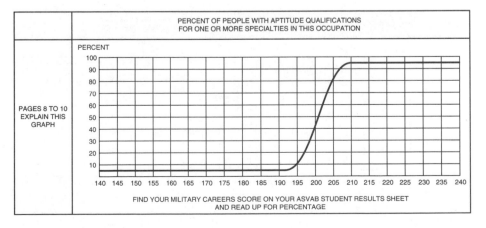

PAGES 8 TO 10 EXPLAIN THIS GRAPH

PERCENT OF PEOPLE WITH APTITUDE QUALIFICATIONS FOR ONE OR MORE SPECIALTIES IN THIS OCCUPATION

PERCENT

FIND YOUR MILITARY CAREERS SCORE ON YOUR ASVAB STUDENT RESULTS SHEET AND READ UP FOR PERCENTAGE

# SALES AND STOCK SPECIALISTS

Navy
Air Force
Marine Corps
Coast Guard

The military operates retail stores and snack bars for its personnel on bases and aboard ships in the United States and overseas. Military stores, called exchanges, sell merchandise similar to that sold in civilian stores but at a discount. Sales and stock specialists operate retail food and merchandise stores for military personnel.

## What They Do

Sales and stock specialists in the military perform some or all of the following duties:

- Operate snack bars, laundries, and dry cleaning facilities

- Order and receive merchandise and food for retail sales

- Inspect food and merchandise for spoilage or damage

- Price and mark retail sales items, using markers and stamping machines

- Stock shelves and racks for the display of products

- Count merchandise and supplies during inventories

- Record and account for money received and prepare bank deposits

## Work Environment

Sales and stock specialists work on land and aboard ships in retail stores, snack bars, and storerooms.

## Physical Demands

The ability to speak clearly is required. Sales and stock specialists may have to lift and carry heavy objects.

## Training Provided

Job training consists of 6 to 7 weeks of classroom instruction for some specialties. For others, training occurs on the job. Course content includes:

- Stock procedures

- Vending machine operation and maintenance

- Record keeping and bookkeeping procedures

Further training occurs on the job.

## Helpful Attributes

Helpful school subjects include bookkeeping, mathematics, and typing. Helpful attributes include:

- Interest in marketing and sales work

- Ability to use cash registers, calculators, and adding machines

- Interest in working with people

## Civilian Counterparts

Civilian sales and stock specialists work in many kinds of retail businesses, such as grocery stores and department stores. They perform duties similar to military sales and stock specialists. They may also be called sales clerks or stock clerks.

## Opportunities

The services have about 2,000 sales and stock specialists. On average, they need about 150 new specialists each year. After job training, sales and stock specialists are assigned to bases or shipboard retail stores and storerooms. Initially, they work under close supervision. With experience, they work more independently, train new workers, and assume more responsibility for sales and stock activities. In time, they may become department supervisors or retail store supervisors.

PAGES 8 TO 10 EXPLAIN THIS GRAPH

PERCENT OF PEOPLE WITH APTITUDE QUALIFICATIONS
FOR ONE OR MORE SPECIALTIES IN THIS OCCUPATION

PERCENT

100
90
80
70
60
50
40
30
20
10

140 145 150 155 160 165 170 175 180 185 190 195 200 205 210 215 220 225 230 235 240

FIND YOUR MILITARY CAREERS SCORE ON YOUR ASVAB STUDENT RESULTS SHEET
AND READ UP FOR PERCENTAGE

# SUPPLY AND WAREHOUSING SPECIALISTS

Army
Navy
Air Force
Marine Corps
Coast Guard

The military maintains a large inventory of food, medicines, ammunition, spare parts, and other supplies. Keeping the military's supply system operating smoothly is an important job. The lives of combat troops in the field may depend on receiving the right supplies on time. Supply and warehousing specialists receive, store, record, and issue military supplies.

## What They Do

Supply and warehousing specialists in the military perform some or all of the following duties:

- Perform inventory and financial management procedures, including ordering, receiving, and storing supplies
- Locate and catalog stock
- Give special handling to medicine, ammunition, and other delicate supplies
- Select the correct stock for issue
- Load, unload, and move stock using equipment such as forklifts and hand trucks
- Keep records on incoming and outgoing stock

## Training Provided

Job training consists of 4 to 6 weeks of classroom instruction, including practice in handling and storing stock. Course content typically includes:

- Stock control and accounting procedures
- Procedures for shipping, receiving, storing, and issuing stock
- Procedures for handling medical and food supplies
- Movement, storage, and maintenance of ammunition

Further training occurs on the job and through advanced courses.

## Work Environment

Supply and warehousing specialists work in large general supply centers, small specialized supply rooms, or ship storerooms.

## Physical Demands

Supply and warehousing specialists may have to lift and carry heavy boxes of ammunition and other supplies. Normal color vision is required for specialties that handle color-coded parts, supplies, and ammunition.

## Helpful Attributes

Helpful school subjects include math, bookkeeping, accounting, business administration, and typing. Helpful attributes include:

- Ability to keep accurate records
- Preference for physical work
- Interest in operating forklifts and other warehouse equipment
- Preference for work requiring attention to detail

## Civilian Counterparts

Civilian supply and warehousing specialists work for factories, parts departments in repair shops, department stores, and government warehouses and stockrooms. They perform duties similar to military supply and warehousing specialists. Civilian supply and warehousing specialists may also be called stock control clerks, parts clerks, or storekeepers.

## Opportunities

The services have about 65,430 supply and warehousing specialists. On average, they need about 5,500 new specialists each year. After job training, specialists stock shelves, learn about different parts and supplies, and fill supply requests. In time, they also estimate needs, order stock, and supervise others. Eventually, they may become superintendents of supply centers.

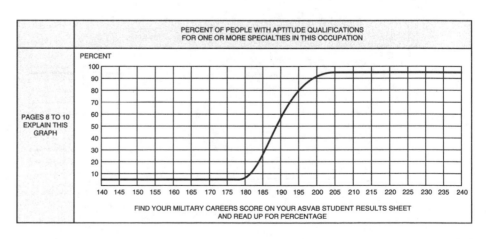

PERCENT OF PEOPLE WITH APTITUDE QUALIFICATIONS
FOR ONE OR MORE SPECIALTIES IN THIS OCCUPATION

PAGES 8 TO 10 EXPLAIN THIS GRAPH

PERCENT

FIND YOUR MILITARY CAREERS SCORE ON YOUR ASVAB STUDENT RESULTS SHEET AND READ UP FOR PERCENTAGE

# TRAINING SPECIALISTS AND INSTRUCTORS

The military trains new personnel in the job skills needed to begin their careers in the service. The military also offers advanced training and retraining to nearly all personnel. Instruction in electronics, health care, computer sciences, and aviation are just a few of the many vocational and technical areas for which the military has training programs. Training specialists and instructors teach classes and give demonstrations to provide military personnel with the knowledge needed to perform their jobs.

## What They Do

Training specialists and instructors in the military perform some or all of the following duties:

- Prepare course outlines and materials to present during training
- Select training materials, such as textbooks and films
- Teach classes and give lectures in person, over closed-circuit TV, or on videotape
- Work with students individually when necessary
- Test and evaluate student progress

## Helpful Attributes

Helpful school subjects include public speaking and English. Helpful attributes include:

- Interest in teaching
- Ability to communicate effectively, in writing and speaking
- Interest in counseling and promoting human relations

## Work Environment

Training specialists and instructors in the military work either indoors or outdoors, depending on the type of training they provide and their specialty area.

## Physical Demands

Training specialists and instructors must be able to speak clearly and distinctly.

## Training Provided

Training consists of 2 to 14 weeks of classroom instruction, including practice teaching. Length of training varies depending on specialty. Course content typically includes:

- Lesson planning
- Instructional methods
- Communications skills

## Civilian Counterparts

Civilian training specialists and instructors work for vocational and technical schools, high schools, colleges, businesses, and government agencies. Their duties are similar to those performed by military training specialists and instructors. Civilian training specialists and instructors may be called teachers, trainers, or training representatives.

## Opportunities

The services have about 4,800 training specialists and instructors. On average, they need about 150 new training specialists and instructors each year. Because training specialists and instructors must have an in-depth knowledge of a subject to be effective, only experienced personnel may become training specialists and instructors. Normally, training specialists and instructors are selected from those workers in each occupation who are both good in their work and have shown an ability to teach. Often, they divide their time between regular work and training duties.

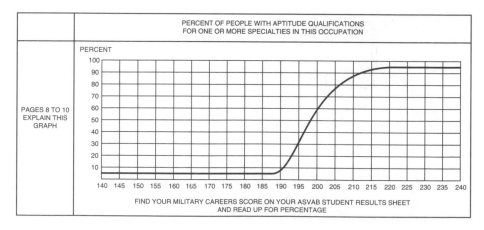

PERCENT OF PEOPLE WITH APTITUDE QUALIFICATIONS FOR ONE OR MORE SPECIALTIES IN THIS OCCUPATION

PAGES 8 TO 10 EXPLAIN THIS GRAPH

PERCENT

FIND YOUR MILITARY CAREERS SCORE ON YOUR ASVAB STUDENT RESULTS SHEET AND READ UP FOR PERCENTAGE

# TRANSPORTATION SPECIALISTS

Army
Navy
Marine Corps
Coast Guard

The military constantly moves passengers and cargo. Personnel often travel to meetings, training sessions, and new assignments. Supplies and equipment to support troops must be shipped regularly. Transportation specialists plan and assist in air, sea, and land transportation for people and cargo. Some assist passenger travel as gate agents and flight attendants.

## What They Do

Transportation specialists in the military perform some or all of the following duties:

- Arrange for passenger travel via plane, bus, train, or boat
- Arrange for shipment and delivery of household goods
- Determine which vehicles to use based on freight or passenger-movement requirements
- Determine transportation and shipping routes
- Prepare transportation requests and shipping documents
- Check in passengers and baggage for military transport flights
- Serve as military airplane flight attendants
- Inspect cargo for proper packing, loading, and marking

## Training Provided

Job training consists of 6 to 9 weeks of classroom instruction, including practice in making transportation arrangements. Course content typically includes:

- Planning transportation for personnel and cargo
- Proper cargo handling, shipping, and storing methods
- Analysis of transportation documents

Further training occurs on the job and through advanced courses.

## Helpful Attributes

Helpful school subjects include mathematics, English, and typing. Helpful attributes include:

- Interest in arranging travel schedules
- Interest in using adding machines, computers, and typewriters
- Interest in serving people

## Civilian Counterparts

Civilian transportation specialists work for airlines, shipping firms, and commercial freight lines. They perform duties similar to military transportation specialists. Civilian transportation specialists may also be called travel clerks, reservation clerks, or transportation agents.

## Work Environment

Transportation specialists usually work in offices. They may work outdoors when escorting passengers or processing shipments. Flight attendants work on land and in airplanes.

## Opportunities

The military has about 13,800 transportation specialists. On average, the services need about 1,600 new specialists each year. After job training, they make travel and shipping arrangements under direct supervision. Some may specialize as flight attendants and gate agents. With experience, they may become supervisors of other transportation specialists. In time, they may manage transportation offices.

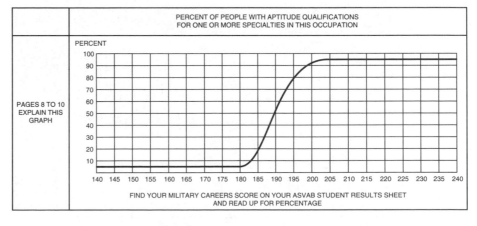

PAGES 8 TO 10 EXPLAIN THIS GRAPH

PERCENT OF PEOPLE WITH APTITUDE QUALIFICATIONS FOR ONE OR MORE SPECIALTIES IN THIS OCCUPATION

FIND YOUR MILITARY CAREERS SCORE ON YOUR ASVAB STUDENT RESULTS SHEET AND READ UP FOR PERCENTAGE

# Service Occupations

- **Firefighters**
- **Food Service Specialists**
- **Law Enforcement and Security Specialists**
- **Military Police**

# FIREFIGHTERS

Military bases have their own protection services, including fire departments. Military firefighting units are responsible for protecting lives and property from fire. Firefighters put out, control, and help prevent fires in buildings, aircraft, and aboard ships.

## What They Do

Firefighters in the military perform some or all of the following duties:

- Operate pumps, hoses, and extinguishers
- Force entry into aircraft, vehicles, and buildings in order to fight fires and rescue personnel
- Drive firefighting trucks and emergency rescue vehicles
- Give first aid to injured personnel
- Inspect aircraft, buildings, and equipment for fire hazards
- Teach fire protection procedures
- Repair firefighting equipment and fill fire extinguishers

## Physical Demands

Good vision without glasses and a clear speaking voice are required to enter some specialties in this occupation. Firefighters have to climb ladders and stairs. They must also be able to lift and carry injured personnel.

## Helpful Attributes

Helpful school subjects include health and general science. Helpful attributes include:

- Ability to remain calm under stress
- Willingness to risk injury to help others
- Ability to think and act decisively

## Work Environment

Firefighters work indoors and outdoors while fighting fires. They are exposed to the smoke, heat, and flames of the fires they fight.

## Training Provided

Job training consists of 7 to 11 weeks of classroom training, including practice in fighting fires. Course content typically includes:

- Types of fires
- Firefighting equipment operations
- Firefighting procedures
- First aid procedures
- Rescue procedures

Further training occurs on the job. The Army and the Navy offer certified apprenticeship programs for some specialties in this occupation.

## Civilian Counterparts

Civilian firefighters work for city and county fire departments, other government agencies, and industrial firms. They perform duties similar to those performed by military firefighters, including rescue and salvage work.

## Opportunities

The services have about 2,200 firefighters. On average, they need about 350 new firefighters each year. After training, new firefighters perform work under close supervision. With experience, they work more independently and may supervise others. Eventually, they may become chiefs of base fire departments or similar units.

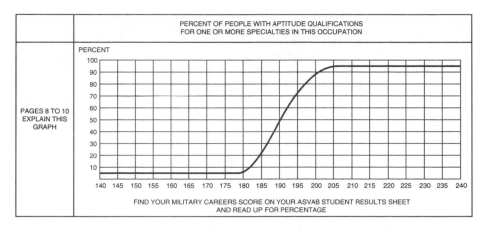

PAGES 8 TO 10 EXPLAIN THIS GRAPH

PERCENT OF PEOPLE WITH APTITUDE QUALIFICATIONS FOR ONE OR MORE SPECIALTIES IN THIS OCCUPATION

FIND YOUR MILITARY CAREERS SCORE ON YOUR ASVAB STUDENT RESULTS SHEET AND READ UP FOR PERCENTAGE

# FOOD SERVICE SPECIALISTS

Every day, more than one million meals are prepared in military kitchens. Some kitchens prepare thousands of meals at one time, while others prepare food for small groups of people. Food service specialists prepare all types of food according to standard and dietetic recipes. They also order and inspect food supplies and prepare meats for cooking. Turn to page 336 for more information about food service specialists.

## What They Do

Food service specialists in the military perform some or all of the following duties:

- Order, receive, and inspect meat, fish, fruit, and vegetables
- Prepare standard cuts of meat using cleavers, knives, and bandsaws
- Cook steaks, chops, and roasts
- Bake or fry chicken, turkey, and fish
- Prepare gravies and sauces
- Bake breads, cakes, pies, and pastries
- Serve food in dining halls, hospitals, field kitchens, or aboard ship
- Clean ovens, stoves, mixers, pots, and utensils

## Helpful Attributes

Helpful school subjects include home economics, health, mathematics, accounting, and chemistry. Helpful attributes include:

- Interest in cooking
- Interest in working with the hands

## Training Provided

Job training consists of 9 to 14 weeks of classroom instruction, including practice in food preparation. Training length varies depending on specialty. Course content typically includes:

- Standard and dietetic menus and recipes
- Preparation and cooking of various foodstuffs and bakery products
- Food and supply ordering
- Storage of meats, poultry, and other perishable items

Further training occurs on the job and through advanced courses. The Army, Navy, and Marine Corps offer certified apprenticeship programs for some specialties in this occupation.

## Work Environment

Food service specialists normally work in clean, sanitary kitchens and dining facilities. They may sometimes work in refrigerated meat lockers. Sometimes they work outdoors in tents while preparing and serving food under field conditions.

## Physical Demands

Food service specialists may have to lift and carry heavy containers of foodstuffs and large cooking utensils.

## Civilian Counterparts

Civilian food service specialists work in cafés, restaurants, and cafeterias. They also work in hotels, hospitals, manufacturing plants, schools, and other organizations that have their own dining facilities. Depending on specialty, food service specialists are called cooks, chefs, bakers, butchers, or meat cutters.

## Opportunities

The services have about 22,930 food service specialists. On average, they need about 2,600 new specialists each year. After job training, food service specialists help prepare and serve food under close supervision. Some food service specialists specialize as bakers, cooks, butchers, or meat cutters. With experience, they work more independently and may train new food service specialists. Eventually, they may become head cooks, chefs, or food service supervisors.

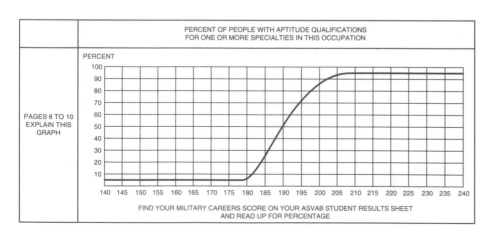

PERCENT OF PEOPLE WITH APTITUDE QUALIFICATIONS
FOR ONE OR MORE SPECIALTIES IN THIS OCCUPATION

PAGES 8 TO 10 EXPLAIN THIS GRAPH

PERCENT

FIND YOUR MILITARY CAREERS SCORE ON YOUR ASVAB STUDENT RESULTS SHEET
AND READ UP FOR PERCENTAGE

# LAW ENFORCEMENT AND SECURITY SPECIALISTS

The military services have their own law enforcement and security specialists. These specialists investigate crimes committed on military property or that involve military personnel. They also guard inmates in military correctional facilities.

## What They Do

Law enforcement and security specialists in the military perform some or all of the following duties:

- Investigate criminal activities and activities related to espionage, treason, and terrorism

- Interview witnesses and question suspects, sometimes using polygraph machines (lie detectors)

- Guard correctional facilities and conduct searches of inmates, cells, and vehicles

- Perform fire and riot control duties

## Training Provided

Job training consists of 5 to 12 weeks of classroom instruction. Training length varies depending on specialty. Course content typically includes:

- Civil and military laws

- Investigation procedures and techniques

- Prisoner control and discipline

## Helpful Attributes

Helpful attributes include:

- Interest in law enforcement and crime prevention

- Willingness to perform potentially dangerous work

- Ability to remain calm under pressure

## Work Environment

Law enforcement and security specialists in the military work mainly indoors; they may work outdoors while conducting investigations or guarding prisoners in exercise yards.

## Physical Demands

Normal color vision is necessary to enter some specialties in this area. Some specialties have minimum age and height requirements.

## Civilian Counterparts

Civilian law enforcement and security specialists work in federal, state, and local prisons, intelligence and law enforcement agencies, and private security companies. They perform similar duties to those performed in the military. They may be called detectives, private investigators, undercover agents, correction officers, or guards.

## Opportunities

The military has about 5,050 law enforcement and security specialists. On average, the services need about 250 new law enforcement and security specialists each year. After job training, they work under the direction of more experienced specialists. In time, they may supervise and train new workers or lead investigations. Eventually, they may become chiefs of detectives or superintendents of correctional facilities.

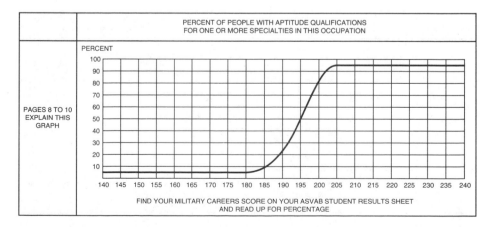

PERCENT OF PEOPLE WITH APTITUDE QUALIFICATIONS FOR ONE OR MORE SPECIALTIES IN THIS OCCUPATION

PERCENT

PAGES 8 TO 10 EXPLAIN THIS GRAPH

FIND YOUR MILITARY CAREERS SCORE ON YOUR ASVAB STUDENT RESULTS SHEET AND READ UP FOR PERCENTAGE

# MILITARY POLICE

The services have their own police forces for many of the same reasons that civilians do: to control traffic, prevent crime, and respond to emergencies. Military police protect lives and property on military bases by enforcing military laws and regulations. Turn to page 346 for more information about military police.

## What They Do

Military police perform some or all of the following duties:

- Patrol areas on foot, by car, or by boat
- Interview witnesses, victims, and suspects in the course of investigating crimes
- Collect fingerprints and other evidence
- Arrest and charge criminal suspects
- Train and walk with police dogs
- Testify in court
- Guard entrances and direct traffic

## Helpful Attributes

Helpful school subjects include government and speech. Helpful attributes include:

- Interest in law enforcement and crime prevention
- Ability to remain calm in stressful situations
- Ability to think and react quickly

## Physical Demands

Normal color vision, hearing, and a clear speaking voice are usually required to enter this occupation. Some specialties have minimum height requirements.

## Work Environment

Military police work both indoors and outdoors. They may work on foot, in cars, or in boats.

## Training Provided

Job training consists of 8 to 12 weeks of classroom instruction, including practice in police methods. Course content typically includes:

- Military and civil laws and jurisdiction
- Crime and accident investigation procedures
- Evidence collection procedures, including fingerprinting and suspect questioning
- Use of firearms
- Traffic and crowd control procedures
- Arrest and restraint of suspects
- Hand-to-hand defense techniques (judo, karate, etc.)

Further training occurs on the job and through advanced courses. The Navy offers a certified apprenticeship program for one specialty in this occupation.

## Civilian Counterparts

Civilian police officers generally work for state, county, or city law enforcement agencies. Some work as security guards for industrial firms, airports, and other businesses and institutions. They perform duties similar to military police.

## Opportunities

The military has about 23,000 military police. On average, the services need about 2,400 new military police each year. After job training, military police guard and patrol bases, and direct traffic. With experience, they question crime suspects and collect evidence. They may also supervise other police officers. In time, they may become station chiefs or police superintendents.

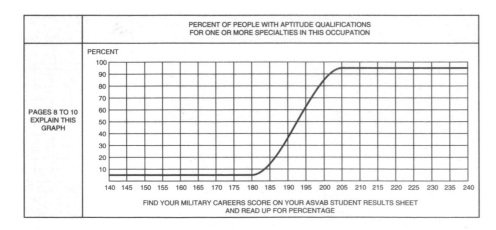

PERCENT OF PEOPLE WITH APTITUDE QUALIFICATIONS
FOR ONE OR MORE SPECIALTIES IN THIS OCCUPATION

PAGES 8 TO 10 EXPLAIN THIS GRAPH

PERCENT

100
90
80
70
60
50
40
30
20
10

140 145 150 155 160 165 170 175 180 185 190 195 200 205 210 215 220 225 230 235 240

FIND YOUR MILITARY CAREERS SCORE ON YOUR ASVAB STUDENT RESULTS SHEET
AND READ UP FOR PERCENTAGE

# Vehicle and Machinery Mechanic Occupations

- **Aircraft Mechanics**
- **Automotive and Heavy Equipment Mechanics**
- **Divers**
- **Heating and Cooling Mechanics**
- **Marine Engine Mechanics**
- **Powerhouse Mechanics**

# AIRCRAFT MECHANICS

Army
Navy
Air Force
Marine Corps
Coast Guard

Military aircraft are used to fly hundreds of missions each day for transport, patrol, and flight training. They need frequent servicing to remain safe and ready to fly. Aircraft mechanics inspect, service, and repair helicopters and airplanes. Turn to page 324 for more information about aircraft mechanics.

## What They Do

Aircraft mechanics in the military perform some or all of the following duties:

- Service and repair helicopter, jet, and propeller aircraft engines
- Inspect and repair aircraft wings, fuselages (bodies), and tail assemblies
- Service and repair aircraft landing gear
- Repair or replace starters, lights, batteries, wiring, and other electrical parts

## Helpful Attributes

Helpful school subjects include mathematics and shop mechanics. Helpful attributes include:

- Interest in work involving aircraft
- Interest in engine mechanics
- Ability to use hand and power tools

## Training Provided

Job training consists of 3 to 17 weeks of classroom instruction, including inspection and repair of aircraft engines and equipment. Training length varies depending upon the specialty. Course content typically includes:

- Engine disassembly and repair
- Repair of hydraulic, fuel, and electrical systems
- Repair of aluminum, steel, and fiberglass airframes and coverings

Further training occurs on the job and through advanced courses. The Army, Navy, and Marine Corps offer certified apprenticeship programs for some specialties in this occupation.

## Work Environment

Aircraft mechanics work in aircraft hangars and machine shops located on air bases or aboard aircraft carriers.

## Civilian Counterparts

Civilian aircraft mechanics work for aircraft manufacturers, commercial airlines, and government agencies. They perform duties similar to military aircraft mechanics. They may also be called airframe or power plant mechanics.

## Physical Demands

Some specialties require moderate to heavy lifting. Normal color vision is required to work with color-coded wiring.

## Opportunities

The services have about 60,675 aircraft mechanics. On average, they need about 4,100 new mechanics each year. After job training, mechanics are assigned to an aircraft maintenance unit, where they perform routine maintenance and simple repair jobs. In time, they may perform more difficult repairs and train and supervise new mechanics. Eventually, they may become inspectors, shop supervisors, or maintenance superintendents.

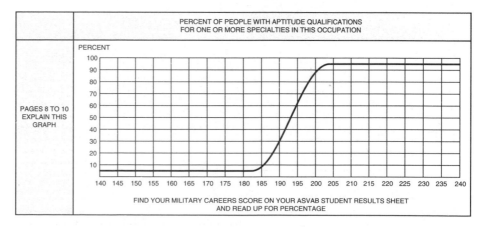

PERCENT OF PEOPLE WITH APTITUDE QUALIFICATIONS FOR ONE OR MORE SPECIALTIES IN THIS OCCUPATION

PAGES 8 TO 10 EXPLAIN THIS GRAPH

FIND YOUR MILITARY CAREERS SCORE ON YOUR ASVAB STUDENT RESULTS SHEET AND READ UP FOR PERCENTAGE

# AUTOMOTIVE AND HEAVY EQUIPMENT MECHANICS

Army
Navy
Air Force
Marine Corps
Coast Guard

Keeping automotive and heavy equipment in good working condition is vital to the success of military missions. Automotive and heavy equipment mechanics maintain and repair vehicles such as jeeps, cars, trucks, tanks, self-propelled missile launchers, and other combat vehicles. They also repair bulldozers, power shovels, and other construction equipment. Turn to page 326 for more information about automotive and heavy equipment mechanics.

## What They Do

Automotive and heavy equipment mechanics in the military perform some or all of the following duties:

- Troubleshoot problems in vehicle engines, electrical systems, steering, brakes, and suspensions
- Tune and repair engines
- Replace or repair damaged body parts, hydraulic arms or shovels, and grader blades
- Establish and follow schedules for maintaining vehicles

## Training Provided

Job training consists of 8 to 29 weeks of classroom instruction. Training length varies depending on specialty. Course content typically includes:

- Engine repair and tune-up
- Troubleshooting mechanical and electrical problems
- Repairing and replacing body panels, fenders, and radiators

Further training occurs on the job and through advanced courses. The Army, Navy, and Marine Corps offer certified apprenticeship programs for some specialties in this occupation.

## Special Requirements

Although some women are automotive and heavy equipment mechanics, some specialties in this occupation are open only to men.

## Work Environment

Automotive and heavy equipment mechanics usually work inside large repair garages. They work outdoors when making emergency repairs in the field.

## Physical Demands

Automotive and heavy equipment mechanics may have to lift heavy parts and tools. They sometimes have to work in cramped positions. Normal color vision is required for some specialties to work with color-coded wiring and to read diagrams.

## Helpful Attributes

Helpful school subjects include auto mechanics and industrial arts. Helpful attributes include:

- Preference for physical work
- Interest in troubleshooting and repairing mechanical problems
- Interest in automotive engines and how they work

## Civilian Counterparts

Civilian automotive and heavy equipment mechanics may work for service stations, auto and construction equipment dealers, farm equipment companies, and state highway agencies. They perform duties similar to military automotive and heavy equipment mechanics. They may also be called garage mechanics, carburetor mechanics, transmission mechanics, radiator mechanics, construction equipment mechanics, or endless track vehicle mechanics.

## Opportunities

The services have about 54,775 automotive and heavy equipment mechanics. On average, they need about 6,450 new mechanics each year. After job training, mechanics begin repairing equipment under the direction of a supervisor. In time, they have the opportunity to supervise other workers and possibly manage repair shops, motor pools, or maintenance units.

PAGES 8 TO 10 EXPLAIN THIS GRAPH

PERCENT OF PEOPLE WITH APTITUDE QUALIFICATIONS FOR ONE OR MORE SPECIALTIES IN THIS OCCUPATION

PERCENT

100
90
80
70
60
50
40
30
20
10

140 145 150 155 160 165 170 175 180 185 190 195 200 205 210 215 220 225 230 235 240

FIND YOUR MILITARY CAREERS SCORE ON YOUR ASVAB STUDENT RESULTS SHEET AND READ UP FOR PERCENTAGE

# DIVERS

Sometimes, military tasks such as ship repair, construction, and patrolling must be done under water. Divers in the military perform this work. They usually specialize either as scuba divers, who work just below the surface, or as deep sea divers, who may work for long periods of time in depths up to 300 feet.

## What They Do

Divers in the military perform some or all of the following duties:

- Inspect and clean ship propellers and hulls
- Patch damaged ship hulls using underwater welding equipment
- Patrol the waters below ships at anchor
- Salvage (recover) sunken equipment
- Assist with underwater construction of piers and harbor facilities
- Survey rivers, beaches, and harbors for underwater obstacles
- Use explosives to clear underwater obstacles

## Physical Demands

Divers must be good swimmers and physically strong.

## Special Requirements

Although there are women divers, some specialties in this occupation are open only to men.

## Helpful Attributes

Helpful school subjects include shop mechanics and building trades. Helpful attributes include:

- Interest in underwater diving
- Ability to stay calm under stress
- A high degree of self-reliance

## Work Environment

Divers work under water. However, they plan and prepare for work on land or aboard ships. Because diving is not usually a full-time job, divers often have another job specialty in which they work.

## Training Provided

Job training consists of 5 to 13 weeks of classroom instruction, including practice in diving and repair work. Training length varies depending on specialty. Course content typically includes:

- Principles of scuba diving
- Underwater welding and cutting
- Use and care of hand and power tools
- Maintenance of diving equipment

Further training occurs on the job and through advanced courses.

## Civilian Counterparts

Civilian divers work for oil companies, salvage companies, underwater construction firms, and police or fire rescue units. They perform duties similar to divers in the military.

## Opportunities

The services have about 350 divers. On average, they need about 10 new divers each year. After job training, divers work in teams headed by experienced divers. Eventually, they may become master divers and supervise diving operations.

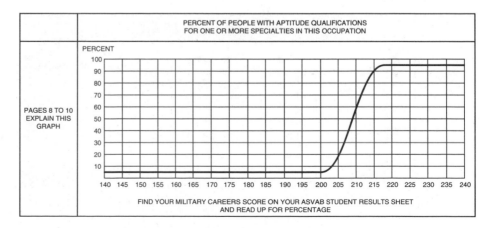

PERCENT OF PEOPLE WITH APTITUDE QUALIFICATIONS FOR ONE OR MORE SPECIALTIES IN THIS OCCUPATION

PAGES 8 TO 10 EXPLAIN THIS GRAPH

FIND YOUR MILITARY CAREERS SCORE ON YOUR ASVAB STUDENT RESULTS SHEET AND READ UP FOR PERCENTAGE

# HEATING AND COOLING MECHANICS

Air conditioning and heating equipment is used to maintain comfortable temperatures in military buildings, airplanes, and ships. Refrigeration equipment is used to keep food cold and to keep some missile fuels at sub-zero storage temperatures. Heating and cooling mechanics install and repair air conditioning, refrigeration, and heating equipment.

## What They Do

Heating and cooling mechanics in the military perform some or all of the following duties:

- Install and repair furnaces, boilers, and air conditioners

- Recharge cooling systems with refrigerant gases

- Install copper tubing systems that circulate water or cooling gases

- Replace compressor parts such as valves, pistons, bearings, and electrical motors on refrigeration units

- Repair thermostats and electrical circuits

## Physical Demands

Heating and cooling mechanics may have to lift or move heavy equipment. They are often required to stoop, kneel, and work in cramped positions. Normal color vision is required for locating and repairing color-coded wiring.

## Helpful Attributes

Helpful school subjects include science, math, and shop mechanics. Helpful attributes include:

- Ability to use hand and power tools

- Interest in working on machines

- Interest in solving problems

## Work Environment

Heating and cooling mechanics may work inside repair shops. Frequently, they work wherever equipment is to be installed or repaired.

## Training Provided

Job training consists of 8 to 22 weeks of classroom instruction, including practice in repair work. Training length varies depending on specialty. Course content typically includes:

- Refrigeration theory

- Installation and repair of refrigeration and air conditioning units

- Installation and repair of furnaces and boilers

- Use of diagrams and blueprints

Additional training is available on the job and in advanced courses. The Army, Navy, and Marine Corps offer certified apprenticeship programs for some specialties in this occupation.

## Civilian Counterparts

Civilian heating and cooling mechanics work for contractors that install home furnaces and air conditioners or for firms that repair refrigerators and freezers in homes, grocery stores, factories, and warehouses. Heating and cooling mechanics in civilian life often specialize more than those in the military. They may be called heating, air conditioning, refrigeration, or climate control mechanics.

## Opportunities

The military has about 6,800 heating and cooling mechanics. On average, the services need about 500 new mechanics each year. After job training, mechanics maintain and repair equipment under supervision. With experience, they may learn to diagnose mechanical problems and perform complicated repairs. Eventually, they may become superintendents of utilities for large bases.

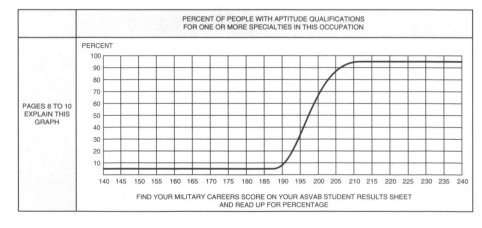

PAGES 8 TO 10 EXPLAIN THIS GRAPH

PERCENT OF PEOPLE WITH APTITUDE QUALIFICATIONS FOR ONE OR MORE SPECIALTIES IN THIS OCCUPATION

PERCENT

100 90 80 70 60 50 40 30 20 10

140 145 150 155 160 165 170 175 180 185 190 195 200 205 210 215 220 225 230 235 240

FIND YOUR MILITARY CAREERS SCORE ON YOUR ASVAB STUDENT RESULTS SHEET AND READ UP FOR PERCENTAGE

# MARINE ENGINE MECHANICS

The military operates many types of watercraft from small motor launches to large ships. Many of these vessels are powered by gasoline or diesel engines. Marine engine mechanics repair and maintain gasoline and diesel engines on ships, boats, and other watercraft. They also repair shipboard mechanical and electrical equipment. Turn to page 342 for more information about marine engine mechanics.

## What They Do

Marine engine mechanics in the military perform some or all of the following duties:

- Repair and maintain shipboard gasoline and diesel engines

- Locate and repair machinery parts, including valves and piping systems

- Repair ship propulsion machinery

- Repair and service hoisting machinery and ship elevators

- Repair refrigeration and air conditioning equipment on ships

- Repair engine-related electrical systems

## Helpful Attributes

Helpful school subjects include shop mechanics. Helpful attributes include:

- Interest in fixing engines and machinery

- Ability to use hand and power tools

- Preference for doing physical work

## Work Environment

Marine engine mechanics work aboard ships, normally in the engine or power rooms. Sometimes they work in repair centers on land bases. Working conditions in engine rooms tend to be noisy and hot.

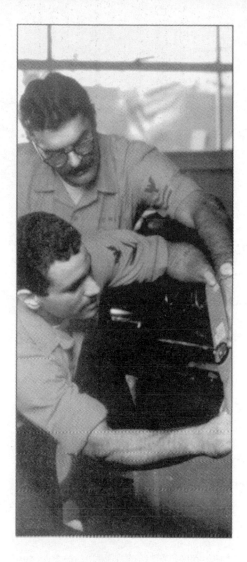

## Physical Demands

Normal color vision is required to work with color-coded diagrams and wiring.

## Training Provided

Job training consists of 9 to 24 weeks of classroom instruction, including practice in marine engine maintenance and repair. Training length varies depending on specialty. Course content typically includes:

- Internal combustion engine theory

- Repair of shipboard electronic and electrical machinery systems

- Service and repair of fuel injection systems

- Use and care of hand and power tools

Further training occurs on the job and through advanced courses. The Army offers a certified apprenticeship program for one specialty in this occupation.

## Civilian Counterparts

Civilian marine engine mechanics work in many industries, including marine transportation, commercial fishing, and oil exploration and drilling. They perform duties similar to military marine engine mechanics.

## Opportunities

The military has about 9,975 marine engine mechanics. On average, the services need about 900 new mechanics each year. After job training, they work under close supervision in repair centers or shipboard engine rooms. With experience, they work more independently and may supervise other mechanics. In time, marine engine mechanics may become supervisors of marine engine repair centers or shipboard maintenance sections.

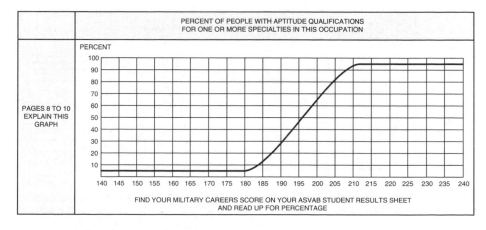

PERCENT OF PEOPLE WITH APTITUDE QUALIFICATIONS FOR ONE OR MORE SPECIALTIES IN THIS OCCUPATION

PAGES 8 TO 10 EXPLAIN THIS GRAPH

PERCENT

FIND YOUR MILITARY CAREERS SCORE ON YOUR ASVAB STUDENT RESULTS SHEET AND READ UP FOR PERCENTAGE

# POWERHOUSE MECHANICS

Power generating stations (powerhouses) provide electric power for military bases, ships, and field camps. There are many types of powerhouses, from small gas generators to large nuclear reactors. Powerhouse mechanics install, maintain, and repair electrical and mechanical equipment in power generating stations.

## What They Do

Powerhouse mechanics in the military perform some or all of the following duties:

- Install generating equipment, such as gasoline and diesel engines, turbines, and air compressors
- Repair and maintain nuclear power plants
- Inspect and service pumps, generators, batteries, and cables
- Tune engines using hand tools, timing lights, and combustion pressure gauges
- Diagnose (troubleshoot) engine and electrical system problems
- Replace damaged parts such as fuel injectors, valves, and pistons

## Physical Demands

Powerhouse mechanics may have to lift and move heavy electrical generators or batteries. Normal color vision is required to work with color-coded wiring and cables.

## Special Requirements

Nuclear power plant specialties are open only to men and require course work in algebra.

## Training Provided

Job training for non-nuclear specialties consists of 12 to 24 weeks of classroom instruction, including practice in repairing power generating equipment. Training length varies depending on the specialty. Course content typically includes:

- Principles of electricity
- Gas and diesel engine theories
- Hydraulic (fluid pressure) and pneumatic (air pressure) system maintenance
- Instrumentation of power generating systems

Nuclear specialties have training programs that last 1 year or more, covering all aspects of nuclear power plant operations. Further training occurs on the job and through advanced courses. The Army offers a certified apprenticeship program for this occupation.

## Work Environment

Powerhouse mechanics work in equipment repair shops, power plant stations, or power generating rooms aboard ships. Sometimes they work outdoors while repairing substation generating equipment.

## Helpful Attributes

Helpful school subjects include shop mechanics and math. Helpful attributes include:

- Interest in repairing machines and equipment
- Preference for doing physical work
- Interest in nuclear power

## Civilian Counterparts

Civilian powerhouse mechanics work for a wide variety of employers, such as utility and power companies, manufacturing companies, and others that operate their own power plants. They perform duties similar to military powerhouse mechanics.

## Opportunities

The services have about 10,475 powerhouse mechanics. On average, they need about 700 mechanics each year. After job training, mechanics are assigned routine tasks maintaining and repairing generating equipment under close supervision. With experience, they perform more complex repair work and operate more independently. In time, they may become powerhouse repair crew supervisors or power plant operations managers.

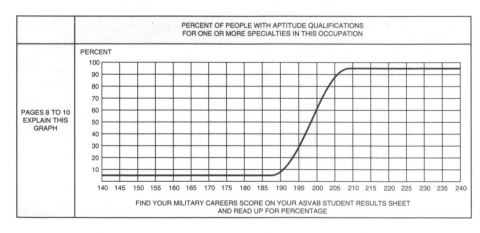

PERCENT OF PEOPLE WITH APTITUDE QUALIFICATIONS
FOR ONE OR MORE SPECIALTIES IN THIS OCCUPATION

PAGES 8 TO 10 EXPLAIN THIS GRAPH

PERCENT

FIND YOUR MILITARY CAREERS SCORE ON YOUR ASVAB STUDENT RESULTS SHEET
AND READ UP FOR PERCENTAGE

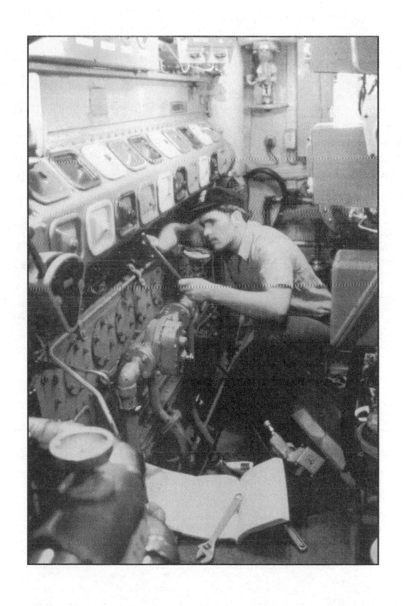

# Electronic and Electrical Equipment Repairer Occupations

- Aircraft Electricians
- Communications Equipment Repairers
- Computer Equipment Repairers
- Electrical Products Repairers
- Electronic Instrument Repairers
- Photographic Equipment Repairers
- Power Plant Electricians
- Precision Instrument Repairers
- Radar and Sonar Equipment Repairers
- Ship Electricians
- Weapons Maintenance Technicians

# AIRCRAFT ELECTRICIANS

Airplanes and helicopters have complex electrical systems. Instruments, lights, weapons, ignition systems, landing gear, and many other aircraft parts are powered by electricity. Aircraft electricians maintain and repair electrical systems on airplanes and helicopters.

## What They Do

Aircraft electricians in the military perform some or all of the following duties:

- Troubleshoot aircraft electrical systems using test equipment

- Repair or replace defective generators and electric motors

- Inspect and maintain electrical systems

- Replace faulty wiring

- Solder electrical connections

- Repair or replace instruments, such as tachometers, temperature gauges, and altimeters

- Read electrical wiring diagrams

## Helpful Attributes

Helpful school courses include math and shop mechanics. Helpful attributes include:

- Interest in solving problems

- Interest in electricity and how electrical equipment works

- Ability to work with tools

## Training Provided

Job training consists of 18 to 25 weeks of classroom instruction, including practice in repairing electrical systems. Training length varies depending on specialty. Course content typically includes:

- Electrical theory

- Troubleshooting procedures

- Soldering techniques

- Electrical system maintenance

Further training occurs on the job and through advanced courses. The Army and the Navy offer certified apprenticeship programs for one specialty in this occupation.

## Work Environment

Aircraft electricians usually work indoors, in aircraft hangars, airplanes, and repair shops. They may also work on aircraft parked outdoors.

## Civilian Counterparts

Civilian aircraft electricians work mainly for airlines and aircraft maintenance firms. They may also work for aircraft manufacturers and other organizations that have fleets of airplanes or helicopters. Their duties are similar to those of military aircraft electricians.

## Physical Demands

Normal color vision is required to work with color-coded wiring.

## Opportunities

The military has about 5,500 aircraft electricians. On average, the services need about 200 new aircraft electricians each year. After job training, aircraft electricians perform maintenance and routine repairs under close supervision. With experience, they are assigned more complicated troubleshooting and repairs and may supervise other electricians. In time, they may become supervisors of aircraft maintenance shops.

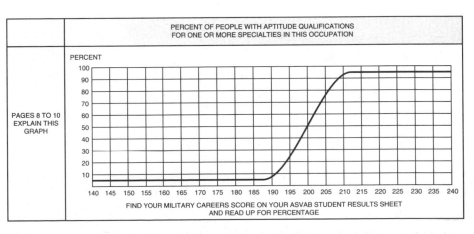

PAGES 8 TO 10 EXPLAIN THIS GRAPH

PERCENT OF PEOPLE WITH APTITUDE QUALIFICATIONS FOR ONE OR MORE SPECIALTIES IN THIS OCCUPATION

FIND YOUR MILITARY CAREERS SCORE ON YOUR ASVAB STUDENT RESULTS SHEET AND READ UP FOR PERCENTAGE

# COMMUNICATIONS EQUIPMENT REPAIRERS

Army
Navy
Air Force
Marine Corps
Coast Guard

The military relies on communication equipment to link ground, sea, and air forces. This equipment allows the military to track and direct troop, aircraft, and ship movements. Communications equipment repairers ensure this equipment operates properly.

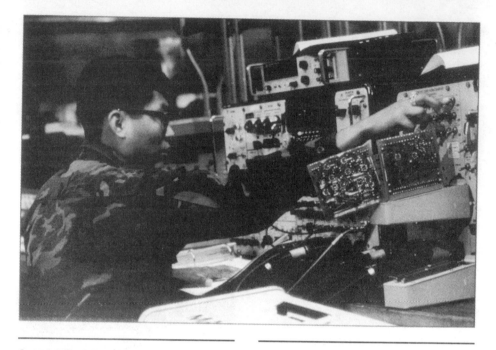

## What They Do

Communications equipment repairers in the military perform some or all of the following duties:

- Maintain, test, and repair communications equipment using frequency meters, circuit analyzers, and other electrical and electronic test equipment

- Install and repair circuits and wiring using soldering iron and hand tools

- Calibrate and align equipment components using scales, gauges, and other measuring instruments

- String overhead communications and electric cables between utility poles

## Physical Demands

For some specialties, normal color vision is required. Some repairers may work from ladders or on tall utility poles.

## Helpful Attributes

Helpful school subjects include math, electricity or electronics repair, and shop mechanics. Helpful attributes include:

- Interest in working with electrical, electronic, and electromechanical equipment

- Interest in solving problems

## Special Requirements

Although there are women communications equipment repairers, some specialties in this occupation are open only to men.

## Civilian Counterparts

Civilian communications equipment repairers often work for firms that design and make communications and electronic equipment. They may also work for the federal government. They perform duties similar to military communications equipment repairers. They may be called radio repairers, radio mechanics, teletype repairers, or station installers and repairers, depending on their specialty.

## Work Environment

Communications equipment repairers usually work in repair shops, laboratories, and outdoors, depending on the specialty.

## Training Provided

Job training consists of 8 to 40 weeks of classroom instruction, including practice with equipment. Course content typically includes:

- Mechanical, electronic, and electrical principles

- Preventive maintenance procedures

- Line installation and wiring techniques

- Communication security policies and procedures

The Army, Navy, and Marine Corps offer certified apprenticeship training programs for some specialties in this occupation.

## Opportunities

The services have about 40,200 communications equipment repairers. On average, the services need about 2,400 new repairers each year. After job training, repairers make simple repairs or installations under close supervision. With experience, they perform more difficult repairs and train other repair personnel. Eventually, they may become supervisors of communications units or maintenance shops.

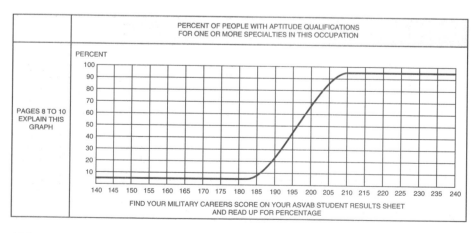

PAGES 8 TO 10 EXPLAIN THIS GRAPH

PERCENT OF PEOPLE WITH APTITUDE QUALIFICATIONS FOR ONE OR MORE SPECIALTIES IN THIS OCCUPATION

PERCENT

FIND YOUR MILITARY CAREERS SCORE ON YOUR ASVAB STUDENT RESULTS SHEET AND READ UP FOR PERCENTAGE

# COMPUTER EQUIPMENT REPAIRERS

Army
Navy
Air Force
Marine Corps

The military relies on computers to support weapons systems, communications, and administration. Keeping systems "up" is crucial for all military operations. Computer equipment repairers install, test, maintain, and repair computers and related data processing equipment.

## What They Do

Computer equipment repairers in the military perform some or all of the following duties:

- Install computers and other data processing equipment
- Inspect data processing equipment for defects in wiring, circuit boards, and other parts
- Test and repair data processing equipment using electrical voltage meters, circuit analyzers, and other special testing equipment
- Locate defective data processing parts using technical guides and diagrams

## Physical Demands

Specialties that involve flying require passing a special physical exam. Normal color vision is required to work with color-coded wiring.

## Helpful Attributes

Helpful school subjects include mathematics and electronic equipment repair. Helpful attributes include:

- Interest in working with electrical and electronic equipment

## Work Environment

Computer equipment repairers usually work indoors in repair shops or data processing centers on land or aboard ships. Some specialties involve flying.

## Training Provided

Job training consists of 25 to 35 weeks of classroom instruction, including practice in repairing computer equipment. Course content typically includes:

- Electronic principles and concepts
- Operation of various computer systems and equipment
- Use of test equipment
- Repair of data processing equipment

The Army, Navy, and Marine Corps offer certified apprenticeship programs for some specialties in this occupation.

## Civilian Counterparts

Civilian computer equipment repairers work for computer manufacturers, repair services, and other businesses with large computer facilities. They perform duties similar to military computer equipment repairers. They may also be called computer service technicians.

## Opportunities

The services have about 4,000 computer equipment repairers. On average, they need about 100 new equipment repairers each year. After job training, repairers are assigned to maintenance units or data processing centers. They perform routine maintenance and simple repair jobs under close supervision. In time, they may perform more difficult repairs and supervise and help train other repair personnel. Eventually, they may become supervisors or managers of computer maintenance departments.

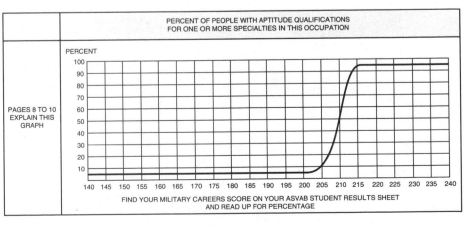

PERCENT OF PEOPLE WITH APTITUDE QUALIFICATIONS
FOR ONE OR MORE SPECIALTIES IN THIS OCCUPATION

PAGES 8 TO 10 EXPLAIN THIS GRAPH

PERCENT

FIND YOUR MILITARY CAREERS SCORE ON YOUR ASVAB STUDENT RESULTS SHEET
AND READ UP FOR PERCENTAGE

# ELECTRICAL PRODUCTS REPAIRERS

Much of the military's equipment is electrically powered. Electric motors, electric tools, and medical equipment require careful maintenance and repair. Electrical products repairers maintain and repair electrical equipment. They specialize by type of equipment.

## What They Do

Electrical products repairers in the military perform some or all of the following duties:

- Maintain, test, and repair electric motors in many kinds of machines, such as lathes, pumps, office machines, and kitchen appliances

- Inspect and repair electrical, medical, and dental equipment

- Inspect and repair electric instruments, such as voltmeters

- Replace worn gaskets and seals in watertight electrical equipment

- Maintain and repair portable electric tools, such as saws and drills

- Maintain and repair submarine periscopes

## Work Environment

Electrical products repairers usually work in repair shops on land or aboard ships.

## Training Provided

Job training consists of 4 to 22 weeks of classroom instruction, including practice in repairing electrical products. Training length varies depending on specialty. Course content typically includes:

- Maintenance and repair procedures

- Use of electrical test equipment

Further training occurs on the job and through advanced courses. The Army, Navy, and Marine Corps offer certified apprenticeship programs for some specialties in this occupation.

## Physical Demands

Normal color vision is required to work with color-coded wiring.

## Helpful Attributes

Helpful school subjects include math, electricity, and shop mechanics. Helpful attributes include:

- Ability to use tools

- Interest in electric motors and appliances

- Interest in solving problems

## Civilian Counterparts

Civilian electrical products repairers work in many industries, including hospitals, manufacturing firms, and governmental agencies. They also work in independent repair shops. They perform duties similar to military electrical products repairers. They may be called electric tool repairers, electrical instrument repairers, electromedical equipment repairers, or electric motor repairers.

## Opportunities

The military has about 4,400 electrical products repairers. On average, the services need about 250 new repairers each year. After job training, they normally make simple repairs under the direction of more experienced workers. With experience, they perform more complicated repairs. In time, repairers may become electrical repair shop supervisors.

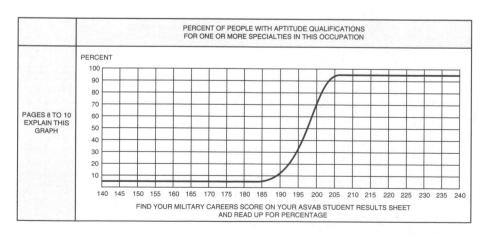

PERCENT OF PEOPLE WITH APTITUDE QUALIFICATIONS
FOR ONE OR MORE SPECIALTIES IN THIS OCCUPATION

PAGES 8 TO 10 EXPLAIN THIS GRAPH

PERCENT

FIND YOUR MILITARY CAREERS SCORE ON YOUR ASVAB STUDENT RESULTS SHEET AND READ UP FOR PERCENTAGE

# ELECTRONIC INSTRUMENT REPAIRERS

Army
Navy
Air Force
Marine Corps
Coast Guard

The military uses electronic instruments in many areas, including health care, weather forecasting, flight control, and combat, to name a few. Electronic instrument repairers maintain and repair electronic instruments, such as precision measuring equipment, navigational controls, photographic equipment, and biomedical instruments. Electronic instrument repairers normally specialize by type of equipment or instrument being repaired. Turn to page 334 for more information about electronic instrument repairers.

## What They Do

Electronic instrument repairers in the military perform some or all of the following duties:

- Test meteorological and medical instruments, navigational controls, and simulators using electronic and electrical test equipment
- Read technical diagrams and manuals in order to locate, isolate, and repair instrument parts
- Replace equipment parts such as resistors, switches, and circuit boards

## Training Provided

Job training consists of 15 to 30 weeks of classroom instruction, including practice in repairing and replacing equipment parts. Training length varies depending on specialty. Course content typically includes:

- Principles of electronics
- Use and maintenance of electrical and electronic test equipment
- Equipment repair exercises

The Navy and the Marine Corps offer certified apprenticeship programs for some specialties in this occupation.

## Work Environment

Electronic instrument repairers usually work in repair shops and laboratories.

## Physical Demands

Normal color vision is required to work with color-coded wiring. Some specialties require a minimum age of 18 to enter.

## Helpful Attributes

Helpful school subjects include math and electronic equipment repair. Helpful attributes include:

- Interest in working with electronic equipment
- Interest in solving problems
- Attention to detail

## Civilian Counterparts

Most civilian electronic instrument repairers work for manufacturing, medical research, satellite communications firms, or commercial airlines. They may also work for government agencies, such as the Federal Aviation Administration, the National Aeronautics and Space Administration, or the National Weather Service. They perform the same kind of duties as military instrument repairers. They are called electronics mechanics, dental equipment repairers, or biomedical equipment technicians, depending on their specialty.

## Opportunities

The services have about 6,000 electronic instrument repairers. On average, they need about 500 new repairers each year. After job training, they are assigned to an operations or equipment maintenance unit. They perform routine maintenance and simple repair jobs. In time, they may perform more difficult repairs and supervise other repair personnel. Eventually, they may become supervisors or managers of electronic equipment maintenance units.

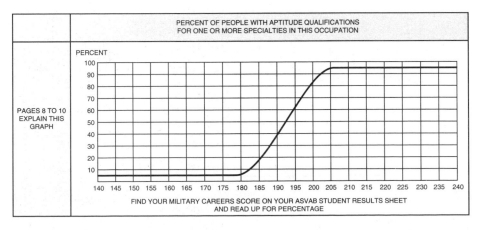

PERCENT OF PEOPLE WITH APTITUDE QUALIFICATIONS
FOR ONE OR MORE SPECIALTIES IN THIS OCCUPATION

PAGES 8 TO 10 EXPLAIN THIS GRAPH

PERCENT

FIND YOUR MILITARY CAREERS SCORE ON YOUR ASVAB STUDENT RESULTS SHEET
AND READ UP FOR PERCENTAGE

# PHOTOGRAPHIC EQUIPMENT REPAIRERS

The photographic equipment used by the military has many sensitive mechanisms. Still cameras, video cameras, and photographic processing equipment need regular attention to stay in working order. Photographic equipment repairers adjust and repair cameras, projectors, and photo-processing equipment.

## What They Do

Photographic equipment repairers in the military perform some or all of the following duties:

- Adjust and repair camera shutter mechanisms, focus controls, and flash units

- Maintain and repair aerial cameras mounted in airplanes

- Maintain aerial sensors that detect foreign military activities

- Maintain and repair motion picture cameras and sound recording equipment

- Repair photoprocessing equipment such as enlargers, film processors, and printers

- Diagnose problems in all types of cameras

## Work Environment

Photographic equipment repairers work in repair shops on land or aboard ships.

## Physical Demands

Normal color vision is required to work with color-coded wiring.

## Training Provided

Job training consists of 9 to 32 weeks of classroom instruction, including practice in repairing photographic equipment. Training length varies depending on specialty. Course content typically includes:

- Test and repair of still cameras and darkroom equipment

- Maintenance and repair of motion picture cameras, tape recorders, synchronizers, and similar equipment

- Test and repair of aerial sensor equipment

Further training occurs on the job and through advanced courses. The Navy offers certified apprenticeship programs for some specialties in this occupation.

## Helpful Attributes

Helpful school subjects include math and science. Helpful attributes include:

- Interest in solving problems

- Ability to use repair tools

## Civilian Counterparts

Civilian photographic equipment repairers work for photographic laboratories, engineering firms, and government agencies. They perform duties similar to those performed in the military. Depending on specialty, they may also be called camera repairers, motion picture equipment machinists, or photographic equipment technicians.

## Opportunities

The services have about 800 photographic equipment repairers. On average, they need about 50 new photographic equipment repairers each year. After job training, photographic equipment repairers make routine adjustments and simple repairs under close supervision. In time, they make more difficult repairs and may supervise others. Eventually, they may become chiefs of one or more military photographic labs.

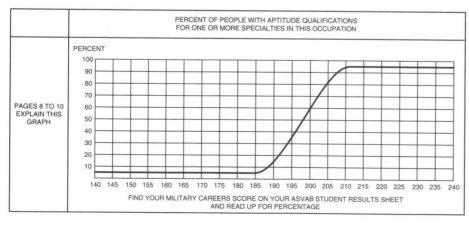

PAGES 8 TO 10 EXPLAIN THIS GRAPH

PERCENT OF PEOPLE WITH APTITUDE QUALIFICATIONS FOR ONE OR MORE SPECIALTIES IN THIS OCCUPATION

PERCENT

FIND YOUR MILITARY CAREERS SCORE ON YOUR ASVAB STUDENT RESULTS SHEET AND READ UP FOR PERCENTAGE

# POWER PLANT ELECTRICIANS

Army
Navy
Air Force
Marine Corps
Coast Guard

Each military base—anywhere in the world—must have its own electricity. Power plant electricians maintain and repair electricity generating equipment in mobile and stationary power plants.

## What They Do

Power plant electricians perform some or all of the following duties:

- Maintain and repair motors, generators, switchboards, and control equipment

- Maintain and repair power and lighting circuits, electrical fixtures, and other electrical equipment

- Detect and locate grounds, open circuits, and short circuits in power distribution cables

- Connect emergency power to the main control board from an emergency switchboard

- Operate standard electrical and electronic test equipment

- Read technical guides and diagrams to locate damaged parts of generators and control equipment

## Work Environment

Power plant electricians work in repair shops on land, aboard ships, or wherever generating equipment needing repair is located.

## Training Provided

Job training consists of 4 to 17 weeks of classroom instruction, including practice in maintaining electrical power systems. Course length varies depending on specialty. Course content typically includes:

- Generator and power plant operations

- Electrical generation and distribution

- Diesel generator operation, disassembly, inspection, and maintenance

- Principles of electrical and electronic circuitry

Further training occurs on the job and through advanced courses. The Army offers certified apprenticeship programs for one specialty in this occupation.

## Special Requirements

Although there are women power plant electricians, some specialties in this occupation are open only to men.

## Physical Demands

Normal color vision is required to work with color-coded wiring.

## Helpful Attributes

Helpful school subjects include electrical and electronic theory, math, and technical drawing. Helpful attributes include:

- Ability to use hand and power tools

- Interest in working with large machinery

- Interest in electricity

## Civilian Counterparts

Civilian power plant electricians often work for construction companies, manufacturers, and utility companies. They perform duties similar to military power plant electricians.

## Opportunities

The services have about 1,100 power plant electricians. On average, they need about 50 new power plant electricians each year. After job training, power plant electricians perform routine maintenance and repairs under supervision. In time, they perform more complex tasks and may help train others. Eventually, they may become supervisors of power plant operations.

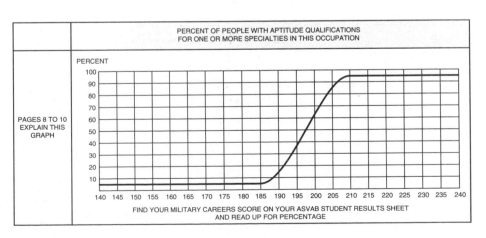

# PRECISION INSTRUMENT REPAIRERS

Precision instruments are measuring devices. They can be as simple as a thermometer or as complex as a gyrocompass. Precision instruments are used by the military to measure distance, pressure, altitude, underwater depth, and many other physical properties. Precision instrument repairers keep measuring devices in good working order. They calibrate (adjust) gauges and meters to give correct readings.

## What They Do

Precision instrument repairers in the military perform some or all of the following duties:

- Calibrate weather instruments, such as barometers and thermometers
- Repair gyrocompasses
- Adjust and repair weapon-aiming devices, such as range finders, telescopes, periscopes, and ballistic computers
- Calibrate engineering instruments, such as transits, levels, telemeters, and stereoscopes
- Calibrate and repair instruments used in aircraft
- Repair watches, clocks, and timers
- Calibrate electrical test instruments

## Work Environment

Precision instrument repairers usually work in repair shops on land or aboard ships.

## Helpful Attributes

Helpful school subjects include math, science, electronics, and shop mechanics. Helpful attributes include:

- Interest in machines and how they work
- Ability to solve mechanical problems
- Ability to work with tools

## Physical Demands

Normal color vision is required to work with color-coded wiring and repair manuals.

## Training Provided

Job training consists of 12 to 34 weeks of classroom instruction, including practice in repairing precision instruments. Training length varies depending on specialty. Course content typically includes:

- Calibration and repair of precision measuring instruments
- Use of blueprints and schematics

The Army and Navy offer certified apprenticeship programs for some specialties in this occupation.

## Civilian Counterparts

Civilian precision instrument repairers work for firms that manufacture or use precision instruments. These include manufacturing firms, airlines, machinery repair shops, maintenance shops, and instrument makers. Civilian precision instrument repairers perform duties similar to military precision instrument repairers. They may also be called instrument mechanics or calibration specialists.

## Opportunities

The services have about 5,700 precision instrument repairers. On average, they need 350 new precision instrument repairers each year. After job training, precision instrument repairers calibrate instruments under the direction of supervisors. With experience, they perform more complicated repairs and may supervise others. In time, precision instrument repairers may become managers of instrument repair shops.

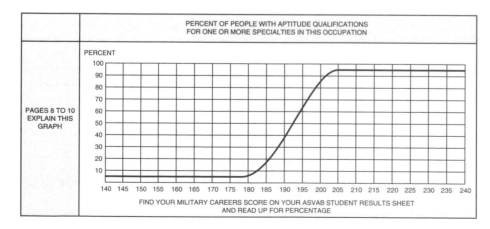

PAGES 8 TO 10 EXPLAIN THIS GRAPH

PERCENT OF PEOPLE WITH APTITUDE QUALIFICATIONS FOR ONE OR MORE SPECIALTIES IN THIS OCCUPATION

PERCENT

FIND YOUR MILITARY CAREERS SCORE ON YOUR ASVAB STUDENT RESULTS SHEET AND READ UP FOR PERCENTAGE

# RADAR AND SONAR EQUIPMENT REPAIRERS

Army
Navy
Air Force
Marine Corps
Coast Guard

Radar and sonar equipment locates objects by bouncing radio and sound waves off them. This equipment is used to detect and track enemy ships, planes, and missiles. It is also used for ship and plane navigation and weather observation. Radar and sonar equipment repairers install, maintain, repair, and operate sonar and radar equipment. Turn to page 350 for more information about radar and sonar equipment repairers.

## What They Do

Radar and sonar equipment repairers perform some or all of the following duties:

- Test radar systems using electronic and electrical test equipment

- Monitor the operation of air traffic control, missile tracking, air defense, and other radar systems to make sure there are no problems

- Repair sonar and radar components (parts), using soldering irons and other special hand and power tools

- Install receivers, transmitters, and other components using technical manuals and guides

- Read wiring diagrams, designs, and other drawings to locate parts and components of radar equipment

## Physical Demands

Specialties involving flying require passing a special physical exam. Normal color vision is required to work with color-coded wiring.

## Helpful Attributes

Helpful school subjects include math and physics. Helpful attributes include:

- Interest in working with electrical and electronic equipment

- Ability to apply electronic principles and concepts

## Work Environment

Radar and sonar equipment repairers work in repair shops and laboratories on land or aboard ships. Some specialties involve flying.

## Special Requirements

Although there are women radar and sonar equipment repairers, some specialties in this occupation are open only to men.

## Training Provided

Job training consists of 20 to 30 weeks of classroom instruction, including practice in repairing radar and sonar equipment. Course content typically includes:

- Application of electronic principles and concepts

- Inspection techniques and procedures

- Use of electrical and electronic test equipment

- Repair and replacement of radar and sonar equipment

The Army, Navy, and Marine Corps offer certified apprenticeship programs for some specialties in this occupation.

## Civilian Counterparts

Civilian radar and sonar equipment repairers work for engineering firms, the federal government, or aircraft and military hardware manufacturers. They perform duties similar to military radar and sonar equipment repairers. They may also be called communications technicians.

## Opportunities

The services have about 16,000 radar and sonar equipment repairers. On average, they need about 250 new equipment repairers each year. After job training, radar and sonar equipment repairers are assigned to a radar or sonar maintenance unit. They perform routine maintenance and simple repair jobs under close supervision. In time, they may perform more difficult repairs and supervise others. Eventually, they may become managers or chiefs of communications units or avionics maintenance shops.

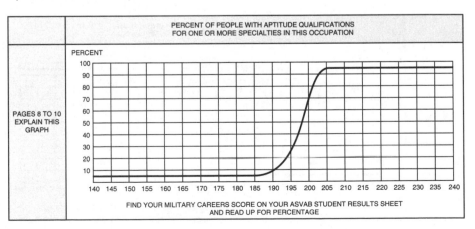

PERCENT OF PEOPLE WITH APTITUDE QUALIFICATIONS FOR ONE OR MORE SPECIALTIES IN THIS OCCUPATION

PAGES 8 TO 10 EXPLAIN THIS GRAPH

PERCENT

FIND YOUR MILITARY CAREERS SCORE ON YOUR ASVAB STUDENT RESULTS SHEET AND READ UP FOR PERCENTAGE

# SHIP ELECTRICIANS

Electrical systems supply power to operate ships and submarines. Lights, radar, weapons, laundry and cooking appliances, and machinery all need electricity. Ship electricians operate and repair electrical systems on ships. They keep electrical power plants, wiring, and machinery in working order.

## What They Do

Ship electricians in the military perform some or all of the following duties:

- Install wiring for lights and equipment
- Troubleshoot electrical wiring and equipment using test meters
- Inspect and maintain devices that distribute electricity throughout ships, such as circuits, transformers, and regulators
- Monitor and maintain electrical devices connected to the ship's main engines or nuclear reactors
- Repair motors and appliances

## Physical Demands

Normal color vision is required to work with color-coded wiring.

## Helpful Attributes

Helpful school courses include math and shop mechanics. Helpful attributes include:

- Interest in electricity and how electrical machines work
- Interest in solving problems
- Ability to use tools

## Training Provided

Job training for non-nuclear specialists consists of 18 to 25 weeks of classroom instruction, including practice repairing electrical systems. Course content typically includes:

- Electrical theory
- Troubleshooting procedures
- Maintenance and repair procedures
- Reading diagrams and calculating amperage, voltage, and resistance levels

Further training occurs on the job and through advanced courses.

## Special Requirements

Nuclear specialties are open only to men and require successful completion of high school algebra.

## Work Environment

Ship electricians usually work indoors, aboard ships or submarines. They also work in ship repair shops on land.

## Civilian Counterparts

Civilian ship electricians work for shipbuilding and drydock firms and shipping lines. They perform duties similar to military ship electricians. Other civilian electricians, such as building electricians and electrical products repairers, also perform similar work. Civilian nuclear power plant electricians perform duties similar to ship electricians who work with nuclear plants on ships and submarines.

## Opportunities

The military has about 2,000 ship electricians. On average, the services need about 50 new ship electricians each year. After job training, ship electricians perform maintenance work and repair electrical problems. Eventually, they may become superintendents of electrical repair shops or of ship electrical systems.

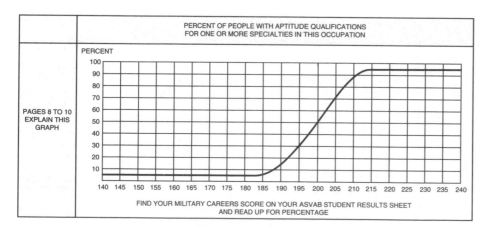

PAGES 8 TO 10 EXPLAIN THIS GRAPH

PERCENT OF PEOPLE WITH APTITUDE QUALIFICATIONS FOR ONE OR MORE SPECIALTIES IN THIS OCCUPATION

PERCENT

FIND YOUR MILITARY CAREERS SCORE ON YOUR ASVAB STUDENT RESULTS SHEET AND READ UP FOR PERCENTAGE

# WEAPONS MAINTENANCE TECHNICIANS

Combat forces use many different types of weapons from small field artillery to large ballistic missiles. Weapons may be fired from ships, planes, and ground stations. Most modern weapons have electronic components and systems that assist in locating targets, aiming weapons, and firing them. Weapons maintenance technicians maintain and repair weapons used by combat forces. Turn to page 360 for more information about weapons maintenance technicians.

## What They Do

Weapons maintenance technicians in the military perform some or all of the following duties:

- Repair and maintain artillery, naval gun systems, and infantry weapons

- Clean and lubricate gyroscopes, sights, and other electro-optical fire control components

- Repair and maintain missile mounts, platforms, and launch mechanisms

- Test and adjust weapons firing, guidance, and launch systems

## Training Provided

Job training consists of 15 to 30 weeks of classroom instruction and practical experience. Training length varies depending on specialty. Course content typically includes:

- Electronic and mechanical principles and concepts

- Use of electronic, electrical, and mechanical test equipment

- Use of schematics, drawings, blueprints, and wiring diagrams

- Operation, testing, and maintenance of specific types of weapons systems

- Operation and maintenance of fire control systems on ships

Further training occurs on the job and through advanced courses. The Army, Navy, and Marine Corps offer certified apprenticeship programs for some specialties in this occupation.

## Special Requirements

Although there are women weapons maintenance technicians, some specialties in this occupation are open only to men.

## Work Environment

Weapons maintenance technicians work in workshops when testing and repairing electronic components. They may work outdoors while inspecting and repairing combat vehicles, ships, artillery, aircraft, and missile silos.

## Helpful Attributes

Helpful school subjects include science and math. Helpful attributes include:

- Interest in working with electronic or electrical equipment

- Ability to do work requiring accuracy and attention to detail

- Interest in working with weapons

## Physical Demands

Some specialties involve moderate to heavy lifting. Normal color vision is required to read color-coded charts and diagrams.

## Civilian Counterparts

Civilian weapons maintenance technicians work for firms that design, build, and test weapons systems for the military. They perform duties similar to military weapons maintenance technicians. They may also be called electronic mechanics, avionics technicians, or missile facilities repairers.

## Opportunities

The services have about 11,000 weapons maintenance technicians. On average, they need about 450 new technicians each year. After job training, they are assigned to weapons operations or maintenance units. They perform routine maintenance and work under close supervision. With experience, they may work more independently and train new personnel. Eventually, they may become managers of missile facilities, avionics, or electronics maintenance units or shops.

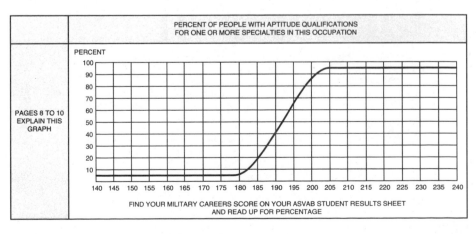

PAGES 8 TO 10 EXPLAIN THIS GRAPH

PERCENT OF PEOPLE WITH APTITUDE QUALIFICATIONS FOR ONE OR MORE SPECIALTIES IN THIS OCCUPATION

PERCENT

FIND YOUR MILITARY CAREERS SCORE ON YOUR ASVAB STUDENT RESULTS SHEET AND READ UP FOR PERCENTAGE

# Construction Occupations

- Building Electricians
- Construction Equipment Operators
- Construction Specialists
- Plumbers and Pipe Fitters

# BUILDING ELECTRICIANS

| Army
Navy
Air Force
Marine Corps
Coast Guard

The military uses electricity to do many jobs, including lighting hospitals, running power tools, and operating computers. Building electricians install and repair electrical wiring systems in offices, repair shops, airplane hangars, and other buildings on military bases.

## What They Do

Building electricians in the military perform some or all of the following duties:

- Install and wire transformers, junction boxes, and circuit breakers, using wire cutters, insulation strippers, and other hand tools

- Read blueprints, wiring plans, and repair orders to determine wiring layouts or repair needs

- Cut, bend, and string wires and conduits (pipe or tubing)

- Inspect power distribution systems, shorts in wires, and faulty equipment using test meters

- Repair and replace faulty wiring and lighting fixtures

- Install lightning rods to protect electrical systems

## Helpful Attributes

Helpful school subjects include science and math. Helpful attributes include:

- Ability to use hand tools

- Preference for doing physical work

- Interest in electricity

## Work Environment

Building electricians usually work indoors while installing wiring systems. They work outdoors while installing transformers and lightning rods.

## Physical Demands

Normal color vision is required for working with color-coded wiring and circuits.

## Training Provided

Job training consists of 8 to 12 weeks of classroom instruction, including practice in the installation and repair of electrical wiring systems. Course content typically includes:

- Fundamentals of electricity

- Electrical circuit troubleshooting

- Safety procedures

- Techniques for wiring switches, outlets, and junction boxes

Further training occurs on the job and through advanced courses. The Army and Marine Corps offer certified apprenticeship programs for some specialties in this occupation.

## Civilian Counterparts

Civilian building electricians usually work for building and electrical contracting firms. Some work as self-employed electrical contractors. They perform duties similar to military building electricians.

## Opportunities

The military has about 1,000 building electricians. On average, the services need about 100 new electricians each year. After job training, building electricians work under close supervision. As they gain experience, building electricians work more independently. In time, they may be promoted to supervisors of one or more work crews. Eventually, they may become construction superintendents.

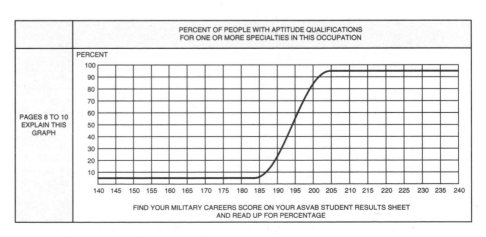

PAGES 8 TO 10 EXPLAIN THIS GRAPH

PERCENT OF PEOPLE WITH APTITUDE QUALIFICATIONS FOR ONE OR MORE SPECIALTIES IN THIS OCCUPATION

FIND YOUR MILITARY CAREERS SCORE ON YOUR ASVAB STUDENT RESULTS SHEET AND READ UP FOR PERCENTAGE

# CONSTRUCTION EQUIPMENT OPERATORS

Army
Navy
Air Force
Marine Corps
Coast Guard

Each year the military completes hundreds of construction projects. Tons of earth and building materials must be moved to build airfields, roads, dams, and buildings. Construction equipment operators use bulldozers, cranes, graders, and other heavy equipment in military construction.

## What They Do

Construction equipment operators in the military perform some or all of the following duties:

- Drive bulldozers, roadgraders, and other heavy equipment to cut and level earth for runways and roadbeds
- Lift and move steel and other heavy building materials using winches, cranes, and hoists
- Dig holes and trenches using power shovels
- Remove ice and snow from runways, roads, and other areas using scrapers and snow blowers
- Operate mixing plants to make concrete and asphalt
- Spread asphalt and concrete with paving machines
- Drill wells using drilling rigs
- Place and detonate explosives

## Helpful Attributes

Helpful school subjects include shop mechanics. Helpful attributes include:

- Interest in operating heavy construction equipment
- Preference for working outdoors

## Training Provided

Job training consists of 4 to 12 weeks of classroom instruction, including practice operating construction equipment. Course content typically includes:

- Operation of different types of construction equipment
- Maintenance and repair of equipment

Further training occurs on the job and through advanced courses. The Army and the Navy offer certified apprenticeship programs for one specialty in this occupation.

## Physical Demands

Some specialties require normal hearing, color vision, and heavy lifting.

## Work Environment

Construction equipment operators work outdoors in all kinds of weather conditions. They often sit for long periods and are subject to loud noise and vibrations. They may work indoors while repairing equipment.

## Civilian Counterparts

Civilian construction equipment operators work for building contractors, state highway agencies, rock quarries, well drillers, and construction firms. Civilian construction equipment operators may also be known as operating engineers, heavy equipment operators, well drillers, or riggers.

## Opportunities

The services have about 5,800 construction equipment operators. On average, they need about 450 new construction equipment operators each year. With time, they have the opportunity to become construction supervisors or construction superintendents.

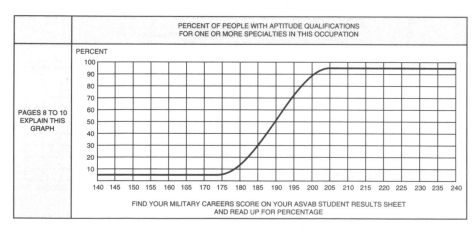

PERCENT OF PEOPLE WITH APTITUDE QUALIFICATIONS FOR ONE OR MORE SPECIALTIES IN THIS OCCUPATION

PAGES 8 TO 10 EXPLAIN THIS GRAPH

PERCENT

FIND YOUR MILITARY CAREERS SCORE ON YOUR ASVAB STUDENT RESULTS SHEET AND READ UP FOR PERCENTAGE

# CONSTRUCTION SPECIALISTS

Army
Navy
Air Force
Marine Corps
Coast Guard

The military builds many temporary and permanent structures each year. Lumber, plywood, plasterboard, and concrete and masonry (bricks, stone, and concrete blocks) are the basic building materials for many of these projects. Construction specialists build and repair buildings, bridges, foundations, dams, and bunkers. They work with engineers and other building specialists as part of military construction teams. Turn to page 332 for more information about construction specialists.

## What They Do

Construction specialists in the military perform some or all of the following duties:

- Build foundations, floor slabs, and walls with brick, cement block, mortar, or stone
- Erect wood framing for buildings using hand and power tools, such as hammers, saws, levels, and drills
- Lay roofing materials, such as asphalt, tile, and wooden shingles
- Install plasterboard, plaster, and paneling to form interior walls and ceilings
- Lay wood and ceramic tile floors and build steps, staircases, and porches
- Build temporary shelters for storing supplies and equipment while on training maneuvers

## Training Provided

Job training consists of 5 to 8 weeks of instruction, including practice with carpentry and masonry tools. Course content typically includes:

- Building construction
- Masonry construction methods
- Types and uses of construction joints and braces
- Interpretation of blueprints and drawings
- How to mix and set concrete, mortar, and plaster

Further training occurs on the job and through advanced courses. The Army, Navy, and Marine Corps offer certified apprenticeship programs in this occupation.

## Physical Demands

Construction specialists may have to lift and carry heavy building materials, such as lumber, plasterboard, and concrete. Sometimes, they climb and work from ladders and scaffolding.

## Helpful Attributes

Helpful school subjects include math, woodworking, and industrial arts. Helpful attributes include:

- Preference for physical work
- Ability to work with blueprints
- Interest in using power tools

## Work Environment

Construction specialists work indoors and outdoors on construction sites.

## Civilian Counterparts

Civilian construction specialists usually work for construction or remodeling contractors, government agencies, utility companies, or manufacturing firms. They perform duties similar to military construction specialists. They may also be called bricklayers, stonemasons, cement masons, cement finishers, carpenters, or cabinetmakers.

## Opportunities

The military has about 6,000 construction specialists. On average, the services need about 700 new specialists each year. After job training, construction specialists work in teams under close supervision. Initially, they perform simple work, such as form building and rough framing. With experience, they perform more difficult tasks. In time, they may supervise and train other specialists. They may become construction superintendents.

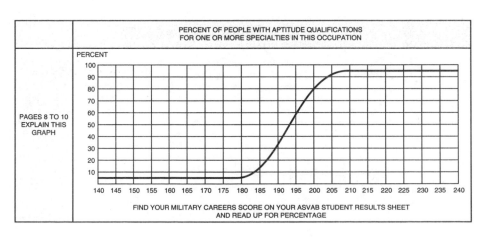

PAGES 8 TO 10 EXPLAIN THIS GRAPH

PERCENT OF PEOPLE WITH APTITUDE QUALIFICATIONS FOR ONE OR MORE SPECIALTIES IN THIS OCCUPATION

PERCENT

FIND YOUR MILITARY CAREERS SCORE ON YOUR ASVAB STUDENT RESULTS SHEET AND READ UP FOR PERCENTAGE

# PLUMBERS AND PIPE FITTERS

Military buildings and equipment require pipe systems for water, steam, gas, and waste. Pipe systems are also needed on aircraft, missiles, and ships for hydraulic (fluid pressure) and pneumatic (air pressure) systems. Plumbers and pipe fitters install and repair plumbing and pipe systems.

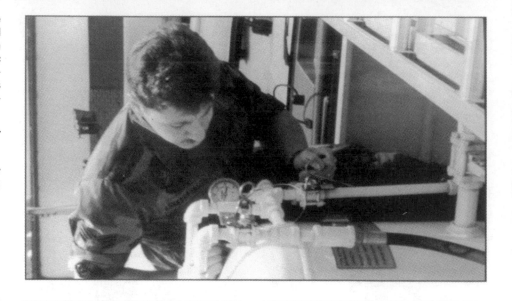

## What They Do

Plumbers and pipe fitters in the military perform some or all of the following duties:

- Plan layouts of pipe systems using blueprints and drawings
- Bend, cut, and thread pipes made of lead, copper, and plastic
- Install connectors, fittings, and joints
- Solder or braze pipe and tubing to join them
- Install sinks, toilets, and other plumbing fixtures
- Troubleshoot, test, and calibrate hydraulic and pneumatic systems
- Keep accurate records of tasks completed and materials used

## Physical Demands

Plumbers and pipe fitters have to lift and carry heavy pipes and tubes.

## Work Environment

Plumbers and pipe fitters work both indoors and outdoors on land and aboard ships.

## Training Provided

Job training consists of 8 to 12 weeks of classroom instruction, including practice in repairing plumbing systems. Course content typically includes:

- Installation, operation, and repair of pipe systems
- Installation and repair of plumbing fixtures and boiler controls
- Installation and repair of water purification and distillation systems
- Maintenance and repair of hydraulic and pneumatic systems
- Methods of soldering, welding, silver brazing, and cutting

The Army, Navy, and Marine Corps offer certified apprenticeship programs for some specialties in this occupation.

## Helpful Attributes

Helpful school subjects include math and shop mechanics. Helpful attributes include:

- Preference for doing physical work
- Ability to work with detailed plans

## Civilian Counterparts

Civilian plumbers and pipe fitters usually work for mechanical or plumbing contractors or as self-employed contractors. Some plumbers and pipe fitters work for public utilities. Civilian plumbers and pipe fitters perform duties similar to those performed in the military.

## Opportunities

The military has about 1,500 plumbers and pipe fitters. On average, the services need about 150 new plumbers and pipe fitters each year. After job training, plumbers and pipe fitters work under close supervision. With experience, they work more independently and may supervise others. Eventually, they may advance to become managers of utilities departments, construction units, or missile maintenance units.

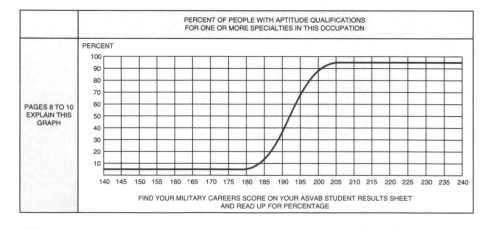

PERCENT OF PEOPLE WITH APTITUDE QUALIFICATIONS
FOR ONE OR MORE SPECIALTIES IN THIS OCCUPATION

PAGES 8 TO 10 EXPLAIN THIS GRAPH

PERCENT

FIND YOUR MILITARY CAREERS SCORE ON YOUR ASVAB STUDENT RESULTS SHEET
AND READ UP FOR PERCENTAGE

# Machine Operator and Precision Work Occupations

- Compressed Gas Technicians
- Dental and Optical Laboratory Technicians
- Machinists
- Power Plant Operators
- Printing Specialists
- Survival Equipment Specialists
- Water and Sewage Treatment Plant Operators
- Welders and Metal Workers

# COMPRESSED GAS TECHNICIANS

Compressed gases have many uses in the military, such as breathing oxygen for jet pilots, divers, and medical patients and fuel for missiles and welding torches. Compressed gas technicians operate and maintain the machinery used to compress or liquefy gases.

## What They Do

Compressed gas technicians in the military perform some or all of the following duties:

- Operate valves to control the flow of air through machinery that compresses or liquefies gases
- Remove impurities, such as carbon dioxide, from gases
- Fill storage cylinders with compressed gas
- Test cylinders for leaks, using pressure gauges
- Operate dry ice plants
- Maintain compressed gas machinery

## Training Provided

Job training consists of 14 to 19 weeks of classroom instruction, including practice working with compressed gases. Course content typically includes:

- Operation and maintenance of systems that produce liquefied and compressed gases
- Storage, distribution, and handling of liquid gas and dry ice
- Procedures for changing and handling compressed gas cylinders
- Safety precautions

The Navy offers a certified apprenticeship program for one specialty in this occupation.

## Physical Demands

Normal color vision is usually required to enter this occupation.

## Helpful Attributes

Helpful school subjects include chemistry and shop mechanics. Helpful attributes include:

- Interest in working with machines
- Preference for doing physical work

## Work Environment

Compressed gas technicians in the military normally work indoors in shops on bases or aboard ships. Working with air compressors may be noisy and hot.

## Civilian Counterparts

Civilian compressed gas technicians work for a wide range of industrial companies and processing plants, especially distilling and chemical firms. They perform duties similar to military compressed gas technicians. They may also be called oxygen plant operators, compressed gas plant workers, or acetylene plant operators.

## Opportunities

The military has about 1,200 compressed gas technicians. On average, the services need about 20 new technicians each year. After job training, compressed gas technicians work under the direction of supervisors. With experience, they work more independently and may eventually manage compressed gas production plants.

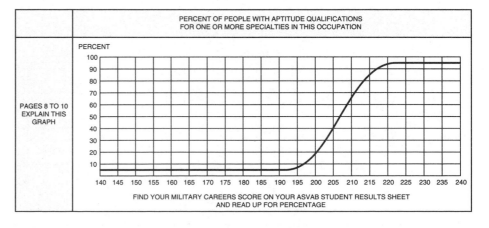

PERCENT OF PEOPLE WITH APTITUDE QUALIFICATIONS
FOR ONE OR MORE SPECIALTIES IN THIS OCCUPATION

PAGES 8 TO 10 EXPLAIN THIS GRAPH

PERCENT

FIND YOUR MILITARY CAREERS SCORE ON YOUR ASVAB STUDENT RESULTS SHEET
AND READ UP FOR PERCENTAGE

# DENTAL AND OPTICAL LABORATORY TECHNICIANS

**Army**
**Navy**
**Air Force**
**Coast Guard**

The military provides dental and optical care as part of its comprehensive health service program. Dental and optical laboratory technicians make and repair dental devices and eyeglasses that are provided for military personnel.

## What They Do

Dental and optical laboratory technicians perform some or all of the following duties:

- Make dentures, braces, and other dental or optical devices

- Construct, assemble, repair, and align dental and optical devices (metal braces and retainers, eyeglass frames and lenses)

- Harden and cure new dentures or lenses using high temperature ovens or other heat-treating equipment

- Grind, polish, and smooth dentures or lenses using hand or power tools

## Training Provided

Job training consists of 21 to 26 weeks of classroom instruction, including practice in making and repairing dental and optical devices. Course content varies depending on specialty, but typically includes laboratory operating procedures (for dental or optical specialty).

Further training occurs on the job and through advanced courses. The Navy offers a certified apprenticeship program for one specialty in this occupation.

## Helpful Attributes

Helpful school subjects include biology, chemistry, and industrial arts. Helpful attributes include:

- Ability to use precision tools and instruments

- Interest in work requiring attention to detail

- Ability to follow detailed instructions and work procedures

- Interest in working with one's hands

## Special Requirements

Successful completion of high school algebra is required to enter some specialties in this occupation.

## Physical Demands

Normal color vision for some specialties is required to match color of artificial teeth with natural tooth color.

## Work Environment

Dental and optical laboratory technicians normally work in dental or optical laboratories and occasionally in examination and dispensing offices.

## Civilian Counterparts

Civilian dental laboratory technicians normally work for small dental laboratories or large dental offices. Optical laboratory technicians work in optical laboratories or for retail opticians. They perform duties similar to military technicians. Civilian optical laboratory technicians may also be called opticians or ophthalmic laboratory technicians.

## Opportunities

The services have about 1,100 dental and optical laboratory technicians. On average, they need about 80 new technicians each year. After job training, technicians work under very close supervision. With experience, they work more independently and perform more challenging tasks. Eventually, they may become supervisors or managers of dental or optical laboratories.

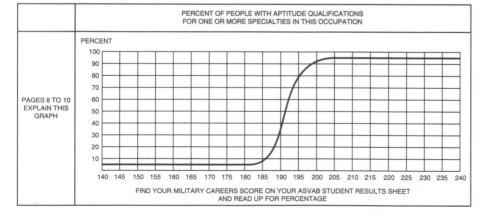

PAGES 8 TO 10 EXPLAIN THIS GRAPH

PERCENT OF PEOPLE WITH APTITUDE QUALIFICATIONS FOR ONE OR MORE SPECIALTIES IN THIS OCCUPATION

PERCENT

FIND YOUR MILITARY CAREERS SCORE ON YOUR ASVAB STUDENT RESULTS SHEET AND READ UP FOR PERCENTAGE

# MACHINISTS

Sometimes when engines or machines break down, the parts needed to repair them are not available. In these cases, the broken parts must be repaired or new ones made. Machinists make and repair metal parts for engines and all types of machines. They operate lathes, drill presses, grinders, and other machine shop equipment. Turn to page 340 for more information about machinists.

## What They Do

Machinists in the military perform some or all of the following duties:

- Study blueprints or written plans of the parts to be made
- Set up and operate lathes to make parts such as shafts and gears
- Cut metal stock using power hacksaws and bandsaws
- Bore holes using drill presses
- Shape and smooth parts using grinders
- Measure work using micrometers, calipers, and depth gauges

## Special Requirements

Although there are women machinists, some specialties in this occupation are open only to men.

## Helpful Attributes

Helpful school subjects include math, general science, metal working, and mechanical drawing. Helpful attributes include:

- Preference for working with the hands
- Interest in making things and finding solutions to mechanical problems
- Ability to apply mathematical formulas

## Work Environment

Machinists work in machine shops, which are often noisy.

## Training Provided

Job training consists of 10 to 12 weeks of classroom instruction, including practice in machine operation. Course content typically includes:

- Machine types and uses
- Machine setup and operation
- Uses of different metals
- Safety procedures

Further training occurs on the job and through advanced courses. The Army and Navy offer certified apprenticeship programs for this occupation.

## Civilian Counterparts

Civilian machinists work for factories and repair shops in many industries, including the electrical product, automotive, and heavy machinery industries. They perform duties similar to military machinists.

## Opportunities

The services have about 1,500 machinists. On average, they need about 150 new machinists each year. After job training, machinists perform routine repairs under close supervision. In time, they perform more difficult repairs and may train others. Eventually, they may become managers of one or more machine shops.

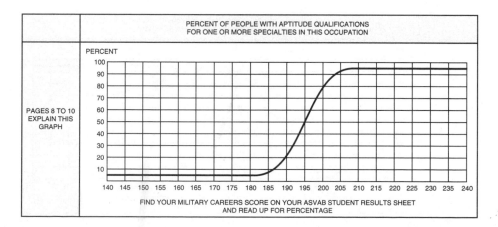

PERCENT OF PEOPLE WITH APTITUDE QUALIFICATIONS
FOR ONE OR MORE SPECIALTIES IN THIS OCCUPATION

PERCENT

PAGES 8 TO 10 EXPLAIN THIS GRAPH

100 90 80 70 60 50 40 30 20 10

140 145 150 155 160 165 170 175 180 185 190 195 200 205 210 215 220 225 230 235 240

FIND YOUR MILITARY CAREERS SCORE ON YOUR ASVAB STUDENT RESULTS SHEET
AND READ UP FOR PERCENTAGE

# POWER PLANT OPERATORS

Power plants generate electricity for ships, submarines, and military bases. The military uses many different types of power plants. Some are fueled by oil, others run on coal. Many ships and submarines have nuclear power plants. Power plant operators control power generating plants on land and aboard ships and submarines. They operate boilers, turbines, nuclear reactors, and portable generators.

## What They Do

Power plant operators in the military perform some or all of the following duties:

- Monitor and operate control boards to regulate power plants

- Operate and maintain diesel generating units to produce electric power

- Monitor and control nuclear reactors that produce electricity and power ships and submarines

- Operate and maintain stationary engines, such as steam engines, air compressors, and generators

- Operate and maintain auxiliary equipment, such as pumps, fans, and condensers

- Inspect equipment for malfunctions

- Operate the steam turbines that generate power for ships

- Operate and maintain auxiliary equipment, including pumps, fans, condensers, and auxiliary boilers

## Special Requirements

Nuclear specialties are open only to men and require successful completion of high school algebra.

## Physical Demands

Power plant operators lift heavy parts or tools when maintaining power plants. They may also have to stoop and kneel and work in awkward positions while repairing.

## Helpful Attributes

Helpful school subjects include math and shop mechanics. Helpful attributes include:

- Interest in working with large machinery

- Interest in nuclear power

## Work Environment

Power plant operators usually work indoors. They are subject to high temperatures, dust, and noise.

## Training Provided

Job training consists of 12 to 25 weeks of classroom instruction, including practice in operating power plants. Course content typically includes:

- Operation of pressure boilers

- Operation and maintenance of reactor control systems

- Operation and maintenance of mechanical systems on nuclear powered ships and submarines

Nuclear specialties have training programs that last 1 year or more, covering all aspects of nuclear power plant operations.

## Civilian Counterparts

Civilian power plant operators work for power companies, factories, schools, and hospitals. They perform duties similar to military power plant operators. Depending on the specialty, power plant operators may also be called boiler operators, stationary engineers, nuclear reactor operators, or diesel plant operators.

## Opportunities

The services have about 11,700 power plant operators. On average, they need about 120 new power plant operators each year. After job training, power plant operators work under the close direction of supervisors. With experience, they may gain greater responsibility for plant operations and supervise other operators. Eventually, they may become superintendents of utilities for large bases or chiefs of ships' engineering departments.

| | PERCENT OF PEOPLE WITH APTITUDE QUALIFICATIONS FOR ONE OR MORE SPECIALTIES IN THIS OCCUPATION |
|---|---|
| PAGES 8 TO 10 EXPLAIN THIS GRAPH | PERCENT — 100, 90, 80, 70, 60, 50, 40, 30, 20, 10 — 140 145 150 155 160 165 170 175 180 185 190 195 200 205 210 215 220 225 230 235 240 — FIND YOUR MILITARY CAREERS SCORE ON YOUR ASVAB STUDENT RESULTS SHEET AND READ UP FOR PERCENTAGE |

# PRINTING SPECIALISTS

The military produces many printed publications each year, including newspapers, booklets, training manuals, maps, and charts. Printing specialists operate printing presses and binding machines to make finished copies of printed material.

## What They Do

Printing specialists in the military perform some or all of the following duties:

- Reproduce printed matter using offset lithographic printing processes

- Prepare photographic negatives and transfer them to printing plates using copy cameras and enlargers

- Prepare layouts of artwork, photographs, and text for lithographic plates

- Produce brochures, newspapers, maps, and charts

- Bind printed material into hardback or paperback books using binding machines

- Maintain printing presses

## Helpful Attributes

Helpful school subjects include shop mechanics and photography. Helpful attributes include:

- Preference for doing physical work

- Interest in learning about printing

## Training Provided

Job training consists of 8 to 20 weeks of classroom instruction, including practice in operating printing presses. Training length varies by specialty. Course content typically includes:

- Photolithography techniques

- Operation of offset presses

- Techniques for making printing plates

- Binding techniques

Further training occurs on the job and through advanced courses. The Army, Navy, and Marine Corps offer certified apprenticeship programs in this occupation.

## Work Environment

Printing specialists work indoors in print shops and offices located on land or aboard ships.

## Civilian Counterparts

Civilian printing specialists work for commercial print shops, newspapers, insurance companies, government offices, or businesses that do their own printing. They perform duties similar to military printing specialists. They may be called offset printing press operators, lithograph press operators, offset duplicating machine operators, lithograph photographers, or bindery workers.

## Physical Demands

Normal color vision is required to enter some specialties in this occupation.

## Opportunities

The military has about 800 printing specialists. On average, the services need about 70 new specialists each year. After job training, specialists normally operate printing and binding machines under direct supervision. With experience, they work more independently, setting up and operating machines. In time, printing specialists may become supervisors of printing plants.

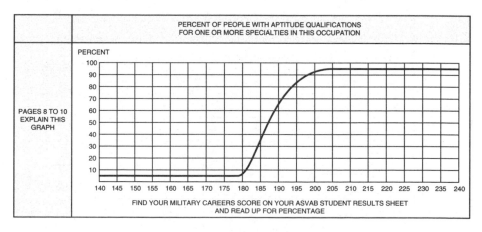

PERCENT OF PEOPLE WITH APTITUDE QUALIFICATIONS FOR ONE OR MORE SPECIALTIES IN THIS OCCUPATION

PAGES 8 TO 10 EXPLAIN THIS GRAPH

PERCENT

FIND YOUR MILITARY CAREERS SCORE ON YOUR ASVAB STUDENT RESULTS SHEET AND READ UP FOR PERCENTAGE

# SURVIVAL EQUIPMENT SPECIALISTS

Army
Navy
Air Force
Marine Corps
Coast Guard

Military personnel often have hazardous assignments. They depend on survival equipment (parachutes, rescue equipment) to protect their lives in case of emergencies. Survival equipment specialists inspect, maintain, and repair survival equipment such as parachutes, aircraft life support equipment, and air-sea rescue equipment.

## What They Do

Survival equipment specialists in the military perform some or all of the following duties:

- Inspect parachutes for rips and tangled lines
- Pack parachutes for safe operation
- Repair life rafts and load them with emergency provisions
- Test emergency oxygen regulators on aircraft
- Stock aircraft with fire extinguishers, flares, and survival provisions
- Train crews in the use of survival equipment
- Repair tents, tarps, and other canvas equipment

## Work Environment

Survival equipment specialists in the military work in repair shops on land or aboard ships.

## Physical Demands

Normal color vision is required to work with color-coded wiring and repair charts.

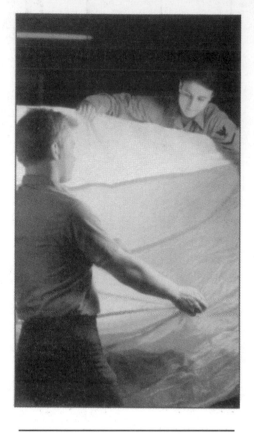

## Helpful Attributes

Helpful school subjects include shop mechanics and science. Helpful attributes include:

- Interest in working for the safety of others
- Ability to do work requiring accuracy and attention to detail

## Training Provided

Job training consists of 6 to 12 weeks of classroom instruction, including practice in working with survival equipment. Course content typically includes:

- Parachute rigging techniques
- Repair of inflatable rafts and other survival equipment
- Maintenance of oxygen equipment
- Maintenance of air-sea rescue equipment

Further training occurs on the job and through additional courses.

## Civilian Counterparts

Civilian survival equipment specialists work for commercial airlines, parachute rigging and supply companies, survival equipment manufacturing firms, and some government agencies. They perform duties similar to military survival equipment specialists. Those that specialize in parachutes are called parachute riggers.

## Opportunities

The military has about 3,050 survival equipment specialists. On average, the services need about 350 new specialists each year. After job training, survival equipment specialists work on survival equipment under the close direction of supervisors. With experience, they work with less supervision and perform more challenging tasks. In time, survival equipment specialists may become supervisors assisting in the management of survival equipment repair facilities.

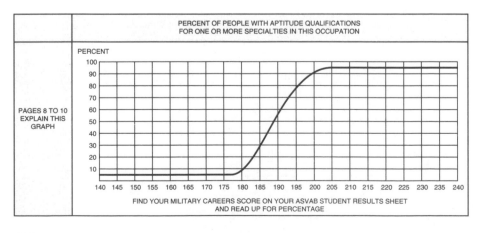

PERCENT OF PEOPLE WITH APTITUDE QUALIFICATIONS FOR ONE OR MORE SPECIALTIES IN THIS OCCUPATION

PAGES 8 TO 10 EXPLAIN THIS GRAPH

PERCENT

FIND YOUR MILITARY CAREERS SCORE ON YOUR ASVAB STUDENT RESULTS SHEET AND READ UP FOR PERCENTAGE

# WATER AND SEWAGE TREATMENT PLANT OPERATORS

**Army
Navy
Air Force
Marine Corps
Coast Guard**

Military bases operate their own water treatment plants when public facilities cannot be used. These plants provide drinking water and safely dispose of sewage. Water and sewage treatment plant operators maintain the systems that purify water and treat sewage.

## What They Do

Water and sewage treatment plant operators in the military perform some or all of the following duties:

- Operate pumps to transfer water from reservoirs and storage tanks to treatment plants

- Add chemicals and operate machinery that purifies water for drinking or cleans it for safe disposal

- Test water for chlorine content, acidity, oxygen demand, and impurities

- Regulate the flow of drinking water to meet demand

- Clean and maintain water treatment machinery

- Keep records of chemical treatments, water pressure, and maintenance

## Helpful Attributes

Helpful school subjects include chemistry, math, and shop mechanics. Helpful attributes include:

- Interest in working with mechanical equipment

- Interest in chemistry and pollution control

## Work Environment

Water and sewage treatment plant operators work indoors and outdoors. They may be exposed to strong odors.

## Physical Demands

Normal color vision is needed to examine water for acidity and impurities.

## Training Provided

Job training consists of 8 to 10 weeks of classroom instruction, including practice operating water and sewage treatment equipment. Course content typically includes:

- Operation of treatment systems

- Water testing and analysis

- Maintenance and repair of pumps, compressors, and other equipment

Further training occurs on the job and through advanced courses. The Army and the Navy offer certified apprenticeship programs for some specialties in this occupation.

## Civilian Counterparts

Civilian water and sewage treatment plant operators work for municipal public works and industrial plants. Their work is similar to military water and sewage treatment plant operators. Civilian plant operators usually specialize as water treatment plant operators, waterworks pump station operators, or wastewater treatment plant operators.

## Opportunities

The services have about 2,000 water and sewage plant operators. On average, they need 200 new plant operators each year. After job training, new operators work under close supervision in water or sewage treatment plants. With experience, they may supervise plant operations. Eventually, they may become base utilities superintendents.

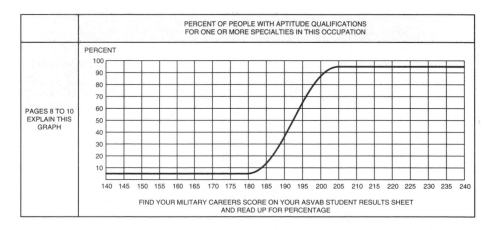

PERCENT OF PEOPLE WITH APTITUDE QUALIFICATIONS FOR ONE OR MORE SPECIALTIES IN THIS OCCUPATION

PAGES 8 TO 10 EXPLAIN THIS GRAPH

FIND YOUR MILITARY CAREERS SCORE ON YOUR ASVAB STUDENT RESULTS SHEET AND READ UP FOR PERCENTAGE

# WELDERS AND METAL WORKERS

**Army**
**Navy**
**Air Force**
**Marine Corps**
**Coast Guard**

Sheet metal is used as a building material in many military construction projects. Ships, tanks, and aircraft are made of heavy metal armor. Welders and metal workers make and install sheet metal products, such as roofs, air ducts, gutters, and vents. They also make custom parts to repair the structural parts of ships, submarines, landing craft, buildings, and equipment.

## What They Do

Welders and metal workers in the military perform some or all of the following duties:

- Weld, braze, or solder metal parts together
- Repair automotive and ship parts using welding equipment
- Measure work with calipers, micrometers, and rulers

## Physical Demands

Welders and metal workers may have to lift heavy metal parts and work in crouching or kneeling positions. Good color vision is required for locating and marking reference points, setting and adjusting welding equipment, and matching paints.

## Helpful Attributes

Helpful school subjects include auto mechanics and industrial arts. Helpful attributes include:

- Preference for physical work
- Interest in working with repair tools

## Work Environment

Welders and metal workers work indoors in metalworking shops and aircraft hangars. They also work outdoors at construction sites, on ships, and in the field.

## Civilian Counterparts

Civilian welders and metal workers may work for metal repair shops, auto repair shops, construction companies, pipeline companies, aircraft manufacturing plants, shipyards, and marine servicing companies. They perform duties similar to military welders and metal workers.

## Training Provided

Job training consists of 4 to 15 weeks of classroom instruction. Training length varies depending on specialty. Course content typically includes:

- Sheet metal layout and duct work
- Procedures for cutting, brazing, and heat treating
- Operation and care of welding, soldering, and brazing equipment

Further training occurs on the job and through advanced courses. The Army, Navy, and Marine Corps offer certified apprenticeship programs for some specialties in this occupation.

## Opportunities

The services have about 6,100 welders and metal workers. On average, they need about 340 new welders and metal workers each year. After job training, welders and metal workers begin to make and repair metal equipment under the direction of a supervisor. With experience, they may become managers of repair shops, maintenance depots, or shipyards.

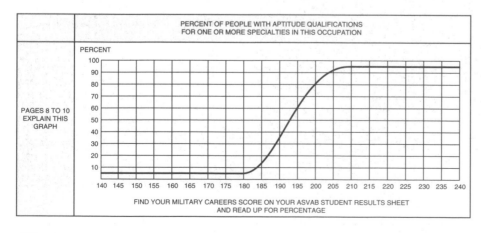

PERCENT OF PEOPLE WITH APTITUDE QUALIFICATIONS
FOR ONE OR MORE SPECIALTIES IN THIS OCCUPATION

PERCENT

PAGES 8 TO 10 EXPLAIN THIS GRAPH

FIND YOUR MILITARY CAREERS SCORE ON YOUR ASVAB STUDENT RESULTS SHEET
AND READ UP FOR PERCENTAGE

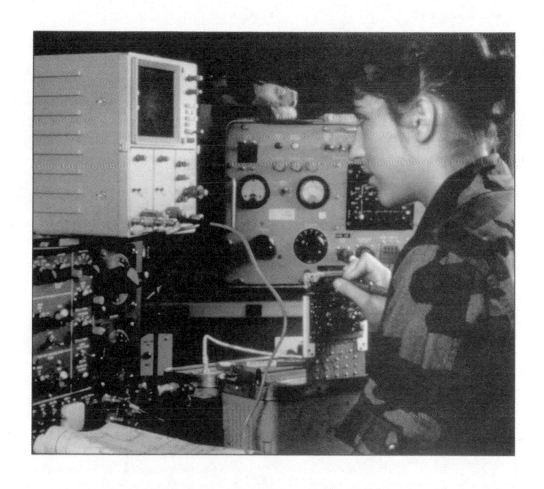

# Transportation and Material Handling Occupations

- Air Crew Members
- Aircraft Launch and Recovery Specialists
- Cargo Specialists
- Flight Engineers
- Petroleum Supply Specialists
- Quartermasters and Boat Operators
- Seamen
- Vehicle Drivers

# AIR CREW MEMBERS

The military uses aircraft of all types and sizes to conduct combat and intelligence missions, rescue personnel, transport troops and equipment, and perform long-range bombing missions. Air crew members operate equipment on board aircraft during operations. They normally specialize by type of aircraft, such as bomber, intelligence, transport, or search and rescue. Turn to page 318 for more information about air crew members.

## What They Do

Air crew members in the military perform some or all of the following duties:

- Operate aircraft communication and radar equipment
- Operate and maintain aircraft defensive gunnery systems
- Operate helicopter hoists to lift equipment and personnel from land and sea
- Operate and maintain aircraft in-flight refueling systems

## Training Provided

Job training consists of 7 to 9 weeks of classroom instruction, including practical experience in aircraft systems operation and maintenance. Course content varies by specialty and may include:

- Operation of aircraft gunnery systems
- Operation of aircraft in-flight refueling systems
- Cargo, munitions, and fuel load planning
- Rescue and recovery operations

Further training occurs on the job through actual flying time. There are additional courses covering air crew survival, scuba diving, parachuting, aircraft maneuvering, and combat crew training. The Army, Navy, and Marine Corps offer certified apprenticeship programs for one specialty in this occupation.

## Special Requirements

Although there are women air crew members, some specialties in this occupation are open only to men.

## Helpful Attributes

Helpful school subjects include mathematics and mechanics. Helpful attributes include:

- Interest in flying
- Ability to work under stress
- Ability to work as a team member

## Work Environment

Air crew members work inside all sizes and types of aircraft based on land or aboard ships. They fly in all types of weather and in both hot and cold climates.

## Physical Demands

Air crew members must be in excellent physical condition and pass a special physical exam in order to qualify for flight duty. They must be mentally sound and have normal hearing.

## Civilian Counterparts

There are no direct civilian equivalents to military air crew members. However, some of the skills gained in the military could be useful in civilian government and private agencies that provide emergency medical services. Also, weight and load computation skills are useful for civilian air transport operations.

## Opportunities

The services have about 6,700 air crew members. On average, they need about 700 new air crew members each year. After receiving their "air crew qualified" rating, air crew members are assigned to a flying unit. They may work on one of many types of aircraft under direction of the aircraft commander. With experience, they may supervise and train other enlisted air crew members. They have the opportunity to become air crew chiefs, combat crew chiefs, or supervisors of rescue and recovery units.

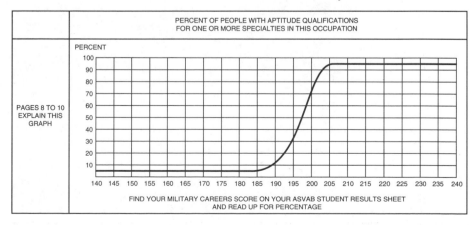

PERCENT OF PEOPLE WITH APTITUDE QUALIFICATIONS FOR ONE OR MORE SPECIALTIES IN THIS OCCUPATION

PAGES 8 TO 10 EXPLAIN THIS GRAPH

FIND YOUR MILITARY CAREERS SCORE ON YOUR ASVAB STUDENT RESULTS SHEET AND READ UP FOR PERCENTAGE

# AIRCRAFT LAUNCH AND RECOVERY SPECIALISTS

**Navy
Marine Corps
Coast Guard**

The military operates thousands of aircraft that take off and land on aircraft carriers all over the world. The successful launch and recovery of aircraft is important to the completion of air missions and the safety of flight crews. Aircraft launch and recovery specialists operate and maintain catapults, arresting gear, and other equipment used in aircraft carrier takeoff and landing operations. Turn to page 322 for more information about aircraft launch and recovery specialists.

## What They Do

Aircraft launch and recovery specialists in the military perform some or all of the following duties:

- Operate consoles to control launch and recovery equipment, including catapults and arresting gear
- Operate elevators to transfer aircraft between flight and storage decks
- Install and maintain visual landing aids
- Test and adjust launch and recovery equipment using electric and mechanical test equipment and hand tools
- Install airfield crash barriers and barricades
- Direct aircraft launch and recovery operations using hand or light signals
- Maintain logs of airplane launches, recoveries, and equipment maintenance

## Special Requirements

This occupation is open only to men.

## Helpful Attributes

Helpful school subjects include shop mechanics. Helpful attributes include:

- Interest in working on hydraulic and mechanical equipment
- Ability to use hand tools and test equipment
- Interest in aircraft flight operations

## Training Provided

Job training consists of 9 to 13 weeks of classroom instruction, including practice in maintaining launch and recovery equipment. Course content typically includes:

- Operating launch and recovery equipment
- Installing crash barriers and barricades
- Maintaining launch and recovery equipment
- Handling aircraft

## Physical Demands

Normal color vision is required to work with color-coded parts and the wiring of launch and recovery equipment.

## Work Environment

Aircraft launch and recovery specialists work outdoors aboard ships while operating and maintaining launch and recovery equipment or holding visual landing aids for incoming aircraft. They are exposed to noise and fumes from jet and helicopter engines.

## Civilian Counterparts

There are no direct civilian counterparts to military aircraft launch and recovery specialists. However, many of the skills learned are relevant to jobs performed by ground crews at civilian airports.

## Opportunities

The services have about 1,400 aircraft launch and recovery specialists. On average, they need about 50 new specialists each year. After job training, specialists are assigned to an aircraft launch and recovery section aboard an aircraft carrier or at an airfield. Initially, they perform maintenance and repair on equipment, working under close supervision. With experience, they perform more complex operation and maintenance activities. In time, they may train and supervise other aircraft launch and recovery specialists. Eventually, they may supervise activities on carrier flight and storage decks.

PAGES 8 TO 10 EXPLAIN THIS GRAPH

PERCENT OF PEOPLE WITH APTITUDE QUALIFICATIONS
FOR ONE OR MORE SPECIALTIES IN THIS OCCUPATION

PERCENT

100
90
80
70
60
50
40
30
20
10

140 145 150 155 160 165 170 175 180 185 190 195 200 205 210 215 220 225 230 235 240

FIND YOUR MILITARY CAREERS SCORE ON YOUR ASVAB STUDENT RESULTS SHEET
AND READ UP FOR PERCENTAGE

# CARGO SPECIALISTS

The military delivers supplies, weapons, equipment, and mail to United States forces in many parts of the world. Military cargo travels by ship, truck, or airplane. It must be handled carefully to ensure safe arrival at the correct destination. Cargo specialists load and unload military supplies and material using equipment such as forklifts and cranes. They also plan and organize loading schedules.

## What They Do

Cargo specialists in the military perform some or all of the following duties:

- Load supplies into trucks, transport planes, and railroad cars using forklifts
- Load equipment such as jeeps, trucks, and weapons aboard ships, using dockyard cranes
- Pack and crate boxes of supplies for shipping
- Inspect cargo for damage
- Plan and inspect loads for balance and safety
- Check cargo against invoices to make sure the amount and destination of material are correct

## Physical Demands

Cargo specialists must lift and carry heavy cargo.

## Training Provided

Job training consists of 2 to 6 weeks of classroom instruction, including practice in loading cargo. Course content typically includes:

- Operation and care of forklifts, power winches, and cranes
- Techniques for loading and storing cargo
- Techniques for planning and scheduling cargo shipments
- Safety procedures for handling potentially dangerous cargo

Further training occurs on the job.

## Helpful Attributes

Helpful school subjects include general office and business mathematics. Helpful attributes include:

- Interest in working with forklifts and cranes
- Preference for physical work

## Civilian Counterparts

Civilian cargo specialists work for trucking firms, air cargo companies, and shipping lines. They perform duties similar to military cargo specialists. Depending on specialty, they may also be called industrial truck operators, stevedores, longshoremen, material handlers, or cargo checkers.

## Work Environment

Cargo specialists work outdoors on loading docks and indoors in warehouses.

## Opportunities

The services have about 2,500 cargo specialists. On average, they need about 300 new cargo specialists each year. After job training, cargo specialists work in teams preparing and loading cargo for shipment under the direction of supervisors. In time, they may advance to become team leaders or supervisors of other cargo specialists. Eventually, they may become warehouse managers.

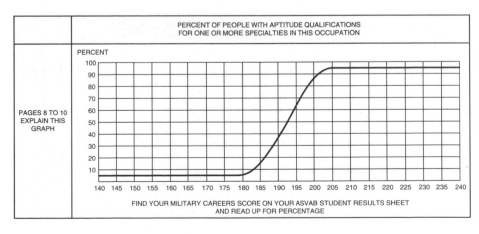

PERCENT OF PEOPLE WITH APTITUDE QUALIFICATIONS FOR ONE OR MORE SPECIALTIES IN THIS OCCUPATION

PAGES 8 TO 10 EXPLAIN THIS GRAPH

PERCENT

FIND YOUR MILITARY CAREERS SCORE ON YOUR ASVAB STUDENT RESULTS SHEET AND READ UP FOR PERCENTAGE

# FLIGHT ENGINEERS

The military operates thousands of airplanes and helicopters. Pilots and air crew members rely upon trained personnel to keep aircraft ready to fly. Flight engineers inspect airplanes and helicopters before, during, and after flights to ensure safe and efficient operations. They also serve as crew members aboard military aircraft.

## What They Do

Flight engineers in the military perform some or all of the following duties:

- Inspect aircraft before and after flights, following pre- and post-flight checklists
- Plan and monitor the loading of passengers, cargo, and fuel
- Assist pilots in engine start-up and shut-down
- Compute aircraft load weights and fuel distribution
- Compute fuel consumption using airspeed data, charts, and calculators
- Monitor engine instruments and adjust engine controls following pilot orders
- Check fuel, pressure, electrical, and other aircraft systems during flight
- Inform pilot of aircraft performance problems and recommend corrective action

## Physical Demands

Flight engineers, like pilots and navigators, have to be mentally alert and physically sound to perform their job. They must be in top physical shape and pass a special physical exam to qualify for flight duty.

## Special Requirements

Although there are women flight engineers in the military, some specialties in this occupation are open only to men.

## Work Environment

Flight engineers live and work on air bases or aboard ships in all areas of the world. They fly in hot and cold climates and in all types of weather.

## Helpful Attributes

Helpful school subjects include general mathematics and shop mechanics. Helpful attributes include:

- Skill in using wiring diagrams and maintenance manuals
- Interest in working with mechanical systems and equipment
- Strong desire to fly
- Ability to work as a member of a team

## Training Provided

Job training consists of 17 to 24 weeks of classroom instruction and practical experience in aircraft inspection. Course content typically includes:

- Operation of electronic, pressure, and fuel systems
- Inspection of aircraft engines, structures, and systems
- Operation of aircraft engine instrument controls
- Preparation of aircraft performance records and logs

Further training occurs on the job during flight operations.

## Civilian Counterparts

Civilian flight engineers work for passenger and cargo airline companies. They perform the same duties as in the military.

## Opportunities

The services have about 1,900 flight engineers. On average, they need about 10 new flight engineers each year. After receiving their "air crew qualified" rating, they are assigned to an airplane or helicopter flying unit. With experience, they work more independently and may supervise or train others. They have the opportunity to become flight engineer chiefs or air crew chiefs.

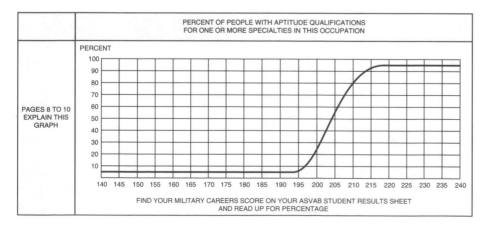

PAGES 8 TO 10 EXPLAIN THIS GRAPH

PERCENT OF PEOPLE WITH APTITUDE QUALIFICATIONS FOR ONE OR MORE SPECIALTIES IN THIS OCCUPATION

PERCENT

FIND YOUR MILITARY CAREERS SCORE ON YOUR ASVAB STUDENT RESULTS SHEET AND READ UP FOR PERCENTAGE

# PETROLEUM SUPPLY SPECIALISTS

Army
Navy
Air Force
Marine Corps
Coast Guard

Ships, airplanes, trucks, tanks, and other military vehicles require large amounts of fuel and lubricants. These and other petroleum products require special storage and handling. Petroleum supply specialists store and ship petroleum products, such as oil, fuel, compressed gas, and lubricants.

## What They Do

Petroleum supply specialists in the military perform some or all of the following duties:

- Connect hoses and valves and operate pumps to load petroleum products into tanker trucks, airplanes, ships, and railroad cars
- Test oils and fuels for pollutants
- Repair pipeline systems, hoses, valves, and pumps
- Check the volume and temperature of petroleum and gases in tankers, barges, and storage tanks
- Prepare storage and shipping records
- Store and move packaged petroleum products using forklifts

## Physical Demands

Petroleum supply specialists may have to perform moderate to heavy lifting.

## Work Environment

Petroleum supply specialists work outdoors in all types of weather while filling storage tanks and refueling airplanes, ships, and tankers.

## Helpful Attributes

Helpful school subjects include shop mechanics and business math. Helpful attributes include:

- Interest in working with machines and equipment
- Ability to follow spoken instructions
- Preference for physical work

## Training Provided

Job training consists of 4 to 8 weeks of classroom instruction, including practice in using petroleum pumping equipment. Course content typically includes:

- Testing oil and fuels
- Operating airplane refueling systems and equipment
- Operating pumps, pipelines, and tanker equipment
- Planning and scheduling petroleum transport
- Safety regulations and procedures for handling dangerous materials

Further training occurs on the job and through advanced courses. The Army, Navy, and Marine Corps offer certified apprenticeship programs for one specialty in this occupation.

## Civilian Counterparts

Civilian petroleum supply specialists work for oil refineries, pipeline companies, and tanker truck and ship lines. They may also refuel airplanes at large airports. They perform many of the same duties as military petroleum supply specialists.

## Opportunities

The services have about 10,000 petroleum supply specialists. On average, they need about 1,200 new specialists each year. After training, specialists work in teams while performing oil and fuel pumping operations. Each team works under the direction of a supervisor. With experience, petroleum supply specialists may become team leaders, pipeline or pump station supervisors, or petroleum storage supervisors.

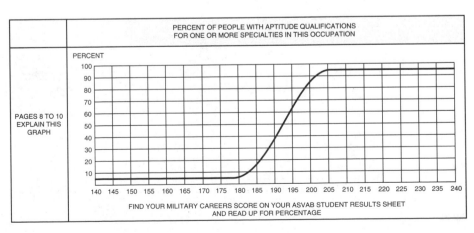

PAGES 8 TO 10 EXPLAIN THIS GRAPH

PERCENT OF PEOPLE WITH APTITUDE QUALIFICATIONS FOR ONE OR MORE SPECIALTIES IN THIS OCCUPATION

PERCENT

FIND YOUR MILITARY CAREERS SCORE ON YOUR ASVAB STUDENT RESULTS SHEET AND READ UP FOR PERCENTAGE

# QUARTERMASTERS AND BOAT OPERATORS

Army
Navy
Marine Corps
Coast Guard

The military operates many small boats for amphibious troop landings, harbor patrols, and transportation over short distances. Quartermasters and boat operators navigate and pilot many types of small watercraft, including tugboats, PT boats, gunboats, and barges.

## What They Do

Quartermasters and boat operators in the military perform some or all of the following duties:

- Direct the course and speed of boats
- Consult maps, charts, weather reports, and navigation equipment
- Pilot tugboats when towing and docking barges and large ships
- Operate amphibious craft during troop landings
- Maintain boats and deck equipment
- Operate ship-to-shore radios
- Keep ship logs

## Training Provided

Job training consists of 6 to 22 weeks of classroom instruction including practice in boat operations. Course content typically includes:

- Boat handling procedures
- Log and message-handling procedures
- Use of compasses, radar, charts, and other navigational aids
- Navigational mathematics

## Physical Demands

Quartermasters and boat operators may have to stand for several hours at a time. They must be able to speak clearly. Some specialties require normal depth perception and hearing.

## Helpful Attributes

Helpful school subjects include mathematics. Helpful attributes include:

- Ability to work with mathematical formulas
- Interest in sailing and navigation
- Ability to follow detailed instructions and read maps

## Work Environment

Quartermasters and boat operators work aboard all types of boats and in all types of weather conditions. When not piloting boats, they may work on or below deck repairing boats and equipment or overseeing cargo storage. When ashore, they may work in offices that make nautical maps or in harbor management offices. Some boats are operated in combat situations.

## Civilian Counterparts

Civilian quartermasters and boat operators may work for shipping and cruise lines, piloting tugboats, ferries, and other small vessels. They perform duties similar to military quartermasters and boat operators. Depending upon specialty, they may also be called tugboat captains, motorboat operators, navigators, or pilots.

## Opportunities

The services have about 4,000 quartermasters. On average, they need about 100 new quartermasters and boat operators each year. After job training, new quartermasters and boat operators assist more experienced enlisted operators in maintaining logs, handling passengers, operating navigational equipment, and keeping charts. After gaining experience, they perform more difficult tasks, such as operating navigational equipment and calculating ship position. In time, they pilot boats and help train new quartermasters and boat operators.

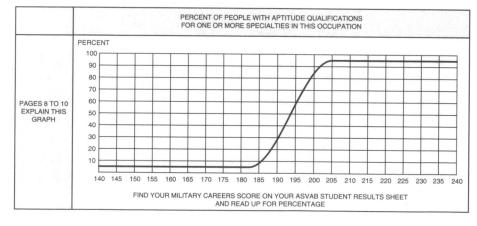

PERCENT OF PEOPLE WITH APTITUDE QUALIFICATIONS
FOR ONE OR MORE SPECIALTIES IN THIS OCCUPATION

PAGES 8 TO 10
EXPLAIN THIS
GRAPH

PERCENT

FIND YOUR MILITARY CAREERS SCORE ON YOUR ASVAB STUDENT RESULTS SHEET
AND READ UP FOR PERCENTAGE

# SEAMEN

All ships must have teams of individuals with "jack-of-all-trades" skills who make things run smoothly above deck. Seamen perform many duties to help operate and maintain military ships, boats, and submarines.

## What They Do

Seamen in the military perform some or all of the following duties:

- Operate hoists, cranes, and winches to load cargo or set gangplanks
- Operate and maintain on-deck equipment and ship rigging
- Supervise firefighting and damage control exercises
- Handle lines to secure vessels to wharves or other ships
- Stand watch for security, navigation, or communications
- Supervise crews painting and maintaining decks and sides of ships

## Physical Demands

Seamen may have to climb ships' rigging and perform work at heights. Their work often involves moderate to heavy lifting.

## Work Environment

Seamen and deckhands work aboard all types of ships and submarines. On ships, they often work outdoors on deck while servicing shipboard equipment.

## Helpful Attributes

Helpful school subjects include mathematics and shop mechanics. Helpful attributes include:

- Ability to work closely with others
- Interest in sailing and being at sea
- Preference for physical work

## Training Provided

Although classroom training of 6 to 12 weeks is provided to seamen, most training occurs on the job. Training programs vary depending on service and specialty.

## Civilian Counterparts

Civilian seamen work primarily for shipping companies, sometimes called the Merchant Marine. They also work for cruise ship lines. They perform many duties similar to military seamen. They are called able seamen, deckhands, or boatswains.

## Opportunities

The services have about 14,000 seamen. On average, the services need about 6,000 new seamen each year. New seamen work together on teams led by experienced supervisors. Through practice, they learn the many tasks they must perform. In time, seamen supervise one or more teams. Eventually, they may become managers responsible for planning and directing the work of many seamen. Often, seamen receive additional training that prepares them for other occupations in their service.

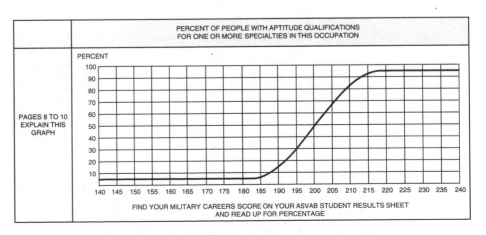

PAGES 8 TO 10 EXPLAIN THIS GRAPH

PERCENT OF PEOPLE WITH APTITUDE QUALIFICATIONS FOR ONE OR MORE SPECIALTIES IN THIS OCCUPATION

FIND YOUR MILITARY CAREERS SCORE ON YOUR ASVAB STUDENT RESULTS SHEET AND READ UP FOR PERCENTAGE

# VEHICLE DRIVERS

The military uses numerous vehicles to transport its troops, equipment, and supplies. Together, the services own and operate about 50,000 heavy trucks and buses. Vehicle drivers operate all types of heavy military vehicles. They drive fuel or water tank trucks, semi-tractor trailers, heavy troop transports, and passenger buses.

## What They Do

Vehicle drivers in the military perform some or all of the following duties:

- Read travel instructions to determine travel routes, arrival dates, and types of cargo
- Make sure vehicles are loaded properly
- Check oil, fuel and other fluid levels, and tire pressure
- Drive vehicles over all types of roads, traveling alone or in convoys
- Keep records of mileage driven and fuel and oil used
- Wash vehicles and perform routine maintenance and repairs

## Helpful Attributes

Helpful school courses include driver education. Helpful attributes include:

- Interest in driving
- Interest in mechanics

## Work Environment

Vehicle driving involves long periods of sitting. Drivers sometimes must change heavy tires.

## Training Provided

Job training consists of 7 to 8 weeks of classroom instruction, including practice in driving heavy military vehicles. Course content typically includes:

- Accident prevention
- Safety check procedures
- International road signs
- Basic vehicle maintenance

The Army and the Marine Corps offer certified apprenticeship programs for one specialty in this occupation.

## Physical Demands

Normal color vision is required to read road maps.

## Civilian Counterparts

Civilian vehicle drivers work for trucking companies, moving companies, bus companies, and businesses with their own delivery fleets. They perform duties similar to military vehicle drivers. They may specialize as tractor-trailer truck drivers, tank truck drivers, heavy truck drivers, or bus drivers.

## Opportunities

The services have about 17,400 vehicle drivers. On average, they need about 2,000 new vehicle drivers each year. After job training, vehicle drivers are assigned to motor pools or motor transport units. They generally work without close supervision. In time, vehicle drivers may advance to supervisory positions assisting in the management of motor transport units.

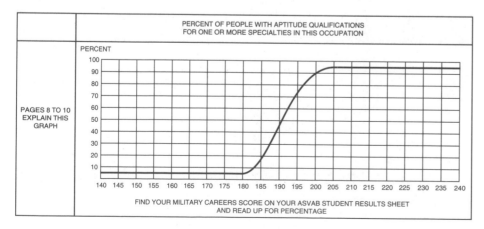

PERCENT OF PEOPLE WITH APTITUDE QUALIFICATIONS
FOR ONE OR MORE SPECIALTIES IN THIS OCCUPATION

PAGES 8 TO 10 EXPLAIN THIS GRAPH

PERCENT

FIND YOUR MILITARY CAREERS SCORE ON YOUR ASVAB STUDENT RESULTS SHEET
AND READ UP FOR PERCENTAGE

# Combat Specialty Occupations

- **Artillery Crew Members**
- **Combat Engineers**
- **Infantrymen**
- **Special Operations Forces**
- **Tank Crew Members**

# ARTILLERY CREW MEMBERS

Artillery includes weapons that fire large shells or missiles. The military uses artillery to support infantry and tank units in combat. Artillery is also used to protect land and sea forces from air attack. Artillery crew members position, direct, and fire artillery guns, cannons, howitzers, missiles, and rockets to destroy enemy positions and aircraft. They normally specialize by type of artillery.

## What They Do

Artillery crew members in the military perform some or all of the following duties:

- Determine target location using computers or manual calculations
- Set up and load artillery weapons
- Prepare ammunition, fuses, and powder for firing
- Fire artillery weapons according to instructions from artillery officers
- Clean and maintain artillery weapons
- Drive trucks and self-propelled artillery

## Physical Demands

Artillery crew members must have physical stamina to perform strenuous activities for long periods without rest. They are also required to have normal color vision to identify color-coded ammunition and to read maps and charts.

## Work Environment

Artillery crew members work outdoors when on land maneuvers. Some work in sheltered fire control stations. At sea, they mainly work below deck.

## Helpful Attributes

Helpful attributes include:

- Ability to think and remain calm under stress
- Ability to work as a member of a team
- Interest in cannon and rocket operations
- Ability to perform a wide variety of duties

## Civilian Counterparts

Although the job of artillery crew member has no equivalent in civilian life, the close teamwork, discipline, and leadership experiences it provides are helpful in many civilian jobs.

## Special Requirements

This occupation is open only to men.

## Training Provided

Job training consists of 10 to 14 weeks of classroom instruction and field training under simulated combat conditions. Course content typically includes:

- Methods of computing target locations
- Ammunition-handling techniques
- Gun, missile, and rocket system operations
- Artillery tactics

Further training occurs on the job and through advanced courses. The Army, Navy, and Marine Corps offer certified apprenticeship programs for one specialty in this occupation.

## Opportunities

The services have about 49,000 artillery crew members. On average, they need about 6,200 new crew members each year. After job training, new crew members work as part of an artillery team. Leadership ability and job performance are the most important factors for advancement in the artillery field. Those with leadership potential may assume supervisory positions. In time, they may lead gun crews or supervise firing batteries consisting of several large guns or missiles.

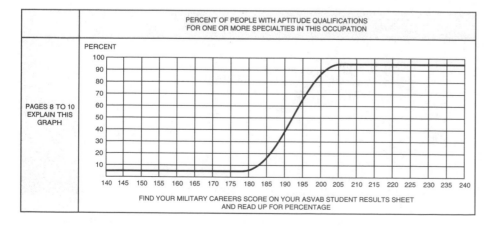

PERCENT OF PEOPLE WITH APTITUDE QUALIFICATIONS FOR ONE OR MORE SPECIALTIES IN THIS OCCUPATION

PAGES 8 TO 10 EXPLAIN THIS GRAPH

PERCENT

FIND YOUR MILITARY CAREERS SCORE ON YOUR ASVAB STUDENT RESULTS SHEET AND READ UP FOR PERCENTAGE

Combat situations often require rapid travel across difficult terrain and swift-flowing rivers. A combination of combat ability and building skill is necessary to do field construction for fighting forces.

## What They Do

Combat engineers perform some or all of the following duties:

- Construct trails, roads, and field fortifications, such as shelters, bunkers, and gun emplacements
- Erect floating or prefabricated bridges
- Lay and clear mine fields and booby traps
- Place and detonate explosives, as needed
- Erect camouflage and other protective barriers for artillery and troop positions
- Load, unload, and move supplies and equipment, using planes, helicopters, trucks, and amphibious vehicles
- Construct airfields and perform ground traffic control duties
- Participate in combat operations as infantrymen

## Physical Demands

Combat engineers must meet very demanding physical requirements. They need agility and balance and must be able to perform strenuous physical activities over long periods of time. Combat engineers lift and move heavy objects. Some specialties require good swimming abilities.

## Special Qualifications

This occupation is open only to men.

## Work Environment

Because combat engineers must be prepared to support operations anywhere in the world, they work and train for long hours under all kinds of weather conditions and in all climates. Combat engineers work, eat, and sleep outdoors during training exercises and in real combat situations. Most of the time, combat engineers are assigned to military bases.

## Helpful Attributes

Helpful school subjects include mathematics, general science, and industrial arts. Helpful attributes include:

- Ability to use hand and power tools
- Ability to think and remain calm under stress
- Preference for working outdoors

## Training Provided

Job training for combat engineers is mainly provided on the job. On-the-job training consists of manual work in a variety of construction projects covering the following:

- Basic construction methods
- Bridge building
- Road maintenance and repair
- Rough carpentry and rigging
- Use of hand and power tools

The Marine Corps offers a 6-week course in basic combat engineering skills. Combat training in infantry skills is also provided to combat engineers.

## Civilian Counterparts

Although the job of combat engineer has no direct equivalent in civilian life, experience as a combat engineer is related to occupations in several civilian fields. These include the logging, mining, construction, shipping, and landscaping industries. Civilians in these jobs are called forestry aides, loggers, blasters, and construction workers.

## Opportunities

The military has about 11,700 combat engineers. On average, the services need about 1,600 new combat engineers each year. After basic training, combat engineers are assigned to jobs requiring the application of basic skills and use of common construction tools. After gaining knowledge and improving skills, they may be selected for additional training in various construction specialties, such as road and bridge building. Eventually, they may supervise others and assist in managing engineering units.

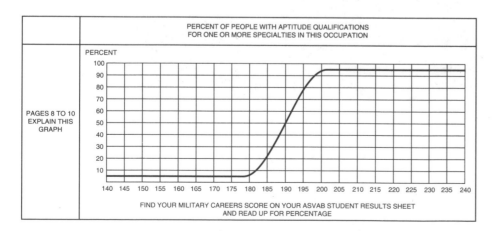

PERCENT OF PEOPLE WITH APTITUDE QUALIFICATIONS
FOR ONE OR MORE SPECIALTIES IN THIS OCCUPATION

PAGES 8 TO 10 EXPLAIN THIS GRAPH

PERCENT

FIND YOUR MILITARY CAREERS SCORE ON YOUR ASVAB STUDENT RESULTS SHEET AND READ UP FOR PERCENTAGE

# INFANTRYMEN

The infantry is the main land combat force of the military. In peacetime, the infantry's role is to stay ready to defend our country. In combat, the role of the infantry is to capture or destroy enemy ground forces and repel enemy attacks. Infantrymen operate weapons and equipment to engage and destroy enemy ground forces. Turn to page 338 for more information about infantrymen.

## What They Do

Infantrymen perform some or all of the following duties:

- Operate, clean, and store automatic weapons, such as rifles and machine guns

- Parachute from troop transport airplanes while carrying weapons and supplies

- Fire armor-piercing missiles from hand-held antitank missile launchers

- Carry out scouting missions to spot enemy troop movements and gun locations

- Operate two-way radios and signal equipment to relay battle orders

- Drive vehicles mounted with machine guns or small missiles

- Perform hand-to-hand combat drills that involve martial arts tactics

- Set firing angles and fire mortar shells at targets

- Dig foxholes, trenches, and bunkers for protection against attacks

## Training Provided

Infantry training starts with basic training of about 7 or 8 weeks. Advanced training in infantry skills lasts for another 8 weeks. While some of the training is in the classroom, most is in the field under simulated combat conditions. In reality, training for an infantry soldier never stops. Infantry soldiers keep their skills sharp through frequent squad maneuvers, target practice, and war games. War games conducted without live ammunition allow soldiers to practice scouting, troop movement, surprise attack, and capturing techniques.

## Physical Demands

The infantry has very demanding physical requirements. Infantrymen must perform strenuous physical activities, such as marching while carrying equipment, digging foxholes, and climbing over obstacles. Infantrymen need good hearing and clear speech to use two-way radios, and good night vision and depth perception to see targets and signals.

## Special Requirements

This occupation is open only to men.

## Helpful Attributes

Helpful attributes include:

- Readiness to accept a challenge and face danger

- Ability to stay in top physical condition

- Interest in working as a member of a team

## Work Environment

Because infantrymen must be prepared to go anywhere in the world they are needed, they work and train in all climates and weather conditions. During training exercises, as in real combat, infantrymen work, eat, and sleep outdoors. Most of the time, however, infantrymen work on military bases.

## Civilian Counterparts

Although the job of infantrymen has no equivalent in civilian life, the close teamwork, discipline, and leadership experiences it provides are helpful in many civilian jobs.

## Opportunities

The military has about 61,300 infantrymen. On average, the services need about 6,500 new infantrymen each year. Leadership ability and job performance are the main factors for advancement in the infantry. Those who have the ability to motivate, train, and supervise others assume greater responsibility. As infantrymen advance in their careers, they become more involved in planning and supervision.

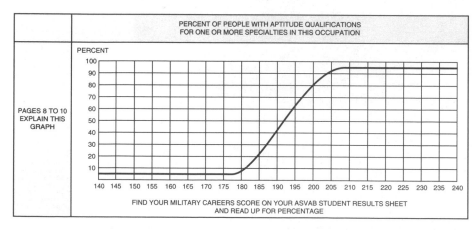

PAGES 8 TO 10 EXPLAIN THIS GRAPH

PERCENT OF PEOPLE WITH APTITUDE QUALIFICATIONS FOR ONE OR MORE SPECIALTIES IN THIS OCCUPATION

PERCENT

FIND YOUR MILITARY CAREERS SCORE ON YOUR ASVAB STUDENT RESULTS SHEET AND READ UP FOR PERCENTAGE

# SPECIAL OPERATIONS FORCES

When the military has difficult and dangerous missions to perform, they call upon special operations teams. These elite combat forces stay in a constant state of readiness to strike anywhere in the world on a moment's notice. Special operations forces team members conduct offensive raids, demolitions, intelligence, search and rescue, and other missions from aboard aircraft, helicopters, ships, or submarines. Due to the wide variety of missions, special operations forces team members are trained swimmers, parachutists, and survival experts, in addition to being combat trained. Turn to page 358 for more information about special operations forces.

## What They Do

Special operations forces team members in the military perform some or all of the following duties:

- Go behind enemy lines to recruit, train, and equip friendly forces for guerrilla raids

- Carry out demolition raids against enemy military targets, such as bridges, railroads, and fuel depots

- Clear mine fields, both underwater and on land

- Conduct missions to gather intelligence information on enemy military forces

- Conduct offensive raids or invasions of enemy territories

- Destroy enemy ships in coastal areas, using underwater explosives

## Special Requirements

This occupation is open only to men.

## Physical Demands

The special operations forces have very demanding physical requirements. Good eyesight, night vision, and physical conditioning are required to reach mission objectives by parachute, overland, or underwater. Also required is excellent hand-eye coordination to detonate or deactivate explosives. In most instances, special operations forces team members are required to be qualified divers, parachutists, and endurance runners.

## Helpful Attributes

Helpful attributes include:

- Ability to work as a team member

- Readiness to accept a challenge and face danger

- Ability to stay in top physical condition

- Ability to remain calm in stressful situations

## Work Environment

Because special operations forces team members must be prepared to go anywhere in the world they are needed, they train and work in all climates, weather conditions, and settings. They may dive from submarines or small underwater craft. Special forces team members may also be exposed to harsh temperatures, often without protection, during missions in enemy-controlled areas. Most of the time, however, they work and train on military bases or ships and submarines.

## Training Provided

Job training consists of up to 72 weeks of formal classroom training and practice exercises. Course content typically includes:

- Physical conditioning, parachuting, swimming, and scuba diving

- Using land warfare weapons and communications devices

- Handling and using explosives

- Bomb and mine disposal

Additional training occurs on the job. Basic skills are kept sharp through frequent practice exercises under simulated mission conditions.

## Civilian Counterparts

Although the job of special operations forces team members has no equivalent in civilian life, training in explosives, bomb disposal, scuba diving, and swimming may be helpful in such civilian jobs as blaster, police bomb disposal specialist, diver, or swimming instructor. The discipline and dependability of special operations forces are assets in many civilian occupations.

## Opportunities

The services have about 10,000 special operations team members. On average, they need about 700 new team members each year. After training, new team members practice their skills under close supervision. With experience, they may supervise and train other team members. They may also work alone on certain missions. Eventually, they may become team leaders.

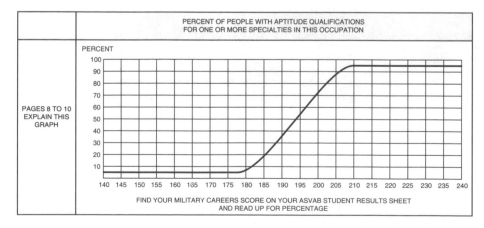

PERCENT OF PEOPLE WITH APTITUDE QUALIFICATIONS
FOR ONE OR MORE SPECIALTIES IN THIS OCCUPATION

PAGES 8 TO 10 EXPLAIN THIS GRAPH

PERCENT

FIND YOUR MILITARY CAREERS SCORE ON YOUR ASVAB STUDENT RESULTS SHEET
AND READ UP FOR PERCENTAGE

# TANK CREW MEMBERS

In peacetime, the role of tank and armor units is to stay ready to defend our country anywhere in the world. In combat, their role is to operate tanks and amphibious assault vehicles to engage and destroy the enemy. Tanks also conduct scouting missions and support infantry units during combat. Tank crew members work as a team to operate armored equipment and fire weapons to destroy enemy positions. Tank crew members normally specialize by type of armor, such as tanks or amphibious assault vehicles.

## What They Do

Tank crew members in the military perform some or all of the following duties:

- Drive tanks or amphibious assault vehicles in combat formations over roadways, rough terrain, and in heavy surf
- Operate target sighting equipment to aim guns
- Load and fire guns
- Operate two-way radios and signaling equipment to receive and relay battle orders
- Gather and report information about the terrain, enemy strength, and target location
- Perform preventive maintenance on tanks, guns, and equipment
- Read maps, compasses, and battle plans

## Special Requirements

This occupation is open only to men.

## Training Provided

Job training consists of 6 to 9 weeks of classroom and field training under simulated combat conditions. Course content typically includes:

- Tank operations
- Armor offensive and defensive tactics
- Tank gunnery
- Map reading
- Scouting techniques

Further training occurs on the job and through training exercises. Tank crews often take part in war games, which simulate combat conditions. They divide into teams and practice battle tactics on military exercise ranges. Instead of firing live ammunition, tanks "shoot" harmless light beams at one another to determine war game victors.

## Physical Demands

Tank crew members must be in good physical condition and have exceptional stamina. They must be able to work inside the confined area of a tank for long periods of time. Good vision and normal color vision are required in order to read maps, drive vehicles around obstacles, and locate targets.

## Helpful Attributes

Helpful attributes include:

- Ability to work as a member of a team
- Readiness to accept a challenge and face danger
- Ability to follow directions and execute orders quickly and accurately

## Work Environment

Tank crew members, like other combat troops, work in all climates and weather conditions. During training exercises, as in real combat conditions, tank crew members work, eat, and sleep outdoors and in tanks.

## Civilian Counterparts

Although the job of tank crew member has no equivalent in civilian life, the close teamwork, discipline, and leadership experiences it provides are helpful in many civilian jobs.

## Opportunities

The services have about 29,400 tank crew members. On average, they need about 3,300 new tank crew members each year. After job training, new tank crew members help operate weapons and control their armored vehicles. Leadership potential and job performance are the most important factors for advancement in this field. In time, crew members may become tank or vehicle commanders.

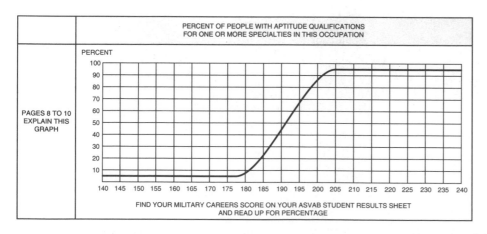

PERCENT OF PEOPLE WITH APTITUDE QUALIFICATIONS FOR ONE OR MORE SPECIALTIES IN THIS OCCUPATION

PAGES 8 TO 10 EXPLAIN THIS GRAPH

PERCENT

FIND YOUR MILITARY CAREERS SCORE ON YOUR ASVAB STUDENT RESULTS SHEET AND READ UP FOR PERCENTAGE

# Military Officer Occupations

# How to Read the Officer Occupational Descriptions

The purpose of *Military Careers* is to introduce students, parents, and counselors to the military world-of-work. *Military Careers* can be used to explore the many employment and training opportunities available in the enlisted and officer forces of the Army, Navy, Air Force, Marine Corps, and Coast Guard.

*Military Careers* contains descriptions of 152 military occupations. The Officer Occupations section contains descriptions of 61 officer occupations. Each officer description has standard sections, as shown in the example on the opposite page. An explanation for each section of the description is also provided.

When reading any of the 61 officer occupational descriptions, remember that it is a summary of similar job specialties across all of the military services. For example, the Air Traffic Control Managers description in the sample represents 10 distinct air traffic controller specialties across four services. Therefore, individual job specialties may differ somewhat from the general occupations described in this book. If you are interested in learning more about a particular service or occupation, you should contact a recruiter for details.

**1 Occupational Title**
The occupational title names the military occupation. An alphabetical listing of titles is in the index beginning on page 420.

**2 Military Service Representation**
The military services listed next to the title offer employment and training opportunities in the occupation. Not all services offer every occupation described in *Military Careers*.

**3 Summary**
The summary contains background information about the military occupation.

**4 What They Do**
"What They Do" describes the main work activities performed by workers in the occupation. Because job specialties vary from one service to another, some of the activities listed may not apply to all services.

**5 Physical Demands**
Some military occupations place physical demands on workers. For example, strength for moderate or heavy lifting is a common physical demand noted in *Military Careers*. Other physical demands include running, climbing, swimming, clear speech, and special vision requirements.

**6 Work Environment**
"Work Environment" describes the typical work settings and conditions for the occupation. Work settings may be indoors or outdoors, on land, aboard ships, or in aircraft.

**7 Helpful Attributes**
"Helpful Attributes" include interests, fields of college study, experience, and other personal characteristics that may be helpful for training and working in the military occupation. These are not requirements.

**8 Special Requirements**
Special requirements must be met to enter certain occupations. College degree requirements, professional certifications, and licenses are examples of special requirements. This section also identifies combat occupations from which women are excluded by law.

**9 Training Provided**
The military provides job training for most of its new officers. Most job training is provided in a classroom setting. For some occupations, training is provided on the job. In "Training Provided," the length of training and course content are summarized. Course content and length of training may vary for each service.

**10 Civilian Counterparts**
Most military occupations are comparable to one or more civilian occupations because they require similar duties and training. "Civilian Counterparts" identifies these civilian occupations and the kinds of companies or organizations in which they are located. The *Dictionary of Occupational Titles* (DOT) Code Index beginning on page 408 provides a listing of counterpart civilian occupations for each military occupation.

**11 Opportunities**
"Opportunities" contains information on the total number of officers working in the occupation and the average annual need for new personnel. Military career advancement in the occupation is also summarized in this section.

# AIR TRAFFIC CONTROL MANAGERS

Army
Navy
Air Force
Marine Corps

 Air traffic control centers often have several sections giving instructions to military aircraft. One section gives take-off and landing instructions. Another gives ground instructions. A third section tracks planes in flight. Air traffic control managers direct the operations of air traffic control centers.

## 4 What They Do

Air traffic control managers in the military perform some or all of the following duties:

- Plan work schedules for air traffic controllers

- Evaluate job performance of controllers

- Manage air traffic control center operations to ensure safe and efficient flights

- Inspect control center facilities and equipment

- Direct tests of radar equipment and controller procedures

- Investigate and find solutions to problems in control center operations

- Control air traffic using radar and radios

- Direct training for air traffic controllers

## 5 Physical Demands

Air traffic control personnel must pass a demanding physical exam as required by the Federal Aviation Administration (FAA).

## 6 Work Environment

Air traffic control managers work in air traffic control towers and centers at airfields and aboard ships.

## 7 Helpful Attributes

Helpful fields of study include aeronautical engineering, computer science, and liberal arts. Helpful attributes include:

- Interest in work requiring accuracy and attention to detail

- Ability to remain calm in stressful situations

- Decisiveness

- Ability to manage in accordance with strict standards

## 8 Special Requirements

A 4-year college degree is normally required to enter this occupation. Certification by the FAA must usually be obtained during military training.

## 9 Training Provided

Job training consists of 6 to 11 weeks of classroom instruction. Training length varies depending on specialty. Course content typically includes:

- Air traffic control management

- Operational procedures for air traffic control

- Communications and radar procedures

- Aircraft recognition

- Take-off, landing, and ground control procedures

## 10 Civilian Counterparts

Civilian air traffic control managers work at commercial airports. They perform duties similar to those performed by military air traffic control managers.

## 11 Opportunities

The services have about 300 air traffic control managers. On average, they need 10 new air traffic control managers each year. After job training, managers are assigned to air traffic control centers at airfields or aboard ships, where they gain experience in air traffic control management. They may advance to senior management and command positions in the aviation field.

# General Information on Officer Occupations

# General Information on Officer Occupations

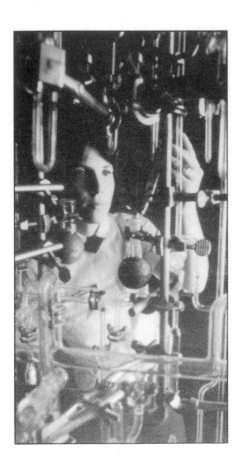

For almost 45 years, the military's personnel requirements and overall strategies had been shaped by the need to be prepared to deal with a short-notice, global war with the former Soviet Union. Given the dramatic developments in Eastern Europe, the former Soviet Union, and Africa, the military services are refocusing their strategy on a peacetime mission and on readiness for regional conflicts and contingencies. As the military plans for the next century, it will reduce the numbers of active-duty officers.

Although the active-duty military services will decline in size, they will still need substantial numbers of new officers. New officers are usually college graduates with bachelor's degrees. They must meet the physical, academic, and moral standards set by their service to be accepted into programs for becoming an officer (commissioning programs). The qualifications required for acceptance into the various programs are described in this section on page 181.

Officers usually begin their careers gaining experience in their chosen occupational field. Working closely with more senior officers, they also begin supervising small groups of enlisted people. As officers become more experienced and advance in responsibility and rank, they direct more enlisted personnel, begin to lead other officers, and may eventually become the senior leaders and managers of the military. Commanding officers are responsible for every detail of U.S. ground and naval forces, ships, flying squadrons, and amphibious assault forces.

## MILITARY OFFICER OCCUPATIONS

Officers lead and manage activities in every occupational specialty in the military. They must be able to learn detailed information quickly to be effective in the changing assignments and environments they will experience during their careers.

One of the characteristics of a successful leader is willingness to serve. Officers serve their country daily, sometimes placing themselves in danger. They are responsible for the well-being, training, and readiness of the people they lead.

Officers are also trained in specific occupational skills. They manage the military supply system and care for the health of combat and support personnel and their dependents. They analyze military intelligence and lead technicians on land or aboard ships.

Some officers, such as infantry and submarine officers, work in jobs directly related to combat. These occupations are open only to men. In other occupations, certain combat-related duty assignments are closed to women. According to federal law and policy, women may not be assigned to duty where there is a high probability of direct exposure to combat.

A large number of men and women in the military work in occupations that support the combat forces. They are essential to the readiness and strength of the combat forces.

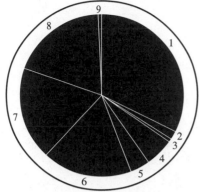

## Figure 5
## Distribution of Officers by Occupational Group

1. Executive, Administrative, and Managerial
2. Human Services
3. Media and Public Affairs
4. Health Diagnosing and Treating Practitioner
5. Health Care
6. Engineering, Science, and Technical
7. Service
8. Transportation
9. Combat Specialty

Together, the five services offer employment opportunities in over 1,500 officer job specialties. To help you explore military officer careers, these specialties are grouped into 61 occupations in this book. The 61 occupations are organized into nine broad groups:

- Executive, Administrative, and Managerial
- Human Services
- Media and Public Affairs
- Health Diagnosing and Treating Practitioner
- Health Care
- Engineering, Science, and Technical
- Service
- Transportation
- Combat Specialty.

Figure 5 shows the distribution of officers across the nine occupational groups.

Over two-thirds of all military officer occupations have counterparts in the civilian world-of-work. For example, there are personnel managers, optometrists, electrical engineers, lawyers, and management analysts in both the military and civilian work forces.

The services offer training and advancement opportunities in each occupation. No matter which occupation newly commissioned officers enter, they find a well-defined career path leading to increased responsibility and higher pay.

## GENERAL QUALIFICATION REQUIREMENTS

Each year, approximately 23,000 men and women become commissioned officers in the military. The term "commissioned" refers to the certification that

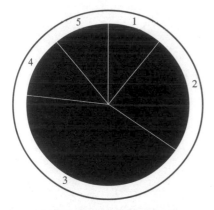

**Figure 6**
**Pathways to Newly Commissioned Officers**

1. Service Academies
2. Officer Candidate School (OCS) and Officer Training School (OTS)
3. Reserve Officers' Training Corps (ROTC)
4. Direct Appointments
5. Enlisted Commissioning Programs

officers receive upon meeting all qualification requirements. The certification confers military rank, authority, and obligation. To join the military as a commissioned officer, applicants must have a four-year college degree. Certain scientific, technical, and professional fields require an advanced degree. In addition, mental aptitude, physical requirements, and moral standards must be met. The general qualification requirements for military officers are presented in Table 5 on page 181. Specific requirements vary by service. For additional information on officer qualification requirements, see the "Service Information on Officer Occupations" section beginning on page 195. For detailed questions, it is necessary to contact a recruiter.

### Pathways to Becoming an Officer

There are four main pathways to becoming a commissioned officer:

- Service Academies
- Officer Candidate School (OCS) and Officer Training School (OTS)
- Reserve Officers' Training Corps (ROTC)
- Direct Appointments.

An indirect pathway to becoming an officer is through Enlisted Commissioning Programs.

Figure 6 shows the percentage of newly commissioned officers who became officers through these pathways. A description of each pathway follows:

## Service Academies

The four service academies are:

- United States Military Academy at West Point, New York (Army)
- United States Naval Academy at Annapolis, Maryland (Navy and Marine Corps)
- United States Air Force Academy at Colorado Springs, Colorado (Air Force)
- United States Coast Guard Academy at New London, Connecticut (Coast Guard)

The competition for entry into the academies is keen. Among candidates who meet all the eligibility requirements, the academies offer admission to only the most qualified. To be eligible for admission to any of the academies, a young person must be at least 17 years of age, a citizen of the United States, of good moral character, and academically and physically qualified. In addition, candidates for the Army, Navy, and Air Force Academies must have a nomination to be considered for admission. Nominations are not necessary for admission to the Coast Guard Academy. Most candidates seek a nomination from their members of Congress. It is not necessary to know Senators or Representatives personally to receive a nomination from them. The recommended time to apply for nomination is the spring of the junior year in high school.

The academies all offer a four-year program of study leading to a bachelor of science degree in one of many disciplines. Students, called cadets or midshipmen, receive free tuition, room, board, medical and dental care, and a monthly allowance. Graduates receive a commission as a military officer and must serve on active duty for at least five years. Each year, about 13 percent of the military's new officers are graduates of these four academies. For more information about the

---

### Table 5 – General Officer Qualifications*

**Age:** Must be between 19 and 29 years for Officer Candidate School (OCS) and Officer Training School (OTS); 17 and 21 years for Reserve Officers' Training Corps (ROTC); 17 and 22 years for the service academies.

**Citizenship Status:** Must be U.S. citizen.

**Physical Condition:** Must meet minimum physical standards listed below. Some occupations have additional physical standards.

| Height – | Maximum | Minimum |
|---|---|---|
| For males: | 6'8"/203.2 cm | 5'0"/152.4 cm |
| For females: | 6'8"/203.2 cm | 4'10"/147.3 cm |

Weight – There are minimum and maximum weights for the various services according to height, wrist size, and/or percentage of body fat.

| | Maximum | Minimum |
|---|---|---|
| For males: | 255 lb/115.66 kg | 100 lb/45.35 kg |
| For females: | 227 lb/102.96 kg | 90 lb/40.82 kg |

Vision – The requirements are specific for each service and are determined by job specialty. In general, service members must have at least 20/400 or 20/200 vision that can be corrected to 20/20 with eyeglasses or contacts lenses. The vision requirements are also based on depth perception as well as color blindness.

Overall Health – Must be in good health and pass a medical exam. Certain diseases or conditions may exclude persons from enlistment, such as diabetes, severe allergies, epilepsy, alcoholism, and drug addiction.

**Education:** Must have a four-year college degree from an accredited institution. Some occupations require advanced degrees or four-year degrees in a particular field.

**Aptitude:** Must achieve the minimum entry score on an officer qualification test. Each service uses its own officer qualification test.

**Moral Character:** Must meet standards designed to screen out persons unlikely to become successful officers. Standards cover court convictions, juvenile delinquency, arrests, and drug use.

**Marital Status and Dependents:** May be either single or married for ROTC, OCS/OTS, and direct appointment pathways. Must be single to enter and graduate from service academies. Single persons with one or more minor dependents are not eligible for officer commissioning.

**Waivers:** On a case-by-case basis, exceptions (waivers) are granted by individual services for some of the above qualification requirements.

---

\* Each service sets its own qualification requirements for officers. For additional information on a particular service's requirements, refer to the "Service Information on Officer Occupations" section beginning on page 195, or contact a military recruiter.

service academies, see the "Service Information on Officer Occupations" section beginning on page 195 and your school counselor.

### Officer Candidate/Training School

Each service offers a program for college graduates with no prior military training who wish to become military officers. These programs are called Officer Candidate School (OCS) or Officer Training School (OTS), depending on the service. Interested candidates should apply through a local recruiter in the fall of their senior year of college. After graduation, young men and women selected for OCS/OTS join the military as enlisted members for the duration of their OCS/OTS training. Depending on the service, OCS/OTS lasts up to 20 weeks. After successful completion, candidates are commissioned as military officers and have a minimum active-duty service obligation of three years. Each year, about 21 percent of the military's new officers are commissioned through OCS/OTS. For more information, contact a recruiter.

### Reserve Officers' Training Corps

Undergraduate students in public or private colleges or universities may receive training to become officers under the Reserve Officers' Training Corps (ROTC). ROTC programs for the Army, Navy, Air Force, and Marine Corps are available in over 1,400 colleges and universities nationwide.

Depending on the service and ROTC option selected, students train for two, three, or four years. Often, they receive scholarships for tuition, books, fees, uniforms, and a monthly allowance. In addition to their military and college course work, ROTC candidates perform drills for several hours each week and participate in military training exercises for several weeks each summer. Graduating ROTC candidates become commissioned as military officers and either go on active duty or become members of Reserve or National Guard units. Each year, about 44 percent of the military's new officers are gained through ROTC programs. For more information about service ROTC programs, see the "Service Information on Officer Occupations" section beginning on page 195. For information on the colleges and universities that offer ROTC programs for a particular service, contact a recruiter from that service.

### Direct Appointments

Medical, legal, engineering, and religious professionals who are fully qualified in their field may apply to receive direct appointments as military officers. These individuals enter military service and begin practicing their profession with a minimum of military training. The service obligation for officers entering through direct appointment is two years. Some scholarship programs are available to assist students in these fields with their professional schooling in return for several years of service. Each year, direct appointments make up about 11 percent of the military's new officers. For information about opportunities for direct appointment in a particular service, contact a recruiter from that service.

### Enlisted Commissioning Programs

In addition to the four main pathways described above, the services each have programs for qualified enlisted personnel to earn commissions as officers. Once selected to an enlisted commissioning program, enlisted personnel must follow one of the four major pathways described above in order to receive their commission. These programs are exclusive, as they account for only 10 percent of newly commissioned officers each year.

## SERVICE SUPPORT FOR CAREER ADVANCEMENT

From the time officers are commissioned until the last day of duty, the services play an important role in supporting their career development. The military offers a wide range of training and development opportunities to help each officer build a career. However, to succeed, officers must take advantage of the opportunities provided.

### Officer Training and Education

Training and education are ongoing throughout a military officer's career. Although each service has its own programs for officer professional development, all services view training and education, followed by practical experience, as the normal course for officer development. The military provides five kinds of training and educational opportunities to its officers:

- Basic officer training
- Job training
- Advanced training
- Professional military education
- Leadership training.

These five types of training are discussed on the following pages.

### 1) Basic Officer Training

An important part of every pathway leading to officer commissioning is training on the basic knowledge required to become an officer. The topics covered in this training include:

• Roles and responsibilities of the officer
• Military laws and regulations
• Service traditions
• Military customs and courtesies
• Career development
• Military science
• Administrative procedures.

In addition, most commissioning pathways involve physical conditioning consisting of calisthenics, running, and drills.

The duration and timing of officer training may vary with the commissioning pathway followed. For example, ROTC candidates receive basic officer training over the course of their two- to four-year ROTC programs. The same is true for cadets or midshipmen at the service academies. In contrast, OCS/OTS candidates receive their basic officer training in the 12- to 20-week OCS/OTS programs they attend after graduation from college or after spending time as an enlisted member.

### 2) Job Training

After earning their commissions, officers normally receive job training in preparation for their first duty assignment. Depending on the occupational field entered, initial job training may last from several weeks to two years. Officer training, however, does not end after this initial training.

Because officers are the professional leaders of the military, they must develop knowledge of the broad areas they might command. For example, supply officers must understand the entire supply system, from contracting to warehouse management, to one day command supply operations for an entire base. Therefore, supply officers are assigned to several different jobs during their careers. Throughout a career, the services provide training to allow officers to maintain and increase their skills. In addition to technical training, the services provide training that focuses on military strategy and history as well as developing the leadership, communication, and management skills required for positions of greater responsibility.

For certain occupations, the military does not provide job training. Doctors, veterinarians, nurses, therapists, dieticians, lawyers, engineers, social workers, and other professionals may only enter the military after they have been fully trained and, in most cases, certified by a state board.

### 3) Advanced Training

There are advanced training courses for virtually every officer occupation. These courses fall into two basic categories. In the first category are those courses that teach the technical or administrative skills needed for an officer's next assignment. For example, transportation officers with truck and vehicle experience may receive training in landing craft maintenance management before they are transferred to a landing craft assignment.

In the second category are the courses that train officers in the overall mission of their occupations. For example, infantry officers need instruction in coordinating combat actions with artillery and aircraft units, while ship officers need to learn how to coordinate operations of ships and aircraft to hunt submarines.

### 4) Professional Military Education

Professional military education (PME) prepares officers for the increasingly challenging leadership, planning, operations, and management responsibilities they assume as they rise in rank. PME is highly recommended for career-oriented officers, regardless of their occupational specialties.

PME courses teach techniques for combat-support operations in battle. Officers study military history, strategy, tactics (how to maneuver forces on the battlefield), planning, and organization. They learn how each service supports the others, and how the services work together to defend our nation.

PME is divided into two courses of study that correspond to specific points in career development. Officers may be selected to attend full-time resident programs to complete PME. If not, they are strongly encouraged to complete the courses by correspondence. Resident PME courses are usually taught at service "war colleges." Each service has its own PME programs, but the levels of instruction and many subjects are similar. There are even opportunities for members of one service to attend full-time resident programs at the school of another service.

### 5) Leadership Training

Officers receive leadership training throughout their careers. There are formal courses of leadership and management, and leadership is discussed in many occupational courses. Additionally, officers receive advice and on-the-job instruction in leadership from more senior officers.

### Continuing Education

Continuing education is an important part of an officer's professional development. It allows officers to broaden their knowledge and earn advanced degrees in military science, technical subjects related to their occupations, management techniques, and subjects in which they are interested. Although having an advanced degree does not guarantee career advancement, it can be an important factor.

The services offer several programs for officer continuing education:

### Service Colleges and Postgraduate Schools

Service-oriented institutions, like the Naval Postgraduate School and the Air Force Institute of Technology, offer advanced degree programs in many fields. Both correspondence courses and resident programs are available. There is intense competition for entrance into these programs, and selections are based on service need as well as officer preference.

## Figure 7
## Officer Insignia of the United States Armed Forces

| PAY GRADE \ SERVICE | ARMY | NAVY | AIR FORCE | MARINE CORPS | COAST GUARD |
|---|---|---|---|---|---|
| O-9 | ★★★★ GENERAL | ★★★★ ADMIRAL | ★★★★ GENERAL | ★★★★ GENERAL | ★★★★ ADMIRAL |
| O-9 | ★★★ LIEUTENANT GENERAL | ★★★ VICE ADMIRAL | ★★★ LIEUTENANT GENERAL | ★★★ LIEUTENANT GENERAL | ★★★ VICE ADMIRAL |
| O-8 | ★★ MAJOR GENERAL | ★★ REAR ADMIRAL (UPPER HALF) | ★★ MAJOR GENERAL | ★★ MAJOR GENERAL | ★★ REAR ADMIRAL (UPPER HALF) |
| O-7 | ★ BRIGADIER GENERAL | ★ REAR ADMIRAL (LOWER HALF) | ★ BRIGADIER GENERAL | ★ BRIGADIER GENERAL | ★ REAR ADMIRAL (LOWER HALF) |
| O-6 | COLONEL | CAPTAIN | COLONEL | COLONEL | CAPTAIN |
| O-5 | LIEUTENANT COLONEL | COMMANDER | LIEUTENANT COLONEL | LIEUTENANT COLONEL | COMMANDER |
| O-4 | MAJOR | LIEUTENANT COMMANDER | MAJOR | MAJOR | LIEUTENANT COMMANDER |
| O-3 | CAPTAIN | LIEUTENANT | CAPTAIN | CAPTAIN | LIEUTENANT |
| O-2 | FIRST LIEUTENANT | LIEUTENANT JUNIOR GRADE | FIRST LIEUTENANT | FIRST LIEUTENANT | LIEUTENANT JUNIOR GRADE |
| O-1 | SECOND LIEUTENANT | ENSIGN | SECOND LIEUTENANT | SECOND LIEUTENANT | ENSIGN |

### Tuition Assistance

Up to 75 percent of tuition costs at state and private institutions may be reimbursed for officers enrolled in night school or correspondence courses. To participate, officers must meet the entrance requirements of the institution and meet service guidelines. In some cases, the service will select officers to attend graduate degree programs full-time and pay all costs plus their salaries. Opportunities are limited, and selections are based on service need.

## OFFICER PROMOTION

Officers can progress through 10 officer pay grades during their careers. Figure 7 contains information on the relationship between pay grade and rank and also illustrates the insignia for the ranks in each service.

Officers in the pay grade of O-1 advance by the action of their local commander. Commanders ensure that all necessary qualifications are being completed and that officers have spent the required time in grade.

Officers are continually evaluated by more senior officers. Individual performance is compared with the performance of all other officers in similar pay grades. A selection board thoroughly examines every aspect of each officer's career performance to select only the best qualified officers for promotion.

Selection boards are made up of experienced senior officers. Each selection board evaluates performance from the time each officer entered the service to the time the board meets. The members of the selection board evaluate each officer's record for promotion. Factors that qualify officers for promotion include:

- Career-long performance of job duties, leadership, and management
- Pursuit of, and success in, positions of increasing responsibility
- Successful completion of required qualifications and professional military education
- Appearance and behavior.

By selecting the best qualified officers for promotions, the services ensure they have the best possible leadership. Excellent performance reports are essential to career advancement. Although a series of excellent performance reports does not guarantee an individual's promotion, a less-than-excellent record severely limits chances for advancement. Since the number of officer positions is limited by Congress, the competition at senior levels is intense.

Figure 8 shows the average time an officer has been in the military (time-in-service) when he or she is promoted to each pay grade. For example, most officers will advance to O-2 in two years and to O-4 in 10 years. A very few outstanding officers may be selected for promotion earlier than indicated.

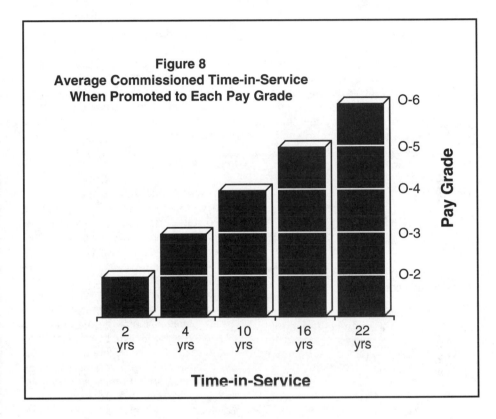

**Figure 8**
**Average Commissioned Time-in-Service When Promoted to Each Pay Grade**

## DUTY ASSIGNMENT

The five services have similar systems for assigning personnel to jobs. Each system is designed to satisfy the present and future staffing needs of the particular service. For example, if the service needs a meteorologist or pilot at a remote location, officers in those occupations will be assigned there. However, at the same time, the services also attempt to meet the desires of individuals and provide the best opportunity for career development. The duty assignment process determines where officers work, how often they move, and the opportunities open to them.

### Assignment Decisions

The services use mid- to senior-level officers who are familiar with a particular occupation to manage assignments for officers in that occupation. Assignment officers try to assign officers to different units to give them a broad range of experience. Both range and depth of experience are important to officer advancement. Although these officers cannot always meet each person's needs or desires, they try to make duty assignments that will enhance each officer's career.

### Length of Tours

The time that an officer spends at a particular duty assignment is called a tour. The length of a tour varies by service and geographic location. Typically, a tour lasts from three to four years, although there are many exceptions.

### Possible Location

All services require their officers to travel. Military officers are stationed in each of the 50 states and in countries all over the world. They are routinely transferred after one-, two-, three-, or four-year tours of duty. To many people, this is one of the attractive parts of service life and they join for the opportunity to travel, live in foreign countries, and see different parts of the United States. Nearly three-quarters of all service personnel are assigned to duty in the United States. Every service also has people stationed overseas; most of them are located in Europe, in countries such as Germany, Great Britain, and Italy. Many officers are also assigned to the Pacific Islands, including countries such as Japan. Typically, officers will have two overseas assignments during their careers.

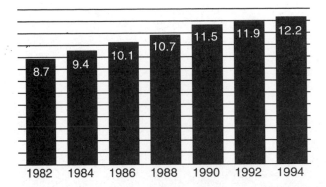

**Figure 9
Percentage of Active
Duty Women Officers
1982 - 1994**

## WOMEN OFFICERS

Military women are recognized today for the important contributions that they make to national defense. As shown in Figure 9, the percentage of active duty officers that are women has increased to about 12 percent.

According to federal laws and policies, women may not be assigned to duty that involves a high probability of exposure to direct combat. Through studies, the services have determined which occupations have the highest probability of exposure to direct combat. Examples of these occupations include infantry officer, artillery officer, and tank officer.

Despite federal laws and policies that restrict women from entering combat-related occupations, the scope of women's opportunities in the military has expanded. Women are currently eligible to enter about 90 percent of military job specialties. Examples of the many occupations in which women serve include airplane pilot, environmental health and safety officer, civil engineer, and intelligence officer. The outlook for women officers in the military suggests that the future will provide even greater opportunities.

# RESERVE FORCES

Seven forces make up the Reserves:

- Army Reserve
- Navy Reserve
- Air Force Reserve
- Marine Corps Reserve
- Coast Guard Reserve
- Army National Guard
- Air National Guard.

## Reserve Forces Role

The Reserves have an important role in our national defense. Their primary mission is to stay prepared to respond to events that threaten our country's security. In a national emergency, the Reserves can be "called up" to serve temporarily on active duty to expand our regular armed forces.

In peacetime, the Reserves perform many duties to support the regular active-duty forces, such as air patrols, search and rescue missions, air defense watch, installation and repair of communications equipment, transport of troops and supplies, and provision of medical services.

In addition to serving the national defense, National Guard units serve their states and communities during natural disasters and civil emergencies. Guard members have been called upon to rescue flood and hurricane victims, fight forest fires, and assist local authorities during evacuations.

## Becoming a Reserve Forces Officer

Currently, there are nearly 160,000 officers in the seven Reserve Forces. Each year, the Reserves need approximately 20,000 new officers. Although most Reserve Forces officers have prior experience as officers in the active-duty forces, young men and women without prior military experience may join the Reserves if they qualify. The basic qualification requirements are the same as for active-duty officers, shown in Table 5 on page 181.

There are several pathways to becoming a Reserve Forces officer, including ROTC and National Guard training. For more information, refer to the "Service Information on Officer Occupations" section beginning on page 195, or contact a military recruiter.

## Service Obligation

To become a Reserve Forces officer, individuals without prior experience as active-duty officers must commit themselves to an eight-year service obligation and undergo an initial training program at a military base. This training lasts between six and 18 weeks, depending on the Reserve Force selected.

After initial training is successfully completed, Reserve Forces officers live and work as civilians in their own communities and train part-time with a nearby Reserve unit.

## Reserve Unit Training

Reservists in organized units are required to attend training assemblies regularly throughout the year. Reserve units are required to conduct a minimum of 48 training assemblies a year. These assemblies are held on the weekends or evenings or a combination of both. One weekend is the equivalent of four training drills.

Reservists must also spend from 12 to 17 days in full-time training each year. The annual training period is normally scheduled during the summer and may be conducted at a site away from the member's community.

## Reserve Pay

A Reservist's pay is based on the same pay grade and length of service as military personnel on active duty. Members receive one day's pay for each drill attended. In addition, they receive one day's pay for each day of annual training.

## PAY AND BENEFITS

Military officers in all five services are paid according to the same pay scale and receive the same basic benefits. Military pay and benefits are set by Congress, which normally grants a cost-of-living pay increase once each year. In addition to pay, the military provides many of life's necessities, such as food, clothing, and housing. The following sections describe officer pay, allowances, and benefits in more detail.

### Officer Pay Grades

Officers can progress through 10 officer pay grades during their careers. Pay grade and length of service determine an officer's pay. Figure 7 on page 186 contains information on the relationship between pay grade and rank and also illustrates the insignia for the ranks in each service.

Most newly commissioned officers begin at pay grade O-1. Those who have certain professional qualifications and receive direct appointment may enter at a higher pay grade. After two years, officers usually move up to O-2. After an additional two years, the military generally promotes officers to O-3 if job performance is satisfactory and other requirements are met.

## Basic Pay

The major part of an officer's paycheck is basic pay. Pay grade and total years of service determine an officer's basic pay. Table 6 contains information on annual basic pay as of 1995. Cost-of-living increases generally occur once a year. Using this table, you can find that a person who has been in the service for eight years, and advanced to pay grade O-3, receives a basic pay of $37,228 per year.

### *Incentives and Special Pay*

The military offers incentives and special pay (in addition to basic pay) for certain types of duty. For example, incentives are paid for submarine and flight duty. Other types of hazardous duty with monthly incentives include parachute jumping, flight deck duty, and explosives demolition. In addition, the military gives special pay for sea duty, diving duty, duty in some foreign countries, and duty in areas subject to hostile fire. Special pay is also provided for officers in certain occupations, such as physicians, dentists, and life scientists.

### Table 6 – 1995 Basic Pay for Officers (Annual Figures)

| Pay Grade | Years of Services | | | | | | | | |
|---|---|---|---|---|---|---|---|---|---|
| | Under 2 yrs | 2 | 3 | 4 | 6 | 8 | 10 | ... | 26 |
| O-10 | * | * | * | * | * | * | * | ... | $115,376 |
| O-9 | * | * | * | * | * | * | * | ... | 101,794 |
| O-8 | * | * | * | * | * | * | * | ... | 92,232 |
| O-7 | * | * | * | * | * | * | * | ... | 81,396 |
| O-6 | * | * | * | * | * | * | $48,463 | ... | 71,514 |
| O-5 | * | * | * | * | * | * | 42,822 | ... | * |
| O-4 | * | * | * | * | * | $38,552 | 41,184 | ... | * |
| O-3 | * | * | $31,000 | $34,297 | $35,939 | 37,228 | 39,244 | ... | * |
| O-2 | $22,615 | $24,696 | 29,675 | 30,672 | 31,306 | * | * | ... | * |
| O-1 | 19,634 | 20,437 | 24,696 | * | * | * | * | ... | * |

\* Military Personnel with this many years of service will probably not be in this pay grade. (Pay scale between 10 and 26 years not shown.)

## Allowances

Many officers and their families live free of charge in military housing on the base where they are assigned. Those living off base receive a quarters (housing) allowance in addition to their basic pay. In 1992, the monthly housing allowance ranged from $329 to $923, depending on pay grade and if the officer had dependents. Each officer also received a subsistence (food) allowance of $134 per month. Because allowances are not taxed as income, they provide a significant tax savings in addition to their cash value.

When added together, housing and food allowances, along with their tax savings, are substantial additions to basic pay. Table 7 contains information on the total value of basic pay, allowances, and tax savings, called Regular Military Compensation. The table represents the amount of pay a civilian worker would have to earn to realize the same "take home" pay as a military officer. These figures provide a more realistic comparison between military and civilian salaries than the figures in Table 6.

### Table 7 – 1995 Regular Military Compensation (Annual Figures)

| Pay Grade | Years of Services | | | | | | | | |
|---|---|---|---|---|---|---|---|---|---|
| | Under 2 yrs | 2 | 3 | 4 | 6 | 8 | 10 | ... | 26 |
| O-10 | * | * | * | * | * | * | * | ... | $131,883 |
| O-9 | * | * | * | * | * | * | * | ... | 122,596 |
| O-8 | * | * | * | * | * | * | * | ... | 112,853 |
| O-7 | * | * | * | * | * | * | * | ... | 101,975 |
| O-6 | $58,830 | * | $66,558 | $66,961 | $66,518 | $66,629 | $66,981 | ... | 85,085 |
| O-5 | 48,857 | $54,687 | 57,650 | 57,673 | 57,626 | 57,646 | 59,061 | ... | * |
| O-4 | 42,107 | 48,076 | 50,307 | 50,307 | 50,980 | 52,631 | 55,392 | ... | * |
| O-3 | 37,816 | 40,951 | 42,939 | 46,153 | 47,752 | 49,008 | 51,045 | ... | * |
| O-2 | 32,313 | 34,517 | 39,804 | 40,782 | 41,402 | * | * | ... | * |
| O-1 | 27,075 | 20,058 | 33,102 | * | * | * | * | ... | * |

Regular Military Compensation reflects basic pay, allowances, and the value of the tax advantage for allowances.

* Military Personnel with this many years of service will probably not be in this pay grade. (Pay scale between 10 and 26 years not shown.)

## Employment Benefits

Military officers receive substantial benefits in addition to their pay and allowances. While they are in the service, officers' benefits include health care, vacation time, legal assistance, recreational programs, educational assistance, and commissary/exchange (military store) privileges. Families of officers also receive some of these benefits. Table 8 contains a summary of these employment benefits.

## Retirement Benefits

The military offers one of the best retirement programs in the country. After 20 years of active duty, officers may retire and receive a monthly payment equal to 40 percent of their average basic pay for their last five years of active duty. Officers who retire with more than 20 years of active service receive higher pay. Other retirement benefits include medical care and commissary/exchange privileges.

## Veterans' Benefits

Veterans of military service are entitled to certain veterans' benefits set by Congress and provided by the Veterans Administration. In most cases, these include guarantees for home loans, hospitalization, survivor benefits, educational benefits, disability benefits, and assistance in finding civilian employment.

## Table 8 – Summary of Employment Benefits for Officers

| | |
|---|---|
| **Vacation** | Leave time of 30 days per year. |
| **Medical, Dental, and Eye Care** | Full medical, hospitalization, dental, and eye care services for officers and most health care costs for family members. |
| **Continuing Education** | Voluntary educational programs for undergraduate and graduate degrees or for single courses, including tuition assistance for programs at colleges and universities. |
| **Recreational Programs** | Programs include athletics, entertainment, and hobbies: <br><br> Softball, basketball, football, swimming, tennis, golf, weight training, and other sports <br><br> Parties, dances, and entertainment <br><br> Club facilities, snack bars, game rooms, movie theaters, and lounges <br><br> Active hobby and craft clubs, book and music libraries. |
| **Exchange and Commissary Privileges** | Food, goods, and services are available at military stores, generally at lower costs than retail stores. |
| **Legal Assistance** | Many free legal services are available to assist with personal matters. |

# Service Information on Officer Occupations

# Army

## OVERVIEW

Today's Army is composed of a highly trained team of individuals. The individual soldier, the noncommissioned officer (NCO), and the officer make the Army's sophisticated technology work. They operate tanks, fly helicopters, and launch missiles. They build bridges, calibrate and operate computers, and apply state-of-the-art tools and methods to solve critical problems. Working together, these elements enable the Army to accomplish its mission to deter war and be prepared to fight and win should deterrence fail.

The Army is made up of nearly 750,000 bright, well-trained men and women, including more than 88,970 officers and 15,307 warrant officers. These men and women compose the best-trained, best-disciplined, and most self-assured Army in recent history. The Army needs about 7,000 new officers each year.

## BECOMING AN OFFICER

You may become an officer in the U.S. Army through one of four commissioning programs: The United States Military Academy, The Army Reserve Officers' Training Corps (ROTC), the Officer Candidate School (OCS), or direct appointment. All require, as a minimum, that the applicant be a high school graduate, pass a medical and physical exam, and be at least 17 years old. In order to be competitive for these programs, an individual needs to be working toward or already have acquired a four-year college degree.

### U.S. Military Academy

The United States Military Academy, located at West Point, New York, offers bachelor of science degrees with majors in both engineering and liberal arts. Graduates earn a commission as a second lieutenant in the U.S. Army.

Admission to the academy is very competitive. Appointments are generally made through nominations from United States Senators and Representatives. Applicants should begin their quest for entry into the academy no later than the middle of their junior year in high school.

### Army Reserve Officers' Training Corps (ROTC)

Army ROTC is the primary source for college-trained officers for the Army. The ROTC program is currently offered at over 300 institutions and through agreements at more than 1,000 colleges and universities.

Army ROTC is divided into two parts—the Basic Course and the Advanced Course. The Basic Course covers the freshman and sophomore years of college. Students may withdraw at any time, and no military obligation is incurred. Selected students may enroll in the Advanced Course during the final two years of college. Students in the Advanced Course receive uniforms,

necessary textbooks, and a subsistence allowance of up to $1,000 each year. Starting September 1995, the subsistence allowance will be increased to up to $1,500 each year. Cadets are scheduled for a six-week Advanced Camp during the summer between their junior and senior years of college.

Educational assistance in the form of highly competitive scholarships are available for two, three, or four years. These scholarships are offered at three different levels of annual payment: $12,000, $8,000, and $5,000. These dollar amounts represent tuition "caps." The scholarship will pay 100 percent of tuition and educational fees up to the cap. Additional scholarship benefits include a designated allowance for textbooks and supplies of $450 per year and the subsistence allowance.

### Officer Candidate School (OCS)

Officer Candidate School (OCS) is a 14-week course to train enlisted personnel, warrant officers, and civilians with a college degree to be Army officers. Enlisted soldiers and warrant officers must have 60 hours of college before applying for OCS. Civilian applicants must have a bachelor's degree.

### Direct Appointment

The Army offers direct appointment opportunities for specialists from selected legal, medical, ministerial, and technical career fields. Professional experience can even earn a higher entry grade for qualified applicants.

### Warrant Officers

An Army warrant officer is an officer appointed by warrant of the Secretary of the Army, based on a sound level of technical and tactical competence. The warrant officer is a highly specialized expert and trainer who gains progressive levels of expertise and leadership by operating, maintaining, administering and managing the Army's equipment, support activities, or technical systems for an entire career.

Becoming a warrant officer requires great skill in a specific occupational specialty. Army warrant officers must demonstrate leadership abilities and have the desire and dedication to perfect their technical proficiency through professional development, training, and education. Through schooling, experience, assignments and promotions, they are trained to perform effectively in the highest, most demanding positions within their career specialties. A local Army recruiter can provide up-to-date information about how to qualify to become a warrant officer.

## OFFICER TRAINING

Newly commissioned officers attend an Officer Basic Course (OBC), which prepares them for their first assignment. OBC contains a mix of classroom education and physical training. Much of the time is devoted to practicing leadership skills in a work-like environment. During OBC, which lasts about four months, lieutenants also participate in a vigorous physical fitness program. OBC instruction is provided by the branch of the Army that utilizes an officer's specialty. For example, newly commissioned infantry officers attend OBC at the U.S. Army Infantry School at Fort Benning, Georgia.

Special skills that may be needed by new officers are developed at a functional training course. Pilots complete their flight training after OBC. Army infantry lieutenants may volunteer for Airborne (parachute) or Ranger training. Some infantry officers complete certification courses as Bradley fighting vehicle commanders if they are being assigned to units equipped with that vehicle.

Army officers are also provided advanced training and refresher instruction to meet the needs of the Army or their next assignment. These courses usually are not more than six months in length. For example, Army supply officers can take advanced courses in material management, air delivery of cargo, and food services management. Specialized courses are available in every career area.

At various points during a career as an Army officer, there are opportunities to participate in professional military education such as the Combined Arms Services Staff School or the Command and General Staff School. These programs prepare officers for the increasing responsibilities associated with career advancement to the more senior grades in the Army. They are primarily the study of how to be an officer and provide the command and staff knowledge required to be a professional officer.

## ADVANCEMENT

Most new Army officers begin their careers as Second Lieutenants. A few officers receive a direct appointment to a higher grade. There are established points (time-in-grade) at which time an officer is considered for promotion. Army officers are selected for advancement based on their being qualified to meet the requirements of the Army. The Army promotion process is designed to ensure advancement of the best officers, promote career development, and promote officers with the greatest demonstrated potential.

Promotion to the grade of First Lieutenant usually occurs at two years of service. After an additional two years of service, the best qualified officers are promoted to Captain. After being in the Army a total of nine to 11 years, an officer becomes eligible for promotion to Major. This and subsequent promotions are more competitive. While all officers compete with each other for promotion, the Army recognizes a need to retain the right number of officers with the skills to meet Army requirements. A selection board evaluates the potential of all eligible officers and recommends the best qualified in each career area for promotion. There are provisions for early promotions of outstanding performers (limited to no more than 10 percent of promotions).

## EDUCATION PROGRAMS

Advanced education is a goal for most Army officers. Some officers may be selected to pursue full-time studies toward a master's or doctorate degree through programs paid by the Army. Many officers pursue advanced education on their own time. Here are some of the programs offered by the Army for the advanced education of its officers:

### Advanced Degree Program

The Army Educational Requirements System determines the Army's need for officers with advanced degrees. Selected officers are provided an opportunity to attend graduate school for up to three years in a discipline required by the Army. After completing their graduate studies, these officers are assigned to positions that utilize their education. These officers can also anticipate future assignments that capitalize on their specialized knowledge. Officers are considered for this program after completing six to eight years of active duty.

### Fully Funded Legal Education Program (FLEP)

The Judge Advocate General's Funded Legal Education Program allows up to 25 officers to be selected each year to attend a regular course of instruction leading to a Juris Doctor (J.D.) or Bachelor of Law (LL.B.) degree at an approved civilian law school. These programs are provided at government expense and usually last three academic years. Upon completion of schooling, the officer is required to accept an appointment in the Judge Advocate General's Corps for the period of active-duty obligation.

### Training With Industry (TWI) Program

The TWI program provides training in industrial procedures and practices not available through military or civilian schools. It provides officers with vital knowledge, experience and perspective in management and operational techniques. This experience is necessary to fill positions of significant responsibility in Army commands and activities that normally deal with civilian industry. Currently, these programs are concentrated in the areas of artificial intelligence, aviation logistics, communications-electronics, finance, marketing, ordnance, physical security, procurement, public affairs, research and development, systems automation, and transportation. These programs are normally one year long, with a predetermined follow-on assignment.

## RESERVE OFFICERS

In thousands of cities and towns across America, men and women work full-time in their communities and serve their nation part-time in one of the Army's reserve components. There are more than 7,000 units of the Army Reserve and the Army National Guard. These units are trained and equipped to accomplish Army missions worldwide on very short notice. They are a vital part of the total Army team, often training alongside active-duty Army personnel at home and overseas.

There are about 11,000 officers currently serving in Army National Guard and Army Reserve units. They serve in all career fields found in the active component of the Army. Often they serve in a career field that is the same as their civilian profession. Many serve in military units that offer them an exciting and demanding change from their full-time job. Most reservists will agree that the skills and qualities that are necessary for success in civilian life are enhanced by their military training and experience.

## FOR FURTHER INFORMATION

Students who wish to learn more about specific military occupations are encouraged to use this book to the fullest. In addition, many career information systems found in high schools and libraries have information about Army careers. The most up-to-date information about Army commissioning programs is available from an Army recruiter. Feel free to contact the one nearest you. There is no obligation.

# Navy

## OVERVIEW

The Navy operates throughout the world to help preserve peace. Navy cruisers, destroyers, frigates, submarines, aircraft carriers, and support ships are ready to maintain the freedom of the seas. Navy sea and air power are available to assist in the defense of our allies or engage enemy forces in the event of war.

The United States Navy is a large and complex organization. It includes nearly 600 ships, 6,000 aircraft, and bases around the world. Over 550,000 officers and enlisted personnel make up today's Navy. Many of the nearly 70,000 officers serve as ship or submarine officers, pilots, flight officers, nuclear power instructors, and special warfare officers. Others perform specialized duties in intelligence, engineering, law, medicine, and scientific careers. Between 6,000 and 7,000 men and women join the Navy as officers every year.

## BECOMING AN OFFICER

A Navy officer must be a mature person capable of assuming a wide variety of duties at sea, in the air, and ashore. Applicants must be physically fit, at least 19 years old, and United States citizens. They must have at least a bachelor's degree. The major fields of study required vary depending on the officer specialty.

There are several ways to become a Navy officer. Commissioning programs are available for students still in college and for college graduates. Specialists in certain professional and scientific fields may qualify for a direct commission. Programs leading to a commission as a Navy officer include the Naval Reserve Officers' Training Corps and the U.S. Naval Academy.

### Naval Reserve Officers' Training Corps

The Naval Reserve Officers' Training Corps (NROTC) program offers tuition and other financial benefits worth up to $70,000 at more than 60 of the country's leading colleges and universities. Two-year and four-year subsidized scholarships are offered. Participants receive a monthly cash allowance.

Two-year and four-year nonsubsidized NROTC programs are also offered. These are referred to as college programs and provide for monthly cash allowances during the junior and senior years.

### U.S. Naval Academy

The United States Naval Academy (USNA) provides a free four-year undergraduate education program. The USNA program leads to a bachelor's degree in a wide range of major subjects and a commission as a Navy or Marine Corps officer. Students are paid a monthly salary while attending the academy.

Students must be single with no children and must serve on active duty for at least five years after graduation, depending on follow-on training and designation. Admission to the Naval Academy is made through nominations from United States Senators, Representatives, the President and Vice President of the United States, and the Secretary of the Navy.

### Nuclear Propulsion Officer Candidate Programs

The Nuclear Propulsion Officer Candidate (NUPOC) program is for college juniors and seniors pursuing a bachelor's degree in physics, chemistry, mathematics, or an engineering discipline. College graduates with a bachelor's or higher degree may also qualify for the NUPOC program. Cash bonuses are offered for joining and completing the Navy's NUPOC program.

The only Navy requirement is that the student maintain excellent grades in required subjects and earn a degree. While in the NUPOC program, the student can enjoy many of the same benefits received by regular Navy officers. Upon graduation from college, NUPOCs begin their naval officer training at Officer Candidate School (OCS) in Newport, Rhode Island.

### Aviation Officer/Naval Flight Officer Programs

Aviation Officer Candidate (AOC) and Naval Flight Officer Candidate (NFOC) programs are for college seniors and graduates interested in becoming Navy pilots or flight officers. If qualified and accepted, they attend the Aviation Officer Candidate School in Pensacola, Florida.

### Warrant Officers

The Warrant Officer Program is open to all enlisted Navy people with the rank of Chief Petty Officer or above and have completed at least 12 years of naval service. Warrant officers are senior to all enlisted Chief Petty Officers and junior to all Ensigns.

### Limited Duty Officers

The Limited Duty Officer Program is open to warrant officers with more than two years of service as warrants and to enlisted people who are petty officers with at least eight years of naval service. If qualified, they earn a Navy officer commission because of their high quality and experience in a specialty, but are limited to duties of that specialty.

### Direct Commission

Direct commission (appointment) may be attained by a professional person who is already established in his or her specialty field, but who is interested in the challenging and rewarding career and lifestyle of a Navy officer. The Navy has programs to help medical, dental, law, and theology students complete their professional training and earn commissions as Navy officers.

## OFFICER TRAINING

Before receiving their first active-duty assignment, all new Navy officers go through a period of initial training. This training is designed to acquaint individuals with the Navy way of life, its rules, regulations, and responsibilities. The training also covers naval operations, organization, and administrative procedures. NROTC candidates and Naval Academy midshipmen receive this training as part of their college program. Other prospective officers are required to go to one of three schools—Officer Candidate School (OCS), Officer Indoctrination School (OIS), or Aviation Officer Candidate School (AOCS).

Each school consists of a full schedule of academic studies and rigorous physical training. OCS is a course for new surface warfare, nuclear submarine, engineering, supply, and diving and salvage officers. OIS is a course for officers who have received a direct commission in the field of medicine or law. AOCS is the training ground for prospective Navy pilots, naval flight officers, intelligence officers, and aviation maintenance duty officers.

Navy officers also go through specialized or technical training before their initial assignment. Initial advanced training after being commissioned an officer is usually at the Navy specialty school that pertains to the officer's major field of education or for which he or she qualified when entering the Navy. Here the new officers learn how to apply that specialty to naval operations.

For instance, cryptology officers go to the Naval Security Group orientation course; intelligence officers go to the Navy and Marine Corps Intelligence School; supply corps officers go to the Navy Supply School; civil engineer corps officers go to the Civil Engineer Corps School; and Navy chaplains go to the Chaplains' School. Pilots and naval flight officers receive their flight training and learn to operate the complex communications and weapons systems on Navy aircraft.

These schools may be several months to more than a year in length, depending on the complexity of the specialty and the advanced training needed. Other than the Navy aviation team, officers in the nuclear power program have the longest overall training period. After OCS, they go to Nuclear Power School in Orlando, Florida, for 24 weeks, then to a nuclear power training unit for 26 weeks, then to either the Submarine Officer Basic Course for 13 weeks or the Surface Warfare Officer School for 17 weeks before being assigned aboard a nuclear-powered vessel. The Navy's nuclear power training program is the broadest and most comprehensive anywhere.

Navy officers are also given short courses of special and refresher instruction to meet the needs of the service and their assignment. These courses usually are not more than six months in length. Specialized courses offered Navy officers are in communications, basic and advanced electronics, civil engineering, transportation management, naval justice, and petroleum products and supply.

Navy officers are also provided an opportunity to attend one of the service colleges. These are considered necessary for higher command leadership. A naval officer should possess a thorough knowledge of the principles and methods of naval strategy and tactics and of joint operations with other branches of the armed forces. To achieve these objectives, courses are given at the Armed Forces Staff College, the Inter-American Defense College, the National Defense University, the Naval War College, and Foreign Service Colleges.

## ADVANCEMENT

Most college graduates begin their Navy officer career as an Ensign. After two years, they are eligible for promotion to Lieutenant Junior Grade. Another two-year period makes them eligible for promotion to Lieutenant. After being in the Navy a total of nine to 11 years, an officer becomes eligible for promotion to Lieutenant Commander. A Lieutenant Commander must have 15 to 17 years of service to be eligible to become a Commander. A Commander must have been in the Navy 21 to 23 years to be promoted to Captain.

Promotion to the ranks of Lieutenant Commander and above are very competitive, and only the best officers are selected for advancement. A selection board evaluates the past performance of each eligible officer and recommends the best qualified for promotions.

Each Navy officer is given a new assignment, or tour, as it is called, every few years. Every effort is made to match personal desires with the needs of the Navy. Assignments may be in the officer's chosen field or in a different field where there is a need.

## EDUCATION PROGRAMS

Education and training are a continuous process throughout a Navy officer's career. As an officer's career develops, he or she may have the opportunity to take advantage of an advanced educational program. Presented below are some of the opportunities offered by the Navy in the professional development of its officers.

### Postgraduate Education Program

The goal of the Navy's Postgraduate Education Program is to provide specialized education at the master's and doctorate level in technical and nontechnical fields of study. The program is conducted mainly at the Naval Postgraduate School in Monterey, California. The program is supplemented by using civilian universities for many courses. It also makes use of appropriate courses provided by other agencies of the Department of Defense.

### Correspondence and Extension Courses

Correspondence and extension courses are encouraged for all Navy officers. Most of the courses are provided by the Naval Correspondence Course Center. Others are offered by the Naval War College, the Industrial College of the Armed Forces, military medical and dental schools, the Defense Intelligence School, and the Naval Submarine School.

Officers may also enroll in courses given by other services and in graduate and undergraduate level education offered by colleges and universities.

## THE NAVAL RESERVE

Navy officers who leave active duty for civilian careers can retain many of the benefits of a Navy career by joining the Naval Reserve Force.

The Naval Reserve Force is a team of highly trained people available in a national emergency to meet the expanded needs of the regular Navy. Most Reservists serve in a part-time status, consisting of one weekend a month and an annual two-week period of duty, called annual training (AT). These training periods can be taken on an individual basis or with a Reserve unit.

A Naval Reserve Force medical program works the same way for medical specialists who wish to serve their country and at the same time continue their civilian medical practice.

The Naval Reserve Force numbered more than 24,000 officers in mid-1986, and rose to approximately 47,000 in 1993.

## FOR FURTHER INFORMATION

The occupational information in *Military Careers* can be useful in exploring career opportunities in the Navy. Many career information systems found in high schools and libraries have similar information about military careers. However, to obtain detailed information about the latest commissioning programs, contact your local officer programs recruiter. There is no obligation. The Navy's toll free number for recruiter information is 1-800-327-NAVY.

# Air Force

## OVERVIEW

The United States Air Force is the primary aerospace arm of our nation's armed forces. The men and women of the Air Force fly, maintain, and support the world's most technically advanced aerospace forces, including long-range bombers, supersonic fighters, Airborne Warning and Control System (AWACS) aircraft, and many others. These forces are used whenever and wherever necessary to protect the interests of the United States and our allies. The Air Force is made up of nearly 400,000 men and women—disciplined, dedicated, and professionally trained officers and airmen—from all walks of life. Some 76,000 officers pilot multimillion-dollar aircraft, launch satellites, gather sensitive intelligence data, manage maintenance and other logistical support, or do one of many tasks vital to the Air Force mission. The Air Force currently commissions about 5,000 men and women each year to fill openings in a wide variety of challenging careers.

## BECOMING AN OFFICER

The Air Force commissions only United States citizens who possess a bachelor's degree from an accredited college. Depending on the career field an applicant selects, additional academic qualifications may be required (e.g., a graduate degree, specific courses). Applicants for a commission must also be physically fit and of high moral character. Typically, men and women may earn a commission through one of three pre-commissioning sources: The U.S. Air Force Academy, Air Force Reserve Officer Training Corps (AFROTC), or Officer Training School (OTS). Individuals in some professions may obtain a direct commission without attending one of the above commissioning programs.

### U.S. Air Force Academy

Located at the foot of the Rocky Mountains near Colorado Springs, Colorado, the Air Force Academy annually accepts about 1,200 young men and women into its four-year program. Graduates earn a bachelor of science degree and an Air Force commission.

The program is intense, with a well-balanced curriculum that includes the physical and social sciences, humanities, and math. In addition, the academy provides cadets with a background in space operations through courses such as astrodynamics and aeroengineering.

Admission to the Air Force Academy is generally made through nominations from United States Senators or Representatives, but other avenues to receive an admission appointment are available.

### Air Force Reserve Officer Training Corps (AFROTC)

This program gives college students a unique opportunity to earn a commission while they complete their degree requirements. The AFROTC offers four- and two-year programs (in selected fields) at more than 750 colleges and universities across the nation. You apply for the four-year AFROTC program by simply enrolling in the aerospace studies course at the time you register for your other freshman courses. You may apply for the two-year AFROTC program if you have at least two years of undergraduate work remaining. Each cadet receives $150 a month tax free during the final two academic years. See your AFROTC representative about details on AFROTC program opportunities.

Scholarships are available for all programs on a competitive basis. Scholarships pay for most tuition, laboratory and incidental fees, and textbooks. Scholarship cadets also receive $150 tax free each month during the school year. High school students interested in the four-year scholarship should apply late in their junior year or early in their senior year of high school. College freshman and sophomores can apply by contacting the professor of aerospace studies at their college or university.

### Officer Training School

The Officer Training School (OTS) at Maxwell AFB near Montgomery, Alabama, is a great opportunity for those who already have a bachelor's degree. Its rigorous 14-week program guides college graduates or degree airmen to commissions as Second Lieutenants. OTS cadets acquire the knowledge to perform as effective Air Force officers.

### Direct Appointment

The Air Force directly commissions men and women in certain professions. Individuals are eligible for direct appointment if they are fully qualified in certain medical, legal, or religious fields. Individuals who believe they may be qualified for a direct commission should contact their nearest Air Force recruiter.

## OFFICER TRAINING

Most new officers attend a technical training course immediately after coming on active duty. Technical training equips new officers with the specific skills required by their job specialty. Depending on the specialty, technical training lasts from a few weeks to over a year. (Some officers go directly to their first assignment without attending technical training.) Technical training centers are located at military installations throughout the United States. Upon completion of initial technical training, officers are assigned to an Air Force unit where they put their newly acquired skills to work.

At various points during a career as an Air Force officer, there is an opportunity to participate in professional military education—such as Squadron Officer School, Air Command and Staff College, and the Air War College. These programs prepare officers for the increasing responsibilities associated with career progression to the more senior grades in the Air Force. In addition, they provide the command and staff knowledge required to be a professional officer. Other educational opportunities are also available to Air Force officers.

## ADVANCEMENT

Most newly commissioned officers enter the Air Force as Second Lieutenants. A few officers receive a direct appointment to a higher grade. There are established points when an officer is considered for promotion. Air Force promotions are based on future potential as demonstrated by past and current performance. Promotion to the grade of First Lieutenant usually occurs after two years of service. After an additional two years of service, most officers are promoted to Captain.

Subsequent promotions are competitive, and only the best qualified officers are selected for promotion. Most officers compete for promotions without regard to their specific career specialty, though some officers (physicians, dentists, nurses, lawyers, chaplains, etc.) compete within their own specialties. There are provisions for early promotion of outstanding performers.

Most young officers (Lieutenants) start out in small units. As they gain experience and progress in rank (Captain), they are assigned to larger units, overseeing the operation of several smaller units. More senior officers (Majors and Lieutenant Colonels) are usually assigned as commanders of squadrons and are responsible for accomplishing that squadron's mission, as well as for the welfare of the men and women under their command. Colonels typically command large units or head major staff functions. Generals command combat organizations and oversee thousands of personnel and hundreds of millions of dollars in aircraft, supplies, and equipment.

## EDUCATION PROGRAMS

The Air Force sponsors advanced education for qualified officers. Officers attending graduate school in their off-duty time can have the Air Force pay up to 75 percent of their tuition. The Air Force also sponsors officers' advanced education at the Air Force Institute of Technology (AFIT) or at one of the many civilian colleges throughout the country. The Air Force pays for all tuition, fees, books, and equipment and continues to provide full pay and benefits. AFIT provides scientific, technological, and other specialized education to satisfy Air Force requirements. Air Force-sponsored education leads to degrees in engineering, management, social sciences, and many other fields.

## RESERVE FORCES

The reserve forces consist of two components, the Air National Guard and the Air Force Reserve. Their primary mission is to provide trained units and qualified personnel for active duty in the Air Force in time of war or national emergency and at such other times as the national security requires.

The reserve forces are highly trained, combat ready, and available for immediate call up to serve on active duty. They train (drill) regularly and provide a significant contribution to the daily operations of the Air Force as a by-product of their training. Guard and Reserve air crews currently fly the Air Force's front line aircraft.

### Air National Guard

The Air National Guard (ANG) provides 89 major flying units and several hundred mission support units, with at least one flying unit in every state. During peacetime, the Guard also has a state mission that includes disaster relief, maintaining peace and order, and civilian defense. Guard units are under the control of the state governors through their Adjutants General. There are approximately 115,000 men and women in the ANG.

Criteria for appointment as an officer in the ANG are similar to those for active Air Force officers and are spelled out in Air Force instructions. However, selection and appointment to fill ANG unit vacancies are prerogatives of the states, with the Air Force granting federal recognition as reserve officers of the Air Force. Nonprior-service line officers selected for appointment in the ANG must attend six weeks of pre-commissioning training at the ANG Academy of Military Science, McGhee-Tyson AB, Knoxville, Tennessee, where they are prepared for their initial commissioned service in the ANG. Upon commissioning, many new ANG officers are scheduled to attend further Air Force training in their specialty. There are approximately 14,000 ANG officers, of which over 4,200 are pilots.

### Air Force Reserve

The Air Force Reserve is a federal force. It provides 58 flying squadrons and nearly 400 mission support units. The Air Force Reserve has both "equipped" units with their own aircraft and "associate" units that fly and maintain active force aircraft and augment their active force counterparts during wartime or times of crisis.

The Air Force Reserve consists of approximately 78,000 men and women who train regularly, either in the units or as Individual Mobilization Augmentees (IMAs). IMAs are individual Reservists who train with active-duty Air Force organizations and who will augment those organizations for wartime, contingency, and limited peacetime requirements. There are approximately 12,400 IMAs.

Criteria for appointment as an officer in the Air Force Reserve are similar to those for active-duty Air Force officers and are discussed elsewhere in this guide. Nonprior-service personnel selected to be candidates for pilot or navigator training or to become engineers are sent to the Officer Training School along with the active-force line officer candidates. Reserve nonprior-service personnel who are not rated attend the Air National Guard Academy of Military Science. Medical officers attend an active-force short course at bases near Montgomery, Alabama. Each year, a small number of "deserving airmen" are selected to be commissioned from the enlisted ranks of the Air Force Reserve. They attend a two-week course at Maxwell AFB, Alabama, to learn officer skills.

There are approximately 15,000 Air Force Reserve officers (including IMAs). Approximately 2,300 are pilots and 350 are navigators. Over 21 percent of Reserve officers are women. The vast majority of the officer corps of the Air Force Reserve consists of prior-service officers who were commissioned through the Air Force Reserve Officer Training Corps, the Air Force Academy, or the Officer Training School and who served several years in the active Air Force before leaving extended active duty and joining the Air Force Reserve.

The focal point for recruiting officers in the Air Force Reserve and Air National Guard is the unit, since officers are basically recruited from each unit's local area. The Military Personnel Flights, located at each flying unit, are aware of all officer vacancies in both the flying units and the mission support units they service.

## FOR FURTHER INFORMATION

High school guidance counselors and Air Force Recruiters can give you advice and information on Air Force ROTC programs, Officer Training School, and the Air Force Academy. Local Air Force selection officers have the latest information on commissioning programs and career opportunities; contact them if you have any questions.

# Marine Corps

## OVERVIEW

The United States Marine Corps was created on November 10, 1775, by a resolution of the Continental Congress. Since then, the Marine Corps has grown to be one of the most elite fighting forces in the world. The Marine Corps' mission is unique among the five services; Marines serve on U.S. Navy ships, protect naval bases, guard U.S. embassies abroad, and serve as an ever-ready strike force to quickly protect the interests of the U.S. and its allies anywhere in the world. To perform the many duties of the Marine Corps, approximately 174,000 officers and enlisted Marines in the Corps fly planes and helicopters; operate radar equipment; drive armored vehicles; gather intelligence; survey and map territory; maintain and repair computers, jeeps, radios, trucks, tanks, and aircraft; and perform hundreds of other challenging jobs. Each year, the Marine Corps accepts approximately 1,600 new officers into its ranks to maintain its approximately 16,500-person officer corps.

## BECOMING AN OFFICER

The Marine Corps recruits young men and women of high moral standards who have or will have a four-year college degree, are physically fit, and have demonstrated potential for leadership. Applicants must be U.S. citizens and pass the initial Marine Corps physical fitness test. Additionally, applicants must take either the SAT, ACT, or ASVAB aptitude tests. Minimum acceptable scores are: SAT – combined verbal and math scores of 1070; ACT – 45; and ASVAB – Electronics Repair composite – 115. The only age requirement is that a person must be at least 20 and less than 30 years of age at the time of commissioning. Applicants for law programs must score a minimum of 30 on a 50-point scale, or 150 on a 180-point scale, of the LSAT.

Marine Corps officers are selected from various sources, including the Naval Reserve Officers' Training Corps (NROTC) Program, the United States Naval Academy, the Platoon Leaders Class (PLC) Program, and the Officer Candidate Class (OCC) Program.

### Naval Reserve Officers' Training Corps

The NROTC Scholarship Program offers tuition and other financial benefits worth as much as $70,000 at one of more than 62 of the country's leading colleges and universities. Four-year NROTC scholarships are available to high school graduates on a competitive selection process in which consideration is given to such factors as high school record, college board scores, extracurricular activities, and leadership qualities.

Two- and three-year NROTC scholarships are available to college freshmen, sophomores, and juniors meeting basic requirements. Recipients are selected in a competitive process similar to that for the four-year scholarship.

### U.S. Naval Academy

Since 1883, Marine Corps officers have been commissioned from the U.S. Naval Academy, where graduating midshipmen earn a bachelor of science degree either in one of seven different engineering programs or in one of eleven disciplines offered apart from engineering programs. Today, nearly 17 percent of each graduating class receives a regular Marine Corps commission.

### Platoon Leaders Class

The Platoon Leaders Class (PLC) Program is for those college freshmen, sophomores, and juniors who have made the decision to pursue a Marine Corps officer commission. Application to this program may be made upon successful completion of the first semester or quarter of the freshman year. Applicants must be pursuing a four-year baccalaureate degree from an accredited college. They are eligible to receive $150 per month in financial assistance after successful completion of their first summer of training.

PLC officer candidates attend summer training sessions at the Marine Corps Officer Candidates School in Quantico, Virginia. Freshmen and sophomores participate in two six-week sessions, and juniors participate in one 10-week session.

Aviation guarantees in the PLC-Aviation Program are available to those who qualify. In this program, individuals can receive real flight experience and instruction to familiarize themselves with flying before military flight training begins.

PLC-Law is a post-baccalaureate degree program for law school attendees. Active duty is postponed until a student obtains a law degree and passes the bar examination.

### Officer Candidate Class

The Officer Candidate Class (OCC) Program is pre-commission training for college seniors and graduates who desire to be Marine Corps officers. Upon graduation from college, candidates attend one 10-week officer training course and receive a reserve commission upon successful completion of training.

### Women Officer Candidate Program

The Women Officer Candidate (WOC) Program is open to women in their junior and senior years of college or who have graduated from a four-year accredited institution. Training consists of a 10-week summer course in consolidated officer candidate companies. Women candidates participate in many of the same rigorous screening programs as their male counterparts, and when they successfully complete training, they receive a reserve commission as well.

In addition to the programs described above, the Marine Corps has programs for qualified enlisted personnel to earn commissions as officers. These programs include the Marine Enlisted Commissioning Education Program (MECEP), the Enlisted Commissioning Program (ECP), and the Meritorious Commissioning Program (MCP).

## OFFICER TRAINING

The Marine Corps has developed career patterns to prepare its officers to assume progressively higher command and staff responsibilities. These career patterns are designed to provide individual training and education, followed by operational assignments. They allow officers to learn their professions and progress to sequentially more demanding assignments.

Officer training can generally be divided into three types. First, the Marine Corps maintains a system of professional military education that is progressive in nature. This education prepares officers for the increasing responsibilities associated with career progression to more senior grades in the Marine Corps. It is primarily the study of how to be an officer and apply the command and staff knowledge required of a professional. Examples of this type of training are the 23-week Basic Officers Course, which all newly commissioned officers attend, and the 43-week Command and Staff College for midgrade officers.

The second type of training encompasses the many specific skill-producing courses that are conducted to enable the officer to perform in a specialized area immediately upon assignment. Most Marine Corps officers attend one of these courses sponsored by the Corps, but they may also attend others conducted by the Navy or another service. An example of this type of initial training is pilot training conducted by the Navy. An example of follow-on skill progression training is the Weapons and Tactics Instructor Course designed for highly qualified aviation and command and control officers.

The third type of training provided to selected officers is either in-house or civilian advanced academic education. This type of training is designed to meet the Marine Corps' need for officers trained in specific technical, scientific, engineering, or managerial fields. Examples of this type of training are the U.S. Naval Test Pilot School and the U.S. Army Management of Defense Acquisition Contracts Course.

Each Marine Corps officer's training begins with the physically and mentally demanding Basic Officers Course and progresses to individual training specifically designed for his or her military occupational specialty (MOS). This unique training of the Marine Corps air-ground team provides all Marine Corps officers with a common background that is independent of their MOS.

## ADVANCEMENT

Marine Corps officers are selected for advancement based on their qualifications to fully meet the needs of the Marine Corps. Each individual's qualifications and performance of duty must clearly demonstrate that he or she would be capable of performing the duties normally associated with the next higher permanent grade. Every aspect of an officer's performance is carefully evaluated during the selection process to ensure that those selected for promotion are truly the best qualified.

The Marine Corps has an established career counseling system to provide officers with proper career guidance and counsel. Broad guidelines help to channel all officers to a rewarding, successful career.

After initial qualification in an MOS, officers are offered continued professional education, various duty assignments, and further MOS training. Junior officers can expect to perform not only as leaders, but as technicians and managers. Commonly, junior officers are put in charge of units consisting of anywhere from three or four, to over 100, Marines.

As junior officers become more proficient in their fields, opportunities arise for more challenging assignments and increased responsibility. Performance in these challenging situations directly relates to the continuance of a Marine Corps career. Although promotion boards review many factors, performance is the key to advancement.

## EDUCATION PROGRAMS

The Marine Corps offers career education at every level in the officer ranks. Not only is formal schooling provided to enhance the professional development of officers, but the Marine Corps has an extensive correspondence course program available to all officers.

Especially inviting are the various graduate education programs made available to qualified officers; the Special Education Program, the Advanced Degree Program, the Excess Leave Program-Law, and the Funded Law Education Program.

### Special Education Program

The Special Education Program (SEP) is a fully funded program designed to build up the Marine Corps' pool of officers with specialties in both technical and nontechnical disciplines. Officers accepted into and completing the program earn master's degrees in designated disciplines by attending the Naval Postgraduate School, the Air Force Institute of Technology, or approved civilian schools.

### Advanced Degree Program

Under the Advanced Degree Program (ADP), expenses for the cost of a master's degree are partially funded. Officers are selected to study in a particular technical or nontechnical discipline and may attend the accredited school of their choice. While in this and the SEP program, officers continue to receive all pay and allowances.

A sample of the types of disciplines officers may study while in either the ADP or the SEP includes space systems operations, defense systems analysis, management, public relations, computer science, electronic engineering, and telecommunications management.

### Excess Leave Program-Law

The Excess Leave Program-Law (ELP-L) provides qualified Marine Corps officers the opportunity to take time off from active duty to attend an accredited law school at their own expense. While participating in the ELP-L, officers receive no pay or allowances.

### Funded Law Education Program

Under the Funded Law Education Program (FLEP), Marine Corps officers attend an accredited law school of their choice, with the Marine Corps paying their tuition and expenses. Full pay and allowances are provided to those officers in the FLEP.

## RESERVE OFFICERS

The Marine Corps Reserve plays a vital role in the augmentation of the regular force. Hard work and dedication are keys to maintaining a combat-ready force capable of responding, at any time, to the call to active duty. Reserve officers have an especially challenging role in maintaining this ready force.

Currently, 8,000 Reserve officers serve on active duty, and 8,054 Reserve officers are assigned to Selected Marine Corps Reserve (SMCR) units or the Individual Ready Reserve (IRR).

Reserve officers serve in the same types of duties and job assignments as their regular counterparts. The main difference is that they serve part-time, one weekend each month and two weeks of continuous duty each year. Regular officers serve full-time, all year round.

## FOR FURTHER INFORMATION

The above information is only a broad overview of the exciting challenges available to Marine Corps officers. Young men and women desiring more information about Marine Corps officer opportunities should contact a local Marine Corps officer selection officer by calling 1-800-MARINES or by sending a message on the Internet to recruiting@MQG-SMTP3.USMC.MIL.

# Coast Guard

## OVERVIEW

The United States Coast Guard regularly performs many functions vital to maritime safety. The Coast Guard's most visible job is saving lives and property in and around American waters. The Coast Guard also enforces customs and fishing laws, protects marine wildlife, fights pollution on our lakes and along the coastline, and conducts the International Ice Patrol. The Coast Guard is also responsible for monitoring traffic in major harbors, keeping shipping lanes open on ice-bound lakes, and maintaining lighthouses and other navigation aides.

The Coast Guard is a part of the U.S. Department of Transportation. In time of war it may be placed under the command of the Navy Department. A vital part of the Armed Services, the Coast Guard has participated in every major American military campaign. The Coast Guard is the smallest of the armed services. Currently there are 5,864 commissioned officers, 1,520 warrant officers, and 29,839 enlisted members. Coast Guard officers perform in many different occupations to support the mission of the Coast Guard. Each year, the Coast Guard has openings for about 300 new officers in a wide range of challenging careers.

## BECOMING AN OFFICER

There are three programs leading to a commission as an officer in the U.S. Coast Guard—the Coast Guard Academy, Officer Candidate School, and direct commissioning. Applicants for all programs must be physically qualified, U.S. citizens, and possess high moral character.

### The U.S. Coast Guard Academy

The U.S. Coast Guard Academy, located in New London, Connecticut, accepts about 250 young men and women into its program each year. The four-year academic program leads to a bachelor of science degree in a variety of majors. Approximately 75 percent of the academy graduates earn degrees in technical areas such as engineering, sciences, and mathematics.

Each major provides a sound undergraduate education in a field of interest to the Coast Guard and prepares the cadet to assume initial duty as a junior officer. Upon graduation, the cadet is commissioned as an ensign in the Coast Guard.

Appointment as a cadet is based solely on an annual nationwide competition. It is not necessary to obtain a nomination from a Senator or Representative. The competition includes either the College Board Scholastic Aptitude Test (SAT) or the American College Testing Assessment (ACT), high school rank in class, community service, and leadership qualities. Interested students should apply during the fall of their senior year in high school.

### Officer Candidate School

The Officer Candidate School (OCS) is pre-commissioning training for college graduates who want to become Coast Guard officers. Candidates attend a 17-week officer training course at Yorktown, Virginia. The physical and academic curriculum is demanding. In addition to physical training, OCS candidates study navigation, ship's operations, seamanship, Coast Guard orientation, and leadership. After completing OCS, candidates are commissioned as Ensigns in the Coast Guard Reserve.

### Direct Commissions

Graduates from a law school accredited by the American Bar Association are eligible to receive commissions as Lieutenant Junior Grade in the Coast Guard Reserve. The applicant must be admitted to the bar of a state or federal court within one year of receiving a commission. Qualified graduates of state and federal maritime academies may also be eligible for a commission as an Ensign or Lieutenant Junior Grade in the Coast Guard Reserve. Engineers are highly sought and may be directly commissioned up to the rank of Lieutenant. Occasionally, direct commissions may be available for ROTC/NROTC/AFROTC students at selected colleges and universities, prior military officers, and qualified military pilots. Qualified military pilots may compete for direct commissions as aviators in the rank of Ensign or Lieutenant Junior Grade in the Coast Guard Reserve.

## TRAINING

Newly commissioned officers are offered a wide variety of mission opportunities for their first assignment. This duty will be in one of the Coast Guard's primary missions, such as search and rescue, marine law enforcement, drug interdiction, or aids to navigation. All officers are encouraged to apply for postgraduate education or specialized training. The Coast Guard provides training in a range of career areas. Coast Guard pilot training is available to selected graduates of the Coast Guard Academy or Officer Candidate School. Pilot trainees attend 14 months of basic and advanced flight training at naval air stations in Pensacola, Florida or Corpus Christi, Texas. Many other courses are provided to instruct officers in specific skills needed for a particular assignment. In addition, there is an opportunity to participate in professional military education such as the Armed Forces Staff College, the Industrial College of the Armed Forces, or one of the colleges run by another branch of the service.

## THE MINORITY OFFICER RECRUITING EFFORT (MORE)

The Coast Guard offers up to two-year scholarships to eligible minority students enrolled full time in selected four-year college programs. Technical majors are preferred but are not essential for participation. Selections are based on nationwide competition with selection announcement in early spring. College sophomores and juniors may compete. Upon successful completion of the MORE program, acceptance into OCS is guaranteed.

## EDUCATION PROGRAMS

The Coast Guard believes strongly in the continued education of its members. The Coast Guard offers several education assistance programs, including:

### Tuition Assistance Program

The Coast Guard sponsors a tuition assistance program for off-duty education within the limits of available funds. This program allows Coast Guard officers to enroll in off-duty courses at accredited colleges and universities. The tuition is paid by the Coast Guard for all courses not in excess of six credits per semester (or quarter) or for any course not extending beyond one semester or a maximum of 17 weeks, whichever is longer.

### Physician's Assistant Program

The Physician's Assistant Program is a two-year, full-time course of study at Sheppard AFB, Wichita Falls, Texas. The program includes 12 months of study and 12 months of clinical rotation at an Air Force hospital. Upon successful completion, Coast Guard graduates receive their certificates as physician's assistants and direct commissions as Ensigns. Completion of the program results in a bachelor's degree in Health Science.

### Postgraduate Education Program

The Coast Guard offers qualified officers an opportunity to obtain advanced education on a full-time basis at Coast Guard expense. Each year, approximately 125 officers are selected for this program. They attend various colleges and universities in over 30 major curriculum areas. Entry into this program is competitive, and only the best qualified officers are selected.

## FOR FURTHER INFORMATION

Although the preceding section gives a general overview of the Coast Guard and its programs, it by no means covers the wide range of opportunities available in the Coast Guard. Use *Military Careers* to begin exploring career possibilities in the Coast Guard. Your local Coast Guard recruiter would be pleased to supply you with current, more detailed Coast Guard career information. There is no obligation.

# Officer Occupational Descriptions

# Executive, Administrative, and Managerial Occupations

- Communications Managers
- Emergency Management Officers
- Finance and Accounting Managers
- Food Service Managers
- Health Services Administrators
- International Relations Officers
- Law Enforcement and Security Officers
- Management Analysts
- Personnel Managers
- Postal Directors
- Purchasing and Contracting Managers
- Recruiting Managers
- Store Managers
- Supply and Warehousing Managers
- Teachers and Instructors
- Training and Education Directors
- Transportation Maintenance Managers
- Transportation Managers

# COMMUNICATIONS MANAGERS

Instant worldwide communication among air, sea, and land forces is vital to military operations. The services operate some of the largest and most complex communication networks in the world. Communications managers plan and direct the operation of military communication systems. They also manage personnel in communications centers and relay stations.

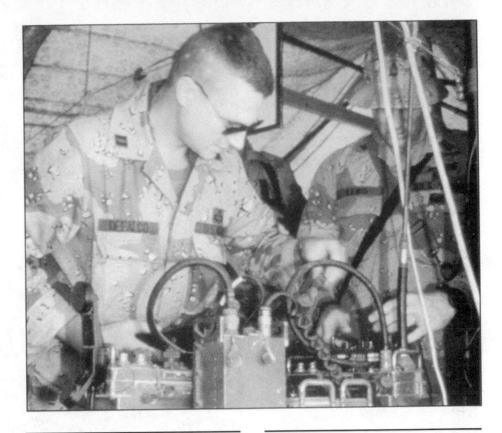

## What They Do

Communications managers in the military perform some or all of the following duties:

- Develop rules or procedures for sending and receiving communications

- Direct personnel who operate computer systems and electronic telecommunications and satellite communications equipment

- Develop ways to track and ensure security of communications

- Direct personnel who maintain and repair communications equipment

- Develop budgets for communications centers

## Special Requirements

A 4-year college degree, preferably in engineering, mathematics, computer science, or related fields, is required to enter this occupation.

## Helpful Attributes

Helpful attributes include:

- Interest in working with computers, radios, and electronic equipment

- Interest in technical work

## Work Environment

Communications managers usually work in communications centers on land or aboard ships.

## Training Provided

Job training consists of 12 to 32 weeks of classroom instruction. Training length varies depending on specialty. Course content typically includes:

- Communications theory and security

- Communications-electronics management

- Satellite communications, including tactical ground terminals

- Electronic principles, technologies, and systems

- Tactical combat communications systems

Further training occurs on the job and through advanced courses.

## Civilian Counterparts

Civilian communications managers work for private firms involved with telephone and telegraph communications, radio and TV broadcasting, and satellite communications. They perform duties similar to those performed by military communications managers. Depending on their specialty, they may also be called station managers, operations managers, or communications superintendents.

## Opportunities

The services have about 4,200 communications managers. On average, they need 100 new communications managers each year. After job training, communications managers are assigned to manage or assist in managing a communications center. With experience, they may advance to senior management or command positions.

# EMERGENCY MANAGEMENT OFFICERS

Army
Navy
Marine Corps
Coast Guard

The military must be prepared for all types of emergencies, from natural disasters, such as floods, earthquakes, and hurricanes, to enemy attacks. Emergency management officers prepare warning, control, and evacuation plans. They also coordinate emergency response teams during natural disasters.

## What They Do

Emergency management officers in the military perform some or all of the following duties:

- Organize emergency teams for quick responses to disaster situations

- Research ways to respond to possible disaster situations

- Conduct training programs for specialized disaster response teams

- Develop joint disaster response plans with local, state, and federal agencies

- Obtain supplies, equipment, and protection equipment

- Develop warning systems and safe shelters

- Direct disaster control centers

## Special Requirements

A 4-year college degree is normally required to enter this occupation.

## Helpful Attributes

Helpful fields of study include physical and environmental sciences, engineering, law enforcement, and business or public administration. Helpful attributes include:

- Interest in developing detailed plans

- Ability to remain calm in stressful situations

- Ability to express ideas clearly and concisely

## Work Environment

Emergency management officers usually work in offices while developing disaster response plans. They work outdoors while inspecting shelters or directing emergency response teams.

## Training Provided

Job training consists of 2 to 9 weeks of classroom instruction. Training length varies depending on specialty. Course content typically includes:

- Disaster planning

- Procedures for nuclear, biological, and chemical decontamination

- Effects of radiation

- Procedures for nuclear accident teams

## Civilian Counterparts

Civilian emergency management officers work for federal, state, and local governments, including law enforcement and civil defense agencies. They perform duties similar to those performed by military emergency management officers.

## Opportunities

The services have about 500 emergency management officers. On average, they need 20 new emergency management officers each year. After job training, emergency management officers are assigned to command centers or planning sections, where they develop emergency plans and training programs. In time, they may advance to senior management positions.

# FINANCE AND ACCOUNTING MANAGERS

**Army**
**Navy**
**Air Force**
**Marine Corps**
**Coast Guard**

Each year, the services spend billions of dollars on personnel, equipment, and supplies. Only through careful management can military funds be put to their best use. Finance and accounting managers direct and manage the financial affairs of the military. They also advise commanders on financial and accounting matters.

## What They Do

Finance and accounting managers in the military perform some or all of the following duties:

- Set policies for the use of military funds

- Direct the preparation of budgets and financial forecasts

- Advise management personnel on accounting, budgeting, and fiscal matters

- Develop ways to track financial transactions

- Prepare and examine financial records and reports

- Direct the activities of finance and accounting staff

## Training Provided

Job training consists of 2 to 16 weeks of classroom instruction. Training length varies depending on specialty. Course content typically includes:

- Financial management techniques, including budget preparation and review

- Financial management techniques

- Military accounting

- Duties of finance and accounting managers

- Personnel management and payroll procedures

- Statistical analysis and fiscal planning

## Special Requirements

A 4-year college degree in accounting, finance, or a related field is required to enter this occupation. Some specialties require a master's degree in business administration or recognition as a Certified Public Accountant (CPA).

## Helpful Attributes

Helpful attributes include:

- Preference for working with numbers and statistics

- Interest in work requiring accuracy and attention to detail

- Interest in planning and directing the work of others

## Work Environment

Finance and accounting managers work in large finance or accounting offices.

## Civilian Counterparts

Civilian finance and accounting managers work for businesses, accounting firms, universities, hospitals, or government agencies. They perform duties similar to those performed by military finance and accounting managers. They usually specialize in certain areas of finance and accounting, such as budgets, internal auditing, or cost accounting. In large business firms, they may be called executive controllers or company treasurers.

## Opportunities

The services have about 2,100 finance and accounting managers. On average, they need 70 new finance and accounting managers each year. After job training, managers are assigned to finance and accounting offices. Initially, they perform work in accounting, auditing, or finance management operations. With experience, they may advance to senior management and command positions.

# FOOD SERVICE MANAGERS

The military serves food to hundreds of thousands of service members each day. Meals must be carefully planned and prepared to ensure good nutrition and variety. Food service managers direct the facilities that prepare and serve food.

## What They Do

Food service managers in the military perform some or all of the following duties:

- Manage the cooking and serving of food at mess halls

- Direct the operation of officers' dining halls

- Determine staff and equipment needed for dining halls, kitchens, and meat-cutting plants

- Set standards for food storage and preparation

- Estimate food budgets

- Maintain nutritional and sanitary standards at food service facilities

## Special Requirements

A 4-year college degree is normally required to enter this occupation.

## Helpful Attributes

Helpful fields of study include food service management, nutrition, and business administration. Helpful attributes include:

- Interest in nutrition and food preparation

- Interest in planning and directing the work of others

## Work Environment

Food service managers usually work in food service facilities. They may manage facilities in field camps or aboard ships.

## Training Provided

Job training consists of 12 to 16 weeks of classroom instruction. Course content typically includes:

- Food service operations and management

- Resource management

- Nutritional meal planning

- Hotel management

## Civilian Counterparts

Civilian food service managers work for hotels, restaurants, and cafeterias. They perform duties similar to those performed by military food service managers.

## Opportunities

The services have about 1,500 food service managers. On average, they need 150 new food service managers each year. After job training, food service managers may work independently or under the supervision of other officers. With experience, they may manage one or more large facilities. In time, they may advance to senior management positions.

# HEALTH SERVICES ADMINISTRATORS

In hospitals and clinics, all of the departments—emergency, X-ray, nursing, maintenance, administration, and food service—must work together to provide quality health care. Health services administrators manage hospitals, clinics, and other health care facilities. They also manage individual departments or specific health care programs within a hospital.

## What They Do

Health services administrators in the military perform some or all of the following duties:

- Develop and manage budgets for health care facilities or programs

- Meet with hospital department heads to plan services and keep the health care facility running smoothly

- Direct personnel activities, such as hiring, employee evaluation, staff development, and recordkeeping

- Plan for delivering health services during emergencies and test these plans during exercises

- Direct the day-to-day operations of the nursing department

- Direct the operations of support departments, such as maintenance, food services, or administration

## Special Requirements

A 4-year college degree in health care, public health, business, nursing administration, or a related field is required to enter most of the specialties in this occupation. Some specialties require further education or prior experience in the health services field.

## Helpful Attributes

Helpful attributes include:

- Interest in planning and directing the work of others

- Interest in working closely with people

- Ability to express ideas clearly and concisely

- Interest in health care

## Work Environment

Health services administrators work in hospitals, clinics, and other health care facilities. Most work at facilities on land, but some work aboard hospital ships and ships with large sick bays.

## Training Provided

Job training is provided for some specialties in this occupation. This training consists of 10 to 12 weeks of classroom instruction and practical exercises. Course content typically includes:

- Planning and directing health services

- Patient unit management

- Nursing service administration

## Civilian Counterparts

Civilian health services administrators usually work for hospitals, clinics, nursing homes, health maintenance organizations (HMOs), or other health care facilities. They may also work for colleges and universities, public health agencies, insurance companies, or health management firms. Civilian health services administrators perform duties similar to those performed in the military. Depending on the programs or facilities they manage, civilian health services administrators may also be called hospital administrators, nursing services directors, emergency medical services coordinators, and outpatient services directors.

## Opportunities

The services have about 3,100 health services administrators. On average, they need 200 new health services administrators each year. After job training, health services administrators may be assigned to a variety of positions depending on their specialty. Usually, they work under the direction of experienced officers. With experience, they may manage one or more departments in a facility. In time, they may direct a health services facility. Eventually, they may advance to senior management positions responsible for planning health services at many facilities.

# INTERNATIONAL RELATIONS OFFICERS

Information about the military capabilities of foreign countries is vital to our national defense. Our leaders need to know the strengths and weaknesses of both friendly and unfriendly countries. International relations officers collect, analyze, and report information about foreign countries to be used for military planning.

## What They Do

International relations officers in the military perform some or all of the following duties:

- Collect and report information about the military forces of foreign countries

- Hold meetings with foreign military and government officials

- Analyze political, social, and economic matters in foreign countries

- Project foreign political trends

- Advise commanders about situations in foreign countries

## Special Requirements

A 4-year college degree is normally required to enter this occupation. Some specialties require an advanced degree. Knowledge of the people and language of one or more foreign countries may be required.

## Helpful Attributes

Helpful fields of study include political science, history, and international affairs. Helpful attributes include:

- Ability to express ideas clearly and concisely

- Interest in collecting and analyzing data

- Interest in living and working in a foreign country

- Interest in working closely with people

## Work Environment

International relations officers work mainly in offices of U.S. embassies and missions located overseas.

## Training Provided

Job training is provided in some specialties. Training length varies by entry requirements and specialty area. Course content typically includes:

- Political and cultural awareness

- Development of foreign area expertise

- Organization and functions of diplomatic missions

Further training occurs on the job.

## Civilian Counterparts

Civilians who perform work similar to the work of international relations officers are employed mainly by government agencies, such as the Department of State. Called foreign service officers, they work in U.S. embassies and missions overseas. Other civilian counterparts include political scientists, university instructors, and advisors to corporations doing business overseas.

## Opportunities

The services have about 200 international relations officers. On average, they need 10 new international relations officers each year. Normally, international relations officers are selected from among officers who have several years of military experience. They are selected from a variety of military career fields. These officers usually return to their main career field after several years of duty as international relations officers.

# LAW ENFORCEMENT AND SECURITY OFFICERS

The military services have their own police forces to protect lives and property on military bases and to patrol our coastal waters. Law enforcement and security officers command military police units that enforce laws and investigate crimes. They also plan and direct programs to protect property, communications, and classified information.

## What They Do

Law enforcement and security officers in the military perform some or all of the following duties:

- Direct the enforcement of military law

- Develop policies and programs to prevent crime and reduce traffic accidents

- Supervise the arrest, custody, transfer, and release of offenders

- Plan and direct criminal investigations and investigations of suspected treason, sabotage, or espionage

- Plan for the security of military bases and office buildings and direct security procedures

- Manage military correctional facilities

- Help in ballistics, forgery, fingerprinting, and polygraph (lie detector) examinations

## Special Requirements

A 4-year college degree is normally required to enter this occupation. Some specialties require further education or prior experience in law enforcement and security.

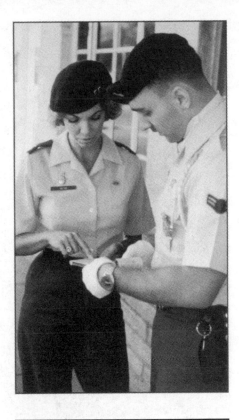

## Helpful Attributes

Helpful fields of study include business administration, criminal justice, psychology, sociology, and public administration. Helpful attributes include:

- Interest in law enforcement and crime prevention

- Interest in planning and directing the work of others

## Work Environment

Law enforcement and security officers in the military usually work in offices while planning and directing law enforcement and security activities. They may work outdoors while directing investigations, observing prisoners, and inspecting security systems.

## Training Provided

Job training consists of 7 to 28 weeks of classroom instruction. Training length varies depending on specialty. Course content typically includes:

- Law enforcement administration

- Management of security problems

- Investigation procedures and reporting

- Military law

## Civilian Counterparts

Civilian law enforcement and security officers work in federal, state, and local prisons, intelligence and law enforcement agencies, and private security companies. Some also operate their own security firms or become private detectives. They perform duties similar to those performed in the military. They may also be called police chiefs, chief inspectors, prison wardens, security managers, or chief deputy sheriffs.

## Opportunities

The services have about 2,400 law enforcement and security officers. On average, they need 125 new law enforcement and security officers each year. After job training, officers are assigned to command police, security, or investigative units. Depending on ability and experience, law enforcement and security officers may be assigned to direct one or more large law enforcement units.

# MANAGEMENT ANALYSTS

Good management minimizes waste and inefficiency. By improving its management techniques, the military makes the best use of its human and material resources. Management analysts study and suggest better ways to organize, staff, and manage military activities.

## What They Do

Management analysts in the military perform some or all of the following duties:

- Measure work load and calculate how many persons are needed to perform the work

- Study the information needs of managers and design manual or computerized systems to satisfy them

- Design organizations for new or existing offices

- Analyze work to be performed and develop an efficient implementation plan

- Design rules or procedures for work activities or information flow

- Gather data for studies by conducting interviews and reviewing records

- Write reports and give briefings on findings

## Special Requirements

A 4-year college degree is normally required to enter this occupation.

## Helpful Attributes

Helpful fields of study include management, operations research, and business or public administration. Helpful attributes include:

- Interest in solving problems

- Interest in collecting and analyzing data

- Ability to express ideas clearly and concisely

## Work Environment

Management analysts normally work in offices, although they sometimes study work that occurs outdoors.

## Training Provided

Job training consists of 6 to 10 weeks of classroom instruction. Training length varies depending on specialty. Course content typically includes:

- Management engineering techniques

- Methods of statistical analysis

- Internal review and analysis techniques

- Systems analysis procedures

## Civilian Counterparts

Civilian management analysts often work in private management consulting firms. Many others work in hospitals, universities, government agencies, or manufacturing firms. Civilian management analysts perform duties similar to those performed in the military. They may specialize in areas such as records management analysis or systems management analysis.

## Opportunities

The services have about 200 management analysts. On average, they need 10 new management analysts each year. After job training, management analysts are assigned to analysis teams. With experience, they may advance to senior management or command positions.

# PERSONNEL MANAGERS

As with civilian employers, the military tries to find the best person for each job and encourages each individual to realize his or her full potential. Personnel managers direct programs to attract and select new personnel for the services, assign them to jobs, provide career counseling, and maintain personnel records.

## What They Do

Personnel managers in the military perform some or all of the following duties:

- Plan recruiting activities to interest qualified young people in the military

- Direct testing and career counseling for military personnel

- Classify personnel according to job aptitude, interest, and service need

- Direct the assignment of personnel to jobs and training

- Direct personnel recordkeeping operations

- Establish standards to determine the number of people to assign to activities

- Study military jobs to see how they can be improved and kept up-to-date with technology

- Plan for hiring, training, and assigning personnel for the future

- Develop programs to prevent and resolve equal opportunity problems

## Special Requirements

A 4-year college degree is normally required to enter this occupation.

## Work Environment

Personnel managers work in offices.

## Helpful Attributes

Helpful fields of study include personnel management, organizational development, industrial psychology, and labor relations. Helpful attributes include:

- Interest in working closely with people

- Interest in planning and directing the work of others

- Interest in working with computers

## Training Provided

Job training consists of 5 to 16 weeks of classroom instruction. Course content typically includes:

- Military personnel policies and objectives

- Automated personnel systems

- Career development programs

- Equal opportunity problems

- Management and organizational concepts

Further training occurs in advanced courses.

## Civilian Counterparts

Civilian personnel managers work for all types of businesses and industries, as well as for government agencies. They perform duties similar to those performed by military personnel managers. Depending on their specialty, they may also be called employment relations directors, employment managers, occupational analysts, industrial relations directors, equal employment opportunity representatives, or affirmative action coordinators.

## Opportunities

The services have about 3,500 personnel managers. On average, they need 100 new personnel managers each year. After job training, personnel managers may be assigned to many different types of work, depending on their specialties. Usually, they begin by working under experienced personnel managers. In time, they may advance to senior management and command positions.

# POSTAL DIRECTORS

The military operates its own postal system, which is an extension of the U.S. Postal Service. This system handles mail sent between the services and civilians. Postal directors manage the postal operations for military bases and naval fleets.

## What They Do

Postal directors in the military perform some or all of the following duties:

- Direct the operation of post offices and mail rooms on military bases and ships

- Work with the U.S. Postal Service to forward service mail

- Keep information on the location and mailing addresses of military personnel

- Prepare reports on postal operations

- Inspect post office activities and records

- Investigate postal irregularities

## Special Requirements

A 4-year college degree is normally required to enter this occupation.

## Helpful Attributes

Helpful fields of study include business or public administration and transportation management. Helpful attributes include:

- Ability to plan and organize

- Interest in administrative work

- Ability to express ideas clearly and concisely

- Interest in working closely with others

## Work Environment

Postal directors usually work in offices and postal facilities.

## Training Provided

Job training consists of 4 weeks of classroom instruction. Course content typically includes:

- Organization of postal operations

- Post office services, such as money orders and certified mail

- Procedures for handling international mail

## Civilian Counterparts

Civilian postal directors work for the U.S. Postal Service. Also called postmasters, they perform duties similar to those performed by military postal directors.

## Opportunities

The services have about 100 officers working as postal directors. On average, they need 10 new postal directors each year. Postal directors are usually selected from among officers who make their career in the various administration or management fields. Postal operations is only one of many administrative specialties they may work in at some time during their military careers. Officers normally do not have a career exclusively in postal operations.

# PURCHASING AND CONTRACTING MANAGERS

Army
Navy
Air Force
Marine Corps
Coast Guard

The military buys billions of dollars worth of equipment, supplies, and services from private industry each year. The services must make sure their purchases meet military specifications and are made at a fair price. Purchasing and contracting managers negotiate, write, and monitor contracts for purchasing equipment, materials, and services.

## What They Do

Purchasing and contracting managers in the military perform some or all of the following duties:

- Review requests for supplies and services to make sure they are complete and accurate

- Prepare bid invitations or requests for proposals for contracts with civilian firms, which specify the type, amount, price, and delivery date for supplies or services

- Review bids or proposals and award contracts

- Prepare formal contracts, specifying all terms and conditions

- Review work to make sure that it meets the requirements of contracts

## Special Requirements

A 4-year college degree is normally required to enter this occupation.

## Helpful Attributes

Helpful fields of study include management and business or public administration. Helpful attributes include:

- Ability to develop detailed plans

- Interest in work requiring accuracy and attention to detail

- Interest in negotiating

## Work Environment

Purchasing and contracting managers work in offices.

## Training Provided

Job training consists of 3 to 10 weeks of classroom instruction. Training length varies depending on specialty. Course content typically includes:

- Purchasing and accounting procedures

- Use of computers in contract administration

- Supply and financial management

Further training occurs through advanced courses.

## Civilian Counterparts

Civilian purchasing and contracting managers work for a wide variety of employers, including engineering, manufacturing, and construction firms. They perform duties similar to those performed by military purchasing and contract managers. They may also be called procurement services managers, purchasing directors, contracts administrators, or material control managers.

## Opportunities

The services have about 7,700 purchasing and contracting managers. On average, they need 200 new purchasing and contracting managers each year. After training, purchasing and contracting managers work with and advise commanders on contract proposals. With experience, they may advance to senior management and command positions.

# RECURITING MANAGERS

Each year, over 300,000 young men and women enlist in the military, making it the country's largest employer of youth. The services recruit young people with the kinds of talent needed to succeed in today's military. Recruiting managers plan and direct the activities of recruiting specialists who provide information to young people about military careers.

## What They Do

Recruiting managers in the military perform some or all of the following duties:

- Plan programs to inform young people about military careers

- Direct staff in local recruiting offices who carry out programs to inform the public about military careers

- Speak with local civic groups, schools, parents, and young people about military careers

- Prepare reports and brief commanders on recruiting goals and results

## Special Requirements

A 4-year college degree is normally required to enter this occupation.

## Helpful Attributes

Helpful fields of study include personnel management, communications, and public relations. Helpful attributes include:

- Interest in working closely with people

- Ability to speak effectively to large and small groups of people

## Work Environment

Recruiting managers usually work in offices.

## Training Provided

No initial job training is provided to officers in this occupation.

## Civilian Counterparts

Civilian recruiting managers work for personnel departments in business and government, searching for employment candidates. They also work for colleges, directing the activities of recruiters in their effort to attract talented high school students.

## Opportunities

The services have about 100 recruiting managers. On average, they need 10 new managers each year. Normally, officers must be in the military for a few years before they are eligible to become recruiting managers. They do not always make a career in the recruiting field. Some spend only a few years in recruiting and then change to another occupation, often in the field of personnel or administration. Officers remaining in recruiting may advance to senior management or command positions in this field.

# STORE MANAGERS

The military operates retail stores for the convenience of service men and women. In some areas, particularly overseas, the goods and services offered at military stores, laundries, and barbershops are not otherwise available. Store managers direct the operation of retail service, food, and merchandise outlets. They also manage personnel who store food, supplies, and equipment.

## What They Do

Store managers in the military perform some or all of the following duties:

- Direct personnel in purchasing, pricing, and selling food, supplies, and equipment

- Direct personnel in receiving, storing, and issuing supplies and equipment

- Supervise the inspection, care, and testing of products before their use or sale

- Plan training programs for new workers

- Direct inventory, accounting, and other record keeping activities

- Plan and prepare store budgets

## Special Requirements

A 4-year college degree is normally required to enter this occupation.

## Helpful Attributes

Helpful fields of study include management, accounting, marketing, business administration, and industrial management. Helpful attributes include:

- Interest in planning work schedules

- Interest in managing a business

- Interest in planning and directing the work of others

## Work Environment

Store managers work in retail stores or warehouses on land and aboard ships.

## Training Provided

Job training consists of 5 to 10 weeks of classroom instruction. Training length varies depending on specialty. Course content typically includes:

- Accounting and record keeping

- Inventory control

- Retail store and warehouse management

- Personnel and office administration

- Budget management

## Civilian Counterparts

Civilian store managers may work in many kinds of retail businesses. Some manage grocery, department, discount, and other large stores. Others manage warehouses that receive, store, and issue merchandise and supplies for retail outlets. Civilian store managers perform duties similar to those performed in the military. They may also be called retail store managers and distribution warehouse managers.

## Opportunities

The services have about 1,000 store managers. On average, they need 70 new store managers each year. After job training, store managers are assigned to supply, exchange, or food service units. With experience, they may advance to senior management and command positions.

# SUPPLY AND WAREHOUSING MANAGERS

The military needs vast amounts of supplies to feed and supply their personnel. Tons of materials such as food, fuel, medicine, and ammunition must be ordered, stored, and distributed each day. Supply and warehousing managers plan and direct personnel who order, receive, store, and issue equipment and supplies. Turn to page 388 for more information about supply and warehousing managers.

## What They Do

Supply and warehousing managers in the military perform some or all of the following duties:

- Analyze the demand for supplies and forecast future needs

- Direct personnel who receive, inventory, store, and issue supplies and equipment

- Manage the inspection, shipping, handling, and packaging of supplies and equipment

- Direct the preparation of reports and records

- Evaluate bids and proposals submitted by potential suppliers

- Study ways to use space and distribute supplies efficiently

## Special Requirements

A 4-year college degree is normally required to enter this occupation.

## Helpful Attributes

Helpful fields of study include business administration, inventory management, and operations research. Helpful attributes include:

- Interest in planning and directing the work of others

- Ability to express ideas clearly and concisely

## Work Environment

Supply and warehousing managers usually work in offices and warehouses. At times, they may be exposed to loud noise from machines and equipment.

## Training Provided

Job training consists of 2 to 16 weeks of classroom instruction. Training length varies depending on specialty. Course content typically includes:

- Warehousing and storage procedures

- Handling and packaging procedures

- Administrative procedures

- Field supply management

- Planning for future supply needs

## Civilian Counterparts

Civilian supply and warehousing managers work for storage companies, manufacturers, hospitals, schools, and government agencies. They perform duties similar to those performed by military supply and warehousing managers. They may also be called warehouse managers or operations managers.

## Opportunities

The services have about 8,300 supply and warehousing managers. On average, they need 400 new managers each year. After job training, supply and warehousing managers are assigned to positions in supply or munitions management. With experience, they may advance to senior management or command positions.

# TEACHERS AND INSTRUCTORS

Army
Navy
Air Force
Marine Corps
Coast Guard

The military provides training and educational opportunities for all personnel. Teachers and instructors conduct classes in such academic subjects as engineering, physical science, social science, and nursing. Teachers and instructors teach military personnel subjects that are related to their military occupations.

## What They Do

Teachers and instructors in the military perform some or all of the following duties:

- Develop course content, training outlines, and lesson plans

- Prepare training aids, assignments, and demonstrations

- Deliver lectures

- Conduct laboratory exercises and seminars

- Give tests and evaluate student progress

- Diagnose individual learning difficulties and offer help

## Special Requirements

A 4-year college degree is normally required to enter this occupation. Some specialties require a master's degree.

## Helpful Attributes

Helpful attributes include:

- Ability to express ideas clearly and concisely

- Interest in teaching

- Preference for working closely with people

## Work Environment

Teachers and instructors usually work in classrooms and lecture halls.

## Training Provided

No initial job training is provided to officers in this occupation.

## Civilian Counterparts

Civilian teachers and instructors work in junior colleges, colleges, and universities. They perform duties similar to those performed in the military. They may teach several different courses within the same field of study.

## Opportunities

The services have about 1,800 officers working as teachers or instructors. On average, 100 officers become military teachers and instructors each year. They are usually selected from officers trained and working in a military occupation. Many officers return to their regular occupations after teaching, but some remain as full-time teachers. Eventually, teachers may become tenured professors at the service academies or other military colleges or managers of education programs.

# TRAINING AND EDUCATION DIRECTORS

The military places great importance on training to prepare service men and women for their military careers. Programs include training in technical skills, physical fitness, and leadership development. Training and education directors plan, develop, and manage education and training programs for military personnel.

## What They Do

Training and education directors in the military perform some or all of the following duties:

- Develop new training courses

- Review and approve course material and training outlines prepared by instructors

- Plan and evaluate new teaching methods

- Assign duties to instructors, curriculum planners, and training aids specialists

- Evaluate the progress of students and instructors

- Train instructors in course subject matter

- Develop training and educational policies and objectives

- Coordinate training for military personnel at civilian schools or through correspondence courses

## Special Requirements

A 4-year college degree is normally required to enter this occupation. Some specialties require a master's degree.

## Training Provided

No initial job training is provided to officers in this occupation.

## Helpful Attributes

Helpful fields of study include education, physical education, organizational development, personnel management, and industrial psychology. Helpful attributes include:

- Interest in developing educational programs

- Preference for working with people

- Interest in work involving many subject areas

## Work Environment

Education and training directors work in offices and classroom training facilities. Those directing physical training work in gyms or outdoor settings.

## Civilian Counterparts

Civilian training and education directors work in schools, colleges, universities, vocational and technical schools, and training departments in business and industry. They perform duties similar to those performed by military training and education directors. They may also be called educational program directors, vocational training directors, and education supervisors.

## Opportunities

The services have about 2,500 officers working as training and education directors. On average, they need 150 officers to become training directors each year. Training and education directors are usually selected from officers in many different occupational fields. They may direct training in their own or another occupational field. This occupation is normally available to officers who have had experience in an occupation besides education.

# TRANSPORTATION MAINTENANCE MANAGERS

The military's transportation system is made up of many different kinds of carriers, including ships, aircraft, trucks, and buses. Repair and maintenance schedules for each type of vehicle must be carefully planned and managed. Transportation maintenance managers direct personnel who repair and maintain the military's transportation equipment.

## What They Do

Transportation maintenance managers in the military perform some or all of the following duties:

- Direct repair shop and garage operations

- Set work schedules for repair shop staff

- Oversee the ordering and use of repair parts, equipment, and supplies

- Check repairs to make sure they are complete and finished on schedule

- Oversee the preparation of maintenance records and reports

- Develop maintenance standards and policies

- Plan and develop training programs for staff

## Special Requirements

A 4-year college degree is normally required to enter this occupation.

## Helpful Attributes

Helpful fields of study include business administration, transportation management, vehicle and maintenance operations, and mechanical engineering. Helpful attributes include:

- Interest in planning and directing the work of others

- Interest in developing detailed plans

## Work Environment

Transportation maintenance managers work in offices located in maintenance yards, shops, and garages.

## Training Provided

Job training consists of 16 to 22 weeks of classroom instruction. Course content typically includes:

- Management of aircraft or aircraft electronics (avionics) maintenance

- Management of vehicle, railroad, and other equipment maintenance

- Use of management information systems

## Civilian Counterparts

Civilian transportation maintenance managers work in auto, bus, truck, and heavy construction equipment repair garages. They also work for aircraft service companies, aircraft builders, and commercial airline companies. They perform duties similar to those performed by military transportation maintenance managers.

## Opportunities

The services have about 4,000 transportation maintenance managers. On average, they need 100 new transportation maintenance managers each year. After job training, transportation maintenance managers gain experience managing maintenance personnel. In time, they may become managers of larger maintenance facilities and advance to command positions.

# TRANSPORTATION MANAGERS

Each year, the military transports thousands of service men and women and tons of material to bases across the U.S. and overseas. Ships, aircraft, trucks, buses, and trains are all part of the military's transportation system. Transportation managers direct the transport of military personnel and material by air, road, rail, and water. Turn to page 390 for more information about transportation managers.

## What They Do

Transportation managers in the military perform some or all of the following duties:

- Determine the fastest and most economical way to transport cargo or personnel

- Direct the packing and crating of cargo

- Direct the loading of freight and passengers

- Schedule shipments to ensure fast and timely deliveries

- Schedule pick-up and delivery of shipments

- Oversee the handling of special items, such as medicine and explosives

- See that transport forms, records, and reports are prepared correctly

## Special Requirements

A 4-year college degree is normally required to enter this occupation.

## Helpful Attributes

Helpful fields of study include transportation management, supply management, operations research, logistics, and business or public administration. Helpful attributes include:

- Interest in planning and directing the work of others

- Ability to work under tight schedules

## Work Environment

Transportation managers work in cargo and passenger terminals and depots.

## Training Provided

Job training consists of between 8 and 12 weeks of classroom instruction. Training length varies depending on specialty. Course content typically includes:

- Transportation management

- Ways to work with civilian and other military service carriers

- Freight classifications

- Handling of special items, such as medicine and explosives

## Civilian Counterparts

Civilian transportation managers work for airlines, railroads, bus lines, trucking companies, and shipping firms. They perform duties similar to those performed by military transportation managers. However, civilian transportation managers normally specialize in one area of transportation, such as air, water, truck, or railroad transportation.

## Opportunities

The services have about 8,000 transportation managers. On average, they need 140 new transportation managers each year. After job training, transportation managers gain experience on the job. In time, they may advance to senior management or command positions in cargo transportation operations.

# Human Services Occupations

- **Chaplains**
- **Social Workers**

# CHAPLAINS

The military provides for the spiritual needs of its personnel by offering religious services, moral guidance, and counseling. Chaplains conduct military worship services for military personnel and perform other spiritual duties covering beliefs and practices of all religious faiths.

## What They Do

Chaplains in the military perform some or all of the following duties:

- Conduct worship services in a variety of religious faiths

- Perform religious rites and ceremonies, such as weddings and funeral services

- Visit and provide spiritual guidance to personnel in hospitals and to their families

- Counsel individuals who seek guidance

- Promote attendance at religious services, retreats, and conferences

- Oversee religious education programs, such as Sunday school and youth groups

- Train lay leaders who conduct religious education programs

- Prepare religious speeches and publications

## Helpful Attributes

Helpful attributes include:

- Ability to express ideas clearly and concisely

- Interest in planning and directing the work of others

- Sensitivity to the needs of others

## Special Requirements

A master's degree in theology is required to enter this occupation. Ordination and ecclesiastical endorsement from a recognized religious denomination are also required.

## Training Provided

Job training consists of 3 to 7 weeks of classroom instruction. Course content typically includes:

- Role and responsibility of military chaplains

- Administration and leadership techniques

- Training and education methods

- Procedures for planning programs

- Pastoral counseling methods

Further training occurs on the job and through advanced courses.

## Work Environment

Chaplains in the military usually work in offices, hospitals, and places of worship. Those assigned to sea duty work aboard ships. Those assigned to land combat units sometimes work outdoors.

## Civilian Counterparts

Civilian chaplains work in places of worship, hospitals, universities, and correctional institutions. They perform duties similar to those performed in the military. However, they are almost always affiliated with a particular religious faith. Chaplains are also called clergy, ministers, preachers, priests, or rabbis.

## Opportunities

The services have about 1,500 chaplains of various faiths. On average, they need 50 new chaplains each year. Military chaplains may advance to become directors of religious programs in their services.

# SOCIAL WORKERS

The military needs close cooperation and a spirit of teamwork among its men and women. Social workers focus on improving conditions that cause social problems, such as drug and alcohol abuse, racism, and sexism.

## What They Do

Social workers in the military perform some or all of the following duties:

- Counsel military personnel and their family members

- Supervise counselors and caseworkers

- Survey military personnel to identify problems and plan solutions

- Plan social action programs to rehabilitate personnel with problems

- Plan and monitor equal opportunity programs

- Conduct research on social problems and programs

- Organize community activities on military bases

## Physical Demands

Social workers need to be able to speak clearly and distinctly to work with clients.

## Special Requirements

A 4-year college degree in social work or related social sciences is required to enter this occupation. Some specialties require a master's degree.

## Work Environment

Social workers in the military usually work in offices or clinics.

## Helpful Attributes

Helpful attributes include:

- Desire to help others

- Sensitivity to the needs of others

- Ability to express ideas clearly and concisely

- Interest in research and teaching

## Training Provided

Job training consists of 16 to 24 weeks of instruction. Course content typically includes:

- Ways of controlling drug and alcohol abuse among military personnel

- Management of equal opportunity programs

## Civilian Counterparts

Civilian social workers work for hospitals, human service agencies, and federal, state, county, and city governments. They perform duties similar to those performed by military social workers. However, civilian social workers usually specialize in a particular field, such as family services, child welfare, or medical services. They may also be called social group workers, medical social workers, psychiatric social workers, and social welfare administrators.

## Opportunities

The services have about 100 social workers. On average, they need 10 new social workers each year. After job training, social workers are assigned to counseling or assistance centers. With experience, they may advance to senior management positions.

# Media and Public Affairs Occupations

- **Audiovisual and Broadcast Directors**
- **Music Directors**
- **Public Information Officers**

# AUDIOVISUAL AND BROADCAST DIRECTORS

Army
Navy
Air Force
Marine Corps

The services produce many motion pictures, videotapes, and TV and radio broadcasts. These productions are used for training, news, and entertainment. Audiovisual and broadcast directors manage audiovisual projects. They may direct day-to-day filming or broadcasting or manage other directors.

## What They Do

Audiovisual and broadcast directors in the military perform some or all of the following duties:

- Plan and organize audiovisual projects, including films, videotapes, TV and radio broadcasts, and artwork displays

- Determine the staff and equipment needed for productions

- Set production controls and performance standards for audiovisual projects

- Direct the preparation of scripts and determine camera-shooting schedules

- Direct actors and technical staff during performances

## Special Requirements

A 4-year college degree is normally required to enter this occupation.

## Helpful Attributes

Helpful fields of study include audiovisual production, cinematography, communications, and graphic arts. Helpful attributes include:

- Interest in organizing and planning activities

- Interest in planning and directing the work of others

- Ability to transform ideas into visual images

## Work Environment

Audiovisual and broadcast directors usually work in studios or offices. They may direct film crews on location in military camps or combat zones.

## Training Provided

Job training consists of 15 to 99 weeks of classroom instruction. Training length varies depending on specialty. Course content typically includes:

- Public information management principles

- Management of military broadcasting facilities

- Motion picture and television production management

## Civilian Counterparts

Civilian audiovisual and broadcast directors work for television networks and stations, motion picture companies, public relations and advertising firms, and government agencies. They perform duties similar to those performed by military audiovisual and broadcast directors.

## Opportunities

The services have about 100 audiovisual and broadcast directors. On average, they need 10 new audiovisual and broadcast directors each year. After job training, audiovisual and broadcast directors work in production units directing the work of audiovisual technicians and specialists. In time, they may advance to management positions in the broadcasting and public affairs fields.

# MUSIC DIRECTORS

Bands have a long tradition in the armed services. Military bands all over the world provide music for marching and parade activities, concerts, and stage presentations. Music directors plan, develop, and direct the activities of military bands. They also conduct band performances during concerts and parades.

## What They Do

Music directors in the military perform some or all of the following duties:

- Plan musical programs

- Lead bands and choirs in performances

- Supervise training and rehearsal of musicians and choirs

- Determine funding needs for bands and choirs

- Plan purchases of instruments, equipment, and facilities

- Provide commanders with ideas for musical programs and ceremonies

## Physical Demands

A "good ear" for musical notes is required.

## Special Requirements

A 4-year college degree in music or music education is required to enter this occupation.

## Helpful Attributes

Helpful attributes include:

- Interest in music theory

- Appreciation for many types of music, including marches, classics, pop, and jazz

- Interest in planning and organizing the work of others

## Work Environment

Music directors usually work in offices and band halls. They may work outdoors when conducting or practicing for parades.

## Training Provided

Job training consists of 20 to 40 weeks of classroom instruction. Training length varies depending on specialty. Course content typically includes:

- Band arranging and conducting

- Concert and marching band styles and techniques

- Band administration and management

## Civilian Counterparts

Many civilian music directors work for college and high school music departments and civic and community orchestras. Others work in the motion picture, television, and studio recording industries. Civilian music directors perform duties similar to those performed in the military. They may also be called band directors, band leaders, orchestra leaders, or conductors.

## Opportunities

The services have about 70 music directors. On average, they need 10 new music directors each year. After job training, music directors are assigned to military band units, where they plan and direct musical programs. With experience, they may assume command of larger military bands or direct the activities of several bands.

# PUBLIC INFORMATION OFFICERS

The services have public information officers to keep the public informed about the military. These officers answer questions from the news media, members of Congress, private citizens, and service personnel. They also prepare reports and news releases about activities on military bases and service policies and operations.

## What They Do

Public information officers in the military perform some or all of the following duties:

- Supervise the preparation of reports and other releases to the public and the military

- Brief military personnel before they meet with the public and the news media

- Provide information to newspapers, TV and radio stations, and civic organizations

- Schedule and conduct interviews and news conferences

- Plan activities to improve public relations

## Special Requirements

A 4-year college degree is normally required to enter this occupation.

## Helpful Attributes

Helpful fields of study include journalism, communications, public relations, and advertising. Helpful attributes include:

- Ability to write clearly and simply

- Ability to speak effectively in public

- Interest in news and current events

## Training Provided

Job training consists of 8 weeks of classroom instruction. Course content typically includes:

- Department of Defense policies

- Principles of public information and community relations

## Civilian Counterparts

Civilian public information officers work for large corporations, government agencies, colleges and universities, and community groups. They perform duties similar to those performed by military public information officers. They may also be called public relations representatives and corporate communications specialists.

## Work Environment

Public information officers usually work in offices.

## Opportunities

The services have about 200 public information officers. On average, they need 10 new public information officers each year. After job training, public information officers normally direct specialists who gather information for reports, respond to requests for information, and write news releases. With experience, public information officers prepare and give briefings, speeches, and interviews. Eventually, they may advance to senior public affairs positions.

# Health Diagnosing and Treating Practitioner Occupations

- **Dentists**
- **Optometrists**
- **Physicians and Surgeons**
- **Psychologists**

# DENTISTS

Dental care is a basic health service provided to men and women in the military. Military dentists examine, diagnose, and treat diseases and disorders of the mouth. They may practice general dentistry or work in one of several specialties.

## What They Do

Dentists in the military perform some or all of the following duties:

- Examine patients' teeth and gums to detect signs of disease or tooth decay

- Examine X-rays to determine the soundness of teeth and the alignment of teeth and jaws

- Locate and fill tooth cavities

- Perform oral (mouth) surgery to treat problems with teeth, gums, or jaws

- Develop and fit dentures (artificial teeth) to replace missing teeth

- Construct and fit dental devices, such as braces and retainers, for straightening teeth

- Plan dental health programs for patients to help prevent dental problems

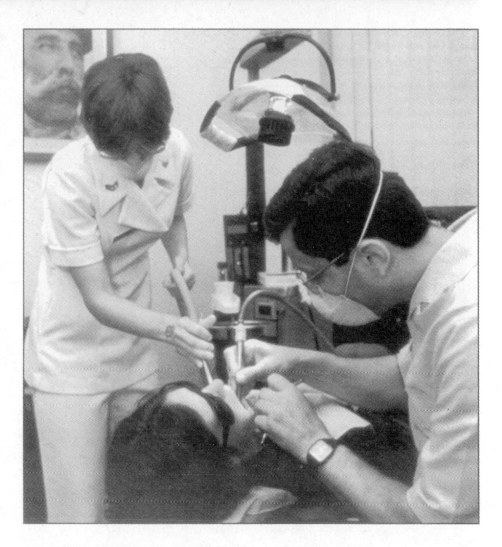

## Special Requirements

A doctor of dentistry degree and additional training in a dental specialty are required to enter this occupation.

## Helpful Attributes

Helpful attributes include:

- Desire to help others

- Good eye-hand coordination

## Work Environment

Dentists work in hospitals and dental clinics on land and aboard ships.

## Civilian Counterparts

Civilian dentists work in private practice, public health facilities, and dental research organizations. They perform duties similar to those performed in the military and specialize in similar areas. Depending on their specialty, dentists may also be called oral pathologists, endodontists, oral surgeons, orthodontists, pedodontists, prosthodontists, periodontists, or public health dentists.

## Training Provided

No initial job training is provided to officers in this occupation.

## Opportunities

The military has about 1,900 dentists. On average, the services need 100 new dentists each year. Newly commissioned dentists are assigned to dental clinics to practice general dentistry or a dental specialty. Positions for dentists in the Coast Guard are filled by U.S. Public Health Service Officers. Dentists who demonstrate leadership and managerial qualities may advance to administer dental facilities and programs.

# OPTOMETRISTS

Eye care is part of the full health coverage provided to military personnel. The most common eye problem is the need for corrective lenses. Optometrists examine eyes and treat vision problems by prescribing glasses or contact lenses. They refer patients with eye diseases to ophthalmologists (eye medical doctors).

## What They Do

Optometrists in the military perform some or all of the following duties:

- Check patient vision using eye charts

- Examine eyes for glaucoma and other diseases

- Measure patient nearsightedness, farsightedness, depth perception, and other vision problems using optical instruments

- Prescribe corrective lenses

- Prescribe training exercises to strengthen weak eye muscles

- Instruct patients on how to wear and care for contact lenses

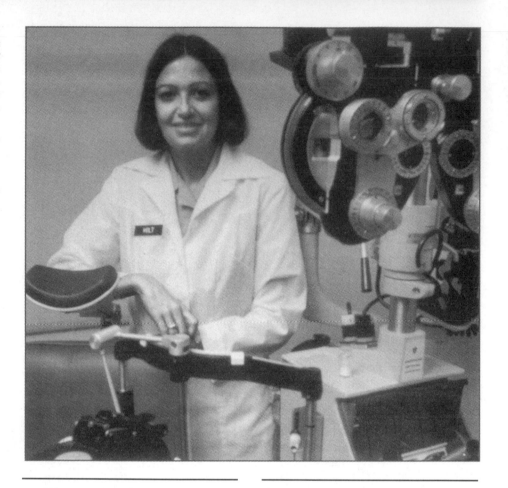

## Special Requirements

A doctor of optometry degree and a state license to practice optometry are required to enter this occupation.

## Helpful Attributes

Helpful attributes include:

- Preference for working closely with people

- Desire to help others

- Interest in work requiring accuracy and attention to detail

## Work Environment

Optometrists work in clinics and hospitals.

## Training Provided

No initial job training is provided to officers in this occupation. The Army has a program to provide financial support to optometry students in return for a period of obligated service.

## Civilian Counterparts

Most civilian optometrists work in private practice. Some work for hospitals, clinics, public health agencies, or optical laboratories. Civilian optometrists perform duties similar to those performed in the military.

## Opportunities

The services have about 250 optometrists. On average, they need 20 new optometrists each year. Newly commissioned optometrists are assigned to clinics or hospitals. In time, they may advance to senior management positions in the health service field.

# PHYSICIANS AND SURGEONS

Army
Navy
Air Force
Coast Guard

Military physicians and surgeons represent all of the major fields of medical specialization. Physicians and surgeons are the chief providers of medical services to military personnel and their dependents. They examine patients, diagnose their injuries or illnesses, and provide medical treatment. Turn to page 382 for more information about physicians and surgeons.

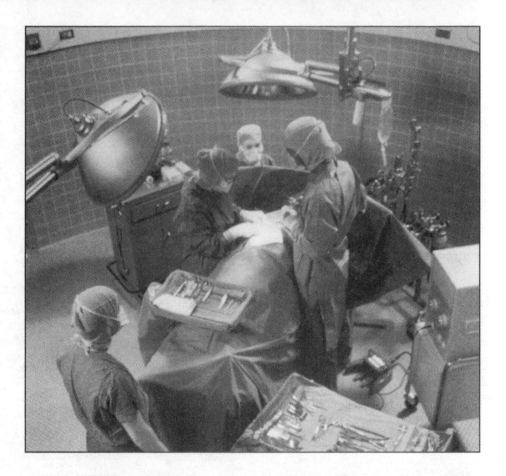

## What They Do

Physicians and surgeons in the military perform some or all of the following duties:

- Examine patients to detect abnormalities in pulse, breathing, or other body functions

- Determine presence and extent of illness or injury by reviewing medical histories, X-rays, laboratory reports, and examination reports

- Develop treatment plans that may include medication, therapy, or surgery

- Perform surgery to treat injuries or illnesses

- Advise patients on their health problems and personal habits

- Coordinate the activities of nurses, physician assistants, medical specialists, therapists, and other medical personnel

- Conduct medical research

## Special Requirements

A doctor of medicine or osteopathy degree and advanced training in a medical specialty are required to enter this occupation.

## Helpful Attributes

Helpful attributes include:

- Desire to help others

- Ability to express ideas clearly and concisely

## Work Environment

Physicians and surgeons work in hospitals and clinics on land and aboard ships.

## Training Provided

No initial job training is provided to officers in this occupation. However, advanced courses and programs in medical specialties are available. In addition, scholarships for advanced medical training are available in return for an obligated period of military service.

## Civilian Counterparts

Civilian physicians work for hospitals or clinics or in private practice. They perform the same duties and work in the same areas of specialization as military physicians.

## Opportunities

The services have a total of about 7,070 physicians and surgeons, including all general practitioners and specialists. On average, they need 760 new physicians and surgeons each year. The services give several hundred scholarships yearly to attend civilian medical schools or the Uniformed Services University of the Health Sciences in Bethesda, Maryland, in return for an obligated period of military service after graduation. The services normally hire physicians who have completed medical school and their internships. However, some services have programs to grant early officer commissions to civilians who are in medical school, internship, or residency status in return for an obligated period of service. Positions for physicians and surgeons in the Coast Guard are filled by U.S. Public Health Service Officers. After gaining experience in the military, physicians and surgeons may advance to senior management or command positions in the services' medical corps.

# PSYCHOLOGISTS

Psychological research and treatment are important to national defense. Research can show how to improve military training, job assignment, and equipment design. Treatment can help personnel cope with stress. Psychologists conduct research on human behavior and treat patients with mental problems.

## What They Do

Psychologists in the military perform some or all of the following duties:

- Conduct research on human and animal behavior, emotions, and thinking processes

- Conduct research on aptitude and job performance

- Give psychological tests and interpret results to diagnose patients' problems

- Treat patients individually and in groups

- Conduct experiments to determine the best equipment design, work procedures, and training course content

- Write research reports

- Direct research projects performed by outside contractors

## Special Requirements

A 4-year college degree in psychology is required to enter this occupation. Some specialties require a master's degree.

## Helpful Attributes

Helpful attributes include:

- Desire to help others

- Interest in scientific research

- Interest in mathematics and statistics

## Work Environment

Psychologists usually work in offices, hospitals, clinics, and other medical facilities on land and aboard ships.

## Civilian Counterparts

Some civilian psychologists treat patients in private practice, hospitals, school systems, and mental health centers. They are called clinical psychologists, counseling psychologists, or educational psychologists. Other civilian psychologists conduct research work for universities, research firms, and government agencies. They are called experimental psychologists, social psychologists, and psychometricians.

## Training Provided

No initial job training is provided for officers in this occupation. Advanced courses are available in some specialties.

## Opportunities

The services have about 300 psychologists. On average, they need 30 new psychologists each year. Positions for psychologists in the Coast Guard are filled by U.S. Public Health Service Officers. With experience, they may lead projects of their own. New clinical psychologists may treat patients in military clinics. Eventually, both research and clinical psychologists may become directors of offices or laboratories.

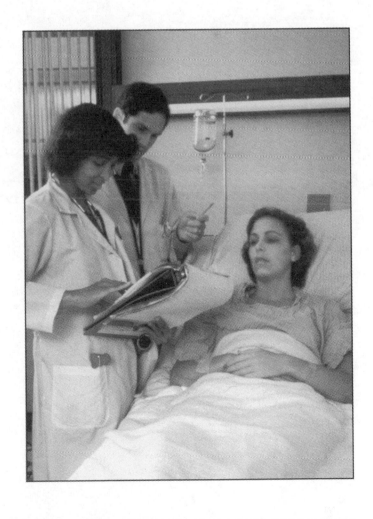

# Health Care Occupations

- Dietitians
- Pharmacists
- Physical and Occupational Therapists
- Physician Assistants
- Registered Nurses
- Speech Therapists

# DIETITIANS

Dietitians are part of the military's health care staff. They are experts in the nutritional needs of hospital patients and outpatients. Dietitians manage medical food service facilities and plan meals for hospital patients and outpatients who need special diets.

## What They Do

Dietitians in the military perform some or all of the following duties:

- Set policies for hospital food service operations

- Inspect hospital food service and preparation areas to be sure they meet sanitation and safety standards

- Plan and organize training programs for medical food service personnel

- Develop special diets for patients based on instructions from doctors

- Plan menus for hospital meals

- Interview patients to determine whether they are satisfied with their diet

- Develop hospital food service budgets

- Provide information on nutrition to the military community

## Special Requirements

A 4-year college degree in food and nutrition or institutional management is required to enter this occupation. Some specialties require completion of a general dietetic internship.

## Helpful Attributes

Helpful attributes include:

- Desire to help others

- Interest in nutrition and food preparation

- Interest in interpreting scientific and medical data

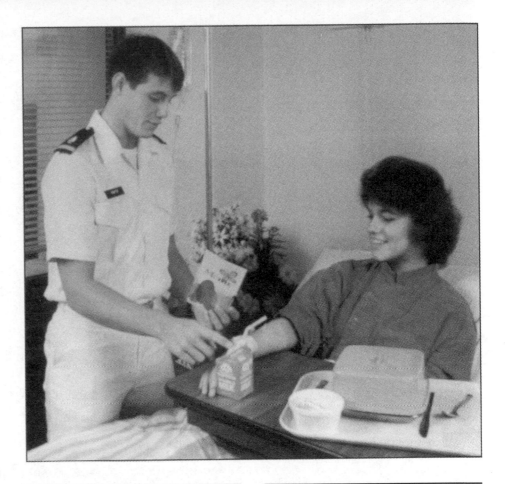

## Work Environment

Dietitians work in hospitals, clinics, and aboard ships.

## Civilian Counterparts

Civilian dietitians work in hospitals, clinics, and other health care facilities. They perform duties similar to those performed by military dietitians. Dietitians also work for college food services, restaurants, industrial food services, and research institutions. Civilian dietitians may specialize in specific areas of dietetics, such as consultation, clinical dietetics, and community health.

## Training Provided

No initial job training is provided to officers in this occupation. However, the Air Force and Army offer internship programs in dietetics that are approved by the American Dietetic Association.

## Opportunities

The services have about 200 dietitians. On average, 20 new dietitians are needed each year. Newly commissioned dietitians are assigned to military hospitals, clinics, or ships, where they plan and direct the work of food service personnel. Positions for dietitians in the Coast Guard are filled by U.S. Public Health Service Officers. They may advance to senior management positions in hospital food service programs.

# PHARMACISTS

Drugs and medicines are sometimes prescribed by doctors when treating patients in military hospitals and clinics. Pharmacists manage the purchasing, storing, and dispensing of drugs and medicines.

## What They Do

Pharmacists in the military perform some or all of the following duties:

- Manage pharmacy technicians who prepare, label, and dispense orders for drugs and medicines

- Advise doctors and patients on the proper use and side effects of drugs and medicines

- Train medical, nursing, and pharmacy staffs on the use of drugs

- Consult on drug and medicine research programs

- Check drug and medicine supplies and reorder when necessary

- Direct pharmacy record keeping

## Special Requirements

A 4-year college degree in pharmacy and a state license to practice pharmacy are required to enter this occupation.

## Helpful Attributes

Helpful attributes include:

- Interest in understanding the effects of drugs and medicines

- Interest in chemical formulas

- Interest in work requiring accuracy and attention to detail

## Work Environment

Pharmacists work in hospitals and clinics on land and aboard ships.

## Civilian Counterparts

Civilian pharmacists work for pharmacies, drug stores, and drug departments of stores and supermarkets. They also work for hospitals, nursing homes, and clinics. They perform duties similar to those performed by military pharmacists. Civilian pharmacists who specialize in radioactive drugs (radioisotopes) are known as radiopharmacists.

## Training Provided

No initial job training is provided to officers in this occupation.

## Opportunities

The services have about 250 pharmacists. On average, they need 25 new pharmacists each year. Newly commissioned pharmacists are assigned to military hospitals or clinics, where they manage daily operations. Positions for pharmacists in the Coast Guard are filled by U.S. Public Health Service Officers. In time, pharmacists plan and direct pharmacy or other health programs.

# PHYSICAL AND OCCUPATIONAL THERAPISTS

Army
Navy
Air Force
Coast Guard

Physical and occupational therapies are programs of treatment and exercise for patients disabled from illness or injury. Physical and occupational therapists plan and administer therapy to help patients adjust to disabilities, regain independence, and prepare to return to work.

## What They Do

Physical and occupational therapists in the military perform some or all of the following duties:

- Test and interview patients to determine the extent of their disabilities

- Plan and manage individual physical or occupational therapy programs

- Consult with doctors and other therapists to discuss appropriate therapy and evaluate patients' progress

- Administer exercise programs and heat and massage treatments

- Counsel patients and their families to help create a positive attitude for recovery

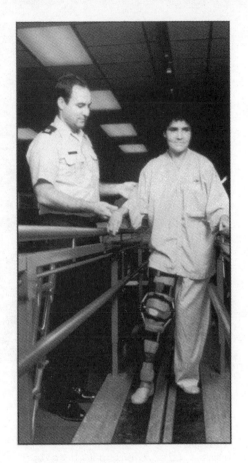

## Special Requirements

A 4-year college degree in physical or occupational therapy and completion of a clinical program in physical or occupational therapy are required to enter this occupation. Depending on specialty, a state physical therapy license or eligibility for registration with the American Occupational Therapy Association may also be required.

## Helpful Attributes

Helpful attributes include:

- Desire to help others

- Interest in developing detailed plans and treatments

- Patience to work with people whose injuries heal slowly

- Ability to communicate effectively

## Physical Demands

Physical and occupational therapists may have to lift and support patients during exercises and treatments.

## Work Environment

Physical and occupational therapists work in hospitals, clinics, rehabilitation centers, and other medical facilities.

## Training Provided

No initial job training is provided to officers in this occupation.

## Civilian Counterparts

Civilian physical and occupational therapists work in hospitals, rehabilitation centers, nursing homes, schools, and community mental health centers. They perform duties similar to those performed by military therapists. Civilian physical and occupational therapists often specialize in treating a particular type of patient, such as children, the elderly, the severely disabled, or those who have lost arms or legs (amputees).

## Opportunities

The services have about 300 physical and occupational therapists. On average, they need 30 new therapists each year. Positions for physical and occupational therapists in the Coast Guard are filled by U.S. Public Health Service Officers. Physical and occupational therapists have the opportunity to advance to senior management or command positions in medical administration.

# PHYSICIAN ASSISTANTS

Army
Navy
Air Force
Coast Guard

Physician assistants provide routine health care for patients, freeing physicians to concentrate on more serious health problems. Physician assistants examine, diagnose, and treat patients under the supervision of medical doctors.

## What They Do

Physician assistants in the military perform some or all of the following duties:

- Record medical histories, examine patients, and make initial diagnoses

- Treat common illnesses or injuries, calling in supervising physicians for serious health problems

- Perform routine physical examinations and collect specimens for laboratory tests

- Order laboratory studies, such as blood tests, urinalysis, and X-rays

- Provide information to patients about diet, family planning, use of drugs, and the effect of treatments

- Provide emergency care in situations where doctors are not available

## Special Requirements

Graduation from an accredited training program for physician assistants that is recognized by the services is normally required to enter this occupation. Depending upon the service, however, military job training may be available.

## Work Environment

Physician assistants work in hospitals and clinics on land and aboard ships.

## Training Provided

Job training, when available from the services, consists of about 40 weeks of classroom instruction, including practice in providing patient health care. Course content typically includes:

- Fundamental medical care procedures

- Principles of behavioral and dental science

- Health care administration techniques

## Civilian Counterparts

Civilian physician assistants work in hospitals, clinics, doctor's offices, and nursing homes. They perform duties similar to those performed by military physician assistants.

## Helpful Attributes

Helpful attributes include:

- Self-confidence and the ability to remain calm in stressful situations

- Patience with others, especially those in pain or stress

- Desire to help others

- Ability to express ideas clearly and concisely

## Opportunities

The services have about 400 physician assistants. On average, they need 20 new physician assistants each year. After job training, physician assistants provide health care under close supervision. With experience, they work more independently, although they remain under the supervision of a doctor. In time, they may advance to management positions in the military health care field.

# REGISTERED NURSES

Nurses are a key part of the staff at military hospitals and clinics. Registered nurses direct nursing teams and give patients individual care to help them recover from illness or injury. Turn to page 384 for more information about registered nurses.

## What They Do

Registered nurses in the military perform some or all of the following duties:

- Help physicians treat patients

- Give injections of pain killers, antibiotics, and other medicines as prescribed by physicians

- Change bandages and dressings

- Assist physicians during surgery

- Provide life support treatment for patients needing emergency care

- Provide care for mental health patients

- Keep records of patients' condition

- Supervise practical nurses, nurse aides, and other support personnel

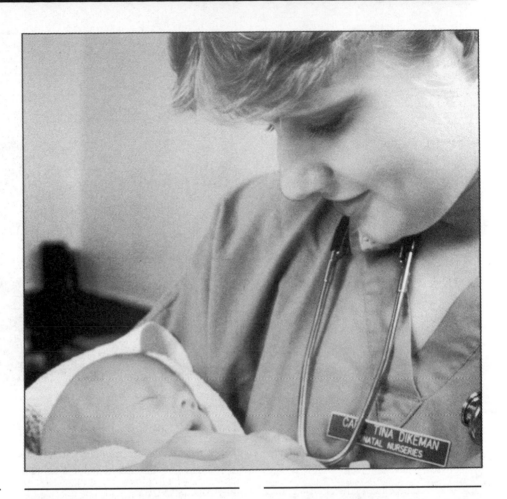

## Helpful Attributes

Helpful attributes include:

- Desire to help others

- Ability to express ideas clearly and concisely

- Self-confidence and the ability to remain calm under pressure

## Civilian Counterparts

Civilian registered nurses work in hospitals, clinics, and private medical facilities. They also work for public health agencies, nursing homes, and rehabilitation centers. Civilian registered nurses perform duties similar to those performed in the military. They often specialize and may be known as public health nurses, nurse practitioners, or general duty nurses.

## Special Requirements

Graduation from an accredited school of nursing and a license to practice nursing are required to enter this occupation.

## Training Provided

Job training consists of 14 to 27 weeks of classroom instruction. Training length varies depending on specialty. Course content typically includes:

- Practices and principles of military nursing

- Care of emotionally disturbed patients

- Health care for children

- Nursing techniques

- Anesthesia, respiratory therapy, and cardiopulmonary resuscitation

## Work Environment

Registered nurses work in hospitals and clinics. Some work in sick bays aboard ships or in mobile field hospitals. Others work in airplanes that transfer patients to medical centers.

## Opportunities

The services have about 5,000 registered nurses. On average, they need 700 new registered nurses each year. Positions for registered nurses in the Coast Guard are filled by U.S. Public Health Service Officers. Depending on the prior experience that nurses bring with them to the military, their job assignments may vary. After job training, inexperienced nurses work under close supervision. Experienced nurses normally work under less supervision. In time, nurses may become nurse supervisors. Eventually, they may become directors of nursing in hospitals or advance to senior health service management positions.

# SPEECH THERAPISTS

Speech therapists work as part of military medical teams. Speech therapists evaluate and treat patients with hearing and speech problems.

## What They Do

Speech therapists in the military perform some or all of the following duties:

- Talk with patients to discuss hearing and speaking problems and possible causes and treatment

- Identify speaking and language problems

- Examine the ears, including the entire auditory (hearing) system

- Evaluate examination and test data to determine the type and amount of hearing loss

- Treat hearing problems using hearing aids and other treatments

- Assist patients in selecting and using hearing aids

- Conduct programs to help patients improve their speaking skills

- Research new techniques for treating hearing and speaking problems

## Special Requirements

A master's degree in either audiology or speech therapy is required to enter this occupation depending on the occupational specialty.

## Training Provided

No initial job training is provided to officers in this occupational group.

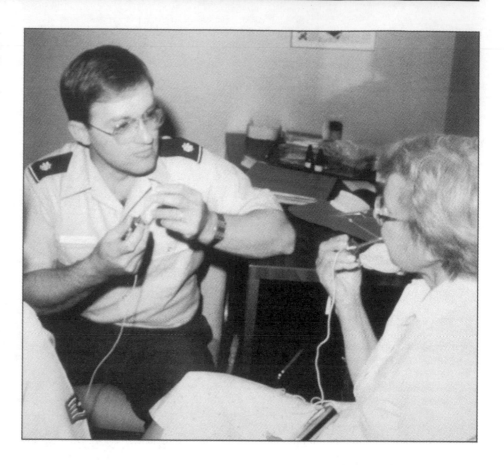

## Helpful Attributes

Helpful attributes include:

- Desire to help others

- Interest in scientific work

- Patience to work with people whose injuries heal slowly

## Work Environment

Speech therapists work in therapy labs, clinics, and medical centers.

## Civilian Counterparts

Civilian speech therapists work in hospitals, clinics, schools, and research centers. They perform duties similar to those performed by military speech therapists. Depending on their specialty, civilian speech therapists may also be called audiologists or speech pathologists.

## Opportunities

The services have about 70 speech therapists. On average, they need 10 new therapists each year. Positions for speech therapists in the Coast Guard are filled by U.S. Public Health Service Officers. After displaying leadership abilities, speech therapists may advance to senior management and command positions in the medical field.

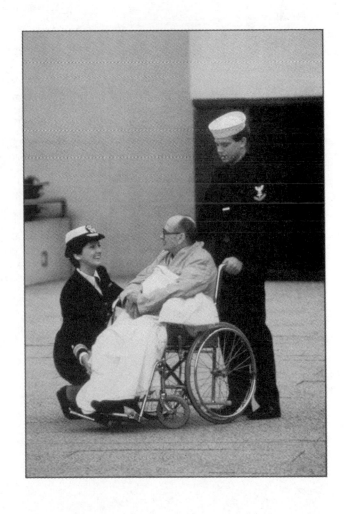

# Engineering, Science, and Technical Occupations

- Aerospace Engineers
- Air Traffic Control Managers
- Chemists
- Civil Engineers
- Computer Systems Officers
- Electrical and Electronics Engineers
- Environmental Health and Safety Officers
- Industrial Engineers
- Intelligence Officers
- Lawyers
- Life Scientists
- Marine Engineers
- Meteorologists
- Nuclear Engineers
- Oceanographers
- Physicists
- Space Operations Officers
- Surveying and Mapping Managers

# AEROSPACE ENGINEERS

Although private companies build the military's aerospace equipment, military engineers are responsible for seeing that all equipment meets service needs. Aerospace engineers design and direct the development of military aircraft, missiles, and spacecraft.

## What They Do

Aerospace engineers in the military perform some or all of the following duties:

- Plan and conduct research on aircraft guidance, propulsion, and weapons systems

- Study new designs for aircraft, missiles, and spacecraft

- Help select private companies to build military aircraft, missiles, and spacecraft

- Monitor production of aircraft, missiles, and spacecraft

- Decide what tests should be conducted of prototypes (full-scale test models)

- Conduct stress analysis and wind tunnel tests with aircraft and missile prototypes

## Special Requirements

A 4-year college degree in aeronautical, astronautical, or mechanical engineering is required to enter this occupation.

## Helpful Attributes

Helpful attributes include:

- Interest in concepts and principles of engineering

- Interest in working with mathematical formulas

- Interest in planning and directing research projects

## Work Environment

Aerospace engineers work in offices or laboratories.

## Civilian Counterparts

Civilian aerospace engineers usually work in the aircraft manufacturing industry. Some work for the Department of Defense, the National Aeronautics and Space Administration (NASA), and other government agencies. As in the military, civilian aerospace engineers may specialize in one type of aerospace product, such as aircraft, missiles, or space vehicles. They may also specialize in engineering specialties such as product design, testing, or production research. Depending on their specialty, they may be called aeronautical engineers, aeronautical test engineers, or stress analysts.

## Training Provided

No initial job training is provided to officers in this occupation.

## Opportunities

The services have about 2,900 aerospace engineers. On average, they need 350 aerospace engineers each year. Newly commissioned aerospace engineers are usually assigned to engineering research and development units or laboratories. They work under the direction of experienced officers conducting research. With experience, they may serve as research and development managers or laboratory managers.

# AIR TRAFFIC CONTROL MANAGERS

Air traffic control centers often have several sections giving instructions to military aircraft. One section gives take-off and landing instructions. Another gives ground instructions. A third section tracks planes in flight. Air traffic control managers direct the operations of air traffic control centers.

## What They Do

Air traffic control managers in the military perform some or all of the following duties:

- Plan work schedules for air traffic controllers

- Evaluate job performance of controllers

- Manage air traffic control center operations to ensure safe and efficient flights

- Inspect control center facilities and equipment

- Direct tests of radar equipment and controller procedures

- Investigate and find solutions to problems in control center operations

- Control air traffic using radar and radios

- Direct training for air traffic controllers

## Physical Demands

Air traffic control personnel must pass a demanding physical exam as required by the Federal Aviation Administration (FAA).

## Work Environment

Air traffic control managers work in air traffic control towers and centers at airfields and aboard ships.

## Helpful Attributes

Helpful fields of study include aeronautical engineering, computer science, and liberal arts. Helpful attributes include:

- Interest in work requiring accuracy and attention to detail

- Ability to remain calm in stressful situations

- Decisiveness

- Ability to manage in accordance with strict standards

## Special Requirements

A 4-year college degree is normally required to enter this occupation. Certification by the FAA must usually be obtained during military training.

## Training Provided

Job training consists of 6 to 11 weeks of classroom instruction. Training length varies depending on specialty. Course content typically includes:

- Air traffic control management

- Operational procedures for air traffic control

- Communications and radar procedures

- Aircraft recognition

- Take-off, landing, and ground control procedures

## Civilian Counterparts

Civilian air traffic control managers work at commercial airports. They perform duties similar to those performed by military air traffic control managers.

## Opportunities

The services have about 300 air traffic control managers. On average, they need 10 new air traffic control managers each year. After job training, managers are assigned to air traffic control centers at airfields or aboard ships, where they gain experience in air traffic control management. They may advance to senior management and command positions in the aviation field.

# CHEMISTS

**Army
Navy
Air Force
Marine Corps**

The military conducts research in chemistry and biochemistry to develop new materials for military equipment, better medicines, and defenses against biological and chemical agents. Chemists conduct and manage research in chemistry, chemical engineering, and biology.

## What They Do

Chemists in the military perform some or all of the following duties:

- Conduct experiments in chemical synthesis, structure, and interactions

- Establish strength and durability standards for materials used to build aircraft, ships, and other equipment

- Test materials to identify defects and determine if they meet minimum military standards

- Conduct chemical research for military and medical uses, such as protecting people from radiation, chemicals, and biological agents

- Oversee research projects under contract to universities and industrial firms

- Prepare technical reports and make research recommendations

## Training Provided

No initial job training is provided to officers in this occupation.

## Helpful Attributes

Helpful attributes include:

- Interest in working with mathematical formulas

- Interest in scientific study and research

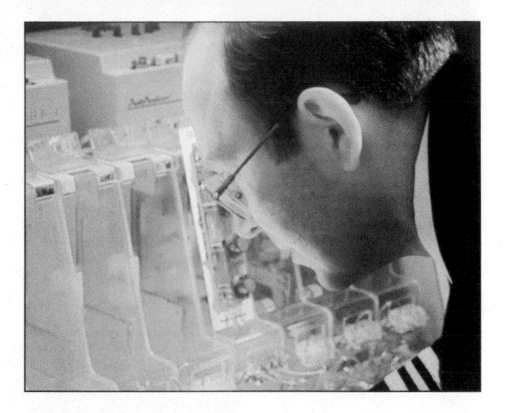

## Work Environment

Chemists work in laboratories and offices. Although they observe strict safety precautions, chemists may be exposed to hazardous substances.

## Civilian Counterparts

Civilian chemists usually work in research and development for private industry, primarily in new product development. They also work for government agencies, colleges, and universities. Civilian chemists perform duties similar to those performed by chemists in the military. They sometimes specialize in areas such as organic chemistry, inorganic chemistry, physical chemistry, or biochemistry.

## Special Requirements

A 4-year degree in chemistry, chemical engineering, or biology is required to enter this occupation.

## Opportunities

The services have about 1,700 chemists. On average, they need 150 new chemists each year. Newly commissioned chemists are usually assigned to military laboratory facilities, where they perform duties in a chemistry specialty area. With experience, they may manage research and development units and advance to command positions.

# CIVIL ENGINEERS

Airfields, roads, bridges, buildings, power plants, docks, and water treatment plants on military bases around the world are continually being built, repaired, and improved. Civil engineers plan, design, and direct the construction of military facilities. Turn to page 370 for more information about civil engineers.

## What They Do

Civil engineers in the military perform some or all of the following duties:

- Study the need for roads, airfields, buildings, and other facilities

- Direct surveys of construction areas

- Design construction projects

- Help select contractors to build facilities

- Check construction progress to see that it meets plans

- Plan and direct facility maintenance and modernization

- Plan temporary facilities for use in emergencies

- Keep master plans for military bases up to date

## Special Requirements

A 4-year college degree in civil, architectural, sanitary, or environmental engineering, or another closely related field is required to enter this occupation.

## Helpful Attributes

Helpful attributes include:

- Interest in engineering principles and concepts

- Interest in working with mathematical formulas

## Training Provided

No initial job training is provided to officers in this occupation. However, advanced courses are offered to support medical service and environmental control building programs.

## Civilian Counterparts

Civilian civil engineers work for engineering firms, construction companies, and government agencies. Some may work for public utilities, railroads, and manufacturing firms. Civilian civil engineers perform duties similar to those performed in the military; however, they often specialize in certain types of projects.

## Work Environment

Civil engineers work in offices when designing projects or reviewing reports. They work outdoors when overseeing survey or construction activities.

## Opportunities

The services have about 4,700 civil engineers. On average, they need 450 new civil engineers each year. Newly commissioned civil engineers usually assist senior engineering officers in planning and design. With experience, they may manage construction projects and, eventually, engineering offices. In time, they may advance to senior management or command positions in the engineering field.

# COMPUTER SYSTEMS OFFICERS

Army
Navy
Air Force
Marine Corps
Coast Guard

The military uses computers in almost every aspect of its operations. Military computers are used to process payroll and personnel information, control the targeting and firing of weapons systems, account for money, and make it easier to communicate around the world. Computer systems officers direct the operations of computer centers and are involved in the planning and development of computer systems.

## What They Do

Computer systems officers in the military perform some or all of the following duties:

- Prepare data processing plans and budgets

- Develop and monitor contracts for data processing equipment and services

- Translate military objectives and needs into computer systems requirements

- Design and maintain computer software and data bases

- Plan and oversee the installation of new equipment

- Direct teams of computer systems specialists and computer programmers

## Special Requirements

A 4-year college degree in computer science, computer or industrial engineering, business administration, or a related field is required to enter this occupation. Some specialties require a master's degree.

## Helpful Attributes

Helpful attributes include:

- Interest in working with computers

- Interest in working with mathematical models and formulas

- Interest in technical work

## Work Environment

Computer systems officers in the military work in offices or at computer sites on military bases or aboard ships.

## Training Provided

Job training consists of 5 to 18 weeks of classroom instruction. Training length varies depending on specialty. Course content typically includes:

- Fiscal and contract management

- Assessment of computer equipment needs

- Computer systems development and project management

## Civilian Counterparts

Civilian computer systems officers work for a wide variety of employers, such as banks, hospitals, manufacturers, financial firms, government agencies and firms that design and test computer systems. They perform duties similar to those performed by military computer systems officers. They may also be called information systems directors, ADP or EDP managers, computer systems engineers, software engineers, or systems analysts.

## Opportunities

The services have about 3,500 computer systems officers. On average, they need 150 new computer systems officers each year. After job training, computer systems officers are assigned to units where they work in teams of engineers, systems analysts, and computer programmers. With experience and demonstrated leadership, they may advance to senior management or command positions in the computer systems field.

# ELECTRICAL AND ELECTRONICS ENGINEERS

Army
Navy
Air Force
Marine Corps
Coast Guard

Equipment such as radar, missile guidance systems, and communication equipment depends on advanced electronics. Electrical and electronics engineers design, develop, and test electrical and electronic equipment. They also direct equipment installation and repair.

## What They Do

Electrical and electronics engineers in the military perform some or all of the following duties:

- Direct research to improve and develop computer, navigation, and other electronic systems

- Direct equipment installation and repair

- Develop test standards and operating instructions for electrical and electronic systems

- Design and develop test instruments

- Test new or modified equipment to check its performance and reliability

- Review test data, report results, and recommend actions

## Special Requirements

A 4-year college degree in electrical, electronic, or communications engineering is required to enter this occupation.

## Helpful Attributes

Helpful attributes include:

- Interest in engineering concepts and principles

- Interest in planning and directing research projects

- Interest in working with mathematical formulas

## Work Environment

Electrical and electronics engineers usually work in offices while planning research studies and designing electronic systems. They may work outdoors when overseeing the installation of new equipment.

## Civilian Counterparts

Civilian electrical and electronics engineers work for manufacturers of electrical and electronic equipment. Many work for government agencies, public utilities, and engineering firms. Civilian electrical and electronics engineers perform duties similar to those performed in the military. However, they usually specialize in product areas, such as computers, communications, or aerospace systems. They may also be called electronics design engineers and electronics test engineers.

## Training Provided

Initial job training is usually provided on the job. Classroom training is provided for some specialties in this occupation. Course content typically includes:

- Combat and tactical communications systems

- Telecommunications center systems

- Signal center site defense systems

## Opportunities

The services have about 1,000 electrical and electronics engineers. On average, they need 50 new engineers each year. After job training, electrical and electronics engineers are usually assigned to engineering research and development units or to communications centers. Initially, they conduct studies and supervise research and development staff. With experience, they may advance to senior management positions, such as engineering staff officer, research and development manager, or communications center director.

# ENVIRONMENTAL HEALTH AND SAFETY OFFICERS

The services take great care to ensure safe working conditions and a clean environment. A clean, safe, and healthy environment results in happier employees and better work. Environmental health and safety officers study the air, ground, and water to identify and analyze sources of pollution and its effects. They also direct programs to control safety and health hazards in the work place.

## What They Do

Environmental health and safety officers in the military perform some or all of the following duties:

- Determine methods to collect environmental data for research projects and surveys

- Analyze data to identify pollution problem areas

- Inspect food samples to detect any spoilage or disease

- Develop pollution control plans and policies

- Conduct health education programs

- Work with civilian public health officials in performing studies and analyzing results

## Special Requirements

A 4-year college degree is normally required to enter this occupation. A degree in biomedical or biological science is required to enter some specialties in this occupation.

## Training Provided

No initial job training is provided to officers in this occupation.

## Helpful Attributes

Helpful fields of study include chemistry, biology, environmental sciences, soil science, civil engineering, and veterinary science. Helpful attributes include:

- Interest in protecting the environment

- Interest in conducting research or analytical studies

- Interest in work requiring accuracy and attention to detail

## Work Environment

Environmental health and safety officers normally work in offices or research laboratories. They work outdoors while conducting environmental studies and surveys or inspecting facilities.

## Civilian Counterparts

Civilian environmental health and safety officers work for engineering firms, manufacturing firms, and government agencies. They perform duties similar to those performed by military environmental health and safety officers. Depending on their specialty, they may be called environmental scientists, air pollution analysts, soil analysts, industrial hygienists, or water quality analysts.

## Opportunities

The services have about 350 environmental health and safety officers. On average, they need 20 new environmental health and safety officers each year. Positions for environmental health and safety officers in the Coast Guard are filled by U.S. Public Health Service Officers. New environmental health and safety officers are assigned to environmental health teams. After demonstrating leadership qualities, they may advance to senior management or command positions.

# INDUSTRIAL ENGINEERS

Because the military is so large, small savings in personnel or equipment costs can result in savings of millions of dollars. Industrial engineers design ways to improve how the military uses its people and equipment.

## What They Do

Industrial engineers in the military perform some or all of the following duties:

- Study how workers and tasks are organized

- Measure work load and calculate how many people are needed to perform work tasks

- Study and improve the way work is done and equipment is used

- Plan and oversee the purchase of equipment and services

- Plan and direct quality control and production control programs

## Special Requirements

A 4-year college degree in industrial engineering, industrial management, or a related field is required to enter this occupation.

## Helpful Attributes

Helpful attributes include:

- Interest in technical work

- Ability to plan and organize studies

- Interest in working with mathematical models and formulas

- Interest in working closely with people

## Work Environment

Industrial engineers usually work in offices. They may work outdoors while performing field studies or overseeing the installation of equipment and systems.

## Training Provided

Job training is offered for some specialties. Training length varies from 8 to 16 weeks of classroom instruction, depending on the specialty. Course content typically includes:

- Management standards, principles, and policies

- Problem analysis and decision making

- Production and purchasing methods

## Civilian Counterparts

Civilian industrial engineers work primarily in manufacturing and consulting firms. They also work in other industries and businesses, including insurance companies, retail stores, banks, public utilities, and hospitals. Civilian industrial engineers perform duties similar to those performed in the military. Depending on the specialty, they may also be called production engineers, safety engineers, production planners, or quality control engineers.

## Opportunities

The services have about 200 industrial engineers. On average, they need 10 new industrial engineers each year. After job training, industrial engineers are usually assigned to an engineering, management evaluation, or procurement unit. With experience, they may advance to command or policy-making positions in engineering, administration, or other fields.

# INTELLIGENCE OFFICERS

Army
Navy
Air Force
Marine Corps
Coast Guard

Information about the size, strength, location, and capabilities of enemy forces is essential to military operations and national defense. To gather information, the services rely on aerial photographs, human observation, and electronic monitoring using radar and supersensitive radios. Intelligence officers gather technical intelligence needed for military planning. Turn to page 374 for more information about intelligence officers.

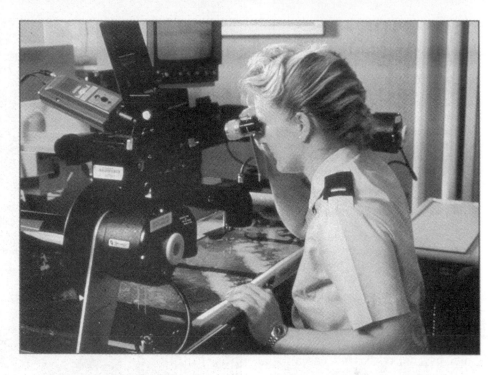

## What They Do

Intelligence officers in the military perform some or all of the following duties:

- Direct sea, ground, and aerial surveillance

- Prepare plans to intercept foreign communications transmissions

- Direct the analysis of aerial photos and other intelligence data

- Oversee the writing of intelligence reports

- Brief commanders on intelligence findings

- Help plan military missions

- Direct the use of computer systems to store and process intelligence data

- Gather and analyze technical intelligence

## Helpful Attributes

Helpful fields of study include cryptology, computer science, mathematics, and engineering. Helpful attributes include:

- Interest in solving problems

- Interest in collecting and analyzing data

- Ability to organize and manage activities

- Ability to work with abstract problems

## Training Provided

Job training consists of 23 to 26 weeks of classroom instruction. Course content typically includes:

- Air, ground, and sea intelligence operations

- Photograph interpretation and evaluation

- Use of radar and electronic surveillance equipment

- Reconnaissance equipment and weapons systems

Further training occurs on the job and through advanced courses.

## Special Requirements

A 4-year college degree is normally required to enter this occupation.

## Physical Demands

Normal color vision is required to work with map overlays and color photos.

## Work Environment

Intelligence officers work in offices on land and aboard ships. They may work in the field on maneuvers and military exercises.

## Civilian Counterparts

Civilian intelligence officers generally work in federal agencies, such as the Central Intelligence Agency (CIA) and Federal Bureau of Investigations (FBI). They perform duties similar to those performed by military intelligence officers.

## Opportunities

The services have about 6,550 intelligence officers. On average, they need 305 new intelligence officers each year. After job training, intelligence officers are assigned to intelligence units, military operations sections, or command posts. With experience, they may become commanders of intelligence units or directors of information gathering sections.

# LAWYERS

Army
Navy
Air Force
Marine Corps
Coast Guard

The military has its own system of laws and courts. Lawyers administer activities within the military judicial system. They also perform legal research, prosecute and defend court cases, and preside over military courts. They provide legal services for military personnel and represent the services in civil and international legal matters. Turn to page 376 for more information about lawyers.

## What They Do

Lawyers in the military perform some or all of the following duties:

- Give legal advice about government real estate, commercial contracts, patents, and trademarks

- Prepare pretrial advice for clients in court-martial cases

- Act as prosecuting attorney, defense attorney, or judge in court cases

- Prepare legal documents, such as wills and powers of attorney

- Interpret laws, directives, regulations, and court decisions

- Preside over court cases and make judgments based on the Uniform Code of Military Justice

- Help train new lawyers

## Special Requirements

A degree in law is required to enter this occupation. In addition, most specialties require a membership to the bar in either federal court or the highest court of a state.

## Helpful Attributes

Helpful attributes include:

- Interest in working with and researching legal concepts

- Ability to write clearly and concisely

- Ability to speak effectively in public

- Sensitivity to the needs of others

## Work Environment

Lawyers work in legal offices and courtrooms on land and aboard ships.

## Training Provided

Job training consists of 8 to 12 weeks of classroom instruction. Training length varies depending on specialty. Course content typically includes:

- Military trial procedures

- Application of the Uniform Code of Military Justice

- Methods of obtaining evidence

- Court-martial advocacy techniques

Further training occurs on the job and through advanced courses.

## Civilian Counterparts

Civilian lawyers work in private practice and for law firms, government, corporations, and nonprofit groups. They perform duties similar to those performed by military lawyers. Civilian lawyers, however, usually specialize in a particular field. There are several fields of civilian law, such as divorce, trade, and antitrust that military lawyers do not practice.

## Opportunities

The services have about 2,500 lawyers. On average, they need 200 new lawyers each year. With experience, lawyers may be appointed military judges. In time, lawyers may advance to senior management positions in the legal field.

# LIFE SCIENTISTS

The military conducts studies of human and animal diseases to understand their causes and to find treatments. Harmful pests and bacteria are studied to find ways to protect people and food against illness or infection. Life scientists study the biology and chemistry of living organisms.

## What They Do

Life scientists in the military perform some or all of the following duties:

- Study bacteria and parasites to determine how they invade and affect humans or animals

- Study the effects of diseases, poisons, and radiation on laboratory animals

- Study the effects of drugs, chemicals, and gases on living organisms

- Study ways of protecting humans through immunization from disease

- Direct blood banks and study blood chemistry

- Study the effects of aerospace flight, temperature, and movement on human physiology

- Study food storage and handling methods

- Study ways of keeping bases and ships free from pests and contagious diseases

- Conduct experiments and write technical reports

## Special Requirements

A 4-year college degree is normally required to enter this occupation. Some specialties require a master's degree or medical degree.

## Training Provided

No initial job training is provided to officers in this occupation. However, advanced courses are available in some specialties.

## Helpful Attributes

Helpful fields of study include biochemistry, biology, microbiology, and pharmacology. Helpful attributes include:

- Interest in scientific work

- Ability to express ideas clearly and concisely

- Interest in mathematics, chemistry, biology, medicine, and medical research

- Interest in collecting and analyzing scientific data

## Work Environment

Life scientists work in medical, clinical, and research laboratories and, at times, in food processing or storage plants. They may work outdoors while conducting field work on land or aboard ships.

## Civilian Counterparts

Civilian life scientists work for universities, government agencies, medical laboratories, blood banks, pharmaceutical firms, chemical companies, or in private practice. They perform duties similar to those performed by military life scientists. Depending on their specialty, civilian life scientists may be called biochemists, biologists, entomologists, immunologists, medical technologists, pharmacologists, physiologists, toxicologists, or veterinarians.

## Opportunities

The services have about 500 life scientists. On average, they need 30 new life scientists each year. Newly commissioned life scientists are normally assigned to a laboratory, where they conduct research under the direction of more experienced scientists. In time, life scientists may manage their own research projects and direct other officers. Eventually, they may become directors of research laboratories or hold other senior management positions in the health research field.

# MARINE ENGINEERS

Ships and submarines must be designed for speed, strength, stability, and safety. Improvements in ship equipment, hull design, and deck layout can improve operations. Marine engineers design ships, submarines, and other watercraft for military use. They also oversee the construction and repair of ships and marine equipment.

## What They Do

Marine engineers in the military perform some or all of the following duties:

- Study new ways of designing and building ship hulls

- Develop and test shipboard combat and salvage equipment

- Oversee the construction, maintenance, and repair of ship hulls and equipment

- Manage research programs to solve naval engineering problems

- Oversee the installation, operation, and repair of marine equipment and systems

- Evaluate marine research data and prepare technical reports

## Special Requirements

A 4-year college degree in marine engineering is required to enter this occupation.

## Helpful Attributes

Helpful attributes include:

- Interest in technical work

- Ability to plan and organize research projects

- Interest in ships and shipbuilding

## Training Provided

No initial job training is provided to officers in this occupation.

## Civilian Counterparts

Civilian marine engineers work in the shipbuilding industry. They also work for government agencies and ship machinery manufacturers. Civilian marine engineers perform duties similar to those performed in the military. They may also be called marine equipment research engineers, marine architects, marine equipment design engineers, marine surveyors, and port engineers.

## Work Environment

Marine engineers do much of their work outdoors at shipyards while overseeing shipbuilding and repair activities. They work in offices while directing vessel design and development activities.

## Opportunities

The services have about 100 marine engineers. On average, they need 10 new marine engineers each year. Newly commissioned marine engineers may be assigned to engineering or marine research and development laboratories. They may also be assigned to work in shipyards with vessel maintenance and repair units. With experience, marine engineers may advance to senior engineering management and command positions.

# METEOROLOGISTS

**Navy**
**Air Force**
**Marine Corps**

Meteorology is the study of the weather and weather forecasting. Military operations such as troop movements, airplane flights, missile launches, and ship movements rely on accurate weather information. Meteorologists study weather conditions and prepare current and long-range weather forecasts. Turn to page 378 for more information about meteorologists.

## What They Do

Meteorologists in the military perform some or all of the following duties:

- Direct personnel who collect weather data

- Observe weather conditions from airplanes

- Interpret weather data received from satellites and weather balloons

- Prepare short-range and long-range weather forecasts

- Relay forecast updates and violent weather warnings to military and civilian authorities

- Train staff in data collection and interpretation

## Physical Demands

Meteorology specialties involving air observation require applicants to pass a demanding flight physical exam.

## Helpful Attributes

Helpful attributes include:

- Interest in scientific work

- Interest in collecting and analyzing data

- Interest in working with mathematical formulas

- Interest in planning and directing the work of others

## Special Requirements

A 4-year college degree, with course work in meteorology, is usually required to enter this occupation.

## Training Provided

Job training consists of 6 to 15 weeks of classroom instruction. Course content typically includes:

- Identification of common weather patterns

- Methods of analyzing weather conditions

- Use of radar and satellite systems for weather data collection

- Use of computers for compiling, analyzing, and plotting weather data

- Techniques and procedures of forecasting

## Work Environment

Meteorologists usually work in weather stations or operations centers where weather information can be collected, analyzed, and plotted using computers. Sometimes they work outdoors while making weather observations.

## Civilian Counterparts

Civilian meteorologists work for government agencies, radio and television stations, and airlines. They perform duties similar to those performed by military meteorologists.

## Opportunities

The services have about 800 meteorologists. On average, they need 40 new meteorologists each year. After job training, meteorologists are assigned to land-based or shipboard weather stations. With experience, they may advance to senior management and command positions.

# NUCLEAR ENGINEERS

The military has been a pioneer in the use of nuclear energy. The military uses nuclear energy for power plants, strategic weapons, and defense systems. Nuclear engineers direct research and development projects to improve military uses of nuclear energy. They also direct nuclear power plant operations. Turn to page 380 for more information about nuclear engineers.

## What They Do

Nuclear engineers in the military perform some or all of the following duties:

- Direct projects to improve nuclear power plants in ships and submarines

- Direct research on the uses and effects of nuclear weapons

- Develop safety procedures for handling nuclear weapons

- Assist high-level officials in creating policies for developing and using nuclear technology

- Direct operations and maintenance of nuclear power plants

## Special Requirements

A 4-year college degree in physics, chemistry, or nuclear engineering is required to enter this occupation. Some specialties in this occupation require a master's degree.

## Work Environment

Nuclear engineers work in offices, research laboratories, and power plant control centers, either on land or aboard nuclear-powered ships and submarines.

## Helpful Attributes

Helpful attributes include:

- Interest in scientific and technical work

- Interest in planning and directing complex research projects

- Interest in working with mathematical formulas

- Interest in concepts and principles of engineering

## Training Provided

No initial job training is provided to officers in this occupation. However, advanced training is available.

## Civilian Counterparts

Civilian nuclear engineers work for firms that build and operate nuclear power plants and that develop and manufacture nuclear weapons. Many also work for public utilities, government agencies, and colleges and universities. Civilian nuclear engineers perform duties similar to those performed in the military.

## Opportunities

The services have about 100 nuclear engineers. On average, they need 10 new nuclear engineers each year. Newly commissioned nuclear engineers are usually assigned to nuclear research laboratories, nuclear power plants (on shore or aboard ships), or other defense facilities. With experience, they may advance to senior management or command positions.

# OCEANOGRAPHERS

The military needs navigational charts and maps to safely travel the oceans. Accurate oceanographic and weather forecasts are also needed to plan military operations. Oceanographers study ocean tides, currents, weather, and the physical features of the ocean floor.

## What They Do

Oceanographers in the military perform some or all of the following duties:

- Direct personnel who collect oceanographic data

- Conduct research on the effects of water and atmosphere on military warning and weapon systems

- Direct the preparation of ocean, sea, and waterway charts, maps, and publications

- Oversee the preparation of oceanographic and weather forecasts

- Collect information on ice conditions in ocean shipping lanes

- Collect information about ocean currents for support of military operational planning

- Advise commanders about ocean and sea conditions to assist in search and rescue missions

## Special Requirements

A 4-year college degree is normally required to enter this occupation.

## Helpful Attributes

Helpful fields of study include oceanography, geology, marine engineering, and hydrology. Helpful attributes include:

- Preference for doing scientific work

- Interest in sailing and being at sea

- Interest in conducting research or analytical studies

## Training Provided

No initial job training is provided to officers in this occupation.

## Civilian Counterparts

Civilian oceanographers usually work for colleges and universities, where they are primarily involved in research. Some work for federal government agencies, such as the National Oceanic and Atmospheric Administration (NOAA) and for state and local governments that border on the ocean. Civilian oceanographers perform duties similar to those performed in the military.

## Work Environment

Oceanographers work outdoors in all climates while collecting oceanographic information. They work in offices while preparing oceanographic publications and charts.

## Opportunities

The services have about 100 oceanographers. On average, they need 10 new oceanographers each year. Newly commissioned oceanographers work in their specialty areas, usually with a senior officer. With experience, they work more independently. In time, they may advance to senior management or command positions.

# PHYSICISTS

The goal of military research is to improve the technologies used for national defense. Through physics research, new materials for building ships, aircraft, and weapons are discovered. Physicists direct research and development projects on physical matter and energy.

## What They Do

Physicists in the military perform some or all of the following duties:

- Plan and conduct experiments in aerodynamics, optics, geophysics, biophysics, and astrophysics

- Conduct research to improve methods of radiation detection and protection

- Analyze strength, flexibility, weight, and other properties of metals, plastics, and other materials

- Conduct studies regarding the use of nuclear-powered engines

- Write technical reports on experiments performed

- Assist in research and development projects to improve radio and other communications equipment

- Oversee research projects under contract to universities and industrial firms

- Manage laboratories or field staff to conduct experiments

## Special Requirements

A 4-year college degree in physics, chemistry, or nuclear engineering is required to enter this occupation. Some specialties require a master's degree.

## Helpful Attributes

Helpful attributes include:

- Interest in scientific and technical work

- Interest in mathematics and physics

- Interest in conducting research and analytical studies

## Work Environment

Physicists usually work in research and development laboratories.

## Training Provided

No initial job training is provided to officers in this occupation.

## Civilian Counterparts

Civilian physicists work primarily in research and development for private industry, colleges and universities, and government agencies. They perform duties similar to those performed by military physicists. Civilian physicists usually specialize in one area of physics, such as nuclear, astronomical, health, or medical physics.

## Opportunities

The services have about 100 physicists. On average, they need 10 new physicists each year. Newly commissioned physicists work as part of research teams. With experience, they may lead research projects of their own. After demonstrating leadership abilities, they may advance to senior management positions in a variety of scientific fields.

# SPACE OPERATIONS OFFICERS

Orbiting satellites and other space vehicles are used for national security, communications, weather forecasting, and space exploration. Space operations officers manage space flight planning, training, mission control, and other activities involved in launching and recovering spacecraft. They may also be astronauts who command space flights or who serve as crew members.

## What They Do

Space operations officers in the military perform some or all of the following duties:

- Manage activities of the flight control facility, including mission planning and training

- Manage operation of guidance, navigation, and propulsion systems for ground and space vehicles

- Develop space flight simulation exercises to train astronauts

- Plan space stations

- Direct space center launch and recovery activities

- Command and pilot space shuttles

- Perform in-orbit tasks and experiments aboard spacecraft

- Monitor foreign space flights and missile launches

## Physical Demands

Astronaut testing and training are very physically demanding. Officers must be in top physical shape to qualify for the astronaut shuttle program. Space operations officers must have normal color vision to read charts, graphics, and control panels.

## Special Requirements

A 4-year college degree in science or engineering is required to enter the space operations field. A bachelor of science degree in engineering, mathematics, physical science, or life science is required to qualify as an astronaut.

## Helpful Attributes

Helpful attributes include:

- Interest in scientific research

- Decisiveness

- Ability to work well as a member of a team

- Interest in space travel and desire to explore new frontiers

## Civilian Counterparts

Most civilian space operations officers work for the National Aeronautics and Space Administration (NASA) in launch and mission control. They perform duties similar to those performed by military space operations officers. Some civilian space operations officers work for private corporations and firms that operate space satellites.

## Work Environment

Launch and mission control space operations officers work in offices. Astronauts are required at times to work in a zero gravity environment in training as well as in space flight.

## Training Provided

Job training for mission control officers consists of about 1 year of classroom instruction and practical experience. Course content typically includes:

- Evaluation of space transport systems

- Development of space mission plans

- Methods for conducting space flight training programs

- Development of space flight simulation exercises

Further training occurs on the job and through academic courses. Astronauts must complete the NASA astronaut candidate training school. They also receive 1 year of practical training in space transport systems.

## Opportunities

The services have about 800 space operations officers. On average, they need 50 new space operations officers each year. After job training, new space operations officers are assigned to space operations, launch and mission control centers, or research facilities. With experience and special training, they have the opportunity to work in various areas such as astronautics or space flight control. Eventually, they may manage a space and ballistic missile warning facility, a satellite command center, a space launch system, a space systems analysis facility, or a manned space flight. Although Marine Corps officers may become astronauts and hold other positions in space operations, at present only the Navy and Air Force have defined career programs in this area.

# SURVEYING AND MAPPING MANAGERS

The military conducts land surveys to construct roads, airfields, and bridges. Land measurements are also needed to make maps and charts of unknown areas. Surveying and mapping managers plan and direct surveying and mapmaking operations.

## What They Do

Surveying and mapping managers in the military perform some or all of the following duties:

- Plan surveys and aerial photography missions

- Direct the activities of survey teams

- Direct the calculation of latitude and longitude, slope, elevation, and other features of the land

- Direct mapmaking and drafting activities

- Advise commanders about distance and location during military operations

## Special Requirements

A 4-year college degree in photographic science, cartography, photogrammetry, or a related field is required to enter this occupation.

## Helpful Attributes

Helpful attributes include:

- Interest in planning and directing the work of others

- Ability to visualize land features from maps and charts

- Interest in construction and engineering

## Physical Demands

Normal color vision is required to read color maps and aerial photographs.

## Work Environment

Surveying and mapping managers usually work in engineering offices. They may work outdoors when assisting survey teams or during military operations.

## Training Provided

Job training consists of 10 to 13 weeks of classroom instruction. Course content typically includes:

- Mapmaking and charting techniques

- Survey methods

- Management of mapmaking programs

## Civilian Counterparts

Civilian surveying and mapping managers usually work for engineering firms, where they manage construction project planning. They perform duties similar to those performed by military surveying and mapping managers. They may also be called land surveyors, cartographic supervisors, or photogrammetric engineers.

## Opportunities

The services have about 400 surveying and mapping managers. On average, they need 10 new managers each year. After job training, surveying and mapping managers are usually assigned to engineering, surveying, or intelligence units or to mapmaking laboratories. Eventually, they may advance to senior management or command positions in the engineering field.

# Transportation Occupations

- **Airplane Navigators**
- **Airplane Pilots**
- **Helicopter Pilots**
- **Ship and Submarine Officers**
- **Ship Engineers**

# AIRPLANE NAVIGATORS

Navy
Air Force
Marine Corps
Coast Guard

Pilots rely on the precision and skill of the navigator to keep the aircraft on course. Airplane navigators use radar, radio and other navigation equipment to determine position, direction of travel, intended course, and other information about their flights. Turn to page 366 for more information about airplane navigators.

## What They Do

Airplane navigators in the military perform some or all of the following duties:

- Direct aircraft course using radar, sight, and other navigation methods

- Operate radios and other communication equipment to send and receive messages

- Locate other aircraft using radar equipment

- Operate bombardier systems during bombing runs

- Inspect and test navigation and weapons systems before flights

- Guide tankers and other airplanes during in-flight refueling operations

- Provide pilots with instrument readings, fuel usage, and other flight information

## Physical Demands

Airplane navigators, like pilots, have a physically and mentally demanding job. Navigators are required to have excellent vision and must be in top physical shape.

## Special Requirements

A 4-year college degree is required to enter this occupation. Although there are women airplane navigators, some specialties are open only to men.

## Work Environment

Airplane navigators perform their work in aircraft. They may be stationed at airbases or aboard aircraft carriers anywhere around the world.

## Training Provided

Job training consists of 6 to 12 months of classroom instruction. Course content typically includes:

- Principles and methods of navigation

- Operation of communication, weapon, and radar systems

- Inspection and testing of navigation equipment and systems

- Combat and bombing navigation procedures and tactics

Practical experience in navigation is gained through training in aircraft simulators and through about 100 hours of actual flying time. Further training occurs on the job and through advanced courses.

## Helpful Attributes

Helpful fields of study include cartography, geography, and surveying. Helpful attributes include:

- Ability to read maps and charts

- Interest in work requiring accuracy and attention to detail

- Ability to respond quickly to emergencies

- Strong desire to fly

## Civilian Counterparts

Civilian airplane navigators work for passenger and cargo airlines. With the exception of duties that are combat-related, their duties are similar to those performed by military navigators.

## Opportunities

The services have about 4,000 airplane navigators. On average, they need 50 new navigators each year. After job training, airplane navigators are assigned to flying sections for duty. They work as officer crewmembers on bombers, tankers, fighters, or other airplanes. In time, they may advance to senior management or command positions.

# AIRPLANE PILOTS

The military operates one of the largest fleets of specialized airplanes in the world. Supersonic fighters and bombers fly combat missions. Large transports carry troops and equipment. Intelligence gathering airplanes take photographs from high altitudes. Military airplane pilots fly the thousands of jet and propeller airplanes operated by the services. Turn to page 368 for more information about airplane pilots.

## What They Do

Airplane pilots in the military perform some or all of the following duties:

- Check weather reports to learn about flying conditions

- Develop flight plans showing air routes and schedules

- Contact air traffic controllers to obtain take-off and landing instructions

- Fly airplanes by controlling engines, rudders, elevators, and other controls

- Monitor gauges and dials located on cockpit control panels

- Perform combat maneuvers, take photographs, transport equipment, and patrol areas to carry out flight missions

## Physical Demands

Airplane pilots must pass the most demanding physical test of any job in the military. To be accepted for pilot training, applicants must have 20/20 vision and be in top physical condition. They must have very good eye-hand coordination and have extremely quick reaction times to maneuver at high speeds.

## Special Requirements

A 4-year college degree is normally required to enter this occupation. Although the military has many women pilots, specialties involving duty in combat airplanes are open only to men. Because all Marine Corps planes are combat planes, there are no women pilots in the Marines.

## Work Environment

Airplane pilots may be stationed at airbases or aboard aircraft carriers anywhere in the world. They fly in all types of weather conditions. Military pilots take off and land on airport runways and aircraft carrier landing decks.

## Training Provided

Pilot training is a 2-year program covering 1 year each in initial and advanced training. Initial training includes time spent in flight simulators, classroom training, officer training, and basic flight training. Course content typically includes:

- Aircraft aerodynamics

- Jet and propeller engine operation

- Operation of aircraft navigation systems

- Foul weather flying

- Federal Aviation Administration (FAA) regulations

This is among the most challenging training given by the services; not everyone who attempts this training can meet the strict requirements for completion. Advanced training begins when pilots successfully complete initial training and are awarded their "wings." Advanced training consists of instruction in flying a particular type of aircraft.

## Helpful Attributes

Helpful fields of study include physics and aerospace, electrical, or mechanical engineering. Helpful attributes include:

- Strong desire to fly airplanes

- Self-confidence and ability to remain calm in stressful situations

- Determination to complete a very demanding training program

## Civilian Counterparts

Civilian airplane pilots who work for passenger airlines and air cargo businesses are called commercial pilots. Other civilian pilots work as flight instructors at local airports, as crop dusters, or as pilots transporting business executives in company planes. Many commercial pilots began their career in the military.

## Opportunities

The services have about 18,000 airplane pilots. On average, they need 150 new pilots each year. After initial and advanced training, most pilots are assigned to flying squadrons to fly the types of aircraft for which they were trained. In time, pilots train for different aircraft and missions. Eventually, they may advance to senior management or command positions.

# HELICOPTER PILOTS

Helicopters can take off from and land on small areas. They can also hover in one spot in the air. The military uses these versatile aircraft to transport troops and cargo, perform search and rescue missions, and provide close combat support for ground troops. Helicopter pilots fly the many helicopters operated by the services.

## What They Do

Helicopter pilots in the military perform some or all of the following duties:

• Prepare flight plans showing air routes and schedules

• Fly helicopters by controlling engines, flight controls, and other systems

• Monitor gauges and dials located on cockpit control panels

• Perform combat maneuvers, spot and observe enemy positions, transport troops and equipment, and evacuate wounded troops

• Check weather reports to learn about flying conditions

## Physical Demands

Helicopter pilots must pass some of the most demanding physical tests of any job in the military. To be accepted for pilot training, applicants must have excellent vision and be in top physical condition. They must have very good eye-hand-foot coordination and have quick reflexes.

## Special Requirements

A 4-year college degree is normally required to enter this occupation. Some specialties in the Army do not require a 4-year college degree, but are only open to personnel who have been in the service for several years and who are selected for a special pilot training program. Although there are women helicopter pilots, some specialties are open only to men. The Marine Corps has no women helicopter pilots because all specialties involve duty in combat aircraft.

## Helpful Attributes

Helpful fields of study include physics and aerospace, electrical, or mechanical engineering. Helpful attributes include:

• Strong desire to fly aircraft

• Determination to complete a very demanding training program

• Self-confidence and ability to remain calm under stress

## Training Provided

Job training consists of 1 to 2 years of academic and flight instruction. Flight training consists of at least 80 hours of flying time. Training length varies depending on specialty. Course content typically includes:

• Principles of helicopter operation

• Principles of helicopter inspection

• Flying techniques and emergency procedures

• Combat skills and tactics

## Work Environment

Helicopter pilots are stationed at military bases or aboard aircraft carriers around the world. They fly in all types of weather conditions. Helicopter pilots take off and land from airports, forward landing areas, and ship landing decks.

## Civilian Counterparts

Civilian helicopter pilots work for police forces, local commuter services, and private businesses. They also work as crop dusters, fire fighters, traffic spotters, and helicopter flight instructors.

## Opportunities

The military has about 3,300 helicopter pilots. On average, the services need 80 new pilots each year. After receiving their pilot rating, helicopter pilots are assigned to flying units. With experience, they may become group leaders or flight instructors. Helicopter pilots may advance to senior management and command positions.

# SHIP AND SUBMARINE OFFICERS

Army
Navy
Coast Guard

Ships and submarines are organized by departments, such as engineering, communications, weapons, and supply. Ship and submarine officers work as team members to manage the various departments aboard their vessels. Turn to page 386 for more information about ship and submarine officers in the military.

## What They Do

Ship and submarine officers in the military perform some or all of the following duties:

- Command vessels of all sizes at sea or in coastal waters

- Plan and manage the operating departments, under the captain's direction

- Plan and manage training exercises, such as target practice, aircraft operations, damage control drills, and searches for enemy submarines

- Evaluate subordinate personnel and recommend awards and promotions

- Direct search and rescue missions

## Physical Demands

Good vision and normal color vision are required for reading color-coded charts and maps and, for submarine duty, for adjusting to red-light vision prior to surfacing at night.

## Special Requirements

A 4-year college degree is normally required to enter this occupation. Although there are women ship officers, some assignments, such as submarine duty, are open only to men.

## Work Environment

Ship and submarine officers work aboard their vessels. Engineering officers are subjected to hot, humid, and noisy environments. Submarine officers work in confined spaces for extended periods.

## Training Provided

Job training consists of classroom instruction and practical experience in one of the following departments: air, weapons, operations, communications, engineering, deck, administration, or supply. Training length varies depending on specialty. Course content typically includes:

- Management and organization of ship or submarine operations

- Responsibilities of the individual departments

- Piloting and navigation of ships

- Interpretation of maritime laws and policies

Further training occurs on the job and through advanced courses.

## Civilian Counterparts

Civilian ship officers work for private maritime passenger, freight, and tanker firms. With the exception of duties that are combat related, their duties are similar to those performed by military ship officers.

## Helpful Attributes

Helpful fields of study include engineering, oceanography, mathematics, and computer science. Helpful attributes include:

- Ability to organize and direct the work of others

- Interest in sailing and being at sea

- Ability to motivate and lead others

## Opportunities

The services have about 3,000 ship and submarine officers. On average, they need 50 new ship and submarine officers each year. After job training, officers are assigned to management positions in one of the ship's departments working under more experienced officers. With experience and demonstrated ability to lead, they assume greater responsibility. Depending on their specialty, ship and submarine officers gain experience in more than one department. Also, they are regularly reassigned to different ships or submarines where they meet and work with new people. Between sea tours, they work and attend training at shore bases. Eventually, ship and submarine officers may be selected to command a vessel.

# SHIP ENGINEERS

Engines are a ship's main source of power for propulsion, heat, and electricity. Ship engines are massive; some are as large as the power plants that generate electricity for small cities. Ship engineers direct the engineering departments aboard ships and submarines. They are responsible for engine operations, maintenance, and repair. They are also responsible for shipboard heating and power generation.

## What They Do

Ship engineers in the military perform some or all of the following duties:

- Direct engine room operations in nuclear or diesel-powered vessels

- Direct crews that inspect and maintain the electrical generators that supply power for lights, weapons, and equipment

- Direct crews that inspect and maintain the heating plants and air conditioning systems

- Direct crews that inspect and maintain ship transmission and propulsion systems

- Direct engine room repairs

## Special Requirements

A 4-year college degree is normally required to enter this occupation. Nuclear specialties require a 4-year college degree in nuclear engineering.

## Helpful Attributes

Helpful fields of study include civil, mechanical, and electrical engineering. Helpful attributes include:

- Interest in planning and directing the work of others

- Interest in engines and machines

## Work Environment

Ship engineers work in engine rooms, where the noise levels and temperatures may be high.

## Training Provided

Job training consists of 3 to 12 months of instruction. Training length varies depending on specialty; the time required for nuclear specialties is the longest. Course content typically includes:

- Inspection and maintenance of marine engines, electrical systems, and fuel systems

- Operation and maintenance of steam plants and related machinery

Further training occurs on the job and through advanced courses. Nuclear specialties involve extensive training in reactor operations.

## Civilian Counterparts

Civilian ship engineers work for shipping lines, transport companies, and some government agencies. They perform duties similar to those performed by military ship engineers. Civilian ship engineers may also be called engineers or marine engineers.

## Opportunities

The services have about 600 ship engineers. On average, they need 10 new ship engineers each year. After job training, ship engineers work as assistant engineers under the direction of a chief engineer. With experience, they may advance to become chief engineer in charge of an engineering department. Eventually, they may advance to senior management and command positions.

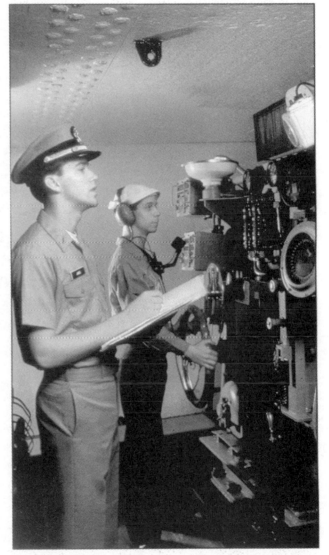

# Combat Specialty Occupations

- **Artillery Officers**
- **Infantry Officers**
- **Missile System Officers**
- **Special Operations Officers**
- **Tank Officers**

# ARTILLERY OFFICERS

The military uses artillery to support infantry and tank units in combat and to protect land and sea forces from air attack. Artillery officers direct artillery crew members as they position, maintain, and fire guns, cannons, howitzers, and rockets at enemy positions and aircraft. They normally specialize by type of artillery.

## What They Do

Artillery officers in the military perform some or all of the following duties:

- Direct training activities of artillery and gun crew members

- Direct fire control operations and firing procedures

- Direct naval gunnery operations

- Select location of artillery and coordinate their use with infantry and tank units

- Direct air defense missile system operations

- Direct maintenance of artillery fire control equipment

## Physical Demands

Physical requirements vary depending upon the type of artillery unit to which the officer is assigned. In most instances, artillery officers must meet very demanding physical requirements. They must be able to perform for long periods of time without rest and to work under stress.

## Special Requirements

A 4-year college degree is normally required to enter this occupation. Although there are women artillery officers, some specialties in this occupation are open only to men.

## Helpful Attributes

Helpful fields of study include engineering, physics, and chemistry. Helpful attributes include:

- Ability to motivate and lead others

- Decisiveness

- Willingness to accept a challenge and face danger

## Training Provided

Job training consists of 3 to 19 weeks of classroom instruction and field training under simulated combat conditions. Training length varies depending on specialty. Course content typically includes:

- Artillery tactics

- Ammunition handling procedures

- Fire direction control procedures

- Air defense artillery duties

Further training occurs on the job and through advanced courses.

## Work Environment

Artillery officers live and work under the same conditions as the personnel they lead. Some artillery officers spend a lot of time in field training exercises, where they work, eat, and sleep outdoors and in tents. Others work and live aboard ships.

## Civilian Counterparts

Although the job of artillery officer has no equivalent in civilian life, the leadership and administrative experiences it provides are similar to those used in many civilian management occupations.

## Opportunities

The services have about 11,200 artillery officers. On average, they need 700 new artillery officers each year. After training, new artillery officers usually assist commanders in directing artillery units. After demonstrating leadership ability, they may advance to command positions.

# INFANTRY OFFICERS

In peacetime, the infantry stays ready to defend the country anywhere in the world. In combat, the infantry is deployed to capture or destroy enemy forces on the ground and to repel enemy invasions. Infantry officers direct, train, and lead infantry units. Turn to page 372 for more information about infantry officers.

## What They Do

Infantry officers in the military perform some or all of the following duties:

- Gather and evaluate intelligence on enemy strength and positions

- Develop offensive and defensive battle plans

- Coordinate plans with armor, artillery, and air support units

- Direct construction of bunkers, fortifications, and obstacles to support and camouflage infantry positions

- Direct the use of infantry weapons and equipment, such as machine guns, mortars, rocket launchers, and armored personnel carriers

- Develop and supervise infantry unit training

- Direct administrative activities

## Physical Demands

Infantry officers must meet the same demanding physical requirements as the infantrymen they command. They must be in excellent physical condition to perform strenuous activities over long periods of time, sometimes without sleep or rest.

## Special Requirements

A 4-year college degree is normally required to enter this occupation. This occupation is open only to men.

## Work Environment

Because infantry officers must be prepared to lead their troops anywhere in the world that the infantry is needed, they work and train in all climates and weather conditions. During training exercises, as in real combat situations, infantry officers work, eat, and sleep outdoors and in tents. When not in the field, infantry officers perform administrative and management duties in offices.

## Training Provided

Job training consists of 8 to 14 weeks of classroom instruction and field training under simulated combat conditions. Training length varies depending on specialty. Course content typically includes:

- Infantry leadership roles

- Infantry squad and platoon tactics

- Modern offensive and defensive combat techniques

## Helpful Attributes

Helpful fields of study include engineering, history, physical education, and business or public administration. Helpful attributes include:

- Ability to motivate and lead others

- Willingness to accept a challenge and face danger

- Interest in land battle history and strategy

## Civilian Counterparts

Although the job of infantry officer has no equivalent in civilian life, the leadership and administrative skills it provides are similar to those used in many civilian managerial occupations.

## Opportunities

The services have about 11,000 infantry officers. On average, they need 700 new infantry officers each year. After job training, infantry officers are assigned to infantry units as platoon leaders. They direct training and tactical exercises for wargames. Advancement in the infantry is based on ability to lead. Infantry officers with proven ability to lead may assume command positions.

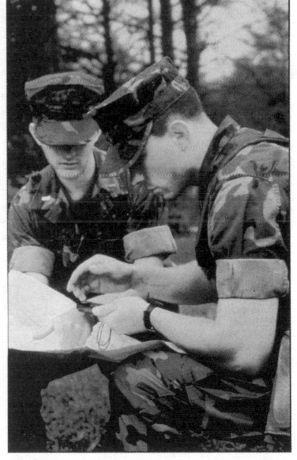

# MISSILE SYSTEM OFFICERS

Ballistic missiles are powerful weapons that travel thousands of miles to their targets. They are fired from underground silos, submarines, and land-based launchers. Missile system officers direct missile crews as they target, launch, test, and maintain ballistic missiles.

## What They Do

Missile system officers in the military perform some or all of the following duties:

- Stand watch as members of missile launch crews

- Direct testing and inspection of missile systems

- Direct missile maintenance operations

- Direct early-warning launch training exercises

- Direct security operations at missile sites

- Direct the storage and handling of nuclear warheads

- Direct operation of fail-safe and code verification systems

## Special Requirements

A 4-year college degree is normally required to enter this occupation. For some specialties, a master's degree in management is preferred.

## Helpful Attributes

Helpful fields of study include engineering, physics, computer science, and business or public administration. Helpful attributes include:

- Ability to motivate and lead others

- Ability to remain calm in stressful situations

- Ability to learn and precisely follow complex procedures

## Work Environment

Missile system officers work in underground launch command centers, in submarines, and in ground-level missile sites.

## Training Provided

Job training consists of 12 to 19 weeks of classroom instruction and training on missile system simulations. Training length varies depending on specialty. Course content typically includes:

- Missile targeting

- Security and code authentication

- Launch operations

- Maintenance programs

Further training occurs on the job and through advanced courses.

## Civilian Counterparts

Although the job of missile system officer has no equivalent in civilian life, the leadership skills it provides are similar to those used in many civilian occupations.

## Opportunities

The services have about 1,000 missile system officers. On average, they need 100 new officers each year. After job training, new missile system officers normally learn the details of missile operations by focusing on one aspect at a time under the direction of experienced officers. In time, they manage one or more divisions at a missile site, assuming more responsibility. Eventually they may advance to senior management and command positions in missile operations or other areas in their service.

# SPECIAL OPERATIONS OFFICERS

Army
Navy
Air Force
Marine Corps

Each service has specially trained forces to perform rapid strike missions. These elite forces stay in a constant state of readiness to strike anywhere in the world on a moment's notice. Special operations officers lead special operations forces in offensive raids, demolitions, intelligence gathering, and search and rescue missions. Due to the wide variety of missions, special operations officers are trained swimmers, parachutists, and survival experts.

## What They Do

Special operations officers in the military perform some or all of the following duties:

• Train personnel in parachute, scuba diving, and special combat techniques

• Plan missions and coordinate plans with other forces as needed

• Train personnel for special missions using simulated mission conditions

• Lead special forces teams in accomplishing mission objectives

• Direct and supervise administrative activities of special forces units

## Physical Demands

Special operations officers must meet very demanding physical requirements. Good eyesight, night vision, and physical conditioning are required to reach mission objectives by parachute, over land, or under water. Good eye-hand coordination is required to detonate or deactivate explosives. In most instances, special operations officers are required to be qualified swimmers, parachutists, and endurance runners.

## Special Requirements

A 4-year college degree is normally required to enter this occupation. Selection as a special operations officer is very competitive. This occupation is open only to men.

## Helpful Attributes

Helpful fields of study include physical education, engineering, physical sciences, history, and business or public administration. Helpful attributes include:

• Ability to remain calm and decisive under stress

• Willingness to accept a challenge and face danger

• Willingness to stay in top physical condition

• Determination to complete a very demanding training program

## Work Environment

Because special operations officers must be prepared to go anywhere in the world they are needed, they train and work in all climates, weather conditions, and settings. They may work in cold water and dive from submarines or small underwater craft. They may also be exposed to harsh temperatures, often without protection, during missions into enemy-controlled areas.

## Training Provided

Job training consists of up to 20 weeks of formal classroom training and practical experience. Training length varies depending on specialty. Course content typically includes:

• Physical conditioning, scuba diving, swimming, and parachuting

• Mission planning techniques

• Handling and using explosives

• Reconnaissance techniques

Additional training occurs on the job. Basic skills are kept sharp through planning and conducting exercises under simulated mission conditions.

## Civilian Counterparts

Although the job of special operations officer has no equivalent in civilian life, the leadership and administrative skills it provides are similar to those used in many civilian management occupations, particularly law enforcement.

## Opportunities

The services have about 1,900 special operations officers. On average they need 20 new special operations officers each year. After training, special operations officers usually assist commanders in directing special operations forces. After demonstrating leadership ability, they may assume command positions.

# TANK OFFICERS

In peacetime, tank and armor units stay ready to defend the country anywhere in the world. In combat, they operate tanks, armored vehicles, and amphibious assault vehicles to engage and destroy the enemy. Tank officers lead tank and armor units. They normally specialize by type of tank unit, such as armor, cavalry, or amphibious assault.

## What They Do

Tank officers in the military perform some or all of the following duties:

- Gather and evaluate intelligence or enemy strength and positions

- Formulate battle plans

- Coordinate actions with infantry, artillery, and air support units

- Plan and direct communications

- Direct operations of tanks, amphibious assault vehicles, and support equipment

- Plan and supervise tactical and technical training of a tank unit

- Direct unit administrative activities

## Physical Demands

Tank officers must meet the same demanding physical requirements as the troops they command. They must be physically fit and able to hold up under the stress of combat conditions.

## Special Requirements

A 4-year college degree is normally required to enter this occupation. This occupation is open only to men.

## Work Environment

Tank officers work and train in all climates and weather conditions. To remain ready for combat, tank units must regularly train under simulated combat conditions. During these exercises, tank officers are on the move, working, eating, and sleeping outdoors and in tents. When not in training, tank officers perform administrative duties in offices.

## Training Provided

Job training consists of 4 to 20 weeks of classroom and field training. Training length varies depending on specialty. Course content typically includes:

- Weapons and equipment maintenance

- Tank and armor operations, principles, and tactics

- Night maneuvers

- Role of the platoon leader

Further training occurs on the job and through specialized courses.

## Helpful Attributes

Helpful fields of study include engineering, geography, physical sciences, history, and business or public administration. Helpful attributes include:

- Ability to motivate and lead others

- Willingness to accept a challenge and face danger

- Decisiveness

- Interest in tanks and battlefield strategy

## Civilian Counterparts

Although the job of tank officer has no equivalent in civilian life, the leadership and administrative skills it provides are similar to those used in many civilian managerial occupations.

## Opportunities

The services have about 5,200 tank officers. On average, they need 350 new tank officers each year. New tank officers are assigned to tank and armor units as platoon leaders. Advancement in armor is based on ability to lead. Tank officers with proven ability to lead may assume command positions.

# Military
# Career Paths

# Introduction to Military Career Paths

The Military Career Paths section provides a general description of the military career development process. This section is divided into two parts—enlisted career path information and officer career path information.

Enlisted personnel are the workers who carry out and maintain the day-to-day operations of the military. They may work as combat engineers, aircraft mechanics, intelligence specialists, or medical care technicians. Enlisted personnel are usually high school graduates and are required to meet minimum physical and aptitude requirements before enlisting. The qualifications for becoming an enlisted service member are described in the General Information on Enlisted Occupations section of *Military Careers* (p. 11).

The enlisted part of Military Career Paths provides descriptions of 23 enlisted career paths for some of the occupations found in the Military Occupations section. Each enlisted career path description includes valuable information such as duty assignment, related military occupations, advancement requirements, specializations, training provided, and a typical career path. Also included in the career path description is a "career profile" summarizing the career progression of an actual service member. Refer to page 313 for more information on Examining Enlisted Career Path Descriptions. The enlisted career path descriptions are located on pages 315 to 361.

Officers are the professional leaders of the military and usually are college graduates. Officers perform duties similar to those of a corporate manager or executive. They develop plans, set objectives, and direct the efforts of other military personnel in meeting the established objectives. Young men and women hoping to become officers must meet the minimum entrance requirements set by the services. The qualifications required for being commissioned as an officer are described in the General Information on Officer Occupations section of *Military Careers* (p. 177).

The officer part of Military Career Paths provides descriptions of 13 of the officer occupations found in the Military Occupations section. Each career path description contains information similar to that provided for enlisted careers. Refer to page 363 for information on Examining Officer Career Path Descriptions. The officer career path descriptions are located on pages 365 to 391.

Also included in Military Career Paths are two exercises to help you use this section more effectively and plan for a career. To use Military Career Paths, begin by reading pages 308 and 309 where you will learn how to read both the enlisted and officer career path descriptions. In addition, you will find suggestions for Developing Your Own Career Plan on page 311.

# How to Read the Career Path Descriptions

The purpose of the Military Career Paths section is to explain military career opportunities to students, counselors, and parents. It can be used to explore enlisted and officer careers in the Army, Navy, Air Force, Marine Corps, and Coast Guard. Military Career Paths describes the typical duties and assignments for a person advancing along the path of a military career. In total, 23 enlisted and 13 officer occupations are illustrated in the Military Career Paths section. Each career path description has standard sections as shown in the example below.

When reading any one of the 36 career path descriptions, remember that it is a summary of career paths in similar job specialties across two or more military services. Individual career paths may differ somewhat from the general descriptions in this book. If you are interested in learning more about a particular service or occupation you should contact a recruiter for details.

### ❶ Career Title
The career title names the military occupation.

### ❷ Military Service Representation
The military services, listed next to the title, offer employment and training opportunities in the occupation.

### ❸ Profile
The "Profile" describes the actual duties and assignments of a military enlisted member or officer during his or her career. Because each individual career path is unique and spans many years, some assignments will not be typical or representative of current policy. However, the flavor and activities of a full career are accurately illustrated in the "Profile." The names in the profiles have been changed for privacy purposes.

### ❹ Introduction
This section summarizes the job duties and the career path for the military occupation.

### ❺ Duty Assignment
Throughout their careers, military personnel are assigned to new duties and locations. This section describes the type of military organizations and installations where people in this career may be assigned. It also discusses the opportunities for overseas assignments. Any major exceptions to the typical career path are noted at the end of this section.

---

❶

## AIR TRAFFIC CONTROLLERS

ARMY
NAVY
AIR FORCE
MARINE CORPS
❷

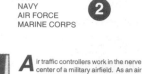

**A**ir traffic controllers work in the nerve center of a military airfield. As an air traffic controller, you direct aircraft into, out of, and around airfields or aircraft carriers. You begin your career under close supervision learning to direct takeoffs, landings, and runway traffic from a control tower or radar center. As you gain experience and skill, you work more independently and take on more difficult tasks. There are opportunities for advancement to supervisor of a control tower or radar center and perhaps to facility supervisor in charge of air traffic control for an entire airfield. ❹

**DUTY ASSIGNMENT** ❺

Air traffic controllers usually work in the control tower or radar center of a military airfield. Some controllers work aboard aircraft carriers or at temporary landing strips near combat zones. The services have airfields all over the United States. There is also good opportunity for assignment at one of the many overseas United States service airfields or at an airfield run by allied forces, where English-speaking controllers are sometimes needed.

**SPECIALIZATION** ❻

Air traffic controllers may specialize in tower or radar operations—although they usually become qualified in both. Tower controllers direct ground and air traffic by sight; radar controllers track aircraft with radar, often at a center away from the control tower. Air traffic controllers may also specialize in combat or aircraft carrier operations. Carrier controllers direct takeoffs and landings on aircraft carriers. Combat controllers set up and run air traffic control centers in combat areas and at temporary landing strips.

❸
**Profile: David Martínez**

David Martínez was concerned about his future career at the hometown paper mill in Maine. "I was married and had children. I needed some education and a job," he explains. So David enlisted in the Marine Corps with a guarantee to work in aviation. He was selected for air traffic control. After basic training, David went to school in Glencoe, GA, to learn tower and radar air traffic control. Since federal licenses are needed for this type of work, he also earned his Federal Aviation Administration (FAA) operator's certificate. Obtaining his FAA operator's license started David on the road toward becoming FAA qualified to work in air traffic control.

At his first assignment in New River, NC, David was a tower air traffic controller trainee. He started in ground control, but soon his duties expanded to include local control (control in the air within a 5-mile radius of the airfield). He also passed his test to become FAA qualified in tower control and for the New River tower. He then became watch supervisor at the facility. In his 2 years at New River, he advanced from private first class through sergeant.

David continued to expand his qualifications at his next duty station in Okinawa.

He became qualified in radar control and facility rated, which meant that he could work any air traffic control position in the facility. He also spent a short time in Yuma, AZ, as a controller and was promoted to staff sergeant.

The next 8 years went fast. David's assignments were split between Japan and New River. Sometimes he only spent a year in one place, and he had to requalify to work at each new facility, but his career was taking off. He was promoted to gunnery sergeant and moved into positions of greater responsibility: from radar controller and assistant approach controller, to facility watch supervisor, to senior enlisted person at his facility. When he was finally assigned to a 3-year tour in Kaneohe, HI, it was as crew chief and radar approach controller.

Now Gunnery Sergeant Martínez is crew chief at Cherry Point, NC. He qualified in the radar air traffic control facility and is working to qualify as a radar approach controller as well. David will be retiring soon, but he believes he has done well in his sometimes hectic career. "I had no prior civilian job experience, but I worked hard and persevered," he says.

320

*Military Careers*

---

## 6 Specialization

This section describes the types of job specialties available in this career and summarizes the career possibilities across the services. The career path and job duties for individual job specialties may differ somewhat from the "Typical Career Path" described in this book.

## 7 Advancement

Military personnel in career paths typically advance through three to five career levels. Promotion to each level requires improving job skills and accepting more responsibility. This section describes the skills, qualities, and abilities needed to advance through the career levels.

## 8 Training

This section summarizes the military training provided to personnel at all career levels. It describes initial job training, advanced skill training, training for job specialties, and leadership training.

## 9 Related Military Occupations

This section identifies other occupations in the military services with similar work and career paths. Descriptions of the related occupations can be found in the Military Occupations section of this book.

## 10 Typical Career Path

This section describes the typical levels of advancement from entry level to supervisor within the occupation. A description of the typical job duties is provided for each level. Because job specialties may differ among the services, some of the job titles and duties listed may not apply to all services. Each title shown in the "Typical Career Path" is descriptive of the duties for that level and is not a specific military job title.

## 11 Timeline

The "Timeline" illustrates the average time it takes to move through career levels. The time for each individual career will differ according to an individual's performance and the needs of the specific military service. It is important to remember that only qualified individuals are promoted to each level.

---

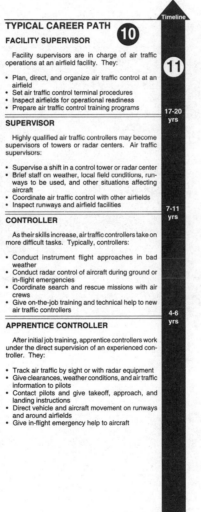

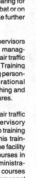

### 7 ADVANCEMENT

The safety of an airfield depends on the ability of the controller to make quick, decisive, and correct judgments under stress. Air traffic controllers must know the many air traffic rules and procedures required to direct the pilots who fly military aircraft. They must also be able to monitor and direct the movement of several aircraft at the same time. At each airfield they are assigned to, controllers must learn the local terrain (mountains, towers, and other obstacles) and prevailing weather conditions to safely direct pilots. Controllers who learn both tower and radar operations increase their chances for advancement.

Air traffic controllers must be certified by the Federal Aviation Administration (FAA) and must maintain this certification throughout their careers. Preliminary certification is awarded at the completion of initial job training; final certification is earned through on-the-job training by an experienced controller. At all levels of this career, air traffic controllers must maintain excellent physical condition to pass stringent physical exams. After mastering the basic skills, the willingness to assume leadership roles helps air traffic controllers advance through the supervisory levels of this career.

### 8 TRAINING

The services provide apprentice controllers with 9 to 15 months of basic and initial job training. It combines classroom instruction and practice using computers that simulate real air traffic control operations. Instruction stresses navigation, air traffic rules, and communication. In addition, trainees receive instruction in radar operations and ground-controlled approach procedures. Air traffic controllers may take advanced training in specialized air traffic and radar operations. Those preparing for specialized work in combat or on aircraft carriers must take further training.

Air traffic control supervisors may receive training in managing the operations of an air traffic control center or tower. Training topics include managing personnel, maintaining operational readiness, and establishing and reviewing work procedures.

During their careers, air traffic controllers learn supervisory skills through leadership training and job experience. This training continues through the facility supervisor level with courses in management and administration. Typically, these courses address budgeting, personnel management, and training program development.

### 9 RELATED MILITARY OCCUPATIONS

If you are interested in air traffic control, you may also want to consider a career as a space operations specialist, flight operations specialist, radar and sonar operator, or aircraft launch and recovery specialist. See the Military Enlisted Occupations section of this book for descriptions of these occupations.

### TYPICAL CAREER PATH 10

Timeline

#### FACILITY SUPERVISOR

11

Facility supervisors are in charge of air traffic operations at an airfield facility. They:

- Plan, direct, and organize air traffic control at an airfield
- Set air traffic control terminal procedures
- Inspect airfields for operational readiness
- Prepare air traffic control training programs

17-20 yrs

#### SUPERVISOR

Highly qualified air traffic controllers may become supervisors of towers or radar centers. Air traffic supervisors:

- Supervise a shift in a control tower or radar center
- Brief staff on weather, local field conditions, runways to be used, and other situations affecting aircraft
- Coordinate air traffic control with other airfields
- Inspect runways and airfield facilities

7-11 yrs

#### CONTROLLER

As their skills increase, air traffic controllers take on more difficult tasks. Typically, controllers:

- Conduct instrument flight approaches in bad weather
- Conduct radar control of aircraft during ground or in-flight emergencies
- Coordinate search and rescue missions with air crews
- Give on-the-job training and technical help to new air traffic controllers

4-6 yrs

#### APPRENTICE CONTROLLER

After initial job training, apprentice controllers work under the direct supervision of an experienced controller. They:

- Track air traffic by sight or with radar equipment
- Give clearances, weather conditions, and air traffic information to pilots
- Contact pilots and give takeoff, approach, and landing instructions
- Direct vehicle and aircraft movement on runways and around airfields
- Give in-flight emergency help to aircraft

---

# Developing Your Own Career Plan

As you read the career profiles that are included in *Military Careers*, remember that each person's career is unique because no one has exactly the same set of experiences—personal, educational, or job-related—as anyone else. Individuals grow, and their interests often change as they gain more knowledge and skills. The work environment also changes, and that has never been more true than in today's world.

Career planning involves exploring careers or work situations that interest you and developing a plan to reach your desired career or work situation. Following the steps listed below, you can begin developing your own plan. Completing these activities will require time and energy on your part. Once you have finished all the steps, you will have developed an initial career plan.

## Step 1: Imagine your ideal career or work situation

- Think of the ideal career or work situation you would like to have five years from now. Describe this as your career goal.

  - You may want to use reference books available from your school counselor such as the *Occupational Outlook Handbook* for information on various occupations, or, if available, you may wish to use your school's computerized career information system or the ASVAB Career Exploration System.

- Outline a plan for obtaining the education/training or skills for reaching your desired career or work situation. Organize the information into the following format:

  *Ideal Work Situation/Career Plan*

  - Career title or work situation

  - Career description

  - Education/training/skills required

  - Plan for reaching my goal.

## Step 2: Share your goals and plan with others for their reactions

- Ask two or three friends for their views about your plan

- Ask your counselor and/or teachers if they think your plan is realistic

- Discuss your career goal and plan with your parents and ask their advice

- Interview one or two people whose work is similar to your career goal to learn the experiences they have had over the years.

Asking for feedback from others tests your ideas and helps you determine how realistic your plans are. Ask specific questions (e.g., Does my plan seem to build on my past experiences? Will this career result in a lifestyle I want? Will I be able to complete the education and training requirements?), and be sure that you understand the reasoning of those advising you.

## Step 3: Revise your goal and plan

- Evaluate the feedback you receive from others and make changes in your plan, if necessary

  - Perhaps you will need to seek more career information before doing so.

## Step 4: Take action

- Begin actions to implement your plan

- Develop a timetable to monitor and evaluate your progress

- Share your timetable and progress with others such as your parents or career guidance counselor

- Continue to review your goal and plan as you learn more.

Developing a career plan is not a one-time experience. It is a process that you will repeat many times in your life as you acquire more information about yourself and careers, and as you experience new problems and opportunities. Your school counselor has additional information available to help you learn more about exploring the world of work and planning for your future.

# Examining Enlisted Career Path Descriptions

Deciding to join the military is typically an initial career decision. However, the career path of each enlisted person is different because it reflects the interests, skills, and abilities of that individual and availability of different military occupations. As you read the specific career descriptions that follow, keep in mind that individuals who choose the military as their work place have many opportunities for change and advancement.

Read the profile for Jeff Picard under "Computer Programmers" on page 330. Several examples mentioned show the uniqueness of Jeff's experiences in the military. For example:

- Jeff did not join the military right after graduating from high school. He tried many things, including college and the National Guard, before deciding to enlist.

- Upon enlistment, Jeff did not start in computer programming. He spent his first four years in the infantry, moving to computer programming after reenlisting.

- After computer school, Jeff started as a programmer/analyst. While working in that position, he learned technical writing—in other words, Jeff was preparing himself for advancement while carrying out his job responsibilities.

- Jeff notes that he likes "interacting with other programmers/analysts." Jeff's ability to work with people as well as computers should help him if he decides to seek advancement into supervisory positions.

- Jeff Picard's first assignment was overseas even though most military computer programmers work in the United States.

## Questions to Consider

Ask yourself questions similar to the following as you read each enlisted career description:

### a) Would I like to have a career in this occupation?

If what you read in the description and typical career path interests you, learn more about it and related enlisted occupations by reading the Computer Programmer description in the Military Occupations section.

### b) How much training and retraining is necessary to succeed in this career?

Computer programmers receive training and retraining throughout their careers because of changing technology. The military is also supportive of those who take the initiative to obtain training on their own.

### c) How can I advance in rank and responsibility?

In computer programming, as in most careers, advancement usually includes taking on supervisory responsibilities. Look at the average timelines for advancement. Remember that not all people advance at this rate—advancement is dependent upon succeeding in training and job performance and receiving the recommendation of one's commanding officer.

# Sample of Military Enlisted Career Path Descriptions

# ADMINISTRATIVE SUPPORT SPECIALISTS

ARMY
NAVY
MARINE CORPS
COAST GUARD

*T*he services need accurate and up-to-date information to make sound planning and management decisions. Written and automated records are kept on almost all aspects of the military, including funds, supplies, personnel, and equipment. As an administrative support specialist, you maintain files, record information, and type reports and correspondence. You begin your career performing typing and clerical duties. As you gain experience, you may help manage office operations. There are opportunities to advance to clerical supervisor and perhaps to office manager positions.

## DUTY ASSIGNMENT

Administrative support specialists usually work in office settings on land and aboard ship. Many work in small groups, giving clerical help to small- or medium-sized military units. Others are assigned to large administrative offices that provide a broad range of clerical services. Those who work in these consolidated offices are likely to work with civilian employees. Many specialists are also assigned to assist in the administration of personnel, finance, or supply units. Most administrative specialists work at military bases in the United States, but opportunities are available for overseas duty.

## ADVANCEMENT

Because administrative support specialists work closely with other people, they must have good communication skills and be able to work easily with others. The ability to do neat and accurate work is essential. Since administrative support specialists must work with many different military forms and regulations, they must be logical, well-organized, and have a good memory for detail. They must also have excellent typing skills and a superior knowledge of spelling, grammar, and punctuation. After mastering the basic skills, the willingness to assume leadership roles and additional responsibilities helps administrative support specialists advance through the supervisory levels of this career.

### Profile: Ray Kanakis

Ray Kanakis joined the Coast Guard on the recommendation of an older brother who had already joined. After boot camp, he was sent for his general duty assignment to the United States Coast Guard (USCG) Yard, Baltimore, MD. As a seaman apprentice, he worked on vessels at the yard and learned basic seamanship. He was also selected to be in the color guard representing the Coast Guard in parades and other ceremonies.

While in Baltimore, Ray took a Coast Guard correspondence course in administrative support and became a trainee in this field. This is when his career really began. He started out in a personnel office, typing correspondence, maintaining service records, preparing forms, and operating computers and word processors. He liked his new career. "I enjoy working with people and I like a desk job," he explains.

After 2 years at the Yard, Ray was assigned to USCG Headquarters, Washington, DC, in the legal administration division, where he worked processing and preparing legal documents. He was selected for a 16-week course at the Defense Race Relations Institute, Patrick Air Force Base, FL, where he trained to be an equal opportunity specialist and military civil rights counselor/facilitator. Ray says, "I enjoy providing a service to people when I help someone or solve a problem." After 5 1/2 years at Headquarters, Ray was assigned to shipboard duty.

To prepare for his new assignment, Ray was given advanced training in the computerized systems used on board Coast Guard ships. He was then assigned to the USCG cutter *Hamilton*. As the cutter's yeoman, he handled 180 service records and maintained and updated all publications for the cutter. Ray was on board when the cutter went on search and rescue, pollution cleanup, and law enforcement missions.

After 2 years on the cutter, Ray was again assigned to USCG Headquarters, this time in the command post exercise division. Working with classified information, he helped coordinate and plan wargames for 2 years. He was then personally selected by the Master Chief Petty Officer of the Coast Guard to be his aide. Since he works for the top enlisted person of the Coast Guard, he feels he must know everything. "I have to be ready to carry on when he's not there," says Ray.

## TRAINING

The services provide administrative support specialists with 10 to 14 months of basic and initial job training. It combines classroom instruction and on-the-job training. Classroom training emphasizes typing and updating manuals and regulations. On-the-job training includes such topics as filing systems, office practices, and special requirements for routing administrative materials. Depending on their assignment, administrative support specialists may be trained to operate computer terminals, teletype machines, or word processing equipment.

During their career, administrative support specialists learn supervisory skills through leadership training and job experience. This training continues through the level of office manager with courses in management and administration. Typically, these courses address budgeting, personnel management, and training program development.

## RELATED MILITARY OCCUPATIONS

If you are interested in administrative support work, you may want to consider a career as a finance and accounting specialist, legal specialist or court reporter, transportation specialist, or personnel specialist. See the Administrative Occupations cluster in the Military Enlisted Occupations section of this book.

## TYPICAL CAREER PATH

### OFFICE MANAGER

Office managers supervise consolidated office facilities or serve as senior supervisors at command or staff headquarters. They:

- Plan and control administrative support
- Implement or recommend new office procedures
- Obtain office furniture, equipment, and supplies
- Develop operating budgets and track expenses

### CLERICAL SUPERVISOR

Administrative technicians may advance to become clerical supervisors responsible for supervising one or more administrative support sections. They:

- Train new personnel
- Prepare directives, job descriptions, and standard operating procedures
- Review and edit correspondence before routing for signature
- Divide the work load among personnel
- Sign for, log, inventory, file, and safeguard classified documents

### ADMINISTRATIVE TECHNICIAN

Administrative technicians perform responsible clerical duties and give technical assistance to administrative clerks. They may:

- Proofread typed material for errors in spelling, punctuation, sentence structure, and missing or unnecessary information
- Route copies of letters, memos, and forms for rework or signature
- Maintain logs, duty rosters, and leave records
- Compose and type routine correspondence
- Take and transcribe dictation

### ADMINISTRATIVE CLERK

After initial job training, administrative clerks perform clerical duties. They:

- Use a word processor to type regulations, directives, requisitions, correspondence, and similar materials from notes, drafts, and instructions
- Check draft and final copies for spelling, grammar, typing errors, proper format, and use of authorized abbreviations
- Greet and direct visitors to the proper office
- Answer telephones and take messages
- Open, sort, route, and deliver mail and messages

**Timeline**

17-19 yrs

9-12 yrs

4-6 yrs

# AIR CREW MEMBERS

**P**ersonnel in each service can "earn their wings" and qualify as a member of a flight crew. Air crew members perform specialized duties for many different military missions. As an air crew member, you may operate in-flight refueling systems, defensive guns on bombers, or submarine detection systems. You may also perform rescue and recovery missions or direct cargo and passenger loading, unloading, and airdrops. You begin your career performing the tasks of your specialty that you will continue to perform throughout your career. As you develop leadership skills, there are opportunities to advance to air crew leader and perhaps to air crew operations supervisor.

## DUTY ASSIGNMENT

Air crew members work in all types of aircraft, from cargo planes and bombers to helicopters. Air crews operate from airfields or ships anywhere in the world, but the specialty an air crew member selects affects the assignments available. For example, loadmasters are assigned to airlift squadrons whose missions of moving cargo and passengers take them on flights all over the world. Gunners, on the other hand, are assigned only to squadrons flying large bombers and usually return to their home base at the end of each mission. Overseas assignment opportunities may be limited for some specialties, but most air crew members travel as part of their job.

---

### Profile: Dennis Nguyen

At 22, Dennis Nguyen had finished high school and had been working for 4 years when he decided to join the Air Force. At first he thought he wanted to be an aircraft mechanic, but during basic training, he volunteered to go to loadmaster school. He says, "That way I could be a mechanic *and* I could fly." He completed 3 months of training in Savannah, GA, and then spent 3 more years maintaining air cargo and airdrop equipment. He also flew missions to drop supplies for use in field exercises.

After 4 1/2 years, Dennis decided he wanted an Air Force career. He liked his job, the security it provided, and the opportunity it gave him to get ahead. By re-enlisting, Dennis also knew he would go overseas on his next assignment. For nearly 2 years, he was on crews that flew out of Okinawa, delivering food, supplies, and troops—sometimes dropping supplies to troops in the field.

For the past 10 years, Dennis has been assigned first to Travis Air Force Base (AFB), CA, then to McGuire AFB, NJ. During both of these assignments, he has held many different jobs and has traveled worldwide. He has also completed an associate's degree through courses offered on base and a bachelor's degree through a special on-base program run by a private college.

Dennis has advanced during his career as a loadmaster. Shortly after arriving at Travis AFB, he became crew leader. He then worked his way up the ladder in his squadron, taking on more responsibility. As a trainer at McGuire AFB, he prepared new loadmasters for work on C-141 aircraft. He advanced to flight examiner and then to assistant chief of loadmasters. After 2 years, Dennis became an air crew operations manager. This position brought him his most challenging assignment—managing all Air Force cargo and passenger equipment from the Mississippi River to Egypt. Dennis made sure that the right type of equipment, from cargo containers to passenger seats, was available at the right airfield when it was needed. For the past several years, Dennis has been the chief of loadmasters for several different squadrons, managing loadmasters carrying supplies throughout the world.

---

## ADVANCEMENT

Air crew members must have a genuine interest in flying and be in excellent physical condition. They must pass periodic flight physical examinations to keep their qualifications to be on a flight crew. Air crew members must master the duties of their specialty to gain the confidence of the aircraft commander and other crew members. They must also be able to work efficiently as a member of a team, sometimes during hazardous and stressful situations. Because there is little room for error in aircraft flight crew operations, they must be able to perform their duties in a calm and deliberate manner. After mastering the basic skills, the willingness to assume leadership roles and to accept additional responsibilities helps air crew members advance through supervisory levels of this career.

## SPECIALIZATION

Air crew members specialize in such areas as:

- In-flight refueling — extending fuel hoses from the tail section of a tanker aircraft to the receiving port of the aircraft to be fueled and operating controls to pump fuel loads
- Defensive gunnery — operating aircraft gun systems to repel and destroy enemy attack aircraft
- Antisubmarine warfare — operating acoustic sensors (machines that detect sounds), airborne radar or sonar, or infrared equipment (machines that detect heat) on jets or helicopters to find and identify submarines
- Rescue and recovery — operating helicopter hoists to lift equipment and personnel from land or sea
- Air transport — planning and directing the loading, unloading, and weight distribution of cargo or personnel, including directing cargo or troop airdrops

## TRAINING

The services provide aircrew members with 8 to 13 months of basic and initial job training. It combines classroom instruction, practical exercises, and on-the-job training. Depending on the air crew specialty, classroom training covers operation and maintenance of equipment as well as flying duties. Specialties may also require courses in air crew survival, scuba diving, combat crew training, or aircraft emergency procedures.

On-the-job training is conducted by air crew leaders. This training continues throughout the career through special mission flight operations and debriefing sessions conducted by the aircraft commander and the air crew operations supervisor. Over the course of their careers, air crew members may return to school for training in new aircraft or airborne equipment used in their specialties.

During their careers, air crew members learn supervisory skills through leadership training and job experience. This training continues through the air crew operations supervisor level with courses in management and administration. Typically, these courses address budgeting, personnel management, and training program development.

## RELATED MILITARY OCCUPATIONS

If you are interested in becoming an air crew member, you might also want to consider a career as a flight engineer or an aircraft launch and recovery specialist. See the Transportation and Material Handling Occupations cluster in the Military Enlisted Occupations section of this book.

## TYPICAL CAREER PATH

### AIR CREW OPERATIONS SUPERVISOR

Highly skilled air crew leaders may become supervisors of air crew operations. They:

- Plan and organize air crew activities
- Assist in planning in-flight operations and training missions
- Conduct mission briefings and prepare operations orders
- Inspect and evaluate unit activities and facilities
- Review air crew records and reports for accuracy and completeness

### AIR CREW LEADER

Skilled air crew members may become crew leaders. At this level, they:

- Plan, schedule, and assign work duties
- Instruct air crew members about equipment changes
- Conduct in-flight and ground air crew training programs
- Conduct inspection of aircraft systems and equipment
- Prepare in-flight mission reports and logs

### AIR CREW MEMBER

Depending on their specialty after initial job training, air crew members may:

- Conduct the preflight check or verify the airworthiness of equipment
- Operate and control tanker aircraft in-flight refueling systems
- Operate aircraft missile or gun systems on strategic bombers
- Operate airborne antisubmarine detection and tracking equipment
- Perform helicopter-assisted rescue and equipment recovery operations
- Prepare plans for loading aircraft fuel, cargo, and passengers
- Perform operational maintenance on specialized aircraft equipment

Timeline

18-21 yrs

6-11 yrs

# AIR TRAFFIC CONTROLLERS

ARMY
NAVY
AIR FORCE
MARINE CORPS

**A**ir traffic controllers work in the nerve center of a military airfield. As an air traffic controller, you direct aircraft into, out of, and around airfields or aircraft carriers. You begin your career under close supervision learning to direct takeoffs, landings, and runway traffic from a control tower or radar center. As you gain experience and skill, you work more independently and take on more difficult tasks. There are opportunities for advancement to supervisor of a control tower or radar center and perhaps to facility supervisor in charge of air traffic control for an entire airfield.

## DUTY ASSIGNMENT

Air traffic controllers usually work in the control tower or radar center of a military airfield. Some controllers work aboard aircraft carriers or at temporary landing strips near combat zones. The services have airfields all over the United States. There is also good opportunity for assignment at one of the many overseas United States service airfields or at an airfield run by allied forces, where English-speaking controllers are sometimes needed.

## SPECIALIZATION

Air traffic controllers may specialize in tower or radar operations—although they usually become qualified in both. Tower controllers direct ground and air traffic by sight; radar controllers track aircraft with radar, often at a center away from the control tower. Air traffic controllers may also specialize in combat or aircraft carrier operations. Carrier controllers direct takeoffs and landings on aircraft carriers. Combat controllers set up and run air traffic control centers in combat areas and at temporary landing strips.

### Profile: David Martínez

David Martínez was concerned about his future career at the hometown paper mill in Maine. "I was married and had children. I needed some education and a job," he explains. So David enlisted in the Marine Corps with a guarantee to work in aviation. He was selected for air traffic control. After basic training, David went to school in Glencoe, GA, to learn tower and radar air traffic control. Since federal licenses are needed for this type of work, he also earned his Federal Aviation Administration (FAA) operator's certificate. Obtaining his FAA operator's license started David on the road toward becoming FAA qualified to work in air traffic control.

At his first assignment in New River, NC, David was a tower air traffic controller trainee. He started in ground control, but soon his duties expanded to include local control (control in the air within a 5-mile radius of the airfield). He also passed his test to become FAA qualified in tower control and for the New River tower. He then became watch supervisor at the facility. In his 2 years at New River, he advanced from private first class through sergeant.

David continued to expand his qualifications at his next duty station in Okinawa.

He became qualified in radar control and facility rated, which meant that he could work any air traffic control position in the facility. He also spent a short time in Yuma, AZ, as a controller and was promoted to staff sergeant.

The next 8 years went fast. David's assignments were split between Japan and New River. Sometimes he only spent a year in one place, and he had to requalify to work at each new facility, but his career was taking off. He was promoted to gunnery sergeant and moved into positions of greater responsibility: from radar controller and assistant approach controller, to facility watch supervisor, to senior enlisted person at his facility. When he was finally assigned to a 3-year tour in Kaneohe, HI, it was as crew chief and radar approach controller.

Now Gunnery Sergeant Martínez is crew chief at Cherry Point, NC. He qualified in the radar air traffic control facility and is working to qualify as a radar approach controller as well. David will be retiring soon, but he believes he has done well in his sometimes hectic career. "I had no prior civilian job experience, but I worked hard and persevered," he says.

## ADVANCEMENT

The safety of an airfield depends on the ability of the controller to make quick, decisive, and correct judgments under stress. Air traffic controllers must know the many air traffic rules and procedures required to direct the pilots who fly military aircraft. They must also be able to monitor and direct the movement of several aircraft at the same time. At each airfield they are assigned to, controllers must learn the local terrain (mountains, towers, and other obstacles) and prevailing weather conditions to safely direct pilots. Controllers who learn both tower and radar operations increase their chances for advancement.

Air traffic controllers must be certified by the Federal Aviation Administration (FAA) and must maintain this certification throughout their careers. Preliminary certification is awarded at the completion of initial job training; final certification is earned through on-the-job training by an experienced controller. At all levels of this career, air traffic controllers must maintain excellent physical condition to pass stringent physical exams. After mastering the basic skills, the willingness to assume leadership roles helps air traffic controllers advance through the supervisory levels of this career.

## TRAINING

The services provide apprentice controllers with 9 to 15 months of basic and initial job training. It combines classroom instruction and practice using computers that simulate real air traffic control operations. Instruction stresses navigation, air traffic rules, and communication. In addition, trainees receive instruction in radar operations and ground-controlled approach procedures. Air traffic controllers may take advanced training in specialized air traffic and radar operations. Those preparing for specialized work in combat or on aircraft carriers must take further training.

Air traffic control supervisors may receive training in managing the operations of an air traffic control center or tower. Training topics include managing personnel, maintaining operational readiness, and establishing and reviewing work procedures.

During their careers, air traffic controllers learn supervisory skills through leadership training and job experience. This training continues through the facility supervisor level with courses in management and administration. Typically, these courses address budgeting, personnel management, and training program development.

## RELATED MILITARY OCCUPATIONS

If you are interested in air traffic control, you may also want to consider a career as a space operations specialist, flight operations specialist, radar and sonar operator, or aircraft launch and recovery specialist. See the Military Enlisted Occupations section of this book for descriptions of these occupations.

## TYPICAL CAREER PATH

### FACILITY SUPERVISOR

Facility supervisors are in charge of air traffic operations at an airfield facility. They:

- Plan, direct, and organize air traffic control at an airfield
- Set air traffic control terminal procedures
- Inspect airfields for operational readiness
- Prepare air traffic control training programs

### SUPERVISOR

Highly qualified air traffic controllers may become supervisors of towers or radar centers. Air traffic supervisors:

- Supervise a shift in a control tower or radar center
- Brief staff on weather, local field conditions, runways to be used, and other situations affecting aircraft
- Coordinate air traffic control with other airfields
- Inspect runways and airfield facilities

### CONTROLLER

As their skills increase, air traffic controllers take on more difficult tasks. Typically, controllers:

- Conduct instrument flight approaches in bad weather
- Conduct radar control of aircraft during ground or in-flight emergencies
- Coordinate search and rescue missions with air crews
- Give on-the-job training and technical help to new air traffic controllers

### APPRENTICE CONTROLLER

After initial job training, apprentice controllers work under the direct supervision of an experienced controller. They:

- Track air traffic by sight or with radar equipment
- Give clearances, weather conditions, and air traffic information to pilots
- Contact pilots and give takeoff, approach, and landing instructions
- Direct vehicle and aircraft movement on runways and around airfields
- Give in-flight emergency help to aircraft

**Timeline**

17-20 yrs

7-11 yrs

4-6 yrs

# AIRCRAFT LAUNCH AND RECOVERY SPECIALISTS

NAVY
MARINE CORPS
COAST GUARD

*T*akeoffs and landings on an aircraft carrier are far from routine, even in the best weather. As an aircraft launch and recovery specialist, you work on the flight deck operating and maintaining catapults (plane launching devices), arresting gear (devices that slow down landing planes), barricades, and other equipment to launch and land aircraft safely. You begin your career working as an apprentice team member performing duties at designated launch or recovery stations. As your skills increase, you take greater responsibility and repair and overhaul equipment. There are opportunities to advance to crew supervisor and perhaps to flight deck supervisor.

## DUTY ASSIGNMENT

Aircraft launch and recovery specialists work on aircraft carriers at sea and at ports of call all over the world. Some launch and recovery specialists also work at advanced-based landing fields set up near infantry training sites or combat zones to provide air support to combat troops. When assigned to airfields on land, launch and recovery workers install land-based crash barriers and barricades and maintain runway lighting systems. They also operate equipment that helps pilots take off or land on short runways.

## RELATED MILITARY OCCUPATIONS

If you are interested in a career as an aircraft launch and recovery specialist, you may also want to consider a career as a flight operations specialist, air traffic controller, or radar and sonar operator. See the Military Enlisted Occupations section of this book for descriptions of these occupations.

### Profile: James DiMarco

James DiMarco's decision to follow his brothers into the service seemed the best answer to limited job opportunities. He joined the Navy with the idea of becoming an electrician, but his first assignment changed his mind. After basic training, he was assigned to the aircraft carrier USS Coral Sea, where he worked on the flight deck with a catapult crew. He enjoyed his work repairing and maintaining the mechanical equipment so much that he asked for formal training in this field. His request was granted, and he went to Philadelphia for classes in becoming a catapult operator.

James liked his new job; still, he left the Navy after his 4-year enlistment to go home and get married. Within 3 months, he had reenlisted because, as he puts it, "There were few jobs that offered me a chance to make something of myself." Following reenlistment, James spent nearly 2 years as catapult crew leader on the USS *Wasp*, where one of his older brothers was also assigned. He then spent a year in Lakehurst, NJ, as a crew leader testing new parts and newly designed catapult systems.

James's next assignment took him to the West Coast and the USS *Bennington*.

He was responsible for a crew of 40 men who maintained and operated two catapults. One big job involved supervising work on the catapult system for a major ship overhaul. He also served aboard the USS Ranger on several cruises to Vietnam as supervisor of a catapult operation.

James was then selected to become an instructor at the Navy's school at Lakehurst. For 4 years, he taught the basics of operating and maintaining catapult systems to 250 students a year. He was also promoted to chief petty officer—the goal he had set for himself when he joined the Navy. Following an assignment on the USS Roosevelt, James was promoted to flight deck supervisor and served on the USS Independence and then the USS Forrestal, where he managed a flight deck crew of up to 550 sailors.

For the past several years, James has been back at Lakehurst managing the launch and recovery school. James enjoys teaching and working with younger people to help them establish themselves in their careers. He believes he has made a significant contribution to the Navy. "But then," he says, "the Navy has rewarded me in turn."

## ADVANCEMENT

Launch and recovery specialists must be accurate and safety-minded because the lives of aviators and flight deck workers depend on their work. They must have the technical skills to maintain and repair one type of flight deck equipment. To advance, specialists need to develop the ability to diagnose problems and repair different types of flight deck equipment. They must also be able to operate this equipment and be prepared to act quickly in case of equipment malfunctions or emergencies.

After mastering the basic skills, the willingness to assume leadership roles helps launch and recovery specialists advance through the supervisory levels of this career. Launch and recovery crew supervisors who apply to become flight deck supervisors must compete with aircraft handling and fueling supervisors for promotion. Hence, a familiarity with and understanding of these other occupations is important; however, the chief consideration for advancement is the individual's ability to give overall direction to carrier flight deck operations.

## TRAINING

The services provide apprentice launch and recovery specialists with 6 to 18 months of basic and initial job training. It starts with a short course covering the basic elements of aviation, including how planes take off and land. Carrier-based personnel take additional courses in operating and maintaining specific types of arresting gear or catapults. These courses also cover hydraulics and the flight deck duties of the launch and recovery specialist. Later in their careers, specialists may take additional training to become familiar with a system used in a new assignment. Advanced training is available covering the operation, inspection, and maintenance of different types of catapults, barricades, and arresting gear.

Individuals who work at expeditionary airfields take the same aviation basics course as those working on aircraft carriers. These individuals then receive specialized instruction in installing, inspecting, and operating land-based arresting gear and barricades.

During their careers, aircraft launch and recovery specialists learn supervisory skills through leadership training and job experience. This training continues through the position of flight deck supervisor with courses in management and administration. Typically, these courses address budgeting, personnel management, and training program development.

## TYPICAL CAREER PATH

### FLIGHT DECK SUPERVISOR

Flight deck supervisors plan and direct operation, maintenance, and safety programs for all aspects of carrier launch and recovery work, including crash rescue, damage control, aircraft handling, and aviation fueling. Flight deck supervisors:

- Organize, schedule, and evaluate training programs
- Administer long-range maintenance programs and monitor maintenance schedules
- Conduct inspections to ensure that scheduled maintenance has been performed
- Predict requirements for personnel, equipment, and materials
- Review the performance of aircraft handling, crash rescue, and damage control crews

### CREW SUPERVISOR

Skilled launch and recovery specialists may become crew supervisors. At this level, they:

- Supervise equipment inspections before and after launch and recovery operations
- Give technical advice and help crew members
- Prepare schedules for preventive maintenance
- Examine faulty parts to determine repair or replacement needs
- Help launch and recovery specialists analyze malfunctions and plan corrective action

### LAUNCH AND RECOVERY SPECIALIST

As their skills increase, launch and recovery specialists perform more difficult tasks. They:

- Perform or direct difficult repairs and machinery and equipment overhauls
- Inspect cables, fittings, and wire-rope sockets
- Prepare weekly preventive maintenance schedules
- Inventory supplies, spare parts, and equipment
- Post changes and additions to maintenance and accounting records

### APPRENTICE LAUNCH AND RECOVERY SPECIALIST

After initial job training, apprentices work under close supervision at designated launch and recovery work stations. They:

- Inspect equipment before and after launch and recovery operations
- Operate controls to fire catapults, raise and lower blast deflectors, or operate arresting gear
- Direct personnel in aircraft launch hookups
- Perform preventive maintenance and complete maintenance records

**This career is open only to men.**

Timeline

19-20 yrs

7-8 yrs

3-4 yrs

# AIRCRAFT MECHANICS

*T*he confidence that military flight crews have in their aircraft is a tribute to the mechanics who maintain them. As an aircraft mechanic, you inspect, service, and repair aircraft to keep them airworthy. You begin your career performing routine maintenance and simple repairs under close supervision. As your skills develop, you may be assigned more difficult duties, such as troubleshooting and performing complicated repairs. There are opportunities to advance to shop supervisor and perhaps to supervisor of an entire aircraft maintenance operation.

## DUTY ASSIGNMENT

Aircraft mechanics work in aircraft hangars and repair shops on air bases and landing fields or aboard aircraft carriers. They may sometimes work outside on runway flight lines and carrier flight decks. Most aircraft mechanics are assigned to aircraft maintenance units in the United States. However, since the services have military airfields throughout the world and carriers at sea, there is good opportunity for overseas or sea duty assignment.

## ADVANCEMENT

Wherever aircraft land or are based, aircraft mechanics are there to keep them safe and ready to fly. Because even a small error may cause a crash, aircraft mechanics must be accurate and thorough in their work. They must have the technical skill to diagnose and fix problems that often affect more than one system of the aircraft. The complexity of aircraft systems and the precision needed to make repairs and adjustments means that mechanics must rely heavily on technical manuals and guides. Aircraft mechanics must be able to find information in the manuals, interpret diagrams, and follow the written work procedures precisely. After mastering the basic skills, the willingness to assume leadership roles helps mechanics advance through the supervisory levels of this career.

---

### Profile: Brian Goelf

When he graduated from high school, Brian Goelf got his parents' permission to join the Air Force. "I wanted to see different places," he says. After 23 years and 15 different locations, travel is still one of the aspects he likes most about his military career. Brian has lived in Canada, England, the Netherlands, Vietnam, Hawaii, and all over the United States.

Being mechanically inclined—he had always enjoyed working on cars—Brian asked to be trained in aircraft mechanics. After basic training, he went to aircraft mechanic's school and was assigned to Andrews Air Force Base (AFB) near Washington, DC. There he also completed an additional field training course on the Air Force T-33 trainer jet aircraft. After 2 years of performing unscheduled maintenance (pilot-reported problems), Brian went to Goose Bay, Canada, for another field training course on the F-102 aircraft.

Brian returned to the United States on an assignment to Scott AFB, IL, to work on the T-39 Saberliner, a private passenger jet. He went on flying status as the chief mechanic and flew around the country. He was also responsible for making or supervising repairs. Brian decided at this time to make his career in the military. Having just married, he saw the Air Force as a chance to get ahead. But, as Brian says, "It was having a job I really liked and being able to fly as well that really sold me."

Brian was promoted to staff sergeant and spent a year in Vietnam. In his first supervisory job, he coordinated flight line maintenance for a fighter squadron. Then, 2 years after his return to the States, he was selected as an instructor in aircraft mechanics. During this time, he earned another promotion and volunteered to go to Europe. Although most of his 4 years was spent in England and the Netherlands, he and his family were able to travel all over Europe.

Brian and his family had been home for only a year when he volunteered to go to Hawaii. He was promoted there to senior manager and served as the Pacific Air Force Command manager for several types of aircraft, ensuring that materials and supplies reached Air Force units in the Pacific. Brian recently returned to the mainland as assistant manager of a maintenance unit capable of supporting F-15 fighters anywhere in the world.

## SPECIALIZATION

Typically, mechanics specialize in a single type of aircraft, such as fighter planes, bombers, cargo or passenger planes, or helicopters. Airplane mechanics specializing on planes often further specialize in particular parts or systems, such as aircraft engines (jet or propeller), airframes (aircraft structural parts), pneudraulic systems, which are a combination of pneumatic (air) and hydraulic (fluid) pressure systems, or aircraft landing gear systems. Depending on the service, a helicopter mechanic may specialize in one system or work on the entire aircraft.

## TRAINING

The services provide apprentice aircraft mechanics with 6 to 13 months of basic and initial job training. It includes instruction in general aviation maintenance practices and procedures. This training stresses practical experience as a way of learning to identify aircraft components and systems, what they do, and how they work. It also covers the use of tools, test equipment, and automated performance analyzers. Additional training covers the skills needed for individual specialties. Engine mechanics learn procedures for inspecting, disassembling, and repairing or replacing engines. Airframe mechanics learn to repair aluminum, steel, titanium, plastic, and fiberglass airframes and coverings. Apprentice mechanics also get training on the type of aircraft they will work on during their first assignment. Throughout their careers, aircraft mechanics may receive training on many different aircraft.

Advanced training is available for mechanics in troubleshooting techniques, certification training for inspectors, and technical training on specific aircraft systems. During their careers, aircraft mechanics learn supervisory skills through leadership training and job experience. This training continues through the level of aircraft maintenance supervisor with courses in management and administration. Typically, these courses address budgeting, personnel management, and training program development.

## RELATED MILITARY OCCUPATIONS

If you are interested in mechanics, you may also want to consider a career as an automotive and heavy equipment mechanic, marine engine mechanic, or powerhouse mechanic. See the Vehicle and Machinery Mechanic Occupations cluster in the Military Enlisted Occupations section of this book for descriptions of these and other similar occupations.

## TYPICAL CAREER PATH

### AIRCRAFT MAINTENANCE SUPERVISOR

Aircraft maintenance supervisors are in charge of large aircraft maintenance and repair facilities. They:

- Plan and direct repair, inspection, maintenance, service, and modification of aircraft
- Analyze reports and meet with supervisors to find and resolve bottlenecks
- Develop training and safety programs
- Prepare technical, personnel, and administrative reports

### SHOP SUPERVISOR

Highly skilled mechanics become shop supervisors in charge of maintenance and repair for specific types of aircraft. They:

- Develop standard operating procedures
- Conduct or direct on-the-job training programs
- Assign and reassign personnel to handle increased work loads and changing work schedules
- Collect data and prepare production and status reports

### MECHANIC

Aircraft mechanics perform more complex repairs and assist other mechanics. At this level, they:

- Help apprentice mechanics identify malfunctions and fix problems
- Perform complicated or unusual tests using special test equipment
- Analyze frequently occurring malfunctions and determine changes that should be made to procedures or equipment
- Disassemble aircraft engines and repair or replace valves, cylinders, and turbine blades

### APPRENTICE AIRCRAFT MECHANIC

After initial job training, new aircraft mechanics work under close supervision and perform routine repair and maintenance duties. Typically, apprentice mechanics:

- Repair airframe parts using drills, rivet guns, welding rigs, and sheet metal machines
- Tighten connections on air and fluid lines and hoses using hand tools
- Flush crankcases, clean screens, and grease moving parts to perform routine aircraft servicing
- Record service, maintenance, and repairs in maintenance log records

**Timeline**

19-21 yrs

8-10 yrs

4-5 yrs

# AUTOMOTIVE AND HEAVY EQUIPMENT MECHANICS

ARMY
NAVY
AIR FORCE
MARINE CORPS
COAST GUARD

**A**utomotive and heavy equipment mechanics repair all types of motor vehicles, from basic jeeps to small attack vehicles. As an automotive and heavy equipment mechanic, you service and repair all parts of a vehicle, including engines, transmissions, and fuel and electrical systems. You begin your career doing simple repairs and servicing on one type of vehicle. As your skills develop, you perform more challenging duties, such as overhauling engines and troubleshooting difficult problems. There are opportunities to advance to shop supervisor and perhaps to vehicle repair supervisor in charge of an entire automotive maintenance organization.

## DUTY ASSIGNMENT

Automotive and heavy equipment mechanics usually work in auto repair shops and garages but may do some outdoor work while making repairs in the field. Mechanics also work in small- to medium-sized motor pools or in larger maintenance and repair centers. Automotive repair units are usually part of a mechanical maintenance organization that services all types of vehicles, including fire trucks, construction equipment, and tanks. Work in these organizations is usually organized by vehicle type(s). Most automotive mechanics are assigned to military bases in the United States; however, since the services have automotive vehicles all over the world, there is good opportunity for overseas assignment.

## SPECIALIZATION

Depending on their assignment, automotive and heavy equipment mechanics often develop specialized skills for working on one or more types of vehicles. A mechanic might specialize, for example, in repairing jeeps, autos, and light trucks; wrecker trucks and forklift equipment; or aircraft towing and ground support equipment.

---

### Profile: Ron Horowitz

When Gunnery Sergeant Ron Horowitz was a senior in high school, he knew he didn't want to go to college, but he wasn't sure what he wanted to do. So Ron enlisted in the Marine Corps. Joining the Marines offered him a break from the routine he saw in civilian life.

Ron entered the infantry even though he knew it was not what he wanted as a career. After basic and initial infantry training, he became a rifleman and was sent overseas to Okinawa, Japan. It was then that he found what he really wanted to do. On many marches, Ron saw trucks parked by the side of the road. When he asked why the trucks were not being used, he was told that they were deadlined (not working) and waiting for repair. He was frustrated because he wanted to be able to fix them. After 4 years in the infantry and reaching the rank of sergeant, he decided to reenlist. At the same time, he asked to switch his occupation to motor transport mechanic.

To qualify for his new occupation, Ron took the basic automotive maintenance course. He then began troubleshooting problems in jeeps, trucks, and trailers at Camp LeJeune, NC. Ron also used his training to help fix his friends' cars. In fact, they started calling him Horowitz, M.D. (for Mechanical Doctor). Because of his good work, Ron was promoted to shop chief, responsible for supervising several mechanics.

After 2 years at Camp Lejeune as a mechanic and another promotion, Ron went back to Okinawa as a maintenance chief. He scheduled all vehicles for maintenance and ensured the safety of the shop. Even though he was overseas, he was able to play his favorite sports—tennis and football—on base. One year later, he moved to the Marine Corps Logistics Base in Albany, GA, as an inspector. He traveled to all the Reserve units from Texas to the East Coast inspecting vehicles. During his 3 years in Albany, Ron took the motor transport staff noncommissioned officer (NCO) course. On the series of tests he took there, he achieved the highest individual average in the school's history and graduated with honors. Ron was recently promoted to gunnery sergeant and reassigned to Marine Corps Headquarters.

---

## ADVANCEMENT

Mechanics must know their vehicles. They need to have the technical skills needed to find out what is wrong and fix it. They must be able to figure out what is wrong with an automobile or truck from driver descriptions, written work orders, or visual inspection of a running vehicle. Good vision, sharp hearing, and hand-eye coordination are needed to spot minor flaws, detect the sounds of faulty operation, and make precise adjustments. Mechanics must also be able to disassemble, inspect, and repair the major systems, such as fuel, brake, transmission, and electrical systems.

After mastering the basic skills, the willingness to assume leadership roles helps automotive and heavy equipment mechanics advance through the supervisory levels of this career. Knowing about many different types of vehicles, including trucks and heavy equipment, is an asset for advancement to vehicle repair supervisor. These senior managers are responsible for the repair and maintenance of all types of vehicles.

## TRAINING

The services provide apprentice auto mechanics with 6 to 13 months of basic and initial job training. It combines classroom and on-the-job instruction. Classroom instruction emphasizes shop procedures, basic repairs, and the use of manuals and repair diagrams. Experienced mechanics provide on-the-job training on a one-to-one basis. This training covers the use of hand tools, power tools, and test equipment and common procedures for repairing brakes, transmissions, carburetors, and fuel and electrical systems. Depending on the first job assignment, additional training may be given on a specific type of vehicle. Throughout their careers, auto mechanics may receive specialized training on many different vehicles. Advanced training is also available for mechanics to sharpen their troubleshooting and fault isolation skills. Shop supervisors may take courses that cover the latest auto and vehicle maintenance techniques.

During their careers, automotive and heavy equipment mechanics learn supervisory skills through leadership training and job experience. This training continues through the vehicle repair supervisor level with courses in management and administration. Typically, these courses address budgeting, personnel management, and training program development.

## RELATED MILITARY OCCUPATIONS

If you are interested in mechanics, you may also want to consider a career as an aircraft mechanic, marine engine mechanic, or powerhouse mechanic. See the Vehicle and Machinery Mechanic Occupations cluster in the Military Enlisted Occupations section of this book for descriptions of these occupations.

## TYPICAL CAREER PATH

### VEHICLE REPAIR SUPERVISOR

Successful shop supervisors may advance to direct repair operations for many different vehicles. At this level, they:

- Coordinate the activities of a major vehicle repair facility
- Identify ways to reduce costs for more effective programs
- Monitor repair orders for recurring problems
- Monitor the use of parts and supplies
- Ensure that proper records are kept on vehicles and shop personnel

### SHOP SUPERVISOR

Qualified mechanics who show leadership potential may advance to become supervisors of repair shops. They:

- Give technical help and advice in troubleshooting difficult problems
- Conduct training on the newest maintenance procedures and techniques
- Design and lay out work stations and equipment
- Assign and schedule work to meet deadlines
- Inspect and approve repaired vehicles

### MECHANIC

By developing their skills and becoming familiar with different vehicles, mechanics take on troubleshooting and more difficult repairs. They:

- Isolate the causes of vehicle problems and determine repair needs
- Conduct on-the-job training for new mechanics in how to use tools and diagnostic test equipment
- Inspect alignments and adjustments of transmissions and electrical systems
- Prepare vehicle maintenance schedules
- Perform major repairs and engine overhauls

### APPRENTICE MECHANIC

After initial job training, apprentice mechanics are assigned to repair shops, where they perform routine maintenance and repairs. At this level, they:

- Perform service on vehicles, following maintenance specifications
- Test vehicles for electrical problems and replace batteries and voltage regulators as needed
- Inspect and replace worn belts, hoses, and wiring
- Change oil and tune engines
- Repair or replace parts as directed on repair orders or by senior mechanics

**Timeline**

19-21 yrs

8-10 yrs

4-5 yrs

# BROADCAST JOURNALISTS AND NEWSWRITERS

ARMY
NAVY
AIR FORCE
MARINE CORPS
COAST GUARD

**B**roadcast journalists and newswriters keep service members, the local community, and the folks back home informed about important events. As a broadcast journalist or newswriter, you prepare news releases, hometown news stories, feature articles, and editorials for publication or radio/television broadcast. You begin your career developing skills in researching, gathering, and organizing information. As you gain experience, you may write feature stories or news scripts. There are opportunities to advance to editor of a military newspaper and perhaps to public affairs coordinator for a large military base.

## DUTY ASSIGNMENT

Broadcast journalists and newswriters work at military bases, but the stories they cover may take them all over the world. Many work at large installations where they write press releases and public relations articles for the public affairs office. Others work for base newspapers, radio/television stations, or magazines. Most broadcast journalists and newswriters work at military bases in the United States, but there is good opportunity for overseas assignment, particularly for those assigned to the Armed Forces Radio/Television Network.

## ADVANCEMENT

Broadcast journalists and newswriters must be able to interpret facts, issues, and opinions and use them to write interesting scripts, stories, and articles. They must relate easily to people with different backgrounds, since they research stories on all aspects of military life. They must also be able to select photographs and illustrations to enhance their stories and articles. Skills in public relations are also important in gaining access to service members and story locations and in dealing with the civilian media. After mastering the basic journalism skills, the willingness to assume leadership roles helps broadcast journalists and newswriters advance through the supervisory levels of this career.

## Profile: Charles Wright

Air Force newswriter Charles (Chuck) Wright described his six month deployment to Saudi Arabia as a combat reporter as the most rewarding experience in his 22-year career. As a senior reporter he had orders allowing him to travel anywhere Air Force personnel were stationed. His stories were carried by the major wire services and appeared in newspapers across the United States. Two things make that experience stand out for Chuck. First, as a military reporter, he was doing everything for which he had been trained. Second, the combat experience allowed him to get to know the many airmen who became the subjects of his stories. Chuck likes being a reporter because he enjoys writing and using his imagination. Being a reporter has allowed him to meet all types of people and deal with different events every day.

In his first assignment, Chuck advanced from "cub" reporter to sports and family page editor for the base paper at Blytheville Air Force Base (AFB), AR. During this assignment, he married his high school sweetheart and found time to complete training at the U.S. Army Information School. Not long after he was married, Chuck and his wife moved to Spain. There, after only 5 years in the Air Force, Chuck became senior reporter of the base newspaper *Alert Strip*. In addition to supervising three reporters, he spent 4 days each week working with Spanish-speaking "cahistas" (typesetters and printers) to print the paper.

Back in his home state of Florida, he spent 3 years managing publicity for over 75 Air Force recruiters. He was responsible for advertisements, managing direct mail campaigns, and working with local newspapers throughout the state. He moved back to Texas as the editor of *The AF Recruiter*, the newspaper of the Air Force Recruiting Command. During this assignment, Chuck also became the speechwriter for the generals who commanded the recruiting service.

For the past 4 years, Chuck has been a public affairs coordinator, first at Osan AFB in Korea and then for the headquarters of the Air Force Reserve at Robins AFB, GA. He manages all aspects of public affairs, including liaison with newspapers and television.

## TRAINING

The services provide broadcast journalists and newswriters with 9 to 12 months of basic and initial job training. It combines classroom instruction and on-the-job training. Classroom instruction focuses on interviewing techniques, research sources, writing style, story lines, and formats. Intensive on-the-job training given by editors and senior broadcast journalists and newswriters helps the individual progress from simple stories to difficult or unusual assignments. Many specialized training courses are available for senior broadcast journalists and newswriters in editing, photojournalism, public affairs, media relations, and radio/television scriptwriting.

During their careers, broadcast journalists and newswriters learn supervisory skills through leadership training and job experience. This training continues through the public affairs coordinator level with courses in management and administration. Typically, these courses address budgeting, personnel management, and training program development.

## RELATED MILITARY OCCUPATIONS

If you are interested in writing and news reporting, you may also want to consider a career as a radio and television announcer, photographer, or audiovisual production specialist. See the Media and Public Affairs Occupations cluster in the Military Enlisted Occupations section of this book for descriptions of these occupations.

## TYPICAL CAREER PATH

### PUBLIC AFFAIRS COORDINATOR

Public affairs coordinators assist staff officers in directing military public affairs operations. They:

- Plan, organize, and direct military news and information operations
- Determine training needs and set up public affairs training programs
- Establish information-gathering procedures and news story reporting and writing standards
- Inspect public affairs units and make recommendations to improve program operations
- Prepare administrative, personnel, and technical reports for officers

### EDITOR

Highly skilled broadcast journalists and newswriters who show leadership ability are assigned supervisory responsibilities. Editors:

- Set work priorities and assign personnel to meet news deadlines
- Review work and give technical assistance
- Coordinate military and civilian news media and public information activities
- Teach classes in the principles of journalism and writing styles and techniques
- Prepare public affairs information and historical program activity records

### SENIOR BROADCAST JOURNALIST NEWSWRITER

As their skills in journalism increase, broadcast journalists and newswriters are given more responsibility. Senior broadcast journalists and newswriters:

- Schedule and conduct special interviews, news conferences, and tours for civilians
- Plan and design layouts for newspapers, bulletins, and magazines
- Proofread news releases and other material for information content and accuracy
- Edit written material and taped interviews for radio and television
- Conduct research to gather information for in-depth feature news stories

### BROADCAST JOURNALIST/NEWSWRITER

After initial training, broadcast journalists and newswriters gather information and prepare news features and stories for military and civilian use. At this level, they:

- Interview individuals and attend meetings and events to gather information
- Write sports and news stories, editorials, and news releases
- Compose scripts for radio/television news reports, speeches, and commentaries
- Process and select photographs for magazines, newspapers, and publicity materials
- Write captions for pictures and compose headlines for news stories

**Timeline**

15-20 yrs

7-8 yrs

3-5 yrs

# COMPUTER PROGRAMMERS

NAVY
AIR FORCE
MARINE CORPS
COAST GUARD

A computer can solve problems in fractions of a second and store vast amounts of information, but it takes a programmer to make it work. As a programmer, you communicate with the computer using language it understands. You begin your career by writing and testing simple programs. As you gain experience, you learn to apply your skills to more difficult programming tasks. There are opportunities to advance to programming supervisor and perhaps to supervisor of an entire data processing facility.

## DUTY ASSIGNMENT

Most programmers work on advanced computer equipment in large data processing centers. These facilities are usually in office settings, but centers may also be located in missile facilities, space command centers, or aboard ships. While there is some opportunity for overseas assignment, most computer programmers work at data processing centers in the United States.

## ADVANCEMENT

Computer programmers need a high level of creativity and intelligence to write and test complex computer programs. Programmers must also have good math skills and the ability to think logically to write the codes that instruct computers. Since the smallest mistake can cause a program to fail, programmers must pay close attention to detail while coding and debugging programs. Keeping up on constantly changing computer technology and being able to work with many different computer systems are important for advancement.

After mastering basic programming skills, the willingness to assume leadership roles helps programmers advance through supervisory levels of this career. A familiarity with the entire range of computer operations (for example, telecommunications, data entry, and specialized equipment) is important to advance to the level of data processing supervisor. Data processing supervisors manage entire computer centers, including programming and computer operations.

### Profile: Jeff Picard

When Jeff Picard joined the Army, he had been out of high school for 6 years. During this time, he had gone to college for 1-1/2 years and had served in the National Guard, but he needed something to get him started. So Jeff decided to enlist.

Jeff did not become a programmer/analyst immediately. During his first 4-year enlistment, he served as a cannon crewman, assistant gunner, and forward observer in the artillery at Fort Campbell, KY, and Camp Essayons, South Korea, where he moved up through the ranks to sergeant. When the time came for Jeff to reenlist, he looked through the Army careers catalogue. The computer career field appealed to him most, so he asked permission to reenlist as a programmer/analyst. His request was granted, and the Army sent him to computer school to learn his new job.

At the 4-month computer school at Fort Benjamin Harrison, IN, Jeff learned COBOL, systems analysis, problem solving, and the Army's job control language. He enjoyed the challenge of learning the latest technology.

Jeff's first assignment in his new career field was at the Army's data processing center in Yongsan, Korea. For 2-1/2 years, Jeff was the analyst in charge of the Standard Army Multi-Command Management Information Systems (STAMMIS). He also programmed in COBOL, worked with the Army's job control language, and, while analyzing problems and reporting them, learned the basics of technical writing. During this tour, he was promoted to staff sergeant.

From Korea, Jeff went to his present assignment at the Army's Information Systems Engineering Command. Working specifically in quality assurance, he monitors the development of new computer systems and gives technical guidance. He also writes documentation, such as user's guides.

Jeff enjoys following the developments of new technology in hardware, especially in microcomputers. "Programming is so complex, no one can know it all," he says. "I like interacting with other programmer/analysts to share knowledge."

## TRAINING

The services provide computer programmers with 6 to 18 months of basic and initial job training. It includes classroom instruction and practical exercises in programming and data processing.

Instruction stresses the different types of programming languages. These languages include operating systems (instructions that control computer operations), assembler, COBOL, and FORTRAN. Hands-on exercises demonstrate the basic tools and techniques used to code, structure, and debug programs.

Training continues on the job under the direction of programmer/analysts and supervisors.

Experienced programmers and programmer/analysts may take advanced training in developing programs to automate manual budgeting and accounting procedures. Instruction emphasizes analysis techniques, such as flow diagrams and decision tables.

Throughout their careers, computer programmers may receive additional training in specific computer systems and computer programming languages. The type of advanced training depends on the skills needed in a duty assignment. For example, programmers

assigned to technical, scientific, or special purpose programming may receive training in special programming languages. This training covers methods for writing input-output routines (data entry and reports) and sub-program call and return statements (special instructions for repetitive program calculations). Programmers often receive training in new computer systems directly from the manufacturer.

During their careers, computer programmers learn supervisory skills through leadership training and job experience. This training continues through the level of data processing supervisor with courses in management and administration. Typically, these courses address budgeting, personnel management, and training program development.

## RELATED MILITARY OCCUPATIONS

If you are interested in working with computers, you may also want to consider a career as a computer systems specialist, or computer equipment repairer. See the Engineering, Science, and Technical Occupations cluster and the Electronic and Electrical Equipment Repair Occupations cluster in the Military Enlisted Occupations section of this book for descriptions of these and other related military occupations.

## TYPICAL CAREER PATH

### DATA PROCESSING SUPERVISOR

Data processing supervisors may manage entire data processing organizations, including programmers and computer operators. They:

- Plan and direct computer operations and programming
- Assign projects, set priorities, and monitor work load
- Develop budgets, track expenses, and predict equipment requirements
- Develop staff training programs

### PROGRAMMING SUPERVISOR

Skilled programmer/analysts who show leadership ability may advance to become programming supervisors. At this level, they:

- Assign staff and organize teams for major projects
- Help programming staff with technical problems
- Review and approve proposed system and program designs
- Train or direct the training of new programmers
- Check user requests and set up project budgets and deadlines

### PROGRAMMER/ANALYST

Experienced programmers may advance to become programmer/analysts who design computer applications for military organizations. Programmer/analysts:

- Meet with supervisors and system users to determine system objectives and needs
- Define inputs, outputs, and data elements for proposed systems
- Write system design and programmer instructions
- Test and debug programs using test data and analysis techniques
- Put new programs and systems into operation

### PROGRAMMER

After initial job training, programmers work with more experienced staff developing routine programs. Programmers:

- Write simple programs using standard, prewritten program segments
- Enter programs using computer terminal input devices
- Prepare documentation for users, computer operators, and other programmers
- Code programs into computer language to perform needed actions
- Help prepare, edit, and test programs

**Timeline**

18-21 yrs

9-12 yrs

4-6 yrs

# CONSTRUCTION SPECIALISTS

**C**onstruction specialists help translate blueprints and drawings into finished structures. As a construction specialist, you may make cabinets, lay floors, roof buildings, erect and finish walls, or build piers, bunkers, and other timber structures. You begin your career performing rough carpentry and masonry, such as framing walls and performing simple repairs. As you develop your skills, you may take on more responsibility and more difficult tasks. There are opportunities to advance to trades supervisor and perhaps to trades superintendent.

## DUTY ASSIGNMENT

Most construction specialists work on military bases, but the actual work site depends on the job. Construction specialists may work in woodworking shops, inside a new building, or outdoors constructing temporary buildings and timber structures. Most construction specialists work at large military bases in the United States, but there is also a good opportunity for overseas assignments maintaining buildings on military installations or working at temporary advanced-base sites used in training exercises or combat.

## ADVANCEMENT

Construction specialists are skilled craftspersons who must learn and master the use of tools of the trade—saws, squares, hammers, and power tools. They must also perform many different construction tasks, such as painting, bricklaying, roofing, masonry, and framing walls and floors. Construction specialists are judged by the quality of their work and their ability to make decisions on how to complete a job. In order to advance, construction specialists must be able to read work orders and estimate the time and materials needed to complete a job. After mastering the many different construction skills, the willingness to assume leadership roles helps construction specialists advance through the supervisory levels of this career.

---

### Profile: Frank Dalton

Frank Dalton worked in construction during his summer breaks from school. He found that he liked working with his hands. So when he joined the Air Force, he asked to sign on as a structural technician. Because of his previous experience, he was able to take a test that allowed him to bypass initial training and go directly to his first duty assignment after basic training.

Frank started as a carpenter's apprentice at Maxwell Air Force Base (AFB), AL. From there, he was sent to Korea, where he renovated buildings and built roads, shelters, and maintenance hangars. Looking back, he feels that this was one of his most interesting experiences in the military. "I really got to see how the people there lived." Back in the States at Seymour Johnson AFB, NC, he performed minor construction and maintenance, such as paneling, patching roofs, and replacing floor tiles. With this experience behind him, Frank then transferred to the planning section where he learned to plan and construct buildings.

Frank's next assignments placed him as crew leader. At Keesler AFB, MS, he was promoted to staff sergeant and led a crew of carpenters who carried out maintenance for the base. At Rhein Mein AB, Germany, he was in charge of a crew that built a hobby shop, a squadron compound, a recreation center, and a communications facility. He then became the noncommissioned officer in charge (NCOIC) of a 3-person shop at the North Charleston Air Force Station, SC. "We did everything—roofing, plumbing, painting, maintenance, and renovation."

Promoted to technical sergeant, Frank became the NCOIC of carpentry shops, first at Homestead AFB and then at Hurlburt Field in Florida. At Homestead, his shop renovated the officers' open mess and the headquarters building, an improvement that won the base an award as the "Best Base in Tactical Air Command of the Air Force." At Hurlburt Field, his crew constructed 11 buildings, renovated the base marina, and rebuilt a Boy Scout camp as a community relations project. Frank is now on temporary duty assignment at Myrtle Beach AFB, SC, where his crew is moving and reconstructing an old hangar.

## TRAINING

The services provide construction specialists with 6 to 12 months of basic and initial job training. It combines classroom instruction and on-the-job experience. Classroom instruction includes the basics of carpentry and masonry: reading blueprints, applying mathematical formulas, using and maintaining hand and power tools, and mixing and pouring concrete. On-the-job training is conducted under the supervision of a more experienced construction specialist on actual repair and construction projects. On these projects, construction specialists gain experience in all carpentry and masonry skills, including performing general maintenance tasks, repairing floors and roofs, making forms for a foundation, and finishing doors and window frames. Crew leaders may take advanced training in basic supervision and planning work projects.

During their careers, construction specialists learn supervisory skills through leadership training and job experience. This training continues through the trades superintendent level with courses in management and administration. Typically these courses address budgeting, personnel management, and training program development.

## RELATED MILITARY OCCUPATIONS

If you are interested in construction work, you may also want to consider a career as a building electrician, or plumber and pipefitter. See the Construction Occupations cluster in the Military Enlisted Occupations section of this book for descriptions of these and other construction occupations.

## TYPICAL CAREER PATH

### TRADES SUPERINTENDENT

Trades superintendents supervise large construction and maintenance units. At this level, they:

- Plan personnel and equipment needs for construction and repair jobs
- Set up and carry out quality control standards and work procedures
- Plan work priorities and timetables
- Direct inspections of completed systems, structures, and facilities
- Develop training programs for construction workers and equipment operators

### TRADES SUPERVISOR

Crew leaders who show skill and motivation may become trades supervisors who oversee the work of several construction trades, including electricians, plumbers, and other construction workers. They:

- Help plan repair and construction projects
- Coordinate construction and support unit operations
- Inspect completed or nearly completed projects
- Carry out training programs and assign trainers for new workers
- Prepare technical, work progress, and cost control records and reports

### CREW LEADER

Skilled construction specialists who show leadership ability may advance to lead carpentry and masonry crews. At this point, they:

- Assign jobs and help in work start-up
- Train new construction specialists in tool and equipment use and carpentry and masonry operations
- Help in on-site construction and carpentry shop inspections
- Interpret drawings and blueprints to plan and lay out work
- Keep records of the time and materials spent on projects and predict future needs

### CONSTRUCTION SPECIALIST

After initial training, construction specialists are assigned to construction and maintenance units. Working under close supervision, they:

- Repair or build piers, timber bridges, bunkers, or temporary structures
- Make forms for pouring concrete and erect wood framing for buildings
- Repair floors and roofs using wood, tile, asphalt, and shingles
- Hang sheetrock or drywall to finish interior walls and ceilings
- Repair and install doors, windows, and cabinets and install locks and doorknobs

**Timeline**

19-20 yrs

8-12 yrs

4-6 yrs

# ELECTRONIC INSTRUMENT REPAIRERS

ARMY
NAVY
AIR FORCE
MARINE CORPS
COAST GUARD

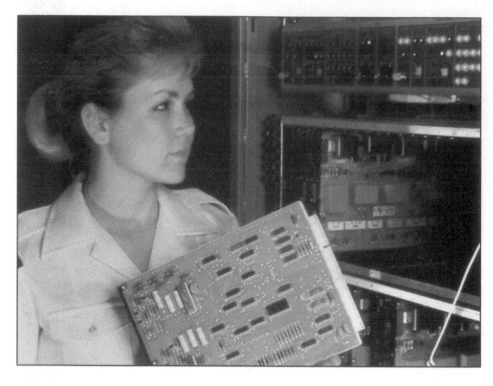

**P**recise electronic instruments are vital in military communications, aircraft navigation, and weapons targeting. They are also used in medical research, weather forecasting, and electronic warfare. As an electronic instrument repairer, you diagnose and repair malfunctions on one type of electronic instrument. You begin your career performing routine maintenance and repair on a single instrument. As you gain experience and skill, you may advance to work on more than one instrument, doing more complicated repairs and helping others solve complex problems. There are opportunities to advance to shop supervisor and perhaps to electronic maintenance superintendent.

## DUTY ASSIGNMENT

Electronic instrument repairers work in electronic repair shops all over the world. The military uses electronic devices in all areas, so repairers are found working aboard ships or aircraft and at most military installations. The instruments that repairers learn to fix may determine their duty assignments. For example, repairers who work on flight control instruments are usually assigned to the electronics section of an aircraft squadron or aircraft maintenance unit. Repairers who work on biomedical equipment (used in medical testing and research) are usually stationed at large medical facilities.

## ADVANCEMENT

Electronic instrument repairers diagnose problems and make repairs to state-of-the-art electronic instruments. To do this, they must understand the electronic principles behind the workings of highly technical equipment. They also need skills in reading schematic diagrams and using test instruments to find faulty parts. To advance, repairers must develop the analytical skills needed to solve complex repair problems and expand their knowledge of related electronic equipment. After mastering the basic skills, the willingness to assume leadership roles helps electronic instrument repairers advance through the supervisory levels of this career.

---

### Profile: Catherine Glidden

Petty Officer First Class Catherine Glidden joined the Navy for travel and an education. The Navy recommended advanced electronics to her because she scored highest in that area on the ASVAB.

Catherine took initial job training courses in electricity and electronics, intermediate avionics, advanced electronics, and ARN52 (navigational gear). She then went on her first duty assignment to Guantanamo, Cuba, where she tested, maintained, and repaired communication navigation gear. There she met her future husband, also an aviation electronics technician in the Navy.

Catherine's next assignment was in Rota, Spain, where she worked on A-3 and P-3 aircraft and maintained electronic countermeasures gear for VQ-2 (fleet air reconnaissance) squadron planes. She worked on control boxes, switching units, and antennae displays. She was also an inspector responsible for checking repaired gear and reviewing the work of others. "When I was in Spain, I bought a Eurail pass and toured Norway, Belgium, Sweden, the Netherlands, France, Germany, Austria, and England," says Catherine.

After completing her assignment in Spain, Catherine trained as an instructor and was then assigned to the Norfolk Naval Air Station, VA, for further on-the-job training. She received her certification, and now, with only 11 years in the Navy, she teaches electronic assembly repair courses (basic and advanced), a supervisor's course, and an instructor's certification course. She also travels to training sites in the southeastern United States to recertify sites and instructors. She enjoys teaching. As she says, "Before, I learned a lot through school and strengthened my technical skills. Now, as an instructor, I'm strengthening my communications skills."

Catherine was not only the first female instructor but also the first woman at her present detachment. She is one of only 10 aviation electronics technicians and the only female aviation electronics technician ever to have reached the "A" level of certification ("A" is the highest of six levels). Catherine has no problem being first. As she says, "I strive to do the best I can in every job I do."

## SPECIALIZATION

From the time they begin their training, electronic instrument repairers specialize in one type of complex equipment. Specialties include avionic systems (electronic systems on aircraft), biomedical equipment (medical diagnostic or research), electronic communications equipment, and electronic warfare systems.

## TRAINING

The services provide electronic instrument repairers with 9 to 24 months of basic and initial job training. It combines classroom instruction and intensive on-the-job training. The classroom instruction consists of two courses. The first covers basic electrical and electronic theory and principles. Trainees also learn how to use and care for electronic tools, instruments, and equipment. The second course gives details about the specific equipment the repairer has selected as a specialty. For example, biomedical equipment repairers learn about X-ray equipment, laboratory instruments, and patient monitoring systems. During on-the-job training, repairers learn how to inspect, maintain, and perform simple, routine repairs on electronic instruments. Advanced classroom training for senior repairers covers advanced electronics, troubleshooting techniques, and new repair procedures.

During their careers, electronic instrument repairers learn supervisory skills through leadership training and job experience. This training continues through the level of electronic maintenance superintendent with courses in management and administration. Typically, these courses address budgeting, personnel management, repair shop operations, and training program development.

## RELATED MILITARY OCCUPATIONS

If you are interested in electronic instrument repair, you may also want to consider a career as a communications equipment repairer, computer equipment repairer, or weapons maintenance technician. See the Electronic and Electrical Equipment Repair Occupations cluster in the Military Enlisted Occupations section of this book for descriptions of these and other related military occupations.

## TYPICAL CAREER PATH

### ELECTRONIC MAINTENANCE SUPERINTENDENT

Highly qualified shop supervisors may advance to plan and manage electronic systems maintenance facilities. They:

* Plan for needed personnel, equipment, parts, and supplies
* Set up quality control guidelines and maintenance and repair standards
* Conduct safety and quality control inspections
* Develop and write technical and administrative reports and orders
* Develop training programs and procedures

**19-21 yrs**

### SHOP SUPERVISOR

Skilled instrument repairers who show leadership ability may become supervisors of electronic repair shops. At this level, they:

* Schedule and make work assignments
* Coordinate repair and support activities to meet work deadlines
* Give technical guidance in electronic system maintenance and repair
* Inspect completed repairs
* Conduct training programs and assign trainers for new repairers

**10-13 yrs**

### SENIOR REPAIRER

As their skills increase, electronic instrument repairers take on more responsibility and perform more complicated repairs. Senior repairers:

* Set up and run electronic testing equipment and machines
* Align and calibrate (adjust) testing equipment and instruments
* Interpret diagrams and use troubleshooting techniques to find faulty parts or wiring
* Test repaired instruments and systems using probes and oscilloscopes (devices that measure variations in electrical current)
* Replace faulty parts, such as loose wires and printed circuit boards (prewired electrical circuits)

**4-8 yrs**

### ELECTRONIC INSTRUMENT REPAIRER

After initial job training, electronic instrument repairers perform routine maintenance and simple repairs on electronic instruments. Working under close supervision, they:

* Use wiring diagrams to find faulty parts and test electronic instrument components (parts)
* Check for faulty wiring and connections using probes and other test instruments
* Replace parts using common and special hand tools
* Repair printed circuits and electric connectors using precision soldering tools
* Clean and maintain electronic testing equipment and instruments

# FOOD SERVICE SPECIALISTS

ARMY
NAVY
AIR FORCE
MARINE CORPS
COAST GUARD

The military serves thousands of meals each day in dining halls, aboard ships, or in tents in the field. As a food service specialist, you help prepare these meals: you may bake the bread, cut the meat, prepare the main courses, or make the sandwiches. You begin your career by preparing food under the close supervision of experienced cooks and chefs. As you gain experience, you may plan meals and order supplies. There are opportunities to advance to chef and perhaps to food service supervisor.

## DUTY ASSIGNMENT

Food service specialists work in clean, sanitary kitchens and dining halls on military bases and ships. They may work in a galley preparing food for a small unit, in a hospital cafeteria, or in a large dining hall where several hundred or several thousand people are served at each meal. Food service specialists may also work under field conditions preparing and serving meals outside in large tents. Most food service specialists work at military bases in the United States, but there is good opportunity for overseas assignment. Food service specialists are likely to work with civilian employees sometime during their careers.

## ADVANCEMENT

The quality of the food prepared for service members affects their health and morale. Food service specialists need to make an extra effort to see that the food they prepare is appetizing and nutritious. To do this, they must master cooking meals using standard recipes. They must also understand the characteristics and nutritional values of ingredients so that they can adjust recipes for large or small volumes and plan menus. At supervisory levels of the career, food service specialists also need to master the basics of managing a food service operation, such as ordering supplies and properly storing food. After mastering the basic cooking skills, the willingness to assume leadership roles helps food service specialists advance through the supervisory levels of this career.

---

### Profile: Dwayne Robinson

Dwayne Robinson joined the Navy right after high school. He and a friend joined the Navy to travel and to learn a trade. Dwayne found his career in his first assignment in Bainbridge, MD, as a seaman apprentice: after spending part of his tour working in the mess hall, he discovered that cooking was what he wanted to do. From Bainbridge, he was assigned to the USS Waldron in Norfolk, VA, where he worked in the ship's galley.

Dwayne reenlisted because the Navy gave him the opportunity to go to cooking school where he learned menu planning and nutrition and improved his cooking skills. After school, he spent a year and a half in the bakery at the Naval Hospital in Guam. From Guam he went to Vietnam where he supervised a team of food service specialists providing meals to tugboat crews. By the end of his tour, Dwayne had been promoted to petty officer first class.

Dwayne spent the next 3 years managing the inventory of a commissary store. He was not sure if his career in the Navy was going anywhere, but after some friendly advice from his Chief, he decided not to leave. His decision paid off. During his next assignment aboard the USS O'Callahan, he was in charge of running the entire mess, something he had always wanted. He was also promoted to chief petty officer. Dwayne says the most important day of his career was the day he "put on the hat." (The lower ranks, Dwayne explains, wear sailor caps; only chiefs may wear "the hat.")

After making chief, Dwayne spent 3 years as an instructor in the Navy cooking school in San Diego. He and his fellow instructors won first place in the San Diego Culinary Show. On Saturdays, Dwayne ran a cooking school for Explorer Scouts. By the end of this assignment, he had been promoted to senior chief.

Dwayne has spent the past 4 years as food services supervisor on several ships. On the USS New Orleans, he managed a 35-person staff that fed 580 crew members and, at times, 1,800 Marines (nearly 7,000 meals a day). Aboard his last ship, the USS Wadsworth, he went on a 7-month cruise of the South Pacific, with stops in Hawaii, Guam, Korea, Hong Kong, the Philippines, Australia, New Zealand, Tonga, and Samoa.

## SPECIALIZATION

While food service specialists typically begin as kitchen workers, they may specialize as bakers, butchers, or cooks. Depending on the military service, they may also spend their careers preparing special meals for hospital patients. These meals, which require special attention, are usually ordered by a physician or a dietitian to meet a patient's special need for low-calorie or salt-free food.

## TRAINING

The services provide cooks with 10 to 18 months of basic and initial job training. It combines classroom and on-the-job training. Classroom training focuses on the basics of kitchen operations, sanitation, food storage, and the use of standard and special diet menus and recipes. Hands-on exercises at the school involve preparing and cooking standard menu meals. Intensive on-the-job training in preparing, arranging, and serving is given by experienced workers and chefs. Most chefs return to school for advanced training in food production and

management of a food service facility. Courses may also be taken in specialized cooking, such as preparing gourmet meals, baking using advanced techniques, or cooking for pilots and flight crews.

During their career, food service specialists learn supervisory skills through leadership training and job experience. This training continues through the food service supervisor level with courses in pricing, nutrition, accounting, sanitation, inventory control, and personnel management.

## RELATED MILITARY OCCUPATIONS

If you are interested in a service career where you work closely with others, you may also want to consider other occupations such as Flight Operations Specialist or Personnel Specialist. See the Administrative Occupations Cluster for descriptions of these and other related Military Enlisted Occupations. The Service Occupation Cluster may also contain related military occupations.

## TYPICAL CAREER PATH

### FOOD SERVICE SUPERVISOR

Highly qualified chefs may advance to direct and control large food service facilities. Food service supervisors:

- Set food service standards, policies, and work priorities
- Plan and develop food service training programs
- Inspect food service facilities and evaluate work procedures
- Plan and prepare budgets and monitor food service expenses
- Determine personnel, equipment, and food supply needs
- Prepare standard operating procedures and administrative reports on food service activities

### CHEF

As their skills in food service increase, cooks take on more responsibility. As chefs, they:

- Plan and prepare standard and dietetic food menus and recipes
- Direct kitchen staff in a food serving facility
- Prepare work schedules and assign food service duties
- Set food serving procedures and plan layouts for dining areas
- Determine food and supply needs and prepare order forms and records
- Conduct training classes and assign trainers to new cooks

### COOK

After initial training, food service specialists begin their careers working as cooks. Working under the supervision of experienced chefs, they:

- Receive, inspect, and store beverages, food items, and food service supplies
- Cook meat, fish, poultry, and vegetables
- Bake cakes, pies, bread, and pastries
- Make soups, salads, and sandwiches
- Serve food in a hospital, dining hall, field kitchen, or aboard ship
- Clean dining areas, kitchen utensils, and equipment

Timeline

15-21 yrs

7-13 yrs

# INFANTRYMEN

ARMY
MARINE CORPS

As an infantryman, you live with a challenge. You learn to push yourself to do things you never thought possible. Your main focus is on teamwork, discipline, and physical conditioning. You begin by learning to read maps, fire weapons, and prepare for enemy attacks. By demonstrating leadership skills, there are opportunities to advance to platoon sergeant and perhaps to company/battalion sergeant.

## DUTY ASSIGNMENT

Infantrymen are most often assigned to infantry units at military bases in the United States, but many are stationed in Western Europe and the Pacific Islands. Not all assignments for infantrymen are with infantry units; at some time in their career, experienced infantrymen are usually assigned to other positions. The most popular assignments include recruiter, drill instructor, and headquarters staff.

## ADVANCEMENT

The nature of combat calls for infantrymen to be able to take charge and lead squad members to reach their goals. Good leadership skills are the key to advancing in the infantry. To advance, infantrymen must show that they could motivate and lead others in combat. They must begin developing these skills at basic training and apply them by leading the men of their squad or platoon in exercises and maneuvers. The willingness to assume leadership roles and take on additional responsibilities helps an infantryman advance through the supervisory levels of this career.

### Profile: Michael Fry

As a civilian, Staff Sergeant Michael Fry had a good job as a pipe layer, but his work was the same every day. Mike joined the Marines because, as he puts it, "I was looking for a challenge and wanted to go different places and do different things." More importantly, Mike says, "I wanted to belong."

For Mike, teaching other Marines the skills he has learned has been the most important part of his infantry career. He believes that leadership and training are the basic roles of all noncommissioned officers (NCOs). During his career, Mike has actively sought assignments that allow him to share what he has learned.

During his initial infantry training, Mike was one of 10 Marines selected for barracks duty. Assigned to the Marine Barracks in Norfolk, VA, for a year, his squad provided security for the many naval installations in that area. From Norfolk, Mike went to marksmanship school at the Dam Neck Rifle Range. He did so well that the school asked him to stay on for a year as an instructor.

When Mike was sent to Okinawa as part of the 3rd Marine Brigade, his experience at the rifle range qualified him to become company armorer in charge of the company's small weapons. While in Okinawa, Mike was promoted to sergeant and volunteered for duty as drill instructor. The following year he recalls as the most rewarding of his career, "I was proud to be able to take someone off the streets and turn him into a Marine." While a drill instructor, he also taught water survival to new recruits. Mike spent the next 3 years as a platoon sergeant in Hawaii training 40 Marines on land and on ship. He led the platoon in many different training exercises and on several cruises.

Mike is currently an instructor at the Marine Corps Officer Candidate School in Quantico, VA, where he trains college students who will one day become officers. He also works at the NCO school teaching leadership to other noncommissioned officers. Mike knows that he is due for another assignment in the near future and says he and his family are trying to decide where they want to go.

## SPECIALIZATION

Infantrymen specialize in parachute jumping to qualify for assignment to an airborne division or in special battle tactics to qualify for assignment to a ranger battalion.

## TRAINING

The services provide infantrymen with 6 to 12 months of basic and advanced infantry training. Following basic training, they continue to develop infantry skills. They learn about weapons, map reading, military law, and hand-to-hand combat techniques. They also undergo a tough physical conditioning program. Advanced training is usually given in specific weapons, such as mortars, machine guns, and truck-mounted weapons. Specialized training is also available in parachute jumping and special battle tactics.

As platoon sergeants, infantrymen receive training in leading an infantry platoon. They learn about infantry combat operations, leadership, communications, and information gathering. Company/battalion sergeants take advanced training in planning and directing infantry operations. They learn about weapons, military tactics, unit readiness, and effective leadership.

## RELATED MILITARY OCCUPATIONS

If you are interested in a combat career, you may also want to consider a career in the special operations forces or as an artillery crew member, combat engineer, or tank crew member. See the Combat Specialty Occupations cluster in the Military Enlisted Occupations section of this book for descriptions of these occupations.

## TYPICAL CAREER PATH

### COMPANY/BATTALION SERGEANT

Company/battalion sergeants plan and direct the several platoons that make up an infantry company or battalion. Typically, they:

- Plan and conduct training programs
- Help decide how and when troops and equipment will be used
- Supervise operation of the unit command post
- Prepare situation briefings, combat orders, and other reports

### PLATOON SERGEANT

Qualified squad leaders are promoted to supervise platoons, each consisting of several squads. At this level, they:

- Supervise a rifle, machine gun, or other infantry group
- Receive and give combat or training exercise orders
- Help develop battle plans
- Coordinate the movement of troops, supplies, and weapons
- Direct the storage and issue of ammunition

### SQUAD OR FIRE TEAM LEADER

Infantrymen who show leadership potential may become squad leaders of small groups of infantrymen. Squad or fire team leaders:

- Motivate and give on-the-job training to new infantrymen
- Coordinate the squad's collection of information about the enemy and the battlefield
- Read maps and photographs taken from aircraft to locate enemy forces
- Request artillery or aircraft support fire
- Carry out combat or training exercise orders

### INFANTRYMAN

After initial job training, infantrymen train and take part in combat exercises. They:

- Fire and maintain rifles, machine guns, and other weapons
- Stand watch at observation posts to observe enemy troop movement
- Stand watch at roadblocks and man bunkers and gun positions
- Drive trucks to transport troops, weapons, and supplies
- Place and arm antipersonnel and antitank mines

**This career is open only to men.**

Timeline

17-20 yrs

7-8 yrs

3-4 yrs

# MACHINISTS

**M**achinists make engine parts so precise that their quality is measured to one one-thousandth of an inch. As a machinist, you make and repair parts for mechanical equipment, such as engines and generators, to keep them in running condition. You begin your career learning to use lathes, grinders, drill presses, and other metalworking machines under close supervision. As your skills develop, you may also learn the art of tool and die making and how to plan machining jobs and lay out work materials. There are opportunities to advance to machine shop supervisor and perhaps to mechanical maintenance superintendent.

## DUTY ASSIGNMENT

Machinists usually work in a machine shop that is part of a larger maintenance organization. Depending on the service, machine shops may be part of an aircraft maintenance unit, a ship tender, or a vehicle repair and maintenance unit. Machinists may also be assigned to the maintenance section of a large combat unit, where they work with mobile equipment during field exercises. Machinists are needed in units all over the world, so there is good opportunity for overseas duty.

## RELATED MILITARY OCCUPATIONS

If you are interested in metalworking or mechanical equipment repair, you may also want to consider a career as a welder and metal worker or communications equipment repairer. See the Machine Operator and Precision Work Occupations cluster in the Military Enlisted Occupations section of this book for descriptions of these occupations. Other related occupations may be found in the Vehicle and Machinery Mechanic or the Electronic and Electrical Equipment Repair Occupations clusters in the Military Enlisted Occupations section.

### Profile: Nancy Tita

Staff Sergeant Nancy Tita has enjoyed her 10 years on active duty. She says her Army career has provided her the opportunity "to travel, meet different people, learn the latest technologies, and just have fun."

Nancy joined the Army Reserves for training so she could do something different from her civilian job as a clerk typist. After basic training, she went to Fort Sam Houston, TX, for training as a medical service technician. For a year, she worked several weekends a month with her Reserve unit; then she volunteered for active duty. "I enjoyed my time on duty, and I saw the Army as a place to get ahead," she explains.

When Nancy joined the Active Army, she asked to receive training as a machinist. She thought the work would be challenging and different and would allow her to prove herself. She went through initial training at Aberdeen Proving Ground, MD, where she learned the basic skills required of all machinists. Her first assignment was at Fort Eustis, VA, where she worked in the maintenance company, helping make repairs to everything from radios to helicopters. She was able to

learn her trade quickly and became familiar with some of the other occupations in the maintenance shop.

At Fort Eustis, VA, Nancy also worked for a year in her second specialty as a medical technician. She was then assigned to a maintenance company in Korea for a year where she was promoted to sergeant. She returned to the States as a shop foreman in the services section of an armored division at Fort Knox, KY. In this position, she supervised a crew that repaired jeeps, tanks, and other armored equipment.

Nancy has been assigned to Aberdeen Proving Ground for the past five years as an instructor and noncommissioned officer in charge of student control. In addition to teaching metalworking courses, she processes students entering training and assigns them to their various classes. Nancy was recently promoted to staff sergeant and looks forward to being one of the top-ranking females in the maintenance field. When asked about being a female in a nontraditional job, Nancy replies, "I like the challenge of being the only female in the unit."

## ADVANCEMENT

Because machinists are called on to make precision parts for sophisticated equipment, they need to develop an attention to detail and craftsmanship not required in many jobs. They must master the methods of crafting various parts, learn the use and properties of different metals, and develop skill in operating the many different machines in a shop. Learning to read blueprints and visualize parts from technical instructions is important in the early part of this career. Pursuing civilian courses in mathematics or applied sciences will help a machinist develop these skills.

After mastering the basic skills, the willingness to assume leadership roles helps machinists advance through the supervisory levels of this career. Learning about other occupations, such as mechanics, increases a machinist's chances for promotion since superintendents manage entire maintenance units.

## TRAINING

The services provide machinists with 6 to 9 months of basic and initial job training. It includes both classroom and on-the-job instruction. Classroom instruction includes the basics of metalworking, including the properties of metals and the use of machine tools, such as lathes, drill presses, and milling machines. Class work also includes training in interpreting blueprints and using precision measuring devices. Expert machinists direct on-the-job training on each machine tool and instruct new machinists in planning, laying out, and completing machining jobs. Advanced training is available for senior machinists interested in more complex machining techniques and the art of tool and die making.

During their careers, machinists learn supervisory skills through leadership training and job experience. This training continues through the mechanical maintenance superintendent level with courses in management and administration. Typically, these courses address budgeting, personnel management, machine shop operations, and training program development.

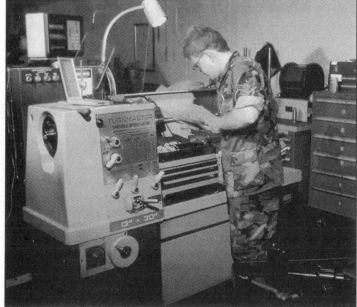

## TYPICAL CAREER PATH

### MECHANICAL MAINTENANCE SUPERINTENDENT

Machine shop supervisors may advance to plan and direct activities of entire mechanical maintenance units. Superintendents:

- Plan personnel needs and organize placement of equipment in the shop
- Develop training programs and procedures for shop personnel
- Set up programs to ensure quality work products
- Manage unit administration, including filing, preparing reports, and maintaining publications that contain part descriptions or work procedures

### MACHINE SHOP SUPERVISOR

Skilled senior machinists who show leadership ability may become supervisors of machine shops. At this level, they:

- Plan and schedule projects to use personnel and equipment efficiently
- Conduct training programs and assign trainers to new machinists
- Oversee shop operations
- Inspect finished machined parts and work pieces for quality
- Design, make, and repair special machine tools, including dies and jigs

### SENIOR MACHINIST

By mastering basic machining skills and abilities, machinists can become senior machinists. They:

- Assign work to machinists to meet work deadlines
- Conduct on-the-job training and show new workers how to operate machines
- Interpret work orders and specifications and help with complex machine jobs
- Perform difficult machine setup and operation for precision work
- Lay out, mark, and make metal and nonmetal parts

### MACHINIST

After initial job training, machinists learn to use metalworking machines to make and repair metal parts. Working under close supervision, they:

- Read blueprints, sketches, diagrams, and work specifications
- Measure and mark parts and materials for machining
- Lay out common work pieces and set up standard machine tools
- Operate lathes, grinders, shapers, and milling machines
- Test completed work using precision devices, such as gauges, calipers, and micrometers

**Timeline**

16-20 yrs

7-8 yrs

3-5 yrs

# MARINE ENGINE MECHANICS

**M**arine engine mechanics keep the ship's engines running. As a marine engine mechanic, you maintain and repair ship or small boat engines, propulsion machinery, and other shipboard mechanical equipment. You begin your career performing routine maintenance and repairs under close supervision. As you gain experience, you take greater responsibility and perform more difficult repairs. There are opportunities to advance to engine room supervisor and perhaps to marine engine superintendent.

## DUTY ASSIGNMENT

Marine engine mechanics work aboard ships or at land-based repair centers. Shipboard duty may involve work anywhere on the high seas or at the ship's home port. A large number of marine engine mechanics work on launches (small boats) and amphibians (vessels able to move on water and over land). Some mechanics work on cutters that patrol the coastal waterways.

## ADVANCEMENT

Marine engine mechanics must understand different kinds of equipment. They must have the technical skills needed to find the cause of a malfunction and fix it. Good eyesight, sharp hearing, and hand-eye coordination are important since mechanics must be able to spot damaged or broken parts, detect the sounds of faulty operation, and make precise adjustments. They must be able to read blueprints and follow standard maintenance procedures. Marine engine mechanics must also have a good job performance record in standing engine room watches. To do this well, they must be alert for unusual conditions and understand emergency procedures. After mastering the basic skills, the willingness to assume leadership roles helps marine engine mechanics advance through the supervisory levels of this career. The opportunity for advancement is usually increased by experience in working on more than one type or class of vessel.

### Profile: George Monch

George Monch grew up in Cape May, NJ, home of the Coast Guard Training Center. His love for the sea and familiarity with the Coast Guard directed him toward a Coast Guard career. Even now, after 16 years, Chief Monch still says, "I can't be too far from the water."

Out of boot camp, George went to Yorktown, VA, for a 4-month course in engineering. His first assignment was back home in Cape May aboard the cutter *Alert*. As George explains it, his first duty assignment was "basic engine cleaning." However, it was not long before he was promoted in both rank and responsibility. He was assigned to overhauling small boilers and maintaining the fresh water system. He also helped repair auxiliary engine equipment (engines that are used in place of the sails).

George's next assignment was a 1-year tour in Japan. He started out as a watchstander and advanced to supervise the overhaul of engines and auxiliary equipment. He then returned to Cape May to become part of the Aids to Navigation Team, responsible for operating and maintaining several boats, lighthouses, and navigation buoys.

George left active duty after 8 years, but stayed in the Coast Guard Reserve, working weekends as a small boat operator on search and rescue missions. Three years later, seeking greater job security, he decided to go back on active duty. He was assigned to the *Eagle*, the Coast Guard Academy's training vessel. In the winter, George supervised the modernization of the ship's auxiliary equipment. In the summer, as the *Eagle* sailed across the Caribbean and the Atlantic to Europe, he gave the cadets instruction in seamanship and the ship's auxiliary equipment.

George's next assignment was on the West Coast where he was the engineering supervisor on the *Point Ledge,* a vessel used for search and rescue and drug enforcement along the California coast.

For the past 2 years, Chief Monch has worked at the Coast Guard shipyard in Baltimore, MD. In charge of equipment for a variety of vessels, he orders parts and advises the ship's crew on how to replace broken parts and repair equipment.

## TRAINING

The services provide apprentice marine engine mechanics with 9 to 14 months of basic and initial job training. It combines classroom instruction and on-the-job training. Classroom instruction includes the theory and operation of internal combustion engines and propulsion machinery. Experienced mechanics and engine room supervisors direct on-the-job training aboard ships or at repair centers. Advanced training is available for experienced marine engine mechanics to increase their troubleshooting skills and refresh their knowledge of maintenance and repair procedures.

During their careers, marine engine mechanics learn supervisory skills through leadership training and job experience. This training continues through the marine engine superintendent level with courses in management and administration. Typically, these courses address budgeting, personnel management, and training program development.

## RELATED MILITARY OCCUPATIONS

If you are interested in working with your hands and with machines, you may also want to consider a career as a machinist, aircraft mechanic, automotive and heavy equipment mechanic, or powerhouse mechanic. These occupational descriptions can be found in the Vehicle and Machinery Mechanic Occupations cluster and the Machine Operator and Precision Work Occupations cluster in the Military Enlisted Occupations section of this book.

## TYPICAL CAREER PATH

### MARINE ENGINE SUPERINTENDENT

Superintendents plan and direct maintenance and repair activities of marine engine mechanics on ships or at repair centers. They:

- Organize training programs and long-range maintenance programs
- Issue orders and instructions for attaining objectives
- Predict personnel, equipment, and material needs
- Develop and monitor safety programs
- Review and update requirements for watchstanding qualifications

**17-20 yrs**

### ENGINE ROOM SUPERVISOR

Marine engine mechanics who master the technical skills and demonstrate leadership qualities can advance to become engine room supervisors. At this level, they:

- Supervise repair of engines, propulsion machinery, and shipboard mechanical equipment
- Prepare reports on machinery repairs and performance
- Give technical advice and help
- Adjust work assignments for personnel development and cross-training
- Supervise an engine room watch and make sure that watchstanders maintain proper qualifications

**8-9 yrs**

### MARINE ENGINE MECHANIC

Mechanics perform more complicated engine repairs and help apprentice mechanics. At this level, they:

- Find the causes for inefficient engine and power plant operations
- Determine repairs needed and perform or direct repair work
- Instruct mechanics in operational procedures and in damage and casualty control
- Check main engine bearing and thrust clearance
- Clean, inspect, and repair mechanical and hydraulic governors (speed limiting devices)

**4-5 yrs**

### APPRENTICE MARINE ENGINE MECHANIC

After initial job training, apprentice mechanics work under close supervision to perform maintenance and repair. They:

- Clean and repair or replace hydraulic filters and fuel oil injectors
- Study blueprints and drawings to trace, locate, and inspect piping systems, valves, and other machinery parts
- Inspect and repair engine parts, such as rings, pistons, bearings, and cylinder heads
- Verify clearances between engine parts, using gauges and micrometers
- Service and repair hoisting machinery, ship elevators, and refrigeration and air conditioning equipment

**Timeline**

# MEDICAL SERVICE TECHNICIANS

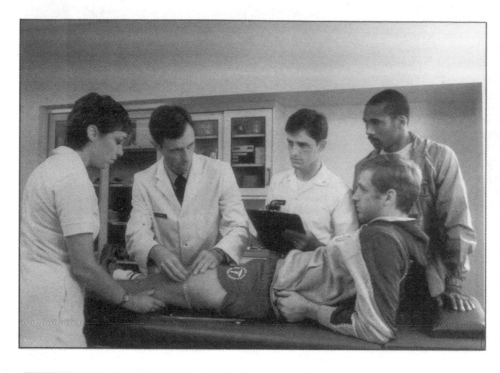

**M**edical service technicians help treat the sick, injured, and wounded. As a medical service technician, you assist doctors and nurses in giving medical care to service members and their families. You begin your career performing medical procedures, such as giving shots, providing emergency first aid, and taking patients' vital signs (pulse, temperature, respiration, and blood pressure). Later you may perform minor surgery, give emergency treatment, or provide treatment for the critically ill. There are opportunities to advance to medical service supervisor and perhaps to medical services coordinator in a large health care facility.

## DUTY ASSIGNMENT

Medical service technicians may be assigned to a hospital, clinic, emergency room, or ship's dispensary. They may also be assigned to a search and rescue unit or field hospital. Medical service technicians are assigned in both the United States and overseas. Technicians who specialize in a particular field of medicine may be limited to hospitals with medical departments in their specialty. As technicians advance in rank, most assignments are made to medical facilities where there are large staffs to manage.

## ADVANCEMENT

Since someone's life may hang in the balance, medical service technicians must be sure and precise in their work. During emergencies or combat, a technician may be called on to make life or death decisions. Medical service technicians must master handling, treating, and caring for patients and assisting medical officers. They must also become skilled at carrying out basic medical procedures.

Medical service technicians who choose one field of medicine as a specialty must complete advanced training and gain additional job experience to qualify in that specialty. After mastering the basic skills, the willingness to assume leadership roles helps technicians advance through the supervisory levels of this career.

### Profile: Larry Roberts

Larry Roberts feels that his career as an Army medical service technician has made the most of his abilities. "I'm good with people," he says, "and I react well in emergencies." His first assignment was with the 65th Medical Group, near Yongsan, Korea. In the beginning, he worked in the dispensary (clinic), caring for patients under the direction of a physician. When needed, he was sent to the demilitarized zone (DMZ) to treat casualties. Within a year, he had been promoted from private first class through sergeant and had become a medical noncommissioned officer (NCO).

From Korea, Larry was assigned to Letterman Army Medical Center, CA, where he cared for patients in special care units and the emergency room. He gave medications, changed dressings, maintained supplies, and helped patients after surgery. Larry liked working in the emergency room best. "There was always something happening," he says. "It kept me sharp and nimble."

Even though he enjoyed his work, Larry decided at this point to leave the Army. He was a civilian for only 83 days. He realized he liked his military career; it interested him more than any others he saw, so he reenlisted.

Larry was sent back to the DMZ in Korea for a year to be in charge of a dispensary. He was then transferred to the 377th Medivac Squadron, a helicopter squadron that picked up patients from all over Korea. His job was to keep the patients alive until they got to the hospital. Back in the States, Larry was assigned to an Army medical center. He started in the emergency room where he performed emergency patient care and went on ambulance runs, and ended his tour in the burn unit.

Larry's next assignments took him more into administration. By this time, Larry had been promoted through staff sergeant to sergeant first class. His best experience, he feels, was at Letterman Army Medical Center, where he was NCOIC of the department of ambulatory care. "Everything came together there," he says. "I had a good group, and I felt good about what I could do."

Larry is now the career advisor NCO for medical service technicians. With 18 years of travel and adventure behind him, he uses his wide knowledge of the field in helping select people for schools and assignments.

## SPECIALIZATION

Just as doctors specialize in specific fields of medicine, so may the medical service technicians who assist them. Medical fields that technicians choose as specialties include neurology (treating brain and nervous system disorders), allergy/immunology (treating patients with allergies), and aerospace physiology (assisting flight surgeons in caring for flight crews). Technicians may also specialize in a particular type of duty, such as emergency room and ambulance service, air search and rescue, or aeromedical evacuation (helping to transport patients and giving in-flight medical care). Some technicians train for independent duty to provide medical care at remote locations where doctors may not be available.

## TRAINING

The services provide medical service technicians with 9 to 24 months of basic and initial job training. It includes both classroom instruction and clinical (on-the-job) experience. Classroom instruction stresses the basics of patient care, emergency first aid, and medical and administrative service procedures. Clinical training, which takes place under a doctor's supervision, gives technicians experience in helping doctors examine and treat patients and teaches the skills needed to give shots, take patients' vital signs, and collect blood, tissue cultures, and other samples for laboratory tests. This training includes the completion of medical history forms and other administrative procedures.

Advanced technical training is available for medical service technicians in surgical procedures, preventive medicine, or medical diagnosis and treatment. At this point, technicians may also train for a specific field of medicine or in a particular duty assignment.

During their careers, medical service technicians learn supervisory skills through leadership training and experience. Specific training emphasizes evaluating personnel, planning and assigning duties, and supervising medical service operations. Such training continues through the medical services coordinator level with courses in management and administration of large hospitals and medical centers. Typically, these courses address budgeting, personnel management, and training program development.

## RELATED MILITARY OCCUPATIONS

If you are interested in a medical career, you may also want to consider other military medical occupations described in the Health Care Occupations cluster in the Military Enlisted Occupations section of this book.

## TYPICAL CAREER PATH

### MEDICAL SERVICES COORDINATOR

Expert supervisors may advance to the most senior level, where they coordinate supply, administrative, and paramedical activities. They:

- Help medical staff plan and direct patient care and treatment
- Plan and set up training, health care, and disaster control programs
- Oversee and inspect training, administrative, and patient care operations
- Set work priorities and procedures for medical service activities
- Recommend ways to improve facility operations and working conditions

### MEDICAL SERVICE SUPERVISOR

Highly skilled medical service technicians who show leadership ability are assigned supervisory responsibilities. Supervisors:

- Plan and schedule work, personnel, and training assignments
- Inspect medical service operations
- Write technical, personnel, and patient reports and records
- Help select sites and set up field medical facilities

### MEDICAL SERVICE TECHNICIAN

By increasing their skills, medical service aides may assume additional duties. As technicians, they:

- Train new workers in basic first aid and emergency medical care
- Treat shock victims and wounded, injured, or critically ill patients
- Drive ambulances and care for patients until they are admitted to a medical facility
- Perform minor surgery, suture wounds, and make and apply casts to broken limbs
- Prepare patients for surgery and perform preoperative and postoperative care

### MEDICAL SERVICE AIDE

After initial job training, medical service aides are assigned to a medical services unit. Working under close supervision, they:

- Fill out patients' medical history forms and other records
- Take and record patients' temperature, pulse, respiration, and blood pressure
- Assist in examining and treating patients who have minor injuries or common diseases
- Collect blood, cultures, and other specimens
- Provide emergency first aid and change bandages and dressings

**Timeline**

18-19 yrs

8-11 yrs

4-6 yrs

# MILITARY POLICE

**M**ilitary police (MPs) must always be ready for the unexpected. As an MP, you stand guard, conduct patrols, control traffic, arrest suspects, and enforce military laws and regulations. You begin your career performing duties as part of a base police force. As you gain experience and develop leadership skills, you may direct a small squad. There are opportunities to advance to law enforcement supervisor and perhaps to law enforcement superintendent.

## DUTY ASSIGNMENT

MPs are most often assigned to a security or law enforcement unit at a military base. The size of the base determines the size of the military police force and the duties of the MPs. At small bases, the force is small, and MPs usually carry out many different duties. At larger bases, where the force is larger, MPs are likely to be assigned to a specific duty. Most MPs are assigned to bases in the United States, but there is good opportunity for assignment to a base overseas, particularly in Europe.

## ADVANCEMENT

MPs must be able to think and react quickly in dangerous situations. They must master skills in patrolling, self-defense, and emergency response. MPs must show good judgment and a sense of responsibility, and remain calm under stress while performing their duties. To advance, MPs must master law enforcement responsibilities, such as crowd control, traffic enforcement, and crime prevention. Experienced police can choose to take additional training to qualify as detectives. After mastering the basic skills, the willingness to assume leadership roles helps MPs advance through the supervisory levels of this career.

In the Navy, a military police career starts at the supervisory level. Individuals may enter the military police at this point from almost any job in the Navy.

---

### Profile: Harold Peters

When Harold Peters joined the military, he knew he wanted to be a Marine. He actually began his career in the infantry. It was not until 14 years after he joined—after serving several tours in Vietnam and Japan and after receiving a number of decorations—that he became a military policeman (MP). "I felt I would be a good MP," he explains, "because I thought I could set a good example."

Harold had some previous experience serving special duty as a patrolman and desk sergeant in Japan, so he knew what to expect on his first assignment at Camp Pendleton, CA. As senior patrol sergeant and desk sergeant, he ensured base security and supervised the units on the base. He also enforced regulations. "As an MP, the only thing I did not like," he says, "was seeing young marines get in trouble, but sometimes I could talk to them and help them."

Harold was next assigned to corrections as a deck warden in the maximum security correctional facility. When he was reassigned back to MP duty, he be-

came operations chief at Camp Pendleton. He moved up to inspector and then to support operations officer in charge of weapons and materials. One assignment during this time was particularly important to him: he was placed in charge of police enforcement for a Vietnamese refugee camp.

Master Gunnery Sergeant Peters is now provost sergeant to the provost marshal for the morale, welfare, and performance of all enlisted personnel at Camp Lejeune, NC. In this position, he serves as liaison to the provost marshal on military police matters, conducts inspections of MPs, and assigns them to their duties.

Harold has given 29 years of service to the Marine Corps and his country. As he approaches his retirement, he says that he has liked helping young Marines, guiding them in their duties and responsibilities, and giving them encouragement. He is looking forward to his next (and last) assignment, which will be in Japan. "I've had an exciting career in the Marine Corps," he says. "I only wish it could last longer."

## SPECIALIZATION

Military police may specialize in one of several areas of law enforcement. For example, some MPs work with specially trained dogs to conduct patrols and detect drugs or explosives. Others work as security specialists to protect aircraft, missiles, nuclear weapons, and property from enemy and terrorist attacks.

## TRAINING

The services provide military police with 9 to 12 months of basic and initial job training. The MP's career begins with a basic law enforcement or security operations course that includes instruction and practical exercises in traffic control, self-defense, security patrols, convoy escorts, and suspect arrest and control. MPs also get on-the-job training from their squad leader and supervisor. Advanced training courses in traffic law enforcement, accident investigation, patrol techniques, and base security activities are available throughout a military police career.

Military police may also receive training focusing on specialized military duties. Dog handlers train to work with and care for their dogs. They learn obedience techniques and how to use a dog in law enforcement or security patrols. Security specialists train in the use of special weapons, security operations, and small unit tactics.

During their careers, MPs learn supervisory skills through leadership training and job experience. Leadership training develops skills in supervising security or general law enforcement programs and scheduling work activities. Training continues through the level of law enforcement superintendent, with courses in planning, managing, budgeting, and evaluating law enforcement activities.

## RELATED MILITARY OCCUPATIONS

If work in the protective services interests you, you may also want to consider a career as a detective, corrections specialist, or firefighter. See the Service Occupations cluster in the Military Enlisted Occupations section of this book for descriptions of these occupations.

## TYPICAL CAREER PATH

### LAW ENFORCEMENT SUPERINTENDENT

Law enforcement superintendents manage military police forces on large bases. At the most senior level, they:

- Decide where military police support is needed
- Coordinate military police work with civilian agencies
- Set police force goals and objectives
- Study accident reports and plan traffic safety programs

### LAW ENFORCEMENT SUPERVISOR

By demonstrating leadership skills, squad leaders advance to supervise several squads. At this level, they:

- Develop crime prevention programs
- Help MPs with problem cases
- Plan work schedules and make duty assignments
- Prepare technical and personnel reports

### SQUAD LEADER

Through experience and training, MPs advance to direct a small squad of police. Squad leaders:

- Give on-the-job training to new MPs
- Carry out traffic safety programs
- Direct crowd control operations
- Inspect squad members for proper uniform and equipment

### MILITARY POLICE

In their first assignments on a base police force after initial training, new MPs:

- Patrol areas on foot, by jeep, or by boat
- Direct the movement of people and traffic
- Investigate traffic accidents
- Arrest crime suspects
- Prepare criminal and accident reports

Timeline

18-20 yrs

8-11 yrs

4-6 yrs

# PERSONNEL SPECIALISTS

*T*he military recruits, trains, promotes, reassigns, and retires over a million people each year. As a personnel specialist, you help in the process of matching service requirements with individual needs. You begin your career performing clerical duties, such as adding information (duty assignments, health information, and promotions) to service records and centralized data bases. As you gain experience, you may enter records into a computer and give advice and assistance to service members and their dependents. There are opportunities to advance to personnel specialist and perhaps to personnel supervisor.

## DUTY ASSIGNMENT

Personnel specialists work in office settings on military bases or aboard ship, although some specialists may accompany their units in the field during special exercises. Personnel offices range in size according to the number of service members assigned to the base or unit; most large personnel offices also have some civilian employees. While most personnel specialists work at military bases in the United States, there is good opportunity for overseas assignment.

## ADVANCEMENT

Since personnel specialists work closely with people, they need to have good communications skills and to be able to work easily with others. To handle the volume of paperwork and detailed information needed for personnel actions, they must be logical, well organized, and have a good memory for details. They must show good judgment when processing requests for duty assignments or training. The ability to type and work with computers is particularly important for advancement in this career. After mastering the basic skills, the willingness to assume leadership roles helps personnel specialists advance through the supervisory levels of this career.

---

### Profile: Donna Grant

Technical Sergeant Donna Grant gets shocked, but positive, reactions when people discover she is a career woman in the military. She likes the opportunities open to her in the military and feels that they are basically the same for women as they are for men. She believes that "if you give it everything you've got, the Air Force will give you all it has to offer."

Donna finished the self-paced initial training course for personnel specialists in just 6 weeks because she already knew how to type. Her first assignment was at Lowry Air Force Base (AFB), CO, where she scheduled testing for personnel eligible for promotion. She quickly advanced to airman and then to airman first class. At Lowry, she met and married her husband, who is also in the Air Force.

On her next assignment at the Royal Air Force in Upper Heyford, England, she was responsible not only for test scheduling, but also for reviewing, maintaining, and organizing records for all the enlisted and officer promotion programs. "At this point, I really dug into the career field, started learning things for myself, and began building a good work reputation." She achieved senior airman and sergeant

and soon became the assistant noncommissioned officer in charge (NCOIC).

Over the next several years, Donna's assignments took her into various areas of personnel administration. At Offut AFB, NE, she was the NCOIC of processing base personnel leaving the Air Force. Here, she received the Meritorious Service Medal for the high quality of her work and was also promoted to staff sergeant. Donna was head of quality force on her next assignment at Thule AFB, Greenland, a small base 600 miles south of the North Pole. "There were only a few people in our office, so we all had a lot of responsibilities and got some really good experience. But our 4th of July baseball game was played in the snow."

Donna worked on separations and retirements on her next assignment at Davis Monthan AFB, AZ. As part of her duties, she implemented computer programs and gave briefings on promotions. Through her efforts, the base personnel office was able to make significant improvements in its promotions and testing process. Technical Sergeant Donna Grant is now the NCOIC of the promotion branch at Scott AFB, IL.

## TRAINING

The services provide personnel specialists with 9 to 11 months of basic and initial job training. It combines classroom instruction and on-the-job training. Classroom training emphasizes typing, interviewing techniques, test interpretation, classification testing, and routing and filing of forms and records. Supervisors give on-the-job training focusing on office procedures and the operation of personnel computer systems. Self-study also helps clerks learn about military careers and the services' needs for personnel in critical job areas.

During their career, personnel specialists learn supervisory skills through leadership training and job experience. This training continues through the personnel supervisor level with courses in management and administration. Typically, these courses address budgeting, personnel management, and training program development.

## RELATED MILITARY OCCUPATIONS

If you are interested in becoming a personnel specialist, you may also want to consider a career as an administrative support specialist, recruiter, or payroll specialist. See the Administrative Occupations cluster in the Military Enlisted Occupations section of this book for descriptions of these and related occupations.

## TYPICAL CAREER PATH

### PERSONNEL SUPERVISOR

Personnel supervisors supervise the staff of a personnel office or advise commanders on personnel matters. They:

- Evaluate personnel office procedures and work load
- Organize and schedule training programs
- Orient new personnel clerks and assign them to supervisors for on-the-job training
- Develop operating budgets and track expenditures
- Advise supervisors and commanders on personnel matters

### PERSONNEL SPECIALIST

Personnel clerks who have mastered the work routine may become personnel specialists. At this level, they:

- Supervise the processing of personnel action forms (promotions, awards, and reassignments) and the maintenance of service record files
- Train and assist new personnel clerks
- Assign work to personnel clerks and monitor their job performance
- Conduct pre-retirement seminars
- Assist servicemembers and dependents who have special problems, such as a need for special medical care

### PERSONNEL CLERK

After initial job training, personnel clerks perform routine clerical and administrative support duties to collect and maintain military personnel records. They:

- Interview incoming personnel, and test and evaluate their qualifications
- Prepare and maintain servicemember personnel record files
- Prepare and type requests for orders, correspondence, personnel action forms, and related records and reports
- Maintain files and review personnel records with servicemembers
- Use computers to store and retrieve personnel information
- Process paperwork for promotions, retirements, reenlistments, separations (discharges), and reclassifications (changes in job specialties)
- Discuss training courses, duty assignments, and educational materials with servicemembers

**Timeline**

**17-21 yrs**

**5-7 yrs**

# RADAR AND SONAR EQUIPMENT REPAIRERS

ARMY
NAVY
AIR FORCE
MARINE CORPS
COAST GUARD

**R**adar and sonar equipment is used to detect objects in the air, under water, or at long distances that could not otherwise be seen. As a radar and sonar equipment repairer, you maintain and repair parts of these complex systems. You begin your career working under close supervision repairing simple parts and units on one system. As you gain experience and skill, you take more responsibility and make more difficult repairs. There are opportunities to advance to repair supervisor and perhaps to electronic repair superintendent.

## DUTY ASSIGNMENT

Radar and sonar equipment repairers work in repair units on military installations or aboard ships or aircraft. They may be assigned to units that use radar and sonar equipment or to large facilities equipped to repair, overhaul, or modify complex systems. Repairers work at military installations across the nation and overseas. There is good opportunity for overseas assignment.

## ADVANCEMENT

Radar and sonar equipment repairers find and fix malfunctions in complex electrical and electronic systems. They start by mastering a single radar or sonar system. To do this, they need to understand the principles of electronics and how the equipment works. They must develop skills in reading schematic diagrams, following detailed work procedures, and using special tools and test instruments. To advance, repairers must develop the analytical skills needed to diagnose the cause of equipment failure. After mastering the basic skills, the willingness to assume leadership roles helps radar and sonar equipment repairers advance through the supervisory levels of this career.

### Profile: Richard Block

Richard Block selected electronics as his occupation when he joined the Air Force because, as he says, "I like working with my hands, and I like to see the results of my efforts." He was assigned to become an aircraft control and warning radar specialist.

After basic training, Richard was sent to Keesler Air Force Base (AFB), MS, for a 10-month training course in repairing aircraft control and warning radar. His first assignment as a radar repairman took him to West Germany where he worked as part of a mobile tactical squadron that was often sent on missions to other parts of Europe. Richard liked the travel—"a big change from high school"—and he also liked working with a small group. He says a NATO exercise in Spain was the highlight of his 3-year tour.

For the next 5 years, Richard's assignments alternated between duty overseas and in the United States. He worked in Ajo, AZ, on height finder radar and then moved up to assistant maintenance support supervisor of repairs on aircraft radar at Palermo, NJ. The Air Force then sent him to Korea for 15 months, where he maintained supporting radar equipment, such as scopes, mappers, trainers, coder/decoders, and interrogator sets. Back in the United States, Richard was assigned to coordinate radar maintenance between his division and the work centers. He then returned overseas to Okinawa for a year as assistant auxiliary maintenance supervisor.

The next 8 years at Cape Charles, VA, were important for Richard. He found himself moving quickly into positions of greater responsibility. Starting as height maintenance radar supervisor for an air division, he advanced to quality control supervisor. In this position, he evaluated personnel, inspected work centers for maintenance, and monitored schemes (which show the placement of equipment).

Richard is now stationed at Warner Robbins AFB, GA, but has retrained to work on air traffic control radar. As maintenance support supervisor, he coordinates the maintenance of radar equipment near the airstrip and air traffic control tower.

## SPECIALIZATION

Radar and sonar equipment repairers usually specialize in equipment designed for a specific purpose, such as:

- Air defense radar used around the world to detect enemy missiles, planes, and satellites
- Air traffic control radar used to identify and manage aircraft takeoffs, landings, and flight patterns
- Submarine or ship sonar used for underwater detection and surveillance

## TRAINING

The services provide apprentice radar and sonar equipment repairers with 6 to 24 months of basic and initial job training. Initial job training is usually provided in two phases. The first phase consists of basic electrical and electronics training, including electronic theory and principles. The second phase consists of both classroom and hands-on training in a single radar or sonar system. Classroom instruction focuses on applying electronic principles to the specific system. Hands-on training with actual equipment gives experience in the practical application of classroom instruction. Radar and sonar repairers may take advanced electronics courses or training on additional systems.

During their careers, radar and sonar repairers learn supervisory skills through leadership training and job experience. This training continues through the level of electronic repair superintendent with courses in management and administration. Typically, these courses address budgeting, repair shop operations, training program development, and personnel and work load management.

## RELATED MILITARY OCCUPATIONS

If you are interested in electronic and electrical equipment repair, you may also want to consider a career as a radio equipment repairer, aircraft electrician, ship electrician, electronic weapons systems repairer, or computer equipment repairer. See the Electronic and Electrical Equipment Repair Occupations cluster in the Military Enlisted Occupations section of this book for a description of these and other related military occupations.

## TYPICAL CAREER PATH

Timeline

### ELECTRONIC REPAIR SUPERINTENDENT

Electronic repair superintendents plan, direct, and control activities at radar or sonar repair shops. They:

- Coordinate repair reports and requests for parts
- Prepare personnel, technical, and administrative reports
- Determine needs for personnel, equipment, and spare parts
- Conduct safety and quality control inspections

**17-20 yrs**

### REPAIR SUPERVISOR

Skilled radar and sonar repairers may advance to become supervisors of electronic repair units. At this level, they:

- Develop standard operating procedures
- Assign and reassign work to reduce slowdowns and meet schedules
- Evaluate and train apprentice repairers
- Inspect work and give technical guidance
- Instruct workers in major changes to existing equipment

**7-12 yrs**

### RADAR AND SONAR REPAIRER

As their skills increase, repairers perform more difficult tasks. Radar and sonar repairers:

- Find problems, using troubleshooting techniques, and test equipment
- Use hand tools to replace broken electrical and electronic parts
- Align and adjust electromechanical assemblies to needed settings
- Test repaired equipment, using special test equipment, such as circuit analyzers (tools that test circuit boards) and continuity meters (tools that trace the flow of electricity)
- Calibrate (adjust) test equipment

**3-6 yrs**

### APPRENTICE RADAR AND SONAR REPAIRER

After initial job training, apprentice radar and sonar repairers work under close supervision. They learn preventive maintenance and simple electronic repairs. At this level, they:

- Read repair tags and maintenance orders to determine work tasks
- Check for loose mountings, poor connections, and cracked resistors
- Replace faulty tubes, wiring, semiconductors, and circuit boards
- Clean and lubricate mechanical parts and connections

# RADAR AND SONAR OPERATORS

ARMY
NAVY
AIR FORCE
MARINE CORPS
COAST GUARD

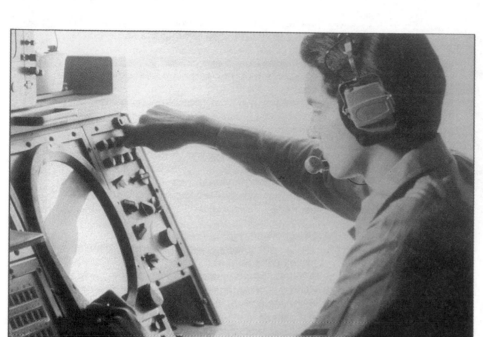

The information provided by radar and sonar operators is used to alert air squadrons; to direct missile, mortar, artillery, and naval gunfire; and to help U.S. forces evade enemy detection. As a radar or sonar operator, you identify, classify, and track objects according to their characteristic echoes (sonar) or displays (radar) on your headphones or screen. You begin your career by working closely with an experienced operator to develop your skills in identifying and classifying objects. As you become more experienced, you work more independently and take greater responsibility. There are opportunities to advance to radar or sonar supervisor and perhaps to operations superintendent.

## DUTY ASSIGNMENT

Radar and sonar operators work in operations centers or command and control facilities on land or aboard aircraft, ships, or submarines. They work at military bases throughout the world, on coastal waterways, and on the high seas. In some radar and sonar specialties, operators must qualify for flight or submarine duty.

## ADVANCEMENT

Tracking objects by radar or sonar requires constant vigilance. Radar and sonar operators must be able to concentrate in order to identify and track one object on a screen full of images. They must be alert for interference, jamming, and masking techniques used by enemy forces to disrupt equipment operations. Once an object has been determined to be a potential enemy threat, it must be rapidly identified; the operators must classify the object and determine the relative strength of the attack. They must then maintain a constant vigil to find the location, course, bearing, and speed of the enemy threat. Operators must also learn to recognize natural objects, such as sea life, land masses, and rain squalls or thunderstorms. After mastering the basic skills, the willingness to assume leadership roles helps operators advance through the supervisory levels of this career.

## Profile: Juan Delgado

Juan Delgado had always been fascinated by submarines. So after enlisting in the Navy in advanced electronics, he volunteered for submarine duty. "After 16 years," Juan says, "I'm still glad I made that decision."

Juan's trip to boot camp was his first airplane ride and his first trip away from home. After this, things began to happen fast. By the time he left boot camp, he had been promoted to seaman. He then went to submarine school for training in electricity, electronics, sonar, and a specific sonar system. On leaving, he was selected class leader and became a petty officer third class.

Juan's first assignment was on the USS *Wahoo,* operating and maintaining the sonar system. Life aboard the submarine was all Juan hoped it would be. He liked the camaraderie among the men, and he enjoyed learning to stand all the different watches. During his second year on the *Wahoo*, he was promoted to petty officer second class and soon after became sonar supervisor. After his tour on the *Wahoo*, Juan went back to school in San Diego for 6 months of training on a new sonar system. He made petty officer first

class soon after he arrived and did so well in the course that he was asked to stay on as an instructor.

Juan went back to sea on the USS *William H. Bates*, a nuclear submarine, as the Leading Petty Officer of a 12-man division. Since he had never operated the ship's particular sonar system, he had to qualify to operate it through on-the-job training. He then became sonar supervisor. When the sonar system was replaced during a ship refit, Juan monitored the installation of the new system and conducted training for other operators. He was able to use this experience on his next assignment—monitoring the installation of sonar equipment on the new PCU *Houston*. He also wrote the training plan for the equipment and trained the entire sonar division. Two years later, he made chief petty officer and remained on board as the chief sonar technician.

Juan likes his career in sonar. "The new technology keeps me challenged," he says. He is also proud to see the success of people he has trained. Juan says he has one last ambition for his Navy career—to be the Chief of the Boat, the top enlisted person aboard a submarine.

## SPECIALIZATION

Operators specialize in either radar or sonar systems, and both types of operators may specialize in a particular military function. Many operators monitor the early warning defense systems at isolated radar posts or in airborne command centers. Others operate long-range air search radar aboard ships or work with field radar units directing mortar, antiaircraft, and artillery fire from helicopters. Some operators conduct antisubmarine searches from helicopters. Others work on ships or submarines to detect enemy ships and navigation obstacles.

## TRAINING

The services provide apprentice radar or sonar operators with 6 to 18 months of basic and initial job training. Through a combination of classroom instruction and on-the-job training, trainees learn how radar and sonar equipment works, how to identify different objects, and how to operate equipment. Most equipment operators are trained to perform some maintenance of the systems they operate; sonar operators are fully trained to maintain and repair their equipment. At any time during their careers, radar and sonar operators can expect to be retrained as new equipment becomes available. For sonar operators, retraining to maintain and repair equipment may be extensive.

During the early part of their careers, operators who will become flight crew members are given specialized training in swimming, parachuting, air crew survival, and aircraft emergency procedures. Sonar operators who want to qualify for submarine duty must also complete specialized training.

During their careers, radar and sonar operators learn supervisory skills through leadership training and job experience. This training continues through the operations superintendent level with courses in management and administration. Typically, these courses address budgeting, personnel management, and training program development.

## RELATED MILITARY OCCUPATIONS

If you are interested in a career as a radar or sonar operator, you may also want to consider a career in a related occupation, such as air traffic controller, weather observer, space systems specialist, radio operator, or radio intelligence operator. See the Engineering, Science, and Technical Occupations cluster in the Military Enlisted Occupations section of this book for descriptions of these occupations.

## TYPICAL CAREER PATH

### OPERATIONS SUPERINTENDENT

Radar and sonar operations superintendents perform administrative and technical duties. They:

- Plan, schedule, and evaluate training programs
- Assign personnel to duty positions and determine work priorities
- Inform and advise superiors on the use and capabilities of personnel, equipment, and material
- Prepare reports, correspondence, and technical instructions

### RADAR OR SONAR SUPERVISOR

Operators who master the work routine and demonstrate leadership qualities may advance to become supervisors of ground, airborne, or shipboard radar or sonar units. They:

- Supervise training of personnel who operate, maintain, and repair radar or sonar equipment
- Give technical advice and assistance to operators
- Help superiors develop tactical procedures (responses to potential war situations)
- Conduct tactical training exercises

### RADAR OR SONAR OPERATOR

Skilled apprentice operators may advance to become radar or sonar operators. At this level, they:

- Ensure that radar or sonar stations are manned during watch and rest periods
- Help operators in multi-target operations and exercises
- Train and instruct operators in the use of equipment
- Operate radar and sonar computer equipment
- Test and replace faulty components (parts) and assemblies (major sections) of equipment

### APPRENTICE RADAR OR SONAR OPERATOR

After initial job training, radar and sonar operators find, classify, and track the movement of airborne, surface, and underwater objects. They:

- Observe objects that appear on radarscope or sonarscope display screens
- Determine the position and movement of objects
- Identify radar or sonar contacts as aircraft, missiles, ships, submarines, or natural objects
- Relay information to pilots, gunners, and navigators by internal communications or radio equipment
- Keep records on objects identified and perform preventive maintenance on equipment

Timeline

18-21 yrs

8-11 yrs

4-6 yrs

# RADIOLOGIC (X-RAY) TECHNICIANS

ARMY
NAVY
AIR FORCE
COAST GUARD

**R**adiology (the use of X-rays) helps doctors detect injuries and illnesses and even treat some diseases. As a radiologic technician, you may take X-rays or give tests using radioisotopes (radioactive liquids) and radiation scanners (Geiger counters). You begin your career performing X-ray procedures under the supervision of a physician. As you develop and master your radiologic skills and work techniques, you are assigned more difficult duties. There are opportunities to advance to radiologic supervisor and radiologic services coordinator.

## DUTY ASSIGNMENT

Radiologic technicians may be assigned to a medical service unit aboard ship, to a base hospital or clinic, or to a mobile medical unit. Nuclear medicine technicians and radiologic supervisors are usually assigned to large hospitals, since the equipment and work load at these facilities require such skilled workers. Most radiologic technicians are assigned to units in the United States, but there is good opportunity for overseas duty, especially early in a career.

## ADVANCEMENT

Since X-rays expose patients to radiation, radiologic technicians must be precise and careful in each procedure. They must be able to work with sick and injured patients and obtain the proper X-rays for study by a doctor. To do this, they must be able to position patients, follow doctors' orders, and operate X-ray equipment. Mastering different techniques, such as X-ray, ultrasound, or computerized scanning, is also important for advancement in this career. Radiologic technicians show their mastery of basic skills through certification by the American Registry of Radiologic Technicians. Certification is awarded to technicians who complete the classroom training given by the military and work for 1 year under the supervision of a radiologist. After mastering the various radiologic techniques and procedures, the willingness to assume leadership roles helps technicians advance through the supervisory levels of this career.

### Profile: Ernie Hughes

When Ernie Hughes joined the Navy, he had a guarantee of training in the medical field. He knew he would eventually specialize, but following boot camp, he first went to school to become a hospital corpsman. At the Great Lakes Naval Training Center, Waukegan, IL, he got what he calls "a working knowledge" of anatomy, nursing, and pharmacological chemistry. His first assignment was at the Naval Regional Medical Center, Millington, TN, caring for patients in the intensive care unit. He also worked in medical records and the dispensary, checking throats, taking temperatures, and sending patients to a doctor if he found a problem.

After a year, Ernie was assigned to the medical records unit at the Naval Regional Medical Center, New Orleans, LA. He also worked part-time in the pediatric clinic and the emergency room. As an extra duty, he flew on sea/air rescue missions with the Coast Guard. For this, he was commended for work done above and beyond the call of duty. "My time spent flying with the Coast Guard," Ernie says, "was some of the best of my career."

With 3 years as a hospital corpsman behind him, Ernie began his training for a specialty in nuclear medicine. The training was in two parts. First, Ernie attended classes in math, chemistry, anatomy, physics, and radiopharmacy at the Naval School of Health Sciences, Bethesda, MD. Then he went to the Naval Regional Medical Center, San Diego, CA, for on-the-job training in his new specialty. Under guidance, he operated and maintained radioactive isotope therapy apparatus to do imaging, blood work, and laboratory tests.

Ernie's first, and current, assignment as a clinical nuclear medicine technician is at the Armed Forces Radiobiology Research Institute, Bethesda, MD. Ernie helps medical officers prepare and conduct radioactive isotope research. His work has included studies of the effects of various levels of radiation on organs of the body and research on neuroreceptors in the brain.

Petty Officer First Class Ernie Hughes likes his specialty. "I had to work hard to get here," he says, "but now I have a respected career that challenges me. I am in a position to make decisions and to work on my own."

## SPECIALIZATION

Radiologic technicians may specialize as either X-ray or nuclear medicine technicians. X-ray technicians operate sensitive equipment to take X-rays for doctors to study. Nuclear medicine specialists help doctors diagnose and treat patients through procedures that use radiation-producing materials. They may administer solutions or operate equipment that gives measured radiation therapy to cancer patients.

## TRAINING

The services provide radiologic technicians with 12 to 24 months of basic and initial job training. It combines classroom instruction and clinical (on-the-job) experience. Classroom instruction stresses developing X-ray film, operating fixed and mobile X-ray units, and taking routine X-rays of the arms, legs, trunk, and skull. Clinical training is conducted under the supervision of a radiologist (M.D.) and a senior radiologic technician. This on-the-job training includes moving and positioning patients, completing and maintaining patients' records, and conducting soft tissue radiographs and bone surveys. Radiologic technicians may take advanced training in specialized techniques, such as angiography (images of blood vessels), xeroradiography (machines producing positive exposures), and computerized axial tomography (CAT) scans (images of a specified level in the body).

Specialists in nuclear medicine need an additional year of training. This training includes 16 weeks of classroom instruction in physics, chemistry, mathematics, and the laboratory procedures needed to work with radioactive liquids. Training also includes operating and maintaining equipment for nuclear medicine diagnosis and therapy. The rest of the year is spent in clinical (on-the-job) training to learn the application of safety, chemical, and medical techniques for different nuclear medicine studies.

During their careers, radiologic technicians learn supervisory skills through leadership training and job experience. This training continues through senior management levels with courses in management, administration, and advanced technical skills. Typically, these courses address budgeting, supervisory techniques, training program development, and recent advances in the field of radiology.

## RELATED MILITARY OCCUPATIONS

If you are interested in using modern technologies to help others with medical problems, you may also want to consider a career as a medical laboratory technician, cardiopulmonary or electroencephalographic (EEG) technician, or an operating room technician. See the Health Care Occupations cluster in the Military Enlisted Occupations section of this book for descriptions of these occupations.

## TYPICAL CAREER PATH

### RADIOLOGIC SERVICES COORDINATOR

At the most senior level, radiologic technicians supervise large radiology departments. At this level, they:

- Plan and direct training programs for radiologic aides and technicians
- Coordinate radiology programs and activities with other health specialists
- Develop guidelines for conducting standard radiologic procedures and setting work priorities
- Inspect radiology departments and monitor work procedures

### RADIOLOGIC SUPERVISOR

Skilled radiologic technicians who show leadership ability may be assigned to supervisory positions. As supervisors, they:

- Give technical help to aides and technicians
- Assist doctors with difficult cases
- Plan and schedule work assignments
- Prepare technical, personnel, and administrative reports
- Supervise radiation surveying, monitoring, and decontamination control duties

### RADIOLOGIC TECHNICIAN

By mastering basic skills and completing additional training, radiologic technicians are assigned more difficult duties. At this level, they:

- Train new personnel to use X-ray equipment
- Maintain and adjust X-ray equipment
- Collect X-rays and other tests for physicians' use
- Complete patients' files and store X-ray film
- Approve the radiograph techniques and computations of new technicians

### RADIOLOGIC AIDE

After initial job training, new radiologic staff are assigned to radiology departments of hospitals, field units, or ship dispensaries. Working under close supervision, they:

- Move patients to and from the radiology unit
- Position patients on X-ray tables
- Load and position film holders, set controls for power and time, and take X-rays
- Move and set up mobile X-ray machines
- Develop X-ray film

Timeline

18-20 yrs

8-10 yrs

4-6 yrs

# RELIGIOUS PROGRAM SPECIALISTS

ARMY
NAVY
AIR FORCE

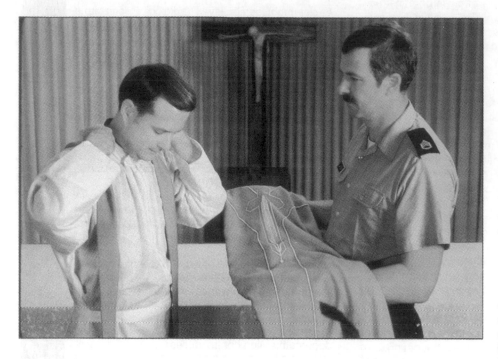

**R**eligious program specialists help chaplains meet the pastoral needs of military personnel and their families. As a religious program specialist, you keep the chaplain's office running smoothly, coordinate religious activities, and manage the chapel. You begin your career typing, filing, and performing clerical duties in chapel offices. As you gain experience, you take more responsibility for organizing religious activities, such as chapel services, weddings, baptisms, and funerals. There are opportunities to advance to chapel supervisor and perhaps to chapel operations coordinator.

## DUTY ASSIGNMENT

Most religious program specialists work on large military bases at base chapels and in chaplains' offices. They may also serve aboard ships or with combat forces in the field. Most religious service specialists work at bases in the United States, but there is opportunity for overseas assignment.

## ADVANCEMENT

Because religious program specialists represent the chaplain in day-to-day activities, they must be mature, sincere, and dependable. They must have good typing and clerical skills and a good command of business math to run the religious program office efficiently. Religious program specialists must understand the principles of different faiths to arrange ceremonies. They must also be able to work easily with people of all backgrounds. Administrative and organizational skills become more important as a service member advances in this career. The willingness to assume leadership roles and take on added responsibility helps religious program specialists advance through the supervisory levels of this career.

### Profile: Michael Kowalski

Sergeant First Class Michael (Mike) Kowalski enlisted in the Army for three reasons: "I wanted to serve God, serve my country, and get experience." As a chaplain assistant, he feels he is doing all three.

In training, Mike learned the two sides of his job: administration and religious support. On his first assignment at Fort Carson, CO, Mike supported the Jewish chapel program, which included maintaining a kosher kitchen. At his second job there, he supported programs at the division artillery chapel. This job also took him with the troops on training exercises. He helped set up the field chapel tent, organize field services, and provide moral support to the troops. "This is what the job is all about," Mike says, "helping support the individual soldier." During this assignment, Mike rose to the rank of sergeant.

Mike was next assigned to a military hospital in Landstuhl, West Germany, where he served as the noncommissioned officer in charge (NCOIC) of the hospital chaplain's office. This was a busy time for Mike and his wife. Not only did they provide support to hospital patients and their families, but they also organized a full-scale chapel program for the Landstuhl community. This included conducting chapel services, religious education programs, and activities in music and drama. Mike also supervised chaplain assistants and was responsible for the chaplains' fund.

Back in the States, Mike went to Fort Knox, KY, as the NCOIC of the main post chapel. As a staff sergeant, he provided support for all the chapel programs, supervised and trained the chaplain assistants, and took care of the chapel and its equipment. When Mike was switched to the staff chaplain's office, he handled budgeting and contracting for material and equipment for the 12 chapels on the post.

Mike is now assigned to the U.S. Army Chaplains' Center and School, Fort Monmouth, NJ, as an instructor. He teaches new chaplain assistants how to support chapel activities. Mike recently returned from the Army Airborne School, where he became parachute qualified.

Mike feels that his career has provided him a unique opportunity. "I love people," he says. "My job has given me a chance to be with them and help them."

## TRAINING

The services provide religious program specialists with 6 to 9 months of basic and initial job training. Training focuses on developing clerical and administrative support skills. Depending on the assignment, training may be given in religious support duties. Chapel supervisors and chapel operations coordinators may receive advanced training in accounting, personnel management, and the preparation of special administrative records and reports.

During their careers, religious program specialists learn supervisory skills through job experience and leadership training. This training continues through the level of chapel operations coordinator with courses in management and administration. Typically, these courses address budgeting, personnel management, and training program development.

## RELATED MILITARY OCCUPATIONS

If you are interested in service-oriented and people-to-people work, you may also want to consider other occupations in the Human Services Occupations cluster or the Service Occupations cluster in the Military Enlisted Occupations section of this book.

## TYPICAL CAREER PATH

### CHAPEL OPERATIONS COORDINATOR

Supervisors may advance to become chapel operations coordinators responsible for religious program activities in subordinate commands. At this level, they:

- Prepare and conduct command briefings on religious programs
- Coordinate worship schedules and educational materials development
- Set goals, objectives, and priorities
- Visit, monitor, and review the performance of religious program specialists
- Prepare and route consolidated reports on religious program activities
- Coordinate programs with hospitals, welfare agencies, and confinement facilities

### CHAPEL SUPERVISOR

Skilled specialists may advance to become chapel supervisors responsible for organizing and leading chaplains' offices. Chapel supervisors:

- Oversee religious program specialists
- Train personnel and assign them their duties
- Coordinate and supervise volunteers and part-time workers
- Review correspondence and reports for accuracy and completeness
- Prepare religious packets for prisoners and hospital patients
- Coordinate recruitment and training of ushers, lay readers, and religious school teachers

### RELIGIOUS PROGRAM SPECIALIST

After initial job training, new personnel are normally assigned to a base chapel where they learn to:

- Type letters, marriage records, certificates, and confirmation, baptism, and funeral records
- Prepare the chapel for religious services or special ceremonies, such as weddings, funerals, and memorial services
- Help the chaplain conduct religious services and ceremonies
- Help recruit and train ushers and religious school teachers
- Schedule the chaplain's appointments and receive visitors in the chaplain's office
- Type bulletins for worshippers and maintain office files

**Timeline**

16-18 yrs

6-8 yrs

# SPECIAL OPERATIONS FORCES

ARMY
NAVY
AIR FORCE
MARINE CORPS

**S**pecial operations teams are small, highly trained combat units. They carry out especially difficult and dangerous missions. To qualify for special operations, you must complete an intense physical conditioning program. As a special operations team member, you practice combat and survival tactics in all types of climates and environments (in jungles, swamps, deserts, or under water). You may raid enemy positions, go on scouting or rescue missions, or undertake demolition operations. There are opportunities to advance to special operations team leader and perhaps to special operations coordinator.

## DUTY ASSIGNMENT

After qualifying for special operations, the new team member is assigned to the special operations unit for his service: the Army Green Berets, the Navy SEALs, the Air Force Pararescue Teams, or the Marine Corps Force Reconnaissance Teams. The units are small select forces, and the number of duty assignments are limited. However, the units may be deployed to train or perform missions anywhere in the world.

## RELATED MILITARY OCCUPATIONS

If you are interested in a special operations career, you may also want to consider the other Combat Specialty Occupations described in the Military Occupations section of this book. Other similar military occupations are found throughout the Military Enlisted Occupations section of this book. These occupations include medical service technician, diver, radio operator, blasting specialist, and air crew member.

## Profile: Thomas Wilson

When Thomas (Tom) Wilson received his draft notice, he could have easily received a student deferment. "But I wanted to do my part," he says, "so I decided to join the Army." Because he was small, his family and friends teased him about enlisting. To prove himself, he decided to enlist for what he thought was the toughest training available—airborne. Then, while he was at Fort Gordon training to be a heavy weapons specialist, he heard about the special forces. He applied because it was an even bigger challenge. "By the time I finished airborne and special forces training," Tom says, "I felt there wasn't anything I couldn't do."

For the next 6 years, Tom was a member of a special forces team with assignments in Fort Bragg (NC), Vietnam, and Fort Devins (MA). He started as a junior demolition man and advanced to team engineer. Tom describes his assignments as continuous training. He went on field exercises all over the world, learning jungle operations in Panama and northern warfare in Alaska. He even went to school to learn French and Spanish. Vietnam, Tom says, was the time he was finally able to put his training to work, a modest statement from a Green Beret

with a purple heart and two bronze stars. Throughout his career, Tom has had further training in operations and intelligence, advanced engineering, and leadership, but he feels that he learned the most during his years as a member of a special forces team.

Tom spent the next 3 years as an engineering sergeant for Army battalions on Okinawa and at Fort Bragg, NC. He coordinated with other Army units to supply equipment and support for battalion activities. At Fort Bragg, Tom was promoted to first sergeant and assigned as operations sergeant for a special forces team. He was then assigned as a first sergeant at the Headquarters of a battalion in Korea. In this job, Tom supervised over 200 people providing administrative support to the battalion. He returned to the States as battalion intelligence sergeant for the 82nd Airborne.

In his current job as a combat development project noncommissioned officer (NCO), Tom evaluates new techniques, equipment, and methods for the special forces. He was recently promoted to sergeant major—a goal he set for himself after returning from Vietnam.

## ADVANCEMENT

The competition for getting into and advancing in the special operations forces is keen. To succeed, special operations team members must be decisive, creative, and self-reliant. They must show resourcefulness and quick action in rapidly changing and dangerous situations. They must be able to communicate ideas effectively, recall detailed instructions, and analyze new problems quickly. In addition, team members must keep themselves in top physical condition.

All special operations candidates are required to complete job training in another military occupation before entering this career. Many serve for several years in another occupation before volunteering for special operations forces. Many also return to their original occupation after serving in special operations.

Advancement to more senior levels of special operations calls for the ability to direct and coordinate several critical activities at the same time. For example, an individual may coordinate the ground activities of a special operations team while directing close tactical air support or cargo delivery.

## SPECIALIZATION

The demanding nature of special operations missions calls for team members to focus their training. Search and rescue missions call for skills in survival, parachuting, and evasion of enemy forces. Underwater demolition missions require skills in scuba diving and the use of explosives. Guerrilla warfare requires training in special weapons and small group combat and infiltration tactics.

In special operations units, each team member usually concentrates on one area, such as engineering, intelligence, communications, or medical services. However, most are trained and skilled in more than one area to back up other team members.

## TRAINING

The services provide 12 to 24 months of special qualifications training to volunteers selected for special operations duty. The initial phase of training stresses physical conditioning. This is among the most challenging training given by the services; not everyone who attempts this training can meet the strict requirements for completion.

In addition to physical conditioning, training is given in reconnaissance, unconventional warfare, small unit tactics, and the use of special weapons. Special skills training may also be given in parachuting, scuba diving, and survival techniques. On-the-job training is conducted through practical field exercises in different climates and terrain, including mountains, swamps, and winter conditions. Specialized training is also given to prepare teams for individual missions.

## TYPICAL CAREER PATH

### SPECIAL OPERATIONS COORDINATOR

Team leaders may advance to coordinate the activities and training of special operations forces teams. At this level, they:

- Plan unit training or formal special operations forces training courses
- Plan and coordinate multiteam operations
- Assign teams to specialized areas of assignment
- Develop and evaluate new procedures and techniques
- Recruit and organize friendly foreign personnel for special operations
- Advise special forces commanders on planning missions

### TEAM LEADER

Highly skilled and motivated team members can advance to become team leaders. Special operations team leaders:

- Train team members in communications, combat tactics, and intelligence gathering
- Assign specific mission tasks to team members
- Instruct allied (friendly) forces in the use of weapons and guerrilla tactics
- Collect, interpret, and distribute intelligence information
- Plan air rescue, air delivery, and other airborne operations
- Plan and lead sabotage and combat raids in enemy territory

### TEAM MEMBER

After initial special operations training, special operations team members are assigned to small elite units where they continually train to improve their special skills. Team members:

- Go on reconnaissance (scouting) missions to identify terrain features and spot enemy troop and gun positions
- Infiltrate (go behind) enemy lines to carry out demolition raids or attack enemy positions
- Plant or clear mine fields on land and under water
- Carry out rescue and recovery operations for stranded or trapped servicemen
- Give regular and emergency medical treatment in the field

**This career is open only to men.**

Timeline

15-20 yrs

6-8 yrs

# WEAPONS MAINTENANCE TECHNICIANS

ARMY
NAVY
AIR FORCE
MARINE CORPS
COAST GUARD

**M**ost modern weapons—from ballistic missiles to field artillery—have electronic parts. As a weapons maintenance technician, you perform electrical, mechanical, and electronic repairs on one type of weapons system. You begin your career performing maintenance and repairs under close supervision. As you gain experience and skill, you work more independently and perform more complicated repairs. There are opportunities to advance to shop supervisor and perhaps to maintenance superintendent.

## DUTY ASSIGNMENT

Weapons maintenance technicians work in specialized maintenance and repair units. These units may be part of the infantry, the artillery, an air squadron, or a ship's crew. Repairs are generally performed in specially equipped workshops, but, depending on the type of weapon, repairers may also work in aircraft hangars, missile silos, or outdoors to inspect, remove, and reinstall electronic parts. Weapons maintenance technicians are assigned wherever military weapons are found. There is good opportunity for overseas assignment.

## ADVANCEMENT

Modern weapons systems are complex; they include electronic guidance and control modules as well as mechanical and electrical parts. To find and fix a problem, technicians must understand how all these parts work together. They need to be able to follow maintenance and repair guides precisely and know how to use special electronic test instruments. They must become skilled at working with hand tools to adjust mechanical parts and replace defective wiring. To advance, technicians must develop the analytical skills needed to diagnose the cause of system failure. After mastering the basic skills, the willingness to assume leadership roles helps weapons maintenance technicians advance through the supervisory levels of this career.

### Profile: Reginald Barnes

Master Sergeant Reginald Barnes sees himself and the other airborne weapons maintenance technicians as a "special breed." They like to work independently, and they enjoy a challenge. Even though they may work on only a few systems in their careers, they are constantly learning. As Reginald says, "We never see the same problem twice."

For his first 11 years in the Army, Reginald worked mainly on one weapon system: the Chaparral. His training on this system began soon after he joined the military. During a series of assignments in the United States and Germany, he advanced from technician to assistant Chaparral system mechanic to senior mechanic. He was also promoted through the ranks to staff sergeant. As senior mechanic, he reported to the Commander on weapon status and supervised training in maintenance and troubleshooting. He also monitored the stock of weapons and made sure that forms and the log book were kept up-to-date. In one assignment, he was the noncommissioned officer-in-charge (NCOIC) of projects to prepare a directory for training and to develop a

mechanic's manual for the Chaparral system.

At this point in his career, Reginald felt that he needed to get experience in another system, so he requested training in the Vulcan weapon system. He also requested parachute training—something he had always wanted to do. Both requests were granted. Reginald is proud of the "wings" on his uniform that show that he is parachute qualified. He earned them when he was 32 years old, 12 years after he joined the military.

Reginald spent the next several years as a senior Vulcan mechanic. Now, with several years of Army experience behind him, he is at Fort Bragg, NC, with the 82nd Airborne, a rapid deployment force. He is maintenance control NCOIC and yard master in charge of all missile support for the division. He supervises over 130 men and controls the work flow of jobs on several weapons systems. Since the division must be ready to deploy at a moment's notice, he and his crew ensure that the weapons are always ready to go.

## SPECIALIZATION

Weapons maintenance technicians usually specialize in one or more weapons systems. They may specialize in:

- Antiaircraft weapons used to protect military positions from attacking aircraft
- Ballistic missiles used for intercontinental (long-range) warfare
- Artillery used for conventional land-based warfare
- Aircraft weapons used for air-to-ground and air-to-air combat

## TRAINING

The services provide weapons maintenance technicians with 9 to 24 months of basic and initial job training. It combines classroom instruction and on-the-job training. Classroom instruction covers basic mechanical, electrical, and electronics theory and principles. It also includes hands-on training in a particular weapons system and in the use of special tools. On-the-job training conducted by senior repairers and shop supervisors emphasizes using technical guides for performing maintenance and repair. Early in their careers, repairers typically return to the classroom for ad-vanced training. These courses help them sharpen their troubleshooting skills and learn maintenance and repair procedures for replacement systems or major equipment modifications. In some cases, repairers return to the classroom for training in other weapons systems.

During their careers, repairers learn supervisory skills through leadership training and job experience. This training continues through the maintenance superintendent level with courses in management and administration. Typically, these courses address budgeting, personnel management, repair shop operations, and training program development.

## RELATED MILITARY OCCUPATIONS

If you are interested in electronic and electrical equipment repair, you may also want to consider a career as a radar and sonar equipment repairer, aircraft electrician, ship electrician, electronic instrument repairer, or computer equipment repairer. See the Electronic and Electrical Equipment Repair Occupations cluster in the Military Enlisted Occupations section of this book for descriptions of these and other related military occupations.

## TYPICAL CAREER PATH

### MAINTENANCE SUPERINTENDENT

Highly qualified shop supervisors may advance to manage electronic weapons systems maintenance units. They:

- Develop training programs and set training priorities
- Help officers plan for maintenance unit personnel and material needs
- Set work priorities and coordinate maintenance and support unit activities
- Develop quality control procedures and conduct maintenance inspections
- Oversee the preparation of inspection reports and personnel and technical records

### SHOP SUPERVISOR

Experienced repairers who show leadership ability may become shop supervisors in electronic maintenance units. At this level, they:

- Schedule and make work assignments
- Inspect repaired electronic weapons systems
- Review maintenance and repair logs for accuracy
- Give technical assistance to shop personnel solving malfunctions in complex weapons systems
- Assign trainers to instruct new weapons maintenance technicians

### SENIOR REPAIRER

As their skills increase, repairers perform more difficult repairs. Senior repairers:

- Set up and run electronic test and weapons system support equipment
- Install and calibrate (adjust) guidance, telemetry, and electronic fire control subsystems
- Use troubleshooting techniques to find faulty parts and causes for system breakdowns
- Use electronic test equipment and performance analyzers to test repaired systems and subsystems
- Train new technicians and help with difficult system repairs

### WEAPONS MAINTENANCE TECHNICIAN

After initial training, weapons maintenance technicians work under close supervision performing simple electronic repairs and routine maintenance. At this level, they:

- Read maintenance manuals and wiring diagrams to find system parts and subassemblies
- Replace sights, gyroscopes (stabilizing devices), printed circuit boards (prewired electrical circuits), and other parts using special hand tools
- Use electronic equipment and test probes to check missile, aircraft, and other fire control and guidance systems
- Repair mounts, launchers, and platforms for computer-controlled guns, torpedoes, artillery, and guided missiles

**Timeline**

18-20 yrs

9-12 yrs

4-7 yrs

# Examining Officer Career Path Descriptions

Officers have typically chosen a career direction before entering the military and usually have a college education. Opportunities to build on this foundation through further education and training enables individuals to advance in their chosen careers while serving their country. As you read the specific career path descriptions that follow, keep in mind that the military offers many opportunities for change and advancement.

Read the profile for Lance Hogan on page 368 in the description of "Airplane Pilots." His experiences illustrate how one person advanced as an officer. For example:

- Lance made a decision early in life to be a military airplane pilot. He prepared by completing college before joining the Air Force.

- Because Lance chose to specialize as an attack flyer, he had several duty assignments overseas.

- Competition for promotion in this field is stiff. Lance demonstrated that he was not only a superior pilot, but also a capable manager.

- Throughout his career, Lance has received continual technical training. In preparation for meeting his goal of commanding a squadron, Lance is completing a master's degree.

- Lance was selected to fly with the Thunderbirds flight demonstration team. This is an accomplishment very few pilots achieve.

## Questions to Consider

Ask yourself questions such as the following as you read each officer career description:

### a) Would I like to have a career in this occupation?

If what you read in the description and typical career path interests you, learn more about it and related officer occupations by reading the Airplane Pilots description in the Military Officer Occupations section.

### b) How much training and retraining is necessary to succeed in this career?

All officers receive training throughout their careers. Lance Hogan not only chose to obtain a great deal of advanced technical training, but also took advantage of graduate education offered through the military.

### c) How can I advance in rank and responsibility?

Military officers must have consistently excellent performance appraisals to advance. In studying the typical career path for an airplane pilot, you find that it indicates that becoming a command pilot requires not only being an outstanding pilot, but also a leader who can handle planning, management, and decision-making responsibilities.

# Sample of Military Officer Career Path Descriptions

# AIRPLANE NAVIGATORS

**A**irplane navigators are vital flight crew members of some of the world's most sophisticated airplanes. As a navigator, you will operate complex electronic navigation systems to bring your airplane safely through its missions. You may also operate weapons systems. You begin your career in a squadron, flying on missions such as air combat, ground attack, submarine hunting, paratroop, or cargo delivery. As you become more experienced and skilled, you will serve in positions of increasing responsibility. There are opportunities to become a squadron commander.

## DUTY ASSIGNMENT

Airplane navigators fly in airplanes to and from military bases in the U.S. and overseas. Some fly in airplanes that take off and land on aircraft carriers at sea. Navigators are usually assigned to flying squadrons made up of 10 to 25 airplanes and the crews needed to fly and maintain them. Navigators who fly on long-range airplanes such as bombers, tankers, and transports are usually assigned to bases in the U.S. These navigators have good opportunities for overseas flights. Navigators of fighter, fighter-bomber, or ground attack airplanes have excellent opportunities for overseas duty, particularly in Europe and the Pacific Islands. At some point in their careers, navigators are usually assigned to jobs that do not require them to fly. These assignments may be with headquarters staff or in a different occupation entirely.

## RELATED MILITARY OCCUPATIONS

If you are interested in a career as an airplane navigator, you may also want to consider a career as a helicopter pilot or airplane pilot. See the Transportation Occupations cluster in the Military Officer Occupations section of this book for descriptions of these occupations. The career of airplane pilot is also described in the next military officer career description.

---

### Profile: Greg Martin

Greg Martin grew up in Oklahoma, the son of a former Marine. He went to college on a football scholarship and after graduation, he decided to become an officer in the Marines. Greg went to Officer Candidate School and says, "The school was all I expected, challenging, to say the least." His career ambition was to fly, and he earned his "wings" as a navigator in Pensacola, FL. Greg and his wife particularly enjoyed their first tour of duty in Hawaii.

Greg flew with several F-4 Phantom squadrons. His assignments took him to the Marine Corps Air Station at Beaufort, SC; Iwakuni, Japan; Europe; and other bases around the United States. Greg also flew with his pilot to learn how to land on Navy aircraft carriers.

Professionally, Greg loved flying, but he also liked leading the maintenance troops in his squadron. He led the radar shop and later the avionics division, handling all electronic equipment. "There is a real sense of accomplishment in taking a group of men, a bunch of parts, and working together to produce 'up' (fully capable) airplanes."

A highlight of Greg's career came when he was selected to attend the Navy Fighter Weapons School, popularly called "Top Gun," in Miramar, CA. He and his pilot spent 5 weeks flying every air combat maneuver possible. They then went on as a team to the Marine Corps Weapons Training Instructor Course in Yuma, AZ. There they practiced F-4 attack missions, including electronic warfare and air combat.

Greg held a number of increasingly responsible jobs in each squadron, ending with an assignment as squadron maintenance officer. This assignment was the best of his career. Greg says, "An officer must be a leader. We manage things, but we lead people. There is nothing more rewarding."

Today Greg is completing a tour at Marine Headquarters in Washington, DC. As a lieutenant colonel, he is looking forward to returning to flight operations and hopes eventually to command a squadron.

## ADVANCEMENT

Airplane navigators must have excellent concentration to operate sophisticated electronic navigation, communications, computer, and radar equipment for long periods of time. They must be able to keep their concentration during strenuous flight maneuvers. They need to know manual navigation techniques as a backup for automated equipment. They may also have to locate and track aerial, submarine, or surface targets and to operate weapons systems. The ability to work as a team with their pilot and other air crew is essential.

To advance in rank, navigators must have superior records of performance throughout their careers and be proven leaders. They must use their initiative to develop their skills, complete advanced education, and seek leadership positions within their squadrons. Their performance in nonflying duty assignments will also be critical for advancement.

Navigators compete with their peers for promotions and career-enhancing assignments. Only the best-qualified personnel are selected for advancement, and competition intensifies with each increase in rank.

## SPECIALIZATION

Airplane navigators usually specialize in one type of airplane throughout their career. The basic airplane types include:

- High-performance jet fighters, fighter-bombers, or ground attack planes
- Long-range, strategic bombers
- Large tanker airplanes that provide in-flight refueling
- Special high-altitude reconnaissance planes
- Medium- or long-range anti-submarine patrol planes

- Long-range, multi-engine heavy transport planes

When assigned to nonflying duty tours, airplane navigators often specialize in areas that will help them in senior staff positions later in their careers. These "second careers" may be in areas such as engineering, computer science, or personnel management.

## TRAINING

Initial training for airplane navigators includes about 12 months of demanding classroom and in-flight training. Training covers navigation, communications, principles of flight, major airplane systems, meteorology, and flight operations. Student navigators are given experience in day, night, aerobatic, and basic military airplane missions. After initial training, navigators are given advanced training in one type of airplane, such as a fighter, ground attack, bomber, reconnaissance, or transport plane. Navigators must continue on-the-job flight training throughout their careers.

Advanced training is available in areas such as ground attack tactics, dogfighting (air-to-air combat tactics), and air battle management. Navigators receive transition training whenever their airplane is modified or replaced by a new airplane. There are opportunities to attend graduate school for advanced technical or management degrees.

Navigators are also given opportunities for professional military education to prepare them for senior officer positions. These programs include study of military subjects such as strategy, tactics, and planning large-scale operations. They may be completed either by correspondence or full-time study.

## TYPICAL CAREER PATH

### SQUADRON COMMANDER

Flight operations directors who have excellent navigation experience and who are outstanding leaders may advance to senior positions. At this level, they:

- Command a squadron, flight operations group, or air facility
- Advise headquarters commanders on squadron operations matters
- Fly missions to maintain their skills
- Direct flight operations of a major command

### FLIGHT OPERATIONS DIRECTOR

Senior navigators who are experts in navigation and their flying missions and who are outstanding leaders may advance to become flight operations directors. At this level, they:

- Plan squadron flight missions
- Teach flight crews advanced mission operations and tactics
- Manage a squadron department, such as maintenance, training, or safety
- Advise squadron commanders on readiness of aircraft and crews
- Evaluate officers' flying, leadership, and management skills

### SENIOR NAVIGATOR

After mastering the requirements of their assigned mission area and gaining experience as leaders, navigators may advance to become senior navigators. At this level, they:

- Plan and accompany their pilots on operational missions
- Instruct new navigators in their squadron duties and responsibilities
- Guide strategic bombers to their targets
- Teach student navigators how to use weapons systems and navigate
- Explain mission plans and assignments to flight crews

### NAVIGATOR

Navigators who earn their wings are assigned to a flying squadron. Depending on the type of airplane and mission, they:

- Locate and track land targets, aircraft, ships, or submarines
- Monitor automated navigational systems using manual navigation techniques
- Operate communications equipment
- Plan missions and tactics with their pilots, considering weather, fuel, and aircraft loading
- Practice normal and emergency operating procedures

**Timeline**

15-18 yrs

9-11 yrs

4 yrs

# AIRPLANE PILOTS

**M**ilitary pilots fly the most sophisticated combat and transport airplanes in the world. As a pilot, you will plan flying missions, brief your air crews, and fly frequently to keep your performance at its peak. You begin your career in a squadron, flying the airplane you were trained to fly—a supersonic jet fighter, high-altitude reconnaissance plane, or huge cargo transport. As you gain experience and skill, you will serve in positions of increasing responsibility. There are opportunities to become a squadron commander.

## DUTY ASSIGNMENT

Airplane pilots fly their airplanes to and from military bases in the U.S. and overseas. Some fly airplanes that take off and land on aircraft carriers at sea. Pilots are usually assigned to flying squadrons made up of 10 to 25 airplanes and the crews needed to fly and maintain them. Pilots of long-range airplanes, such as bombers, tankers, and transports are usually assigned to bases in the U.S. These pilots have good opportunities for overseas flights. Pilots of fighter, fighter-bomber, or ground attack airplanes have excellent opportunities for overseas duty, particularly in Europe and the Pacific. At some point in their careers, pilots are usually assigned to jobs that do not require them to fly. These assignments may be with headquarters staff or in a different occupation entirely.

## RELATED MILITARY OCCUPATIONS

If you are interested in a flying career, you may also want to consider a career as a helicopter pilot or an airplane navigator. See the Transportation Occupations cluster in the Military Officer Occupations section of this book for descriptions of these occupations. The career of airplane navigators is also described in the previous military officer career description.

---

### Profile: Lance Hogan

Lieutenant Colonel Lance Hogan knew he wanted to be a fighter pilot from the time he was young. Hearing the stories of his two uncles who had flown fighter planes in World War II and seeing the Thunderbirds flight demonstration team sparked his interest. Lance worked his way through college in Louisiana. When he received his degree, he joined the Air Force.

Lance was first in his flight training class. He chose to specialize in the A-7 Corsair II attack fighter, flying as the on-scene commander for search and rescue operations. His first assignment was to one of the original Flying Tiger squadrons.

Lance really enjoyed the demanding search and rescue missions. He practiced ground attack and coordinating artillery, naval gunfire, air strikes, and other resources required to rescue air crews shot down in enemy territory. During this tour he was promoted to captain.

After a year of special staff training in Washington, DC, Lance went back to flying, this time in the F-4 Phantom II. Lance served a 1-year tour at Taegu Airbase in Korea. As the squadron scheduling officer, he managed all flight training requirements for the squadron. During this tour, he was promoted to major.

His duties at Taegu prepared him for his next assignment at MacDill Air Force Base (AFB), FL. Here, Lance taught pilots who had just earned their wings air-to-ground combat tactics. He also learned to fly the new F-16 fighter and became one of the first instructor pilots for this aircraft.

At MacDill, Lance was selected for very special duty. He and his family moved to Nellis AFB, NV. In an unusual tour, Lance flew 4-1/2 years with the elite Thunderbirds flight demonstration team. Normally, pilots who are selected to join the Thunderbirds stay only 2 years. Lance toured Europe, South America, and almost all 50 states, including Alaska and Hawaii.

Now with Air Force staff at Langley AFB, VA, Lance coordinates all activities of Air Force tactical demonstration aircraft and squadrons worldwide. In his off-duty time, he is completing a master's degree in aerospace science. "I like my job now," he says, "but I am looking forward to flying again." He hopes to command a squadron sometime in the near future.

## ADVANCEMENT

Airplane pilots must be outstanding fliers. They must be able to fly their airplanes safely through the maneuvers required by their missions. They must be experts in their plane's fuel, flight control, electrical, and weapons systems. All pilots are regularly tested on their knowledge of airplane systems in written examinations, "check flights," and in-flight simulators.

To advance, pilots must be superb aviators and maintain their skills throughout their careers. They must have consistently excellent flying records and be proven leaders. Pilots are expected to use their initiative to develop their skills, complete advanced education, and seek leadership positions in their squadron. Their performance in nonflying duty assignments will also be critical for advancement.

Pilots compete with their peers for promotion and career-enhancing assignments. Only the best-qualified personnel are selected for advancement, and competition intensifies with each increase in rank.

## SPECIALIZATION

Airplane pilots usually specialize in one type of airplane throughout their careers. The basic airplane types include:

- High-performance jet fighters, fighter-bombers, or ground attack planes
- Long-range, strategic bombers
- Large tanker airplanes that provide in-flight refueling
- Special high-altitude reconnaissance planes
- Medium- or long-range anti-submarine patrol planes
- Long-range multi-engine heavy transport planes
- Lightweight utility planes

When assigned to nonflying duty tours, airplane pilots often specialize in areas that will help them in senior staff positions later in their careers. These "second careers" may be in areas such as engineering, computer science, or personnel management.

## TRAINING

Initial training for pilots includes up to 18 months of demanding classroom and in-flight training. Student pilots learn principles of aerodynamics, major airplane systems, meteorology, navigation, communications, and federal and service flight rules and regulations. They practice flying in all types of weather, day and night. They also practice flying in formation and basic aerobatics. After initial training, pilots are given advanced training in one type of airplane, such as a fighter, ground attack, bomber, reconnaissance, or transport plane. Pilots must continue on-the-job flight training throughout their careers.

Advanced training is available in areas such as ground attack tactics, dogfighting (air-to-air combat tactics), and directing air strikes. Pilots receive transition training whenever their airplanes are modified or replaced by new generation airplanes. There are opportunities to attend graduate school for advanced technical and management degrees.

Pilots are also given opportunities for professional military education to prepare them for senior officer positions. These programs include study of military subjects such as strategy, tactics, and planning large-scale operations. They may be completed either by correspondence or full-time study.

## TYPICAL CAREER PATH

### COMMAND PILOT

Excellent flight leaders who have broad experience in flying operations and who are outstanding leaders may advance to senior positions. At this level, they:

- Command a squadron, flight operations group, or air facility
- Direct flight operations of a major flying unit
- Fly missions to maintain expert flying skills
- Advise headquarters commanders on squadron operations

**15-18 yrs**

### FLIGHT LEADER

Pilots who are expert in their flying mission and demonstrate outstanding leadership qualities may advance to become flight leaders. At this level, they:

- Lead several airplanes on flying missions, such as airstrikes, patrols, or transporting cargo
- Instruct pilots in squadron missions and tactics
- Evaluate pilots' flying, leadership, and management skills
- Manage a squadron department, such as maintenance, training, or safety
- Manage combat missions, planning target selections and personnel utilization

**9-11 yrs**

### SENIOR PILOT

After mastering the requirements of their assigned mission area and gaining experience as leaders, pilots may advance to become senior pilots. Senior pilots:

- Plan and fly operational missions
- Fly as first pilot in a large airplane
- Lead flights of two or more aircraft on missions
- Instruct new pilots in their squadron duties and responsibilities
- Teach student pilots to fly
- Explain mission plans and assignments to flight crews

**4 yrs**

### PILOT

Pilots who earn their wings are assigned to a flying squadron. Depending on the type of aircraft and mission, they:

- Plan flights, considering weather, fuel, and aircraft loading
- Fly missions alone, as part of a group of airplanes, or as copilot in a large airplane
- Plan missions and tactics
- Practice emergency and normal operating procedures

# CIVIL ENGINEERS

*C*ivil engineers are the military's builders. In their varied careers they may: build air strips in the jungle; direct construction or maintenance of military bases; or work alongside combat troops, physically altering the battlefield to help them advance or hold their positions. You begin your career managing construction contracts, directing base utility and maintenance services, or leading a group of enlisted combat engineers. As you gain experience, you will serve in positions of increasing responsibility. There are opportunities to become director of engineering at a military base or to command a battalion of combat engineers.

## DUTY ASSIGNMENT

Civil engineers work primarily in engineering offices or temporary construction facilities on military bases in the U.S. and overseas. Civil engineers assigned to combat engineering units may spend much time in the field during combat exercises and field maneuvers. Most have opportunities for overseas assignment, particularly in Europe and the Pacific Islands.

## SPECIALIZATION

Civil engineers typically spend their career developing expertise in several areas. Major areas include combat engineering, contract management, and public works. In each assignment, civil engineers use their engineering background, career experience, and increasing leadership ability.

## RELATED MILITARY OCCUPATIONS

If you are interested in a career as a military civil engineer, you may also want to consider a career in another technical field. See the Engineering, Science, and Technical Occupations cluster in the Military Officer Occupations section of this book for descriptions of these occupations.

---

### Profile: Philip Thompson

Phil Thompson joined the Navy Reserves while he was in college studying civil engineering. "I looked into the Navy's Civil Engineer Corps," he says, "and liked what I saw." After graduation, he went to Officer Candidate School in Newport, RI, and then to Civil Engineer Corps Officer School in Port Hueneme, CA.

Phil's first assignment was to Guam. As a new Civil Engineer Corps ensign (O-1), Phil had 400 civilians working for him. He also had a large budget and responsibility for maintaining all Navy and Marine buildings and housing on the island. In his second year he was assigned as the Activities Civil Engineer (ACE). He managed a budget of $4 million and a large number of civilian workers. Phil liked the job so much that he asked to extend his tour of duty.

Phil enjoyed the public works side of civil engineering. For his next assignment, he went to the Naval Air Station Whidbey Island, WA. There, he directed facility maintenance forces, maintained three runways, two outlying airfields, roads, water, power, transportation, and everything needed to keep the base operating year-round.

Assigned next to Vietnam, he directed the construction of housing for Vietnamese military personnel and their dependents. His crews for this project were the famous Navy "SeaBee" construction battalions.

Phil's most memorable tour was at the naval base at Guantanamo Bay, Cuba. He directed contractors building a water desalination plant and an addition to the power plant. But his greatest satisfaction came from completely remodeling every home on the base. "We gutted and remade hot, uncomfortable houses into modern, fully air-conditioned units. It was really appreciated by the Navy and Marine Corps personnel and dependents living at Guantanamo," Phil says.

From his post in the Pentagon, where he monitors Navy planning and construction in the entire continental United States, Commander Phil Thompson is looking forward to taking some time off when he retires this fall. Looking back he says, "It's been 22 years of fun."

## ADVANCEMENT

To perform their wide range of duties, military civil engineers must be flexible, excellent leaders, and have superior analytical and communications skills. They may come from any of several engineering backgrounds. They apply their education and abilities to solve problems, supervise contractors, lead troops, and give advice on contracts and designs.

To advance, civil engineers must have excellent professional skills and managerial abilities. To build a record of excellent performance, they must win the confidence of the people for whom they work and those who work for them. As they gain experience, they serve in positions of greater responsibility. They manage larger contracts, lead more people, and direct projects of increasing complexity. An excellent performance record is essential to success. An advanced engineering or management degree may increase chances for promotion.

Engineers compete with their peers for promotion and career-enhancing assignments. Only the best-qualified personnel are selected for advancement, and competition intensifies with each increase in rank.

## TRAINING

Initial training for civil engineers is a combination of classroom and field training. Courses are taught in: managing contracts, budgeting, combat engineering techniques, and leadership. To prepare for their next assignment, some engineers receive specialty training in such areas as environmental protection, fire prevention/protection, or mapping (cartography).

Advanced training is available in leadership and combat engineering. Civil engineers may earn a graduate engineering degree in a program funded by their service. Many others obtain degrees on their own time.

Civil engineers are also given opportunities for professional military education to prepare them for senior officer positions. These programs include study of military subjects such as strategy, tactics, and planning large-scale operations. They may be completed by correspondence or full-time study.

## TYPICAL CAREER PATH

### DIRECTOR OF ENGINEERING

Engineering staff officers with outstanding records of leadership and technical expertise may be selected to direct major engineering activities or units. At this level, they:

- Command combat engineering or construction battalions of 500 to 750 military personnel
- Direct civil engineering operations at a military base
- Advise base or area commanders on civil engineering matters
- Evaluate construction bids submitted by civilian contractors
- Direct planning and management of major engineering projects

### ENGINEERING STAFF OFFICER

Senior engineers who show excellent leadership and technical ability may advance to become engineering staff officers. At this level, they:

- Analyze and recommend design specifications for buildings, bridges, roads, and other structures
- Determine construction project costs
- Lead other civil engineers in managing construction and maintenance contracts for a military base
- Advise senior commanders on combat engineering and related matters

### SENIOR ENGINEER

Civil engineers who have performed well in their first assignments may advance to become senior engineers. At this level, they:

- Command combat engineering companies of 65 to 200 enlisted personnel
- Plan and manage programs to maintain utilities, buildings, or roads on a military base
- Train new civil engineer officers
- Review plans and designs for engineering projects

### CIVIL ENGINEER

After initial training, civil engineers are given their first duty assignment. Here they may:

- Direct military and civilian personnel in maintaining and constructing buildings
- Lead combat engineers in missions such as building fortifications, assembling mobile bridges, or preparing mine fields
- Monitor contractors to ensure their work meets contract specifications
- Lead and train enlisted personnel in construction techniques

Timeline

15-18 yrs

9-11 yrs

4 yrs

# INFANTRY OFFICERS

*I*nfantry officers lead their troops through rigorous training and maneuvers. As an infantry officer, you will make sure your men are in top shape, well trained, and properly equipped. You begin your career leading a platoon of 30 to 50 infantrymen. As you gain leadership and tactical experience, you will serve in positions of increasing responsibility. There are opportunities to become battalion commander.

## DUTY ASSIGNMENT

Infantry officers serve in infantry units at military bases in the U.S. and overseas. They work in offices and spend much time in the field. The new officer's first assignment is to train and lead a platoon of 30 to 50 soldiers. Later in their career, infantry officers command a company of 100 to 200 soldiers and perhaps a battalion of 500 to 1,000 soldiers. There are excellent opportunities for overseas assignment in Europe and the Pacific Islands.

## SPECIALIZATION

Infantry officers may specialize in amphibious warfare (attacking land from the water), airborne operations (parachuting into battle), special operations, or Ranger operations. (Rangers are special units skilled in combat in many different geographical areas.) Infantry officers may also develop secondary career specialties through advanced education or special experience.

## RELATED MILITARY OCCUPATIONS

If you are interested in a combat career, you may also want to consider a career as an artillery, tank, missile systems, or special operations officer. See the Combat Specialty Occupations cluster in the Military Officer Occupations section of this book for descriptions of these occupations.

---

### Profile: Wayne Garvey

Growing up in a small town in Texas, Wayne Garvey enjoyed working outdoors and knew he would like the life of a soldier. During his ROTC training at the Virginia Military Institute (VMI), Wayne heard an infantry officer talk about his profession. "I was impressed by his orientation to people and the emphasis the Army places on individual and team effort, professionalism, and dedication."

Wayne graduated from VMI, earning a commission in the Reserves. He qualified for a delayed entry to active duty, and used the time to go to law school. After admission to the bar, he began active duty. His first assignment following basic infantry and airborne training was to the 101st Airborne, Fort Campbell, KY, as a weapons platoon leader. Wayne also served as a company executive officer and as battalion adjutant, monitoring administration.

His next tour was in Vietnam, as a platoon leader with the 1st Air Cavalry. Wayne led his platoon in many combat actions and earned several decorations, including the silver star, the nation's third highest award for gallantry. He also spent part of his tour on the headquarters staff before returning home. During this tour, he advanced to captain.

With his service obligation complete, Wayne left the Army. He practiced law and was very successful. "But," he says, "I missed the Army every day of those 2 years." He and his wife made the decision together to return to Army life.

Back on active duty, Wayne returned to Vietnam, commanding a rifle company. He again earned several decorations. Following this tour, Wayne returned to the States to teach tactics at the Army Military Academy at West Point.

Since West Point, Wayne has served several tours on various Army staffs; in one tour he assigned infantry officers to positions throughout the world. He also commanded an infantry battalion in Korea. "This was a real milestone," he says, "a real highlight of my career to date."

Recently selected for the highest level officers' courses at the Army War College, Wayne says about his service, "Even the bad days have been good. I have really enjoyed my career!"

## ADVANCEMENT

Infantry officers must be quick-thinking, aggressive leaders to be able to train and motivate the soldiers they command.

To be successful platoon leaders, infantry officers must master infantry operations and weapons and show outstanding leadership abilities. To advance to company commander, they must master all tactical aspects of the infantry, and demonstrate ability to coordinate combat actions with artillery, armor, airlift, and air strike support units. To advance to senior command positions, they must have successfully commanded and demonstrated potential at the company level. Outstanding performance in every duty assignment is essential for advancement. Officers with the broadest range of infantry skills and best records of leadership have the best chance for promotion.

Infantry officers compete with their peers for promotion and career-enhancing assignments. Only the best-qualified personnel are selected for advancement, and competition intensifies with each increase in rank.

## TRAINING

Initial training for infantry officers includes up to 6 months of training in the classroom and in the field. Training covers infantry weapons, combat tactics, infantry organization, and military leadership. Many officers also receive specialized training to prepare them for their first assignment. They may be trained in combat skills such as parachute jumping, Ranger training, or amphibious landings.

Advanced training is provided to prepare infantry officers for more senior leadership roles. Courses are taught primarily in coordinating infantry and mechanized infantry with other combat units.

Infantry officers are also given opportunities for professional military education to prepare them for senior officer positions. These programs include study of such military subjects as strategy, tactics, and planning large-scale operations. They may be completed by correspondence or full-time study.

## TYPICAL CAREER PATH

### BATTALION COMMANDER

Outstanding officers with a broad range of infantry experience may advance to senior officer positions. At this level, they:

- Command an infantry battalion of 500 to 1,000 men
- Plan training exercises or missions
- Instruct company commanders on mission assignments and objectives
- Coordinate battle plans with armor, artillery, and air support units

### INFANTRY STAFF OFFICER

Company commanders with demonstrated leadership skills may advance to become infantry staff officers. In this position, they:

- Assist their battalion commander in administration and management duties
- Manage a specialized function such as logistics or operations for a battalion or headquarters staff
- Teach infantry courses
- Resolve unit supply, maintenance, or personnel problems
- Advise senior commanders on infantry operations and readiness

### COMPANY COMMANDER

Platoon leaders who have shown leadership ability may advance to become company commanders. At this level, they:

- Command an infantry company consisting of several platoons
- Develop and carry out battle plans to support battalion objectives
- Develop, schedule, and carry out training plans and field exercises
- Explain battle plans and assign objectives to platoon leaders

### PLATOON LEADER

After initial training, infantry officers are assigned to lead a platoon. Platoon leaders:

- Train and lead an infantry platoon of 30 to 50 soldiers
- Inspect troops, barracks, and equipment
- Plan daily conditioning programs for the platoon or the entire company
- Lead the platoon on combat training exercises
- Direct the care and maintenance of weapons, radios, and other equipment assigned to the platoon

**This career is open only to men.**

Timeline

15-18 yrs

9-11 yrs

4 yrs

# INTELLIGENCE OFFICERS

ARMY
NAVY
AIR FORCE
MARINE CORPS
COAST GUARD

Intelligence officers are the eyes and ears of the military. The information they deal with is vital to our national security. As an intelligence officer, you will analyze information on the military forces, governments, and people of other countries. You begin your career collecting and giving combat commanders briefings on information from sources such as satellite and aerial photographs, intercepted communications, and observers in the field. As you gain experience, you will serve in positions of increasing responsibility. There are opportunities to become intelligence operations director of an intelligence-gathering unit or of a large combat force on land or sea.

## DUTY ASSIGNMENTS

Most intelligence officers work at military bases in the U.S. and overseas. Many work in electronic data processing and evaluation centers or photographic interpretation labs. Some work aboard ships or airplanes with sophisticated intelligence-gathering equipment. Many intelligence officers have an opportunity to work in Washington, DC, where much intelligence planning and evaluation takes place. Intelligence officers have good opportunities for overseas duty.

## SPECIALIZATION

Intelligence officers typically specialize in one area of intelligence early in their careers. They expand on the foundation as they advance. Areas of specialization include communications intelligence (information from intercepted radio voice communications), signals intelligence (data from non-voice coded radio and radar signals), imagery intelligence (information from satellite and aircraft images), combat intelligence, and human intelligence (information provided by agents and other individuals in the field).

## Profile: Teresa Alvarez

Teresa (Teri) Alvarez signed up for a Marine training program one summer in college. "It sounded interesting," she says, "and it carried no obligation." Teri and 6 friends went to training that summer. After graduation, 3 of them went on to Officer Candidate School and became Marine officers.

Teri decided to enter the intelligence field as an interrogator/translator. She was assigned to Hawaii as an intelligence analyst for Southeast Asia. As part of her duties, she prepared and gave briefings to senior officers served by her unit.

To further develop her leadership abilities, she was assigned to the Officer Candidate School in Quantico, VA. There, Teri taught several classes and counseled women officer candidates. She says, "I watched the women walk in and become Marine officers—leaving more confident and professional. It was one of my most enjoyable assignments."

After attending a special 9-month intelligence school to prepare her for assignment to the Defense Intelligence Agency (DIA), Teri reported for duty in Washington, DC as a Marine captain. In this post she developed a situational model to alert intelligence planners to developing threats all over the world. She also prepared a training course for threat analysts in different intelligence agencies. For her work during this tour, she was awarded the newly authorized Defense Meritorious Service Medal.

After being selected for promotion to major, Teri went full-time to Command and Staff College. She was then assigned as the first woman to hold a position as a division level (G-2) intelligence officer. She directed the group that provided intelligence services to the 2nd Marine Division, roughly one-third of the Marine Corps fighting force.

Later assignments included Okinawa and the Marine Headquarters in Washington, DC, where she works now, planning and analyzing Marine Corps intelligence activities. As a lieutenant colonel, she is looking forward to her next assignment. She says, "I am eager for more responsibility. I really like the challenge and the opportunity to advance in a field that is so important to the Marine Corps and the nation."

## ADVANCEMENT

Intelligence officers serve in positions of great sensitivity. They analyze information vital to national security and prepare it for combat commanders around the world. Intelligence officers must be aggressively resourceful and analytical, and have excellent speaking and writing ability. In perhaps no other occupation is so much trust placed in individuals so early in their careers. After mastering the basic analytical skills, intelligence officers apply them in positions of increasing responsibility.

To advance, intelligence officers must have a record of consistently superior performance. Because military operations depend on accurate intelligence, there is no room for mistakes. Intelligence officers must win the respect and trust of their commanders and prove themselves as good leaders. They must often learn computer and related skills.

Intelligence officers compete with their peers for promotion and career-enhancing assignments. Only the best-qualified personnel are selected for advancement, and competition intensifies with each increase in rank.

## TRAINING

Initial training for intelligence officers includes up to 6 months of intensive classroom study. Officers learn how to analyze data and prepare briefings. They are trained in techniques for gathering intelligence and learn the kinds of information combat commanders need to make decisions in battle. They also are briefed on world situations. Intelligence officers may receive specialized training in areas such as electronics, communications, or satellite photographic intelligence gathering.

Advanced training is available, usually to prepare intelligence officers for a specific assignment. Other advanced courses may be in special analysis of intelligence information from many sources.

Intelligence officers are also given opportunities for professional military education to prepare them for senior officer positions. These programs include study of military subjects such as strategy, tactics, and planning large-scale operations. These military courses may be completed either by correspondence or full-time study.

## TYPICAL CAREER PATH

### INTELLIGENCE OPERATIONS DIRECTOR

Outstanding intelligence staff officers may advance to become intelligence operations directors. Here they:

- Direct intelligence services for air, land, or sea commands
- Coordinate their intelligence with other military and civilian intelligence agencies
- Determine the intelligence needed to support large combat forces
- Evaluate intelligence sources for accuracy and usefulness
- Brief top-level military leaders in areas of personal expertise

### INTELLIGENCE STAFF OFFICER

Senior intelligence officers with excellent records of performance and leadership ability may advance to become intelligence staff officers. Typically, they:

- Brief senior-level staff and combat commanders on activities of enemy forces
- Direct a team of officers and enlisted personnel, compiling and analyzing intelligence information from all sources
- Confer with intelligence officers from other services and nations to share information
- Teach military intelligence courses

### SENIOR INTELLIGENCE OFFICER

Intelligence officers with an excellent performance record may advance to become senior intelligence officers. At this level, they may:

- Analyze information from many sources of intelligence and prepare briefings or reports
- Gather information to support combat exercises and maneuvers
- Analyze potential security problems
- Train new intelligence officers in job duties

### INTELLIGENCE OFFICER

After initial training, intelligence officers are assigned to specialized intelligence units or to air, sea, or ground combat units. Here they may:

- Research enemy force locations, size, and capability
- Analyze weaknesses and strengths of enemy forces
- Brief combat commanders or air crews on research results
- Direct a small team of enlisted personnel intercepting and analyzing voice or other radio signals
- Interpret aerial and satellite photographs
- Debrief air crews or ground combat teams returning from missions or patrols

Timeline

15-18 yrs

9-11 yrs

4 yrs

# LAWYERS

**M**ilitary lawyers, known as Judge Advocates General's (JAG) Corps officers, work for the largest "legal firms" in the world. As a military lawyer, you will prosecute or defend military personnel in courts-martial, counsel personnel on legal problems, and advise commanders in matters of law. You begin your career handling trials and providing legal services. As you gain experience, your assignments will become more challenging. There are opportunities to become a legal services director or a judge in a military court.

## DUTY ASSIGNMENT

Most military lawyers work in legal offices and courtrooms on military bases in the U.S. and overseas. Some serve aboard large ships at sea or on the flagship of a fleet commander. Legal services officers and directors normally work at major command headquarters, on large military bases, or in Washington, DC. There are good opportunities for overseas assignments.

## SPECIALIZATION

Lawyers may gain special expertise through experience or advanced education. They may specialize in contract, labor, international, maritime, or criminal law.

---

### Profile: Leighton Pierce

After college, Leighton Pierce was not challenged by his job with a large computer firm. After talking with a Marine officer friend, he decided to give the Marines a try. He graduated near the top of his officer training class and then spent a tour in Vietnam, after which he decided to make the Marine Corps his career.

However, cancer forced him from active duty. The Marine Corps treated him and, while he was on a temporary retirement, provided him with 100 percent medical disability pay and benefits. He took the opportunity to go to law school.

When he was given a clean bill of health, the Marines asked him if he would like to return to active duty as a lawyer. "My wife and I enjoyed the friends we had made and the travel," Leighton says, "so we decided to go back," leaving behind a successful civilian law practice.

He started his Marine law career with Naval Justice School before practicing law for the military.

Leighton especially enjoyed courtroom practice in prosecution and defense, but was challenged by other legal service assignments as well. A high point in his career was a tour in Okinawa. "We loved the life there," he says. In that tour, he served as senior defense counsel directing all trial defense cases and acting as the lead defense lawyer in many trials.

Since then, he and his family have enjoyed assignments in the United States and a tour in the Philippines. Leighton is now a lieutenant colonel in charge of legal support services, 2nd Force Service Support Group, directing 34 lawyers and 83 enlisted legal specialists. His group handles all military justice and administrative law for thousands of Marine Corps personnel stationed at Camp Lejeune, NC. He is looking forward to continuing his challenging and rewarding career.

## ADVANCEMENT

Military lawyers must speak and write with ease and authority. They must be familiar with civilian and military law, as well as courtroom strategy. Creativity and perseverance are essential to research complex legal rulings and use them in court cases.

To advance, lawyers must continue to increase their knowledge of military, criminal, and civil law. They should have excellent legal performance and leadership records. Most lawyers obtain advanced degrees or specialties. However, they are also encouraged to broaden their experience through a variety of assignments. In later assignments, lawyers lead junior JAG officers as well as enlisted legal personnel.

Lawyers with a legal specialty and outstanding records of performance in a variety of assignments have the best opportunities to advance to senior positions. Only the best-qualified personnel are selected for advancement, and competition intensifies with each increase in rank.

## TRAINING

Lawyers entering the military must be graduates of an accredited law school. Initial training for lawyers is conducted by the service JAG school. Courses include introduction to military law, the military justice system, and officer leadership and management responsibilities. New lawyers train on the job in courtrooms and legal service offices.

Lawyers are expected to keep up with changes in laws, regulations, and legal procedures. They must continue to study and attend symposiums, conferences, and seminars throughout their careers. Many lawyers have opportunities to acquire specialties and advanced degrees. Advanced training typically opens up a range of assignments that would otherwise be unavailable.

Lawyers are also given opportunities for professional military education to prepare them for senior officer positions. These programs include study of military subjects such as strategy, tactics, and planning large-scale operations. These military courses may be completed by correspondence or occasionally by full-time study.

## TYPICAL CAREER PATH

### LEGAL STAFF DIRECTOR

Legal staff officers with outstanding records of leadership and legal expertise may advance to become legal services directors. Here they may:

- Direct all activities of a legal services JAG office supporting local operational commands
- Set up prosecution or defense in courts-martial
- Advise senior staff and combat commanders on legal matters
- Serve as a judge on courts-martial

### LEGAL STAFF OFFICERS

Outstanding senior lawyers may advance to become legal staff officers. At this level, they may:

- Advise commanders on specific legal topics (contract, labor, maritime, or international law)
- Defend or prosecute personnel in courts-martial that require lawyers of senior rank and expertise
- Direct lawyers and enlisted legal specialists in providing services to military personnel and their dependents
- Review contracts to determine if they meet legal requirements

### SENIOR LAWYER

Lawyers who demonstrate the ability to interpret and work with law may advance to become senior lawyers. At this level, they:

- Advise commanders and senior staff officers on general legal issues
- Make sure policies and procedures comply with civil and military law
- Investigate liability claims
- Advise military personnel on legal matters

### LAWYER

Following initial training, lawyers are assigned to JAG offices. Here they:

- Prosecute and defend military personnel in courts-martial
- Research cases using law libraries and computerized references
- Interview defendants and witnesses
- Prepare wills, adoption papers, and other personal legal documents

Timeline

15-18 yrs

9-11 yrs

4 yrs

# METEOROLOGISTS

**A**ccurate weather forecasts can save lives and equipment in military operations. As a meteorologist, you supervise enlisted weather observers and forecasters and advise operational commanders on changing weather conditions. You begin your career directing data collection and interpreting weather maps, observation data, and satellite information. As you gain leadership and forecasting skills, you will serve in positions of increasing responsibility. There are opportunities to become director of a major meteorological center in charge of a group of weather stations.

## DUTY ASSIGNMENT

Most meteorology officers work in weather stations or weather support units at military bases in the U.S. and overseas. Some work in global weather centers. Others work in command and control centers aboard ships at sea. There are good opportunities for overseas assignment to military bases and outposts throughout the world, from the tropics to the North and South Poles.

## SPECIALIZATION

Meteorologists may specialize in the field in which they have an advanced degree. Specialties include oceanography, astrophysics, geophysics, and computer science. Typically, meteorologists serve in a variety of assignments, returning periodically to their specialty.

## RELATED MILITARY OCCUPATIONS

If you are interested in a career as a meteorologist, you may also want to consider a career in oceanography or some other scientific or technical occupation. See the Engineering, Science, and Technical Occupations cluster in the Military Officer Occupations section of this book for descriptions of these occupations.

---

### Profile: Brian Christopher

As a child, Brian Christopher lived on a small farm and liked to watch the weather. He remembers when he was just 8 years old trying to figure out what the weather would be. However, it was not until he was working his way through college that Brian really decided meteorology was the career he wanted. He also had another goal — to serve in the Air Force.

His first assignment was to Plattsburg Air Force Base (AFB) in northern New York. There he developed and briefed weather forecasts for B-52 bomber and KC-135 tanker air crews. The air crews depended on the accuracy of his forecasts to fly safely and to protect planes on the ground from damage by severe weather. After 15 months, Brian became a weather officer for all of the bomber squadrons at the base. He briefed the wing commander daily and made sure the squadrons received good support concerning weather conditions.

Brian applied and was selected for fully funded studies at St. Louis University and earned a master's degree in meteorology. "After my degree, the technical assignments really opened up," he says. He became a technical consultant at Andrews AFB, MD, near Washington, DC. There he developed new methods for using satellite data to predict weather in areas of the world with no ground observation stations. He also kept himself informed on what was going on in civilian meteorological science.

As he advanced, Brian filled more leadership roles. He played a part in the weather service's support in developing new weapons systems. As a major, he commanded a large weather station serving the Tactical Air Command's busiest training base, Luke AFB, AZ. He worked with the North American Air Defense Command in Colorado Springs, and he was a key individual in efforts to modernize Air Force weather service equipment.

Today, Lieutenant Colonel Brian Christopher leads 65 meteorologists and enlisted weather specialists at the Global Weather Center at Offut AFB in Omaha, NB. His group serves all the armed services and supports missions ranging from major NATO exercises to missile launches and testing all over the world. "I enjoy my role as a leader," he says, "but I still like to pit my forecasting skills against Mother Nature."

## ADVANCEMENT

Meteorologists must be able to forecast the weather accurately and to apply their expertise to research, military exercises, and strategic planning. Meteorologists begin by practicing short-term and extended forecasting, briefing flight crews, and directing enlisted weather observers. After mastering these skills, they work in larger weather stations serving more people and missions. In the Navy, meteorologists will also apply their knowledge to the field of oceanography.

To advance, meteorologists must make consistently accurate forecasts and show excellent leadership and management skills. Most senior meteorologists have an advanced degree in areas such as math, geophysics, astrophysics, oceanography, meteorology, and computer science. Outstanding performance and advanced education are keys to advancement in meteorology.

Meteorologists compete with their peers for promotion and career-enhancing assignments. Only the best-qualified personnel are selected for advancement and competition intensifies with each increase in rank.

## TRAINING

Initial training for meteorologists includes up to 12 months of classroom instruction in weather observation, analysis, and forecasting. Instruction is also given on the impact of weather on military operations and the information needed by combat commanders. Military leadership is an important part of initial training.

Advanced training is given in such areas of specialization as interpreting satellite weather data and computer applications to forecasting. Most meteorologists earn advanced degrees in areas such as meteorology, oceanography, geophysics, astrophysics, or computer science. They may specialize in such fields as environmental effects on electronic equipment, solar forecasting, or acoustics in water. Some attend schools in programs funded by their service, while others obtain degrees on their own time.

Meteorologists are also given opportunities for professional military education to prepare them for senior officer positions. These programs include military subjects such as strategy, tactics, and forecasting requirements for planning large-scale operations. They may be completed by correspondence or full-time study.

## TYPICAL CAREER PATH

### METEOROLOGY DIRECTOR

Meteorology staff officers with superior technical expertise and leadership ability may advance to direct meteorological centers. At this level, they may:

- Direct personnel predicting and monitoring global weather patterns
- Advise top-level military commanders on weather conditions
- Manage staff and weather planning for large geographic areas (such as northern Europe)
- Inspect weather facilities under their command

### METEOROLOGY STAFF OFFICER

Senior meteorologists with records of excellent performance may advance to become meteorology staff officers. They may:

- Command large weather stations
- Advise scientists and technicians designing, developing, and testing new weapons systems
- Direct weather computer centers
- Confer with oceanographers to support operations at sea
- Advise combat commanders and their staffs on weather conditions

### SENIOR METEOROLOGIST

Meteorologists who have excellent technical and leadership skills advance to become senior meteorologists. At this level, they may:

- Command a small weather station or outlying weather facility
- Train and evaluate new meteorologists and enlisted personnel
- Send hazardous weather warnings
- Direct preparation of weather forecasts and local advisories

### METEOROLOGIST

After initial training, new meteorologists are assigned to base weather stations or outlying weather support facilities. Here they:

- Direct enlisted personnel gathering weather data from surface instruments, balloons, radar, and satellites
- Analyze data and information from charts and other weather stations
- Prepare short-term and long-range weather forecasts
- Brief air crews on weather conditions

Timeline

15-18 yrs

9-11 yrs

4 yrs

# NUCLEAR ENGINEERS

ARMY
NAVY
MARINE CORPS

*C*areer nuclear engineers conduct research and develop projects using the most advanced technology. As a nuclear engineer, you may work with lasers, particle beams, weapons effects, or space environments. Your contributions will be vital to maintaining the nation's defense. You begin your career in a laboratory. You will work with and learn from some of the world's foremost nuclear engineers. As you develop your knowledge and leadership abilities, you will take on greater responsibility. There are opportunities to advance to director of a military research laboratory.

## DUTY ASSIGNMENT

Nuclear engineers work in laboratories, offices, and sometimes in the field. During a typical career, a nuclear engineer performs and directs research and serves with military staffs. Almost all assignments are in the United States. However, there are a few opportunities for assignment abroad.

## SPECIALIZATION

Nuclear engineers specialize in military applications of nuclear energy. They conduct research, direct design and development projects, and manage purchasing contracts. Most seek to become an expert in one area of the field. Some areas of research are:

- Nuclear reactor design for ships, submarines, or land (safety, performance, theory, and testing)
- Nuclear reactor operation
- Nuclear safety (storage and handling of fuel, reactors, and weapons)
- Nuclear effects on electronic and other equipment
- Technical aspects of nuclear weapons policy

As nuclear engineers advance to senior officer positions, they maintain their specialized knowledge and increase their general knowledge of the field.

## Profile: Peter Flambeau

Lieutenant Colonel Peter (Pete) Flambeau enjoyed physics in high school. The man who was his physics teacher and football coach suggested college and a major in physics. Pete decided to take his advice and graduated with honors from a college in Massachusetts.

Pete joined the ROTC in his junior year in college. When he completed his bachelor's degree, he requested and received a delayed entry to active duty so he could complete a master's degree in nuclear physics. When he entered active duty as a second lieutenant, the Air Force needed many officers as weapons controllers. He trained at Tyndall Air Force Base (AFB), FL, and then for 2 years controlled fighter interceptors from MacDill, FL, and Myrtle Beach, SC.

Pete and his family enjoyed Air Force life. When his service obligation ended, he decided to continue a career in the service. Pete wanted to redirect his career to physics, so he applied to the Air Force Institute of Technology in Dayton, OH. He was accepted and completed studies for a doctoral degree (Ph.D.) in nuclear effects. He was promoted to captain while he was at school.

To conduct research for his Ph.D., he was assigned to the Air Force Weapons Laboratory in Albuquerque, NM. He also worked on other projects, including computer predictions of nuclear weapons effects.

Once Pete earned his Ph.D., his leadership duties increased. He led research for several important projects, including the MX ballistic missile program. He also spent a tour teaching physics at the Air Force Academy. "I really enjoyed working with the cadets," Pete says. "It was a rewarding tour." Promoted to major, he was selected to attend Air Force Command and Staff College full time for advanced professional military education.

Today Pete is deputy director of Space Physics at the Air Force Geophysics Laboratory in Hanscom, MA. Smiling, he says, "After assignments all over North America, I now live 5 miles from the place I was born and raised."

Pete says his career has been exciting. "I have had variety and challenges conducting research and leading the scientists who worked for me." He looks forward to being the chief director of critical space systems projects over the next several years.

## ADVANCEMENT

Nuclear engineers conduct research, design weapons and related systems, and manage projects critical to the nation's defense. They must understand the fundamental principles of physics, math, and other areas of science. They must master the most recent advances of an incredibly complex technological profession. They also need to become excellent leaders and managers.

To advance, nuclear engineers must develop their research skills. They must be able to design research programs, tests, and experiments. They work constantly to keep abreast of innovations in the field. It is essential for nuclear engineers to have an advanced degree (master's or doctorate), and there are many opportunities for fully-funded education to achieve this career milestone. Nuclear engineers must also develop their leadership skills to advance to the most senior levels in the profession.

The Air Force is the only service with a distinct career path in nuclear engineering. In the Army, Navy, and Marine Corps, officers typically enter nuclear engineering after qualifying in another occupation. They most often enter the field after 6 to 10 years of service and attending graduate school for a nuclear engineering degree. In these cases, nuclear engineering is a secondary occupational specialty and not a career, although officers may periodically return to assignments related to nuclear engineering.

## RELATED MILITARY OCCUPATIONS

If you are interested in a career in nuclear engineering, you may also want to consider a career as a physicist, computer systems engineer, electrical and electronics engineer, or chemist. See the Engineering, Science, and Technical Occupations cluster in the Military Officer Occupations section of this book for descriptions of these occupations.

## TRAINING

Initial training for most nuclear engineers is on the job at a military-run laboratory. Nuclear engineers typically enter the service with a master's or bachelor's degree in physics, nuclear engineering, or a related field. After one or two tours in a laboratory, most nuclear engineers attend graduate school funded by their service. They earn a Ph.D. or a master's degree. The course work for their degree usually includes research in an area of direct interest both to them and to the service.

Nuclear engineers are encouraged to complete professional military education programs to prepare them for senior officer positions. These programs involve study of military subjects such as leadership, strategy, tactics, and planning large-scale operations. They may be completed by correspondence or full-time study.

## TYPICAL CAREER PATH

### LABORATORY DIRECTOR

Outstanding nuclear engineering staff officers with career-long records of top performance as leaders, managers, and expert nuclear engineers may advance to become laboratory directors. At this time in their career, they:

- Command a research laboratory, monitoring research, directing research, and leading teams of scientists and technicians
- Develop and consult on military service research and development strategy
- Provide expert advice to national-level staffs
- Manage government weapons acquisition programs

**15-18 yrs**

### NUCLEAR ENGINEERING STAFF OFFICER

Senior nuclear engineers who have excellent research and managerial skills may advance to become nuclear engineering staff officers. Here they:

- Manage research projects, directing civilian and military scientists
- Provide senior military staffs with expert advice on matters concerning nuclear weapons
- Assist scientists from many other disciplines in solving shared research or production problems
- Conduct independent research in a special area of expertise

**9-11 yrs**

### SENIOR NUCLEAR ENGINEER

Nuclear engineers who have demonstrated technical proficiency and the potential to become excellent researchers and leaders may advance to become senior nuclear engineers. At this level, they may:

- Conduct basic and applied research in a laboratory
- Complete a master's degree or Ph.D. in an area of nuclear engineering
- Teach courses in their field or specialty
- Provide technical direction for research performed by contractors, universities, or government research laboratories.

**4 yrs**

### NUCLEAR ENGINEER

Following initial training, new nuclear engineers are assigned to research and development laboratories, test sites, or nuclear reactor prototypes. Nuclear engineers:

- Work with experienced research scientists on projects such as effects of the outer space electromagnetic environment on people and electronic equipment, laser and particle beam technology, weapons design, or effects of nuclear weapons on military equipment
- Develop professional research skills
- Give technical support to projects demanding knowledge in nuclear engineering

**Timeline**

# PHYSICIANS AND SURGEONS

ARMY
NAVY
AIR FORCE
COAST GUARD

**M**ilitary physicians and surgeons lead health care teams in the field and in military hospitals and clinics around the world. As a physician or surgeon you will diagnose and treat military personnel and their family members. You begin your career treating patients under the direction of an experienced staff doctor. As your knowledge and skills increase, you will specialize in a medical field. There are opportunities to become medical director of a hospital or clinic.

## DUTY ASSIGNMENT

Most physicians and surgeons work in clinics, hospitals, and medical centers at military bases in the U.S. and overseas. Some work aboard naval vessels or hospital ships. Many serve temporary duty assignments in field hospitals during combat exercises and maneuvers. The military services strive to provide doctors with a stable work environment. As a result, physicians and surgeons often serve extended duty assignments at a single hospital in the U.S., Europe, or the Pacific. Positions for physicians and surgeons in the Coast Guard are filled by U.S. Public Health Service Officers.

## SPECIALIZATION

Physicians and surgeons specialize as they gain experience and education. For physicians, typical specialties include family practice, pediatrics (providing care from birth to adolescence), and endocrinology (treating disorders caused by imbalances and diseases of the body's system of internal glands). Surgeons begin in general surgery and typically specialize in neurosurgery (surgery involving the brain and central nervous system), heart surgery, or cosmetic/reconstructive surgery.

### Profile: Anthony Rugieri

Anthony Rugieri enjoyed biology and wanted to become a doctor. He chose the Army because of the educational opportunities it offered for obtaining a medical degree. "The Army internship gave doctors a chance to rotate in departments and to practice many medical specialties," he says. Anthony's first assignment was directing emergency room services at a large hospital near Washington, DC.

In his next assignment, Anthony went to Vietnam. He found the life of a combat doctor challenging. He earned two bronze stars; one for valor and one for exceptionally meritorious service. After this tour, he decided to "stay awhile" in Army medicine.

Returning from Vietnam, Anthony was selected for a fully-funded advanced training program in internal medicine. He stayed on at the hospital where he trained and served a year as staff physician in internal medicine.

After a tour with the Office of the Army Surgeon General in Washington, DC. Anthony and his family enjoyed a tour in Germany together. Anthony was the chief of internal medicine at an Army hospital and followed this assignment with a position as chief of hospital clinics and community health services.

In Germany, Anthony qualified for certification in family practice medicine. This was a new program in military medicine. As one of the first doctors qualified, Anthony returned to the United States and became the chief of family services at a large hospital on the East Coast. He also directed a residency program for doctors in advanced training.

Today, Anthony is a colonel, directing quality assurance for the Surgeon General of the Army. Anthony says, "One of the best things about my career has been the opportunity to work in many different jobs. I am always looking forward to my next assignment."

## ADVANCEMENT

Military physicians and surgeons must have outstanding stamina, perseverance, and a desire to serve others. They must be scientifically astute and able to communicate well in speaking and writing. They are expected to learn and train continually throughout their career.

To advance, physicians and surgeons must be superb medical practitioners. They must be expert observers to diagnose illness or injury. They need excellent skills in gathering, organizing, and analyzing information to make accurate diagnoses and plan treatments. Their professional skills must continue to develop, and they must demonstrate their ability to lead and train younger doctors. When assigned to teaching hospitals, doctors are evaluated on their ability to instruct in both classroom and patient situations.

Physicians and surgeons who have excellent records of performance, leadership, and continuing education may advance to senior positions. Only the best-qualified personnel are selected for advancement, and competition is intense for promotions and career-enhancing duty assignments.

## RELATED MILITARY OCCUPATIONS

If you are interested in a medical career, you may also want to consider other military medical occupations. See the Health Diagnosing and Treating Practitioner Occupations cluster in the Military Officer Occupations section of this book for descriptions of these occupations. The nursing career is also described in the next military officer career path description.

## TRAINING

Initial training for physicians and surgeons includes basic orientation in military medical service administrative, professional, and military policies. Throughout their careers, physicians and surgeons are expected to keep pace with advances in medicine by attending professional symposiums and seminars and by reading technical literature.

Almost all physicians and surgeons will attend fully funded programs to obtain advanced medical specialties. Physicians specialize in a nonsurgical branch of medicine, and surgeons in a branch of surgery. Specialty education may take place in military or civilian teaching hospitals. Programs may require 1 or more years to complete.

Physicians and surgeons are also given opportunities for professional military education to prepare them for senior officer positions. These programs include study of military subjects such as strategy, tactics, and planning large-scale operations. These courses are usually completed by correspondence, but a few doctors attend full-time courses.

## TYPICAL CAREER PATH

**Timeline**

### MEDICAL DIRECTOR

Staff doctors with outstanding medical or surgical ability and outstanding records of leadership may advance to become medical directors. Typically, they:

- Direct medical services at a military hospital or large clinic
- Conduct a limited practice to maintain their skills
- Direct training of interns and residents
- Confer with staff doctors to verify diagnoses and treatments
- Evaluate staff doctors

**15-18 yrs**

### STAFF DOCTOR

Resident doctors who complete specialty training may become staff doctors. At this level, they may:

- Practice in their specialty
- Supervise and advise residents, general medical officers, interns, and students
- Serve as chief of a clinic or medical department
- Evaluate resident doctors

**9-11 yrs**

### RESIDENT DOCTOR

General medical officers with 1 to 3 years of excellent performance return to military or civilian teaching hospitals to gain medical specialties. As residents, they may:

- Complete rigorous programs of study in a specialty
- Instruct interns and medical students
- Conduct medical "rounds" to supervise interns and students and care for their own patients
- Meet with hospital staff to discuss cases and procedures

**2-4 yrs**

### GENERAL MEDICAL OFFICER

Doctors who complete their internships are usually assigned to hospitals, clinics, or, possibly, large ships as general medical officers. They:

- Examine patients, and diagnose and treat illnesses
- Order X-rays, tests, and medication
- Conduct medical "rounds"

**1-2 yrs**

### INTERN

Medical school graduates who have not completed their internship training serve as interns in a supervised program of medical practice training. Here they:

- Work in a teaching hospital, diagnosing and treating patients
- Accompany resident and staff doctors on medical "rounds" to evaluate patient condition
- Help train medical students

# REGISTERED NURSES

ARMY
NAVY
AIR FORCE
COAST GUARD

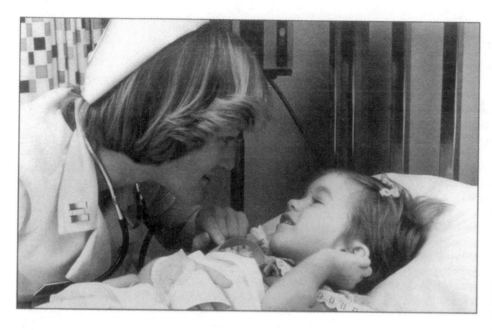

**M**ilitary registered nurses care for the sick, injured, and wounded. They are a vital part of the military health care team. As a military nurse, you begin your career administering medications prescribed by doctors, monitoring patients' progress, and training and directing enlisted medical technicians. As you gain experience and your skills increase, you will serve in positions of increasing responsibility. There are opportunities to become director of nursing care activities at a hospital or clinic.

## DUTY ASSIGNMENT

Most military nurses work in clinics, hospitals, and medical centers at military bases in the U.S. and overseas. Some work aboard naval vessels and hospital ships. Many are assigned to temporary duty in field hospitals during combat exercises and field maneuvers. Others serve in ambulances, evacuation helicopters, or medivac transport planes. There are good opportunities for overseas assignments, particularly in Europe and the Pacific Islands. Positions for registered nurses in the Coast Guard are filled by U.S. Public Health Service Officers.

## ADVANCEMENT

Military registered nurses must want to serve others. They must be able to deal with their patients' emotional well-being as well as their medical needs. They also need to develop leadership and training skills. Initiative is needed to maintain a high level of patient care.

To advance, nurses must be highly skilled professionals. They must master basic nursing and leadership skills quickly. Seeking varied assignments will increase their professional expertise. Almost all nurses specialize, either by acquiring an advanced degree or through specialty training programs. An excellent performance record, combined with specialization and a variety of increasingly responsible positions, is the key to advancement.

Nurses compete with their peers for promotion and career-enhancing assignments. Only the best-qualified personnel are selected for promotion, and competition intensifies with each increase in rank.

### Profile: Janice Kendall

When she was 3 years old, Navy captain Janice Kendall had an attack of appendicitis. She spent months in the hospital. She says, "I was so impressed with the nurses who cared for me that I knew I wanted to be one too."

Janice, a Canadian, went to diploma school, then did more work to train in psychiatric nursing. After practicing several years, she tried nursing in the United States. There, an uncle in the Navy suggested she try Navy nursing. Feeling the 2-year commitment wasn't too bad, Janice joined.

Because of her previous experience, Janice was commissioned as a lieutenant, junior grade (O-2). She began her career monitoring seven psychiatric wards as part of a close-knit team with the psychiatrist at the Navy hospital in San Diego.

Her second tour was in Subic Bay, the Philippines. She used her emergency skills there, handling many cases from the Vietnam conflict. The hours were long but rewarding. During this assignment she used her leave to tour the Far East—Hong Kong, Bangkok, India, and Japan. She also met her husband when he was on leave from Vietnam.

Janice was recognized not only as an outstanding nurse, but as an excellent leader. Her next few tours took her to hospitals where she directed other nurses and trained Navy hospital corpsmen. Training the hospital corpsmen has been a favorite activity for Janice. Navy corpsmen are often the only medical people on board submarines, small ships, and marine combat units.

Janice was selected for further education. After earning her baccalaureate degree in nursing, she was assigned to Camp Pendleton, CA, and then to Okinawa, a Japanese island. In Okinawa she served as assistant director of nursing services and director of family advocacy for all Navy and Marine Corps families on the island.

Today, Janice assists the admiral who directs the Navy Nurse Corps. She has been at the hub of Navy nursing activity over the past several years. She says, "My experience has given me a lot to share with the young nurses I will be directing in my next tour." She is looking forward to serving as assistant director of nursing at one of the largest naval hospitals in the world.

Looking back over 24 years of service, she says, "I like everything about it. It's never the same, you constantly gain experience, see new places, and never lose seniority."

## TRAINING

Initial training for nurses includes orientation in military medical administration, nursing programs and procedures, and leadership. Nurses continue to attend seminars, short formal courses, and conferences throughout their careers to improve their nursing and patient care skills. In addition to these programs, they study on their own to stay abreast of advancements in the field.

Almost all nurses have opportunities to obtain nursing specialties and advanced degrees, often in fully-funded programs. Clinical programs educate nurses in anesthesiology, pediatric nursing, or other clinical specialties. Educational specialties enable nurses to teach other nurses, patients, or enlisted medical technicians. Special programs in administration train them to manage nursing and hospital programs. Many military nurses will have the opportunity to pursue an advanced degree in a nursing specialty.

Nurses are also given opportunities for professional military education to prepare them for senior officer positions. These programs include study of military subjects such as strategy, tactics, and planning large-scale operations. They are usually completed by correspondence.

## SPECIALIZATION

After gaining experience as staff nurses, registered nurses may specialize in such fields as mental health, anesthesiology, operating room nursing, nursing education, pediatrics, or nursing administration.

## RELATED MILITARY OCCUPATIONS

If you are interested in a medical career, you may also want to consider other military medical occupations. See the Health Care Occupations cluster in the Military Officer Occupations section for descriptions of these occupations. The career of physician and surgeon is also described in the previous military officer career description.

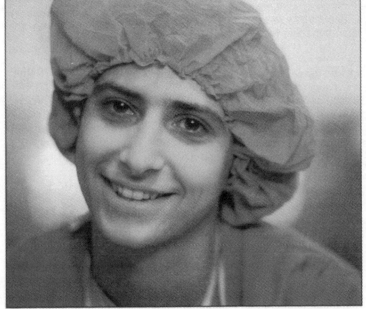

## TYPICAL CAREER PATH

### DIRECTOR OF NURSING CARE

Nurses with outstanding performance records and managerial skills may become directors of nursing care activities at hospitals or other medical treatment facilities. At this level, they:

- Manage all nursing services at their hospital or facility
- Advise medical staff and hospital administration on nursing services
- Direct nursing staff in maintaining approved standards of patient care
- Direct nursing orientation and training programs

### PATIENT CARE COORDINATOR

Charge nurses who have excellent managerial skills may advance to coordinate nursing services for wards or clinics. Here they:

- Assign nurses to shifts and wards
- Determine the adequacy of nursing care
- Inspect rooms and wards
- Accompany doctors on medical "rounds" to keep informed of special orders
- See that drugs, solutions, and equipment are ordered and records are maintained
- Investigate problems of patients, nurses, and enlisted medical technicians

### CHARGE NURSE

Staff nurses with excellent patient care skills who show leadership ability may advance to become charge nurses. They are responsible for all nursing activity on a hospital ward. At this level, they:

- Discuss patient conditions and nursing activities during change-of-shift meetings
- Assign staff nurses to patients
- Consult with the patient care coordinator on unusual nursing problems
- Participate in nursing orientation and training programs
- Evaluate performance of staff nurses

### STAFF NURSE

After initial training, registered nurses are assigned to patient care duty at a clinical service ward of a hospital or medical center. Typically, staff nurses:

- Take and record "vital signs" of patients, such as temperature, pulse, and blood pressure
- Administer medication prescribed by doctors
- Observe patient condition and reaction to drugs
- Assist doctors during examinations and treatments
- Change or direct the changing of bandages and dressings
- Direct enlisted medical and nursing technicians in routine patient care

**Timeline**

15-18 yrs

9-11 yrs

4 yrs

# SHIP AND SUBMARINE OFFICERS

ARMY
NAVY
COAST GUARD

**S** hip and submarine officers sail the world's most powerful vessels, from fast-attack submarines to huge aircraft carriers. As a ship or submarine officer, you will lead highly trained enlisted specialists in maintaining and operating the ship's systems. You begin your career leading a team of 10 to 50 enlisted personnel. You may be responsible for maintaining and operating the ship's power plant, missiles and guns, or radar. You will learn to navigate the ship in all weather, day and night. As you gain experience, you will serve in positions of increasing responsibility. There are opportunities to become captain of a surface ship or submarine.

## ADVANCEMENT

Ship and submarine officers direct the sailing and combat operations of their vessels. They must complete extensive qualifications programs, learning to navigate and operate their ships in all weather, in any area of the world's oceans. They direct enlisted specialists who maintain and operate the ship's radar, power plants, or weapons systems. Ship and submarine officers must be aggressive, self-motivated, and excellent leaders.

To advance, ship and submarine officers must complete all shipboard qualifications and have outstanding leadership and management records. They must also develop special skills. They may get training in a warfare specialty, such as hunting submarines, or they may pursue an advanced degree.

Ship and submarine officers compete with their peers for promotion and career-enhancing assignments. Outstanding performance in every assignment is the key to success. Only the best-qualified personnel are selected for advancement, and competition intensifies with each increase in rank.

Only the Navy offers a career in submarines. In the Army there are duty assignments involving directing units of landing craft and tugboats. However, there is no typical career path for ship officers.

## Profile: James Stoddard

From the time James (Jim) Stoddard was in high school in New York City, he wanted to be a Navy submarine officer, and then he qualified for the Naval Academy. "I felt the discipline at the academy would help me get the most out of my education." Adapting well to academy life, he graduated near the top of his class with a degree in Naval Architecture.

After submarine school in Groton, Connecticut, he went on his first submarine to the Western Pacific. Here, he felt the first thrill of command responsibility as an Officer of the Deck. On watch, he directed the "sailing" and safe operations of his submarine. "The Officer of the Deck is completely trusted by the submarine's captain," Jim says, "I was representing the captain and in charge of the vessel and her crew."

Jim worked hard and advanced rapidly. As a lieutenant, he was assigned to graduate studies at the Massachusetts Institute of Technology and the Woods Hole Oceanographic Institution. He went on to nuclear power school and tours in several nuclear-powered ballistic missile submarines.

Jim served tours in all the major departments of a submarine. He mastered engineering, weapons, and operations. As he gained experience, he became a master tactician and assisted the captains of the submarines on which he served. They used their knowledge of the underwater environment to keep their submarine hidden while carrying out missions assigned to their vessel. He was decorated several times for submarine operations and leadership.

During his career Jim and his wife have enjoyed a unique part of Navy life, and a special commitment to each other. Whenever possible, she joined him at the ports his submarines would visit. They spent time together in Australia, England, Germany, and many ports elsewhere in the world.

Today he is the captain of a nuclear attack submarine. Jim says he has most enjoyed the responsibility of each assignment. "And," he adds, "I have really seen the world."

## DUTY ASSIGNMENT

Ship and submarine officers live and work in their vessels at sea. While in port, they spend the workday aboard their ships. They may travel to locations around the world, and some ships and submarines have "home ports" in the Pacific Islands or Scotland. At regular points in their careers, officers are assigned to a job on shore, usually in offices. Ship and submarine officers typically serve a number of tours on sea duty throughout their careers.

## SPECIALIZATION

Officers of surface ships must have a broad knowledge of their vessels. In addition, they usually focus on one specific area of their ships, such as engineering (power plants, pumps, or fuel systems), combat systems (weapons or electronics operation and maintenance), or operations (tactics and navigation). Some ships are nuclear-powered and require officers trained in nuclear reactor operation. All submarine officers are nuclear qualified. As they advance to senior-level assignments, ship officers are expected to learn about more areas in greater depth.

Because a submarine is a smaller self-contained unit, submarine officers must have a detailed knowledge of their vessels and all its systems.

When assigned ashore, officers often specialize in areas that will help them in senior staff positions later in their careers. These "second careers" may be in personnel management, fleet operations planning, or management of programs to develop or buy large weapons systems.

## TRAINING

Initial training for ship officers includes 15 weeks of classroom instruction. Training covers ship operations, naval tactics, navigation, and the responsibilities of each department aboard ships. After they attend "Surface Warfare Officer School," officers may be further trained for their first assignment aboard ships such as cutters, destroyers, battleships, or aircraft carriers.

Training for submarine officers begins with 12 months of courses on nuclear power. Following nuclear power school, they attend submarine basic school to learn submarine operations and tactics.

Both ship and submarine officers receive advanced training throughout their careers. They often get technical training in such areas as sonar, radar, missile systems, and power plants. They may attend graduate school for advanced degrees.

Ship and submarine officers also have opportunities for professional military education to prepare them for senior officer positions. These programs include study of military subjects such as strategy, tactics, and planning large-scale operations. They may be completed either by correspondence or full-time study.

## RELATED MILITARY OCCUPATIONS

If you are interested in a career as a ship or submarine officer, you may also want to consider a career in transportation management or some other transportation occupation. See the Transportation Occupations and Executive, Administrative, and Managerial Occupations clusters in the Military Officer Occupations section of this book for descriptions of these occupations.

## TYPICAL CAREER PATH

### SHIP CAPTAIN

Executive officers who have consistently shown outstanding leadership and technical ability may be selected to be ship or submarine captains. At this level, they:

- Command the operations of a ship or submarine and crew
- Study orders and plan exercises and maneuvers to carry out missions
- Direct daily operations and plan tactics
- Direct the planning of fleet operations exercises as part of a naval staff

**15-18 yrs**

### EXECUTIVE/STAFF OFFICER

Department heads with broad experience and outstanding leadership abilities may advance to second-in-command (executive officer) of a ship or submarine. At this level, they:

- Issue orders and instructions to assist the ship's captain in daily operations
- Manage administrative and maintenance activities
- Command the ship or submarine in the captain's absence
- Plan fleet exercises as part of a naval staff

**9-11 yrs**

### DEPARTMENT HEAD

Division officers who show leadership potential in several ship divisions may advance to become department heads. Department heads:

- Manage a major department such as engineering, navigation/operations, or combat systems
- Train new officers in seamanship and leadership
- Plan and coordinate the department's activities
- Conduct drills to evaluate the department's performance in emergency or combat situations
- Evaluate the performance of division officers

**4 yrs**

### DIVISION OFFICER

After initial training, new ship and submarine officers are assigned to their first vessels as division officers. Here they:

- Lead a division of 10 to 50 sailors
- Stand watches in the engine room, ship's bridge, or ship's weapons systems control center
- Plan daily and long-term work schedules
- Plan and monitor the training of sailors in their division
- Evaluate performance of enlisted personnel

# SUPPLY AND WAREHOUSING MANAGERS

ARMY
NAVY
AIR FORCE
MARINE CORPS
COAST GUARD

**N**o military force can function without supplies. Supply and warehousing managers make sure our military units around the world have the food, weapons, uniforms, trucks, airplanes, fuel, and spare parts they need to fulfill their missions. As a supply and warehousing manager, you will buy, store, issue, and keep track of vast quantities of equipment and material. You begin your career leading a small group of enlisted specialists in one type of supply such as food, petroleum, or parts. As you gain experience, you will serve in positions of increasing responsibility. There are opportunities to become the supply and warehousing director of a large military base or major command area.

## DUTY ASSIGNMENT

Most supply and warehousing managers work in offices, warehouses, and material-handling facilities at military bases in the U.S. and overseas. They work in facilities similar to wholesale, retail, and warehouse operations in the civilian world. Some supply and warehousing managers are assigned to ships or air units. Many serve temporary duty assignments in the field during combat exercises and maneuvers. There are significant opportunities for overseas assignments, particularly in Europe and the Pacific Islands.

## RELATED MILITARY OCCUPATIONS

If you are interested in a career as a supply and warehousing manager, you may also want to consider a career in purchasing and contract management, transportation management, or a related field. See the Executive, Administrative, and Managerial Occupations cluster in the Military Officer Occupations section of this book for descriptions of these occupations. The career path of a transportation manager is described in the next military officer career path description.

---

### Profile: Benjamin Travis

Benjamin (Ben) Travis wanted to serve in the military. He also wanted a college education and a chance to play college basketball. So he applied for and was selected to attend the U.S. Coast Guard Academy, where he lettered in basketball 3 years.

Like many Coast Guard officers, Ben served two tours of general duty before he specialized. He requested for his first assignment a tour as gunnery (or weapons) officer on a Coast Guard cutter going to Vietnam. His ship gave gunfire support to U.S. soldiers and Marines on land.

Back in the States, Ben married his girlfriend whom he had met while he was a cadet at the Academy. They enjoyed living in Miami Beach, the site of his next tour. Here, Ben commanded a 95-foot patrol boat and a crew of 15 men. He and his crew rescued stranded boats and enforced customs and maritime law in the Miami area.

Ben's next assignment was to graduate school, where he earned an M.B.A. in one intense year of study. Always interested in finance, he specialized in supply and warehousing management. (The Coast Guard calls supply officers "comptrollers.")

As a lieutenant, his first comptroller assignment was with the 7th Coast Guard District in Miami, developing and managing a budget of $35–$45 million. Ben says, "I really enjoyed the independence and responsibility of that job."

As he advanced, he served in positions of more authority. As a lieutenant commander in Washington, DC, he briefed congressmen, senators, and other government officials on Coast Guard budget and procurement plans. He also enjoyed several general duty tours outside his occupational specialty. He especially enjoyed a tour as executive officer of a large Coast Guard cutter.

Now in Washington, DC, with the rank of commander, Ben develops comptroller policies for the Coast Guard and oversees procurement of every item the Coast Guard buys, anywhere in the world. Reflecting on his career he says, "So far, I honestly haven't had an assignment that I didn't enjoy. The variety, the challenges, and the responsibility have been tremendously rewarding."

## ADVANCEMENT

Supply and warehousing managers are vital to every military operation. They must be excellent planners, organizers, and leaders. From the first, they are entrusted with large quantities of valuable materials. They must become expert at using the supply system. Basic skills include purchasing, storage, and accounting for supply items.

To advance, supply and warehousing managers must have excellent records of performance. Their accounting skills must be outstanding, supplies must arrive at the right places at the right time, and they must show excellent leadership. As they master the supply system, they are assigned to positions of greater responsibility. They manage larger areas and lead more supply personnel. To advance to the most senior positions, supply and warehousing managers must seek out, and do well in, leadership and command positions. An advanced degree is helpful when combined with a record of outstanding performance.

Supply and warehousing managers compete with their peers for promotion and career-enhancing assignments. Only the best-qualified personnel are selected for advancement, and competition intensifies with each increase in rank.

## SPECIALIZATION

Supply and warehousing managers may specialize in such areas as bulk petroleum storage and handling, aerial delivery of supplies, or supply and material management. With an advanced degree, they may also specialize in such areas as computer science, financial management, or weapons and material contracting and purchasing.

## TRAINING

Initial training for supply and warehousing managers includes 3 to 6 months of intensive classroom instruction. Officers are trained to use and manage their services' supply system. Budget management, ordering, storage, distribution, and leadership are some of the subjects they study. Depending on their assignment, supply and warehousing managers may also be trained in petroleum management, food management, or aerial cargo delivery.

Advanced training prepares supply and warehousing managers for more responsible positions. Officers may be trained to operate computerized inventory and planning systems, to manage large warehouses and storage depots, or to prepare and manage major contracts with companies supplying the armed forces.

Almost all supply and warehousing managers earn advanced degrees. Some attend schools in programs funded by their service, others obtain degrees on their own after duty time. Degrees in computer sciences, industrial management, and business administration are particularly helpful.

Supply and warehousing managers are also given opportunities for professional military education to prepare them for senior officer positions. These programs include study of military subjects such as strategy, tactics, and planning large-scale operations. They may be completed either by correspondence or full-time study.

## TYPICAL CAREER PATH

### SUPPLY AND WAREHOUSING DIRECTOR

Supply staff officers with outstanding records may advance to direct major supply and warehousing activities. At this level, they:

- Command a supply facility or direct the supply operations at a military base
- Advise senior service commanders on logistics and supply management
- Evaluate bids and proposals submitted by suppliers
- Conduct inspections of supply units

### SUPPLY STAFF OFFICER

Senior supply officers who have demonstrated leadership in a series of assignments may advance to become supply staff officers. At this level, they:

- Assist the supply and warehousing director in administrative and management duties
- Help headquarters staff officers plan supply requirements for operational missions
- Analyze purchasing and distribution patterns
- Direct and evaluate studies to improve supply methods

### SENIOR SUPPLY OFFICER

Supply officers who do well in a variety of supply assignments advance to more demanding supply management duties. At this level, they:

- Manage a supply or warehouse operation, directing other officers and enlisted personnel
- Train new supply officers
- Advise commanding officers of supply requirements
- Inspect their supply facilities

### SUPPLY OFFICER

After initial training, new supply officers are assigned to a supply unit where they gain experience in supply and warehouse operations. At this level, they:

- Direct civilian or military personnel in ordering, receiving, and issuing equipment and supplies
- Direct task assignments and prepare duty assignment and management reports
- Inspect storage facilities, giving instructions on material handling and safety
- Evaluate the performance of personnel working under their leadership

Timeline

15-18 yrs

9-11 yrs

4 yrs

# TRANSPORTATION MANAGERS

**T**ransportation managers run the trucking, air, rail, and sea transportation system that moves military equipment, supplies, and personnel all over the world. As a transportation manager, you will direct a part of that system. You begin by leading a team of trained enlisted specialists. You may direct heavy trucking, landing craft, or air terminal operations. As you gain experience, you will serve in positions of greater responsibility, directing larger operations. There are opportunities to become director of transportation for a group of military bases or a major command area.

## DUTY ASSIGNMENT

Transportation managers work in a variety of locations at military bases in the U.S. and overseas. Their "office" may be the deck of a large landing craft or the flight line of an air cargo terminal. They may also work in an office at a port or a truck motor pool. Many transportation managers support troops in the field during combat exercises and maneuvers. Some managers work in Washington, DC, where most of the military's logistics planning takes place. There are good opportunities for overseas assignments, particularly in Europe and the Pacific Islands.

## RELATED MILITARY OCCUPATIONS

If you are interested in a career in transportation management, you may also want to consider a career in transportation maintenance or supply and warehousing management. See the Executive, Administrative, and Managerial Occupations cluster in the Military Officer Occupations section of this book for descriptions of these occupations. The career in supply and warehousing management is also described in the previous military officer career description.

---

### Profile: Douglas Kronchek

Douglas (Doug) Kronchek went to work on an automobile assembly line right after high school. Knowing he would probably be drafted, he chose the Army and enlisted. Doug did so well in aircraft maintenance training, he was encouraged to apply for Officer Candidate School where he earned his commission. He chose the transportation corps because he wanted to stay close to aircraft and maintenance.

Doug spent his first tour in Vietnam, leading a platoon in aircraft maintenance. After that tour he held several more responsible positions in the United States.

At the end of his obligated service, Doug went back to civilian life and attended school full-time on the GI Bill. After 2 years, the Army offered him the chance to return to active duty. He and his wife thought it over. Remembering the variety and challenge of Army life, they decided to return.

Doug spent a year in Vietnam, then a long tour in Okinawa where his family joined him. He then returned to the States where he completed his bachelor's degree with full funding from the Army and the GI Bill, and his master's degree in transportation management with partial funding from the Army.

Doug also earned a secondary specialty in the supply field and began a series of assignments leading units of increasing size. In one of these jobs he directed the transportation of all personnel and supplies for an armored division.

A high point in his career was a 2-year tour as Army port and air terminal expert with the Navy. Doug arranged the transportation to move people and supplies to and from the U.S. scientific research stations in Antarctica. He says, "I worked with private and government transportation agencies and officials from the United States, Australia, and New Zealand."

Doug has spent the past several years at the Pentagon in Washington, DC, as chief logistician for the Pacific. He is the expert on all Army transportation and supply activity in the Pacific.

Just selected for his next assignment, Lieutenant Colonel Doug Kronchek will assume command of one of the 6 Army transportation movement control centers in the world. "It's going to be fun," he says. "It's a new challenge in a new area for me. My command will control movement of Army personnel, equipment, and supplies through the transportation network to destinations around the world."

---

## ADVANCEMENT

Transportation managers must be excellent leaders, planners, organizers, and problem solvers. They must understand military and civilian air, land, and water transportation systems. Good judgment and careful coordination are needed to avoid costly and time-consuming "bottlenecks" in the system.

To advance, transportation managers must have an outstanding performance record in positions of increasing responsibility. They must get people and cargo to the right destination at the right time. As they master the transportation system, they are assigned positions directing larger and more diverse transportation units. Many transportation managers obtain advanced degrees. An advanced degree, when combined with excellent performance, increases the chances for promotion.

Transportation managers compete with their peers for promotion and career-enhancing assignments. Only the best-qualified are selected, and competition intensifies with each increase in rank.

In the Navy and Coast Guard, there are duty assignments involving transportation management. However, there is no true career path for transportation managers in those two service branches.

## SPECIALIZATION

Some transportation managers specialize in a particular mode or type of transportation operation. Specialties include ground and rail transportation; air, marine, and sea terminal operations; and traffic management.

## TRAINING

Initial training for transportation managers includes up to 5 months of both classroom and field instruction. Training covers transportation policy, maintenance and operation of vehicles and equipment, planning, and leadership. This instruction prepares officers for their first assignments.

Transportation officers have opportunities for advanced training to prepare them for future assignments. Courses may include budgeting, combined transportation specialty operations, or management development. Many transportation managers also receive specialty training in areas such as marine terminal operations, air transportation management, or truck transportation.

Most transportation managers earn master's degrees. Some attend school in a program funded by their service; others obtain degrees on their own after duty time. Degrees in transportation management, computer sciences, logistics management, and systems analysis are particularly helpful.

Transportation managers are also given opportunities for professional military education to prepare them for senior officer positions. These programs include study of military subjects such as strategy, tactics, and planning large-scale operations. They may be completed either by correspondence or full-time study.

## TYPICAL CAREER PATH

### TRANSPORTATION DIRECTOR

Outstanding transportation staff officers may advance to become transportation directors. At this level, they may:

- Command a truck or boat transportation battalion
- Direct an air transport terminal at a major air base
- Advise major base and senior area commanders on transportation matters
- Direct inspection programs for transportation activities they command

### TRANSPORTATION STAFF OFFICER

Senior transportation officers with leadership experience and excellent records of performance may advance to become transportation staff officers. Here they may:

- Coordinate with other military services to transport supplies from air, sea, or land bases to troops in the field
- Develop long-range plans for use of transportation equipment and personnel
- Evaluate new transportation procedures and equipment
- Advise combat commanders on transportation matters
- Teach transportation courses

### SENIOR TRANSPORTATION OFFICER

Transportation officers who perform well and who are good leaders may advance to become senior transportation officers. At this level, they:

- Inspect transportation, maintenance, or operations facilities
- Command companies of trucks, landing craft, or tugboats
- Plan missions and operations to support base and field operations
- Evaluate the performance of transportation officers and senior enlisted personnel

### TRANSPORTATION OFFICER

After initial training, transportation officers are assigned to truck, air, boat, port (harbor), or terminal units. Typically, they:

- Direct enlisted personnel in operating and maintaining transportation equipment
- Schedule equipment use
- Train personnel in transportation procedures
- Prepare reports showing the use and costs of operations

Timeline

15-18 yrs

9-11 yrs

4 yrs

# Career Mapping

As you progress in your career, you will probably move to new jobs or positions. For civilians, this often means changing employers. For those in the military, this involves a change in duty assignments, or jobs, every few years.

It is often assumed that change must mean advancement—taking on more difficult work assignments or added responsibilities, such as supervising others. In addition to moving upward in organizations, some people also make lateral and downward moves at some time in their lives. Not all people are motivated by change to a higher status position or one offering more responsibility and money. For some people, it is more important to learn additional skills or to work in an area that is personally satisfying.

One way to analyze a person's work experiences is to create a "career map." On the following pages are the career maps of four individuals. Figures A and B illustrate the job changes of two individuals who began their careers as apprentice carpenters. Gerardo Rodríguez is a civilian; Frank Dalton has been with the Air Force since he enlisted in 1970. Their profiles appear on page 394. Roberta Matthews and Peter Chen, whose career maps are shown in Figures C and D, are engineers. Roberta is a civilian, while Peter has spent his entire work life in the Navy. Their profiles are on page 395.

To understand the career maps, begin on the left side of the page. The individual's first jobs, employer or location, and the time spent there are shown in the first column. Each new job or position is indicated by a different box. If the person changed employers or locations, this change appears in a new column. If the change was an upward, downward, or lateral move, this is reflected by showing it at a higher, lower, or similar place either within or across columns.

As you review these four maps, look for the following:

- Types of changes made — note that all made lateral and upward moves. Figure A shows that Gerardo Rodríguez also made a downward move when he left Eckman Construction, Inc. and joined KLM Land Developers.

- Number of changes made — because people in the military change duty assignments every few years, the career maps of Frank Dalton and Peter Chen have more columns than their civilian counterparts. This continuing opportunity for change in work type and location is what attracts many people to the military. Roberta Matthews had fewer employers, but she made changes within the organizations for which she worked.

- Future changes — these maps only reflect the past and present. It is also useful to create career maps that include the future. Imagine next steps for each of the four individuals. At some point Frank and Peter will leave the military. What options do you think they will have when they return to civilian life?

You can use the "Typical Career Path" and "Profile" sections to create career maps for any of the career path descriptions in this book. You can also develop career maps by interviewing people whose careers interest you. Finally, you may want to create your own career map. It is another resource to help you as you plan for your future.

# Figure A
## Career Map for Gerardo Rodríguez

### Employer

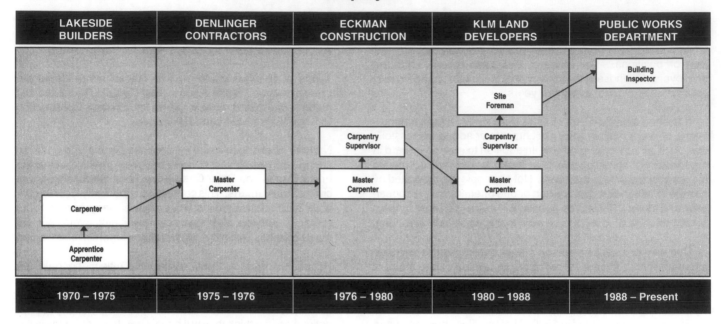

| LAKESIDE BUILDERS | DENLINGER CONTRACTORS | ECKMAN CONSTRUCTION | KLM LAND DEVELOPERS | PUBLIC WORKS DEPARTMENT |
|---|---|---|---|---|
| 1970 – 1975 | 1975 – 1976 | 1976 – 1980 | 1980 – 1988 | 1988 – Present |

Years

# Figure B
## Career Map for First Sergeant Frank Dalton

### Duty Location

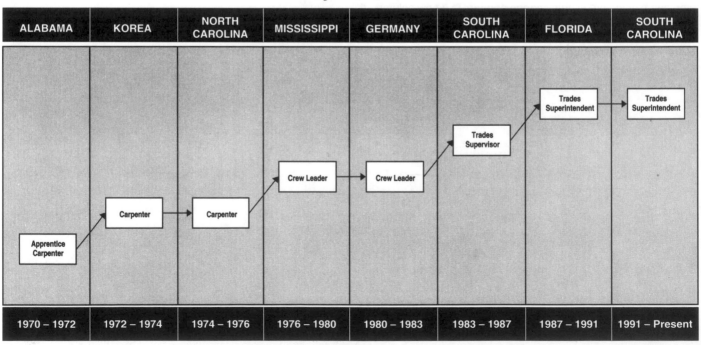

| ALABAMA | KOREA | NORTH CAROLINA | MISSISSIPPI | GERMANY | SOUTH CAROLINA | FLORIDA | SOUTH CAROLINA |
|---|---|---|---|---|---|---|---|
| 1970 – 1972 | 1972 – 1974 | 1974 – 1976 | 1976 – 1980 | 1980 – 1983 | 1983 – 1987 | 1987 – 1991 | 1991 – Present |

Years

## Figure C
## Career Map for Roberta Matthews

### Employer

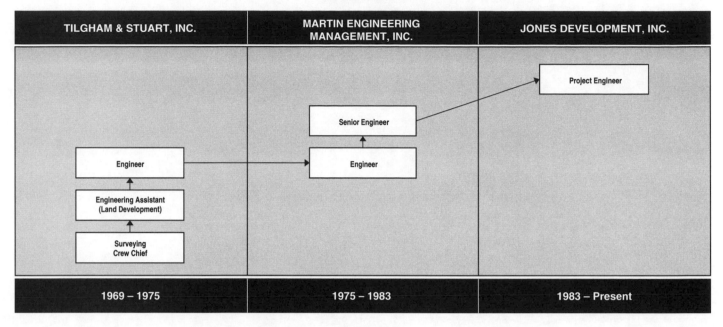

| TILGHAM & STUART, INC. | MARTIN ENGINEERING MANAGEMENT, INC. | JONES DEVELOPMENT, INC. |
| --- | --- | --- |
| 1969 – 1975 | 1975 – 1983 | 1983 – Present |

### Years

## Figure D
## Career Map for Commander Peter Chen

### Duty Location

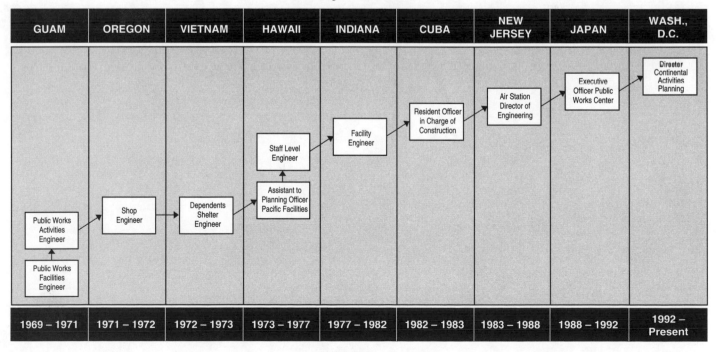

| GUAM | OREGON | VIETNAM | HAWAII | INDIANA | CUBA | NEW JERSEY | JAPAN | WASH., D.C. |
| --- | --- | --- | --- | --- | --- | --- | --- | --- |
| 1969 – 1971 | 1971 – 1972 | 1972 – 1973 | 1973 – 1977 | 1977 – 1982 | 1982 – 1983 | 1983 – 1988 | 1988 – 1992 | 1992 – Present |

### Years

# Glossary

# Glossary of Military Terms

**Active Duty** - Continuous duty on a daily basis. Comparable to "full-time" as used in reference to a civilian job.

**Allowances** - Money, other than basic pay, to compensate in certain specified situations for expenses such as meals, rent, clothing, and travel. Also, compensation is given for maintaining proficiency in specific skill areas such as flying or parachuting.

**Artillery** - Large cannons or missile launchers used in combat.

**ASVAB** - Armed Services Vocational Aptitude Battery. A test that provides students with academic and vocational aptitude scores to assist them in career exploration and decision-making. ASVAB scores are used by the military services to determine enlistment eligibility and to assign occupational specialties.

**Base** - A locality or installation on which a military force relies for supplies or from where it initiates operations.

**Basic Pay** - The amount of pay a military member receives, as determined by pay grade and length of service. Basic pay does not include other benefits such as allowances and bonuses.

**Basic Training** - A rigorous orientation to the military, lasting from six to ten weeks, which provides a transition from civilian to military life.

**Civilian** - Anyone not on active duty in the military.

**Commissary** - A store on a military base that sells groceries and other items at a substantial discount to military personnel.

**Commissioned Officer** - A member of the military holding the rank of second lieutenant or ensign or above. This role in the military is similar to that of a manager or executive.

**DEP** - Delayed Entry Program. A military program that allows an applicant to delay entry into active duty for up to one year, for such things as finishing school, etc.

**Drill** - To train or exercise in military operations.

**Duty** - Assigned task or occupation.

**Enlisted Member** - Military personnel below the rank of warrant or commissioned officers. This role is similar to that of a company employee or supervisor.

**Enlistee** - A service member, not a warrant or commissioned officer, who has been accepted by the military and has taken the Oath of Enlistment.

**Enlistment Agreement/Enlistment Contract** - A legal contract between the military and an enlistment applicant, which contains information such as enlistment date, term of enlistment, and other options such as a training program guarantee or a cash bonus.

**GI Bill Benefits** - A program of education benefits for individuals entering the military. This program enables service persons to set aside money to be used later for educational purposes.

**Inactive Reserve Duty** - Affiliation with the military in a non-training, non-paying status after completing minimum obligation of active duty service.

**Infantry** - Units of men trained, armed, and equipped to fight on foot.

**Job Specialty** - A specific job or occupation in one of the five services.

**MEPS** - Military Entrance Processing Stations, which are located around the country. The enlistment process occurs at each of these stations.

**NCO -** Non-commissioned Officer. An enlisted member in pay grades E-4 or higher.

**Obligation** - The period of time one agrees to serve on active duty, in the reserve, or a combination of both .

**OCS** - Officer Candidate School. Program for college graduates with no prior military training who wish to become military officers. Also, qualified enlisted members who wish to become officers may attend OCS. After successful completion, candidates are commissioned as military officers.

**OTS (OTG)** - Officer Training School (Group). See OCS, Officer Candidate School.

**Officer** - See commissioned officer.

**Pay Grade** - A level of employment, as designated by the military. There are 9 enlisted pay grades and 10 officer pay grades through which personnel can progress during their career. Pay grade and length of service determine a service member's pay.

**Quarters** - Living accommodations or housing.

**Recruit** - See enlistee.

**Regular Military Compensation** - Total value of basic pay, allowances, and tax savings, which represents the amount of pay a civilian worker would need to earn to receive the same take home "pay" as a service member.

**Reserves** - The Reserves are those people in the military who are not presently on full-time, active duty. In a national emergency, reservists can be called up immediately to serve on active duty because they are highly trained by the services and drill regularly. During peacetime, they perform functions in support of the active duty forces in our country's defense, such as installation and repair of communications equipment. Reservists are also entitled to some of the employment benefits available to active military personnel.

**ROTC** - Reserve Officers' Training Corps. Training given to undergraduate college students who plan to become military officers. Often they receive scholarships for tuition, books, fees, uniforms, and a monthly allowance.

**Service Classifier** - A military information specialist who helps applicants select a military occupational field.

**Service Obligation** - The amount of time an enlisted member agrees to serve in the military, as stated in the enlistment agreement.

**Station** - A place of assigned duty.

**Tour of Duty** - A period of obligated service. Also used to describe a type of duty tour, such as a "Mediterranean tour."

# Indexes

# DOT Code Index (by DOT Number)

This index lists civilian counterparts to the 152 military occupations described in the Military Occupations section. The 572 civilian occupations listed here are in numerical order by their *Dictionary of Occupational Titles* (DOT) codes. The DOT, published by the U.S. Department of Labor, defines and classifies over 12,000 civilian occupations found in the U.S. labor force. Civilian occupations involve performance of essentially the same tasks and require the same knowledge, skills, and abilities as their counterpart occupations in the military.

The page number listed for each DOT code and title indicates the location of that military occupational description in the Military Occupations section. This index is useful when you know a DOT code and want to find out whether it has a military counterpart. The index is also useful as a general reference list of civilian occupations that have military counterparts described in the Military Occupations section.

# DOT Code Index (by Occupation)

This index lists civilian counterparts to the 152 military occupations described in the Military Occupations section. (The organization of this index is similar to the organization of the military occupations in the Table of Contents.) Below each military occupation, the counterpart civilian occupations are listed according to their *Dictionary of Occupational Titles* (DOT) codes.

The DOT Code Index is useful when you want to find civilian counterparts to the military occupations described in this guide. Knowledge of how military training and employment relates to civilian employment may be helpful in career planning. DOT codes may also be used to help locate additional information in other publications about any civilian counterpart occupation (for example, the *Dictionary of Occupational Titles* and *Occupational Outlook Handbook*).

# ENGINEERING, SCIENCE, AND TECHNICAL OCCUPATIONS

## ADMINISTRATIVE OCCUPATIONS

# ELECTRONIC AND ELECTRICAL EQUIPMENT REPAIR OCCUPATIONS

# EXECUTIVE, ADMINISTRATIVE, AND MANAGERIAL OCCUPATIONS

# TRANSPORTATION OCCUPATIONS

# Title Index

This index is an alphabetical listing of occupational titles that represent military occupations described in *Military Careers*. The page number listed next to each title indicates where the occupation is described. The titles in capital letters and bold print are the main titles of the 197 military occupations described in the book. The remainder of the titles are alternate names for these occupations or specialties within them. The alternate titles were drawn from several sources including: (1) *Dictionary of Occupational Titles* occupations; (2) titles found in civilian career information resources, such as the *Occupational Outlook*

*Handbook* and computerized career information delivery systems (CIDS); and (3) commonly used job titles.

The Title Index is useful if you know the name of an occupation and want to find out whether it is available in the military. For any title listed in the index, you can read the description of what the occupation is like in the military by turning to the page number listed next to it. If you do not find the exact title you are interested in, try to find a similar title under which the same occupation might be listed.

# The Very Quick Job Search,
## Second Edition
### Get a Better Job in Half the Time!
*By J. Michael Farr*

Mike Farr, one of the most important architects of the self-directed job search, has done it again! Nowhere else will you find such excellent, timeless job search information. This award-winning title has been an important resource for more than 150,000 people just like you!

✦ Thorough coverage of all career planning and job search topics—in one book
✦ Proven, effective advice for *all* job seekers
✦ Latest information on market trends and results-oriented search techniques

**ISBN: 1-56370-181-2 • $16.95 • Order Code: LP-J1812**

---

# The Quick Resume & Cover Letter Book, Second Edition
### Write and Use an Effective Resume in Only One Day
*By J. Michael Farr*

A hands-on, total job search guide! The author understands you don't have a lot of valuable time to waste preparing your job search. This award-winning title offers tips on

✦ Writing a "same-day resume"
✦ Job searching
✦ Interviewing
✦ Cover and follow-up letters
✦ And much, much more!

**ISBN: 1-56370-634-2 • $14.95 • Order Code: LP-J6342**

---

# The Quick Interview & Salary Negotiation Book
### Dramatically Improve Your Interviewing Skills in Just a Few Hours!
*By J. Michael Farr*

Time is money. And, in just a few hours, you could be on your way to earning more! America's premier job search and career author shares simple, fast, effective techniques for handling unusual and difficult interview situations and negotiating salaries and pay increases. No matter what your level of job experience, you literally cannot afford to miss this book!

**ISBN: 1-56370-162-6 • $14.95 • Order Code: LP-J1626**

# Best Jobs for the 21ˢᵗ Century

## Expert Reference on the Jobs of Tomorrow

*By J. Michael Farr and LaVerne L. Ludden, Ed.D.*

Whether you're preparing to enter the job market for the first time or simply wish to remain competitive in your current field, this information-packed reference contains data on the latest employment trends.

✦ Contains over 50 lists of jobs with best pay, high growth, and most openings by numerous categories

✦ Describes 686 jobs with fast growth or high pay

✦ Based on expert analysis of labor and economic trends

**ISBN: 1-56370-486-2 • $16.95 • Order Code: LP-J4862**

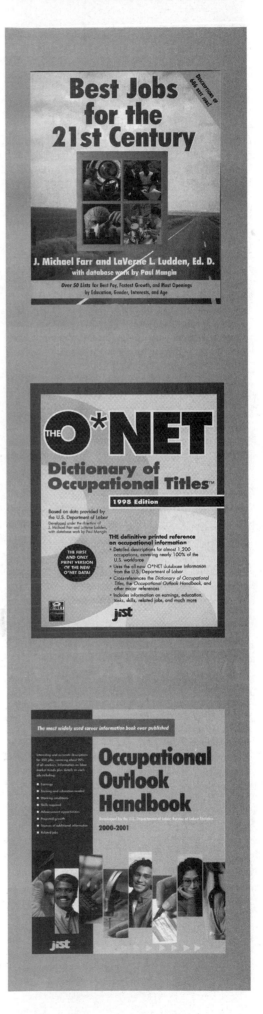

---

# The O*NET Dictionary of Occupational Titles

## Based on Information from the U.S. Department of Labor

*Compiled by J. Michael Farr and LaVerne L. Ludden, Ed.D., with Paul Mangin*

JIST is the first publisher to use the U.S. Department of Labor's new O*NET data, which was developed to replace the 1991 edition of the *Dictionary of Occupational Titles*. The O*NET presents a major change in occupational information systems, and this new reference includes

✦ Descriptions of all major jobs—more than 1,100—in the new O*NET database

✦ User-friendly introduction to the O*NET system

**ISBN: 1-56370-510-9**
**$39.95 Softcover**
**Order Code: LP-J5109**

**ISBN: 1-56370-509-5**
**$49.95 Hardcover**
**Order Code: LP-J5095**

---

# Occupational Outlook Handbook, 2000-2001 Edition

*By the U.S. Department of Labor*

The *OOH* is the most widely used career exploration resource. This is a quality reprint of the government's *OOH*, only at a less-expensive price. It describes 250 jobs—jobs held by 90% of the American workforce—making the book ideal for students, counselors, teachers, librarians, and job seekers.

✦ Well-written narrative with many charts and photos

✦ Gives DOT numbers for the occupation and related occupations

✦ Sections on nature of the work, working conditions, training, job outlook, earnings

**ISBN: 1-56370-676-8**
**$18.95 Softcover**
**Order Code: LP-J6768**

**ISBN: 1-56370-677-6**
**$23.95 Hardcover**
**Order Code: LP-J6776**

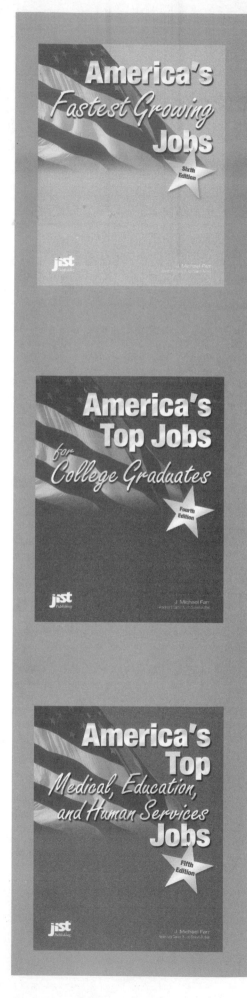

# ...est Growing
## ...on

**Details on the Best Jobs at All Levels of Education and Training**

*By J. Michael Farr*

Essential information for all job seekers, including descriptions of the 138 fastest growing jobs in the U.S., labor market trends, and a section on career planning and job search skills.

✦ Thorough job descriptions based on the latest data from the U.S. Department of Labor and the *Occupational Outlook Handbook*

✦ Career planning and job search techniques that outline results-oriented career planning and job search advice

✦ Additional resources, including recommended books and Internet resources on careers, job seeking, and education

**ISBN: 1-56370-718-7 • $16.95 • Order Code: LP-J7187**

---

# America's Top Jobs® for College Graduates, Fourth Edition

**Detailed Information on 112 Major Jobs Requiring Four-Year and Higher Degrees**

...scriptions for 112 jobs on career planning

...he fastest growth, highest

...nds every job seeker

...der Code: LP-J7209

---

# ...ical,
# ...man Services

...obs with Excellent
...s

...nore than 73 of the top
...h all levels of education

...Medical, Education, &
...ptions for all major jobs in

**ISBN: 1-56370-721-7 • $16.95 • Order Code: LP-J7217**